www.wadsworth.com

www.wadsworth.com is the World Wide Web site for Thomson Wadsworth and is your direct source to dozens of online resources.

At *www.wadsworth.com* you can find out about supplements, demonstration software, and student resources. You can also send e-mail to many of our authors and preview new publications and exciting new technologies.

www.wadsworth.com
Changing the way the world learns®

Sense and Nonsense about Crime and Drugs

A Policy Guide

Sixth Edition

SAMUEL WALKER

University of Nebraska, Omaha

THOMSON

WADSWORTH

Australia • Brazil • Canada • Mexico • Singapore
Spain • United Kingdom • United States

*Sense and Nonsense about Crime and Drugs:
A Policy Guide,* **Sixth Edition**
Samuel Walker

Senior Acquisitions Editor, Criminal Justice:
  Carolyn Henderson Meier

Assistant Editor: *Jana Davis*

Editorial Assistant: *Rebecca Johnson*

Technology Project Manager: *Susan DeVanna*

Marketing Manager: *Terra Schultz*

Marketing Assistant: *Gregory Hughes*

Marketing Communications Manager: *Stacey
  Purviance*

Project Manager, Editorial Production: *Jennie
  Redwitz*

Creative Director: *Rob Hugel*

Art Director: *Vernon Boes*

Print Buyer: *Barbara Britton*

Permissions Editor: *Joohee Lee*

Production Service: *Graphic World Inc.*

Copy Editor: *Graphic World Inc.*

Illustrator: *Graphic World Inc.*

Cover Designer: *Bill Stanton*

Cover Printer: *Phoenix Color Corp*

Compositor: *Graphic World Inc.*

Printer: *Webcom*

Library of Congress Control Number:
2005928204

ISBN 0-534-61654-2

Thomson Higher Education
10 Davis Drive
Belmont, CA 94002-3098
USA

For more information about our products,
contact us at:
Thomson Learning Academic Resource
Center
1-800-423-0563

For permission to use material from this
text or product, submit a request online at
http://www.thomsonrights.com.
Any additional questions about permissions
can be submitted by e-mail to
thomsonrights@thomson.com.

Brief Contents

Contents

IV REFORM: THE LIBERAL PRESCRIPTION   215

11 TREAT 'EM!   217

❖

Propositions

❖

Foreword

Shortly after its initial publication, Samuel Walker's *Sense and Nonsense about Crime* was recognized as an important new book, a substantive contribution to the literature on crime and justice. Over the years, he has reworked its themes and developed its arguments in five more editions (in the third edition updating the title to reflect an expanded discussion of drugs and drug policy), and the field's appreciation of this book has only increased. Today, it is a major text in the study of crime and justice; some call it a nascent classic work in its field. It is a respected argument about our knowledge base for crime and justice, and it is one of those rare books that is deeply respected by scholars and policy makers alike.

It is, therefore, with extraordinary pleasure that I welcome the Sixth Edition to the Wadsworth Contemporary Issues in Crime and Justice Series. The series is devoted to giving detailed and effective exposure to important or emerging issues and problems that ordinarily receive insufficient attention in traditional textbooks. The series also publishes books meant to provoke thought and change perspectives by challenging readers to become more sophisticated consumers of crime and justice knowledge. If you are looking for a book that will make you an informed student of crime and justice policy and practice, you could not do better than the one you are now holding.

Why is this book so important? There are two reasons. First, so much of what is commonly believed about crime—and so much of what shapes public policy on crime—is nonsense. Second, Walker's book was the first (and is still the most effective) book written to point that out. The book provides a masterful critique of the American penchant for short-sighted, metaphorical strategies to prevent crime (boot camps are a good example) or feel-good rhetoric about crime priorities (end poverty, end crime) that have, over the years, not gotten us very far in our pursuit of a safer society. Today, we are enjoying a welcome, sustained national drop in crime rates. But this drop still leaves us with higher rates of crime than we want, and (perhaps more to the point) the source of the drop in crime is more of a mystery to us than a lesson in crime prevention policy.

The contribution of this book—what makes this book special—is its willingness to show evenhandedly how favorite strategies of diverse political agendas have as their foundation some degree of "nonsense." If there is a lesson this book brings to us repeatedly, it is that cherished images of crime and justice are flawed, inaccurate, and doomed to fail for particular reasons of the more or less well-known facts we so often want to ignore to sustain our favorite ideologies. This book challenges us where we need to be challenged: in our willingness to ignore reality in order to nurture our frequently inadvisable pet ideas about crime and crime fighting.

You want your police to be tough, to chase dangerous criminals, to make lifesaving arrests? Well, Professor Walker points out that you have to contend with the fact that police spend very little of their time acting this way, and even when they do, not much in the way of crime control seems to result. You want your judges to lock 'em up and throw away the key? Walker shows all the ways that this belief is expensive and ineffective, even counterproductive. You think we need to save money through closer surveillance of the people convicted of crime? Make our lives safer by treating juveniles as though they were adults? End drug abuse through an all-out war on drugs? Here again, the book sheds cool light on hot emotions, showing how such strategies can backfire.

This book is not, however, just about nonsense in crime and justice. Perhaps nonsense gets the majority of the attention because so much of what we do is based on faulty thinking. But Walker is willing to tell us what makes "sense" as well. Big proposals lack much support, and politically popular proposals may be downright silly. But there are smaller, less ambitious ways we can contribute to a safer society, and we can do so without suspending our constitutional rights or giving up our public freedoms. One of the ways we have learned to be smarter about crime is through the philosophy of evidence-based practice. This approach asks hard questions about criminal policy, seeking to base crime strategies on established studies that show those policies will work. Professor Walker applies the evidence-based criterion to his review of crime and justice policy, and what emerges is a powerfully dispassionate analysis that gives us a carefully crafted challenge to start "making sense" in the way we talk about crime and the way we develop policies to cope with it.

If you are getting ready to read this book, chances are you are contemplating a career in the field of criminal justice. At the very least, you have an informed citizen's interest in the problems of crime and justice. In either case, you have come to the right place to become more knowledgeable in your pursuits. After you read this book, you will join a large number of its alumni, dedicated to crime policies that make sense. I commend you.

Todd R. Clear
Series Editor

Preface

This Sixth Edition marks the 20th anniversary of *Sense and Nonsense about Crime.* As with earlier editions, this is an occasion to reflect on the profound changes in the world of criminal justice since 1985. In that year, the drug crack had just begun to appear on the streets of America. Community policing was still a new and untested idea. Boot camps were also a new idea. Crime rates were high, and the juvenile homicide rate was about to soar even higher. I doubt that any knowledgeable professionals in the criminal justice field would have predicted that the already high American prison population would soar to its current level.

In the past decade, the crime rate has dropped significantly, and in cities such as San Diego and New York City violent crime rates have dropped to levels not seen since the 1960s. Something very positive is happening in this country, and not just in the area of crime. Teenage pregnancy rates have also fallen. Unemployment is at record low levels. New AIDS cases are down. Across the board, social indicators have been moving in a positive direction.

An important new element in this edition is the application of the formal standards of evidence-based policy making. The first edition of this book essentially adopted this approach: to test crime policies against the available evidence. This approach has now become an international movement in criminal justice, health care, education, and other fields. I have applied it more rigorously in this edition than in the past, supplementing it with information made available by recent research:

- Chapter 1 incorporates new material on the evidence-based crime policy movement and also features an expanded discussion of the fall in crime rates over the past decade, with updated coverage of drug use, crime victimization, and incarceration trends.

- Chapter 4 includes new material on the difficulty of predicting violent behavior.

- Chapter 5 presents new evidence on the impact of the COPS program and the hiring of more police officers.

- Chapter 6 introduces new information on the effectiveness of "Scared Straight" anti-crime programs.

- Chapter 7 features updated material on the impact of three-strikes laws.

- Chapter 10 expands the discussion of the Brady Law, the Assault Weapons Ban, and the Right-to-Carry laws, and also contains new material on the phenomenon of drug courts.

- Chapter 11 addresses the success rate of recent rehabilitation initiatives, such as faith-based treatment programs.

- Chapter 13 offers new evidence on the effectiveness of anti-drug media campaigns.

The most significant change in this edition is a more hopeful tone about our capacity to control crime. This reflects important new developments in the field, in particular the growing emphasis on community-focused crime policies, which is supported both by advances in theoretical criminology and by empirical data from experimental programs. The later chapters now incorporate a detailed look at some of these policies:

- Chapter 11 examines domestic violence batterers' treatment programs.

- Chapter 12 brings forward new material on the phenomenon of procedural justice, leading into a discussion of building its legitimacy as a crime prevention strategy.

- Chapter 14 presents a trio of new community-focused programs and new material on community prosecution and offender reentry programs, as well as expanded coverage of problem-oriented policing.

As the final chapter makes clear, however, the evidence is still preliminary, and many questions about the effectiveness of such programs remain unanswered.

The emergence of community-focused crime policy and the evidence-based policy-making approach are manifestations of a more general development: the increased application of social scientific evidence in the field of criminal justice. In brief, research makes a difference, and as many of the changes to this edition indicate, the growing awareness of this fact has begun to visibly influence policy making.

The basic argument of the First Edition was that most crime control proposals are nonsense. That includes the ideas of putting more police on the street, locking up more offenders, and implementing drug treatment and education programs. To a great extent, most crime control policies still are nonsense. But not all are. The best research has discredited many old ideas and provided support for more reasonable proposals. Crime policies are inevitably influenced by political considerations, and science has a hard time making its influence felt. But there are at least some signs of hope.

The First Edition was written primarily as a response to the conservative crime control agenda that dominated public policy at the time. This conservative agenda stressed crime control through tougher law enforcement policies, including new policy initiatives using incapacitation, deterrence, and programs targeting career criminals. The book examined those proposals in light of what was then known about the administration of criminal justice. In the interest of fairness, I subjected liberal crime control policies to the same critical scrutiny. I found them equally lacking in empirical support.

By the time of the Third Edition, the wheel of the policy debate had turned in one significant respect: The conservative/liberal dichotomy that provided the framework for the first two editions was no longer as clearly defined as it was originally. Basically, the liberal perspective had collapsed, and most politicians who defined themselves as liberals had adopted most of the traditional conservative policy agenda: more police, more imprisonment, and so on. Meanwhile, some prominent conservatives had embraced the idea of legalizing drugs, a traditionally liberal proposal. In short, the world of criminal justice policy has become more complex than it was when the first edition of this book appeared.

SUPPLEMENTS

The following supplements are available to accompany this text. (Available to qualified adopters. Please consult your local sales representative for details.)

Instructor's Resource Manual by Dr. Marny Rivera of Southern Oregon University. The *Instructor's Resource Manual* contains the following for each chapter: Chapter Objectives, Key Terms, Detailed Chapter Outlines, Class Activities, and a Test Bank with Multiple Choice, True/False, Fill in the Blank, and Short Answer/Essay Questions. Available on eBank as Microsoft Word files only; please contact your Thomson Wadsworth representative to obtain a copy.

InfoTrac® College Edition Now available with this text: FREE four-month access to InfoTrac College Edition's online database of more than 18 million reliable, full-length articles from 5000 academic journals and periodicals (including the *New York Times, Science, Forbes,* and *USA Today*). Access also includes **Info-Marks®**—stable URLs that can be linked to articles, journals, and searches. Info-Marks allow you to use a simple copy-and-paste technique to create instant and continually updated online readers, content services, bibliographies, electronic "reserve" readings, and current topic sites. In addition, ask about other InfoTrac College Edition resources available, including InfoMarks print and online readers with readings, activities, and exercises hand-selected to work with the text. To help students use the research they gather, their free four-month subscription to InfoTrac College Edition includes access to **InfoWrite,** a complete set of online critical thinking and paper-writing tools. To take a quick tour of InfoTrac College Edition, visit http://www.infotrac-college.com/ and select the User Demo. (Journals subject to change. Certain restrictions may apply. For additional information, please consult your local Thomson Wadsworth representative.)

InfoTrac College Edition Student Guide for Criminal Justice This brief booklet provides a user guide for students on how to get the most out of InfoTrac College Edition and includes login help, search tips, and frequently asked questions, as well as a list of suggested keyword search terms specific to the discipline.

Opposing Viewpoints Resource Center This online center helps you expose your students to all sides of today's most compelling social and scientific issues, from environmental policy to prejudice, health care reform to violence in the media, and much more. The Opposing Viewpoints Resource Center draws on Greenhaven Press's acclaimed social issues series, popular periodicals and newspapers, and core reference content from other Gale and Macmillan Reference USA sources. The result is a dynamic online library of current events topics—the facts as well as the arguments as articulated by the proponents and detractors of each position. Special sections focus on critical thinking (walking students through the critical evaluation of point-counterpoint arguments) and researching and writing papers. To take a quick tour of the OVRC, visit http://www .gale.com/OpposingViewpoints. For college and university adopters only.

DEDICATION

I would like to dedicate this book to Mary Ann Lamanna, who has been a wonderful companion over the past quarter of a century. As I am completing this Sixth Edition, she is working on the Ninth Edition of her book (so I guess I have some work to do). But despite the demands of publishing deadlines, she knows that there is always time for a movie.

ABOUT THE AUTHOR

Samuel Walker is Isaacson Professor of Criminal Justice at the University of Nebraska, Omaha, where he has taught for more than 30 years. He is the author of 13 books on policing, criminal justice history and policy, and civil liberties. His most recent books include *Police Accountability* (Wadsworth, 2001) and *The Police in America* (McGraw-Hill, 2002). His current research involves police accountability, focusing primarily on citizen oversight of the police, and police Early Warning (EW) systems. Professor Walker currently serves on the Panel on Policing of the National Research Council of the National Academy of Sciences.

Samuel Walker

PART I

Thinking Clearly about Crime

1

Crime and Policy:
A Complex Problem

CRIME AT A 30-YEAR LOW

Crime in America hit a 30-year low in 2003. The National Crime Victimization Survey (NCVS) reported that in 2003 crime rates reached the lowest level recorded since the NCVS was initiated in 1973. The NCVS data marked a continuation of the dramatic crime drop that began in 1993. The reduction in crime occurred in all major categories of both violent and property crime. The robbery rate fell from 6.2 per 1,000 in 1992 to 2.4 in 2003. The household burglary rate fell from 58.7 to 28.7 per 1,000 in the same years (Figure 1.1).[1]

These are substantial reductions, and they mean that Americans are much safer today than they were 10 or 12 years ago. The meaning of the crime drop becomes clearer when we look at certain cities. Murders in Chicago hit a 38-year low in 2004. New York City, Boston, and San Diego also enjoyed low violent crime rates they had not seen since the 1960s. In Boston, for example, the number of murders went from 57 in 1965 to a peak of 152 in 1990, and then down to 39 in 2003. In San Diego, the robbery rate followed a similar trajectory: from 0.58 per 1,000 in 1965 to 3.87 in 1990 and then down to 1.28 in 2003.[2]

The crime drop seems like a miracle to many Americans. For the first time in a generation, there is good news about crime and violence. Since crime rates began to soar around 1963, crime has ripped the social fabric of American society and has been a major issue in American politics. In addition to the harm

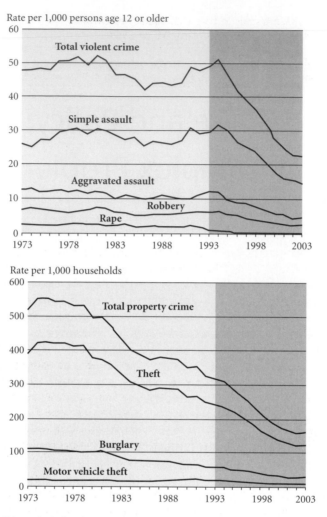

FIGURE 1.1 Crime victimization, 1973–2003

SOURCE: Bureau of Justice Statistics, *Criminal Victimization 2003* (Washington, DC: Department of Justice, 2004).

inflicted by particular crimes—a murder or a rape—crime ripped the fabric of our communities, instilling fear and causing people to move out of their neighborhoods. And in politics, the issue of "crime" has been intertwined with race and has contributed to the racial polarization of American society.

Is It Genuine?

Some skeptics wonder whether the crime drop is genuine or just a temporary blip or the result of a statistical artifact. All of the evidence indicates that it is indeed real. First, the NCVS is regarded as a very reliable measure of criminal

Table 1.1 Positive trends in two U.S. social indicators: Teenage births and infant mortality, 1970–2001

Teenage births Births to women, ages 15–17 per 1,000		Infant mortality Deaths per 1,000 live births	
1972	39	1970	20.0
1977	33.9	1975	16.1
1982	32.2	1980	12.6
1987	31.7	1985	10.6
1992	37.6	1990	9.2
1997	31.4	1995	7.6
2001	24.7	2000	6.9

victimization. No one has ever suggested that the data are manipulated or methodologically flawed. (Check the many NCVS reports on the website of the National Criminal Justice Reference Service [NCJRS].) Second, the downward trend reported by the NCVS is now a decade old and cannot be dismissed as a temporary phenomenon. Third, a similar trend is reported by the Uniform Crime Reports (UCR) of the Federal Bureau of Investigation (FBI). (For the most recent reports, go to the FBI website.) Although the NCVS and the UCR differ on some specific points, they basically agree on the national trend in the past decade—in effect, with these two data systems we are taking the nation's temperature with two different thermometers and getting the same reading. This is powerful confirmation. It might be possible for one city to manipulate its crime data, or for one city to have a very unusual increase or decrease in crime, but the NCVS gives us a very comprehensive national estimate using a methodology that is free of potential manipulation by local officials.

Finally, many other social indicators have also been moving in a positive direction over the past decade, such as decreases in teenage pregnancy and infant mortality (Table 1.1). These trends suggest a general improvement in the quality of life in American society as the result of subtle but important changes in people's behavior in many different areas.[3]

A Notable Exception

Not every city has enjoyed a crime drop, however. Camden, New Jersey, won the label of the nation's most dangerous city in 2004, as murders soared 56 percent, from 34 in 2002 to 53 in 2004. Conditions in Camden resembled those in other cities in the late 1980s during the height of the crack cocaine epidemic: open-air drug dealing, gangs, and high rates of murder and other violent crime. Federal officials promised help for the beleaguered city in late 2004, with a plan to prosecute gun-related crimes (federal sentences are much harsher than state ones) and target gang members. The state government in Trenton had sent in state police officers to help patrol the streets a few years earlier.[4]

Explaining the Crime Drop

The great American crime drop demands an explanation. Why did it happen? What are the causes? Criminologists have been at a loss to provide definite answers to these questions. Blumstein and Wallman in their introduction to *The Crime Drop in America,* argue that "no single factor can be invoked as *the* cause of the crime decline in the 1990s."[5] Their book, which is still the only comprehensive assessment of the subject, examines a number of different possible causes: changes in policing and/or sentencing, the rejection of crack by a new generation of young people, the strength of the economy and new job opportunities, gun control efforts, and so on. Criminologist Richard Rosenfeld suggests a general cultural shift away from violence, which might explain the improvement in other social indicators besides crime.[6]

Explaining the crime drop is a central theme of this book. There is no shortage of people claiming that *their* favorite crime policy deserves credit. The advocates of community policing claim that the adoption of innovative police strategies replaced old and ineffective policies. These new strategies were facilitated by the addition of tens of thousands of new police officers (approximately 70,000) under the 1994 Violent Crime Control Act. Other police experts argue that problem-oriented policing, community policing's first cousin, involves focused strategies that effectively address specific crime and disorder problems. New York City officials, meanwhile, claim that the NYPD's "zero tolerance" policy reduced crime in that city.[7]

Other experts believe that tough new sentencing laws and increased incarceration had the combined effect of both incapacitating many repeat offenders and deterring potential criminals. Still others argue that changes in drug use and drug markets caused much of the reduction in serious crime. Most important is the decline in the use of crack cocaine, which was closely associated with an upsurge in violent crime in the late 1980s. In New York City, for example, the number of cocaine-related emergency admissions to hospitals declined by 33 percent just between early 1998 and early 2002.[8] Why the use of crack declined is not clear, however. Was it innovative police strategies? Tougher sentences? Or was it just a cultural shift away from one drug? Finally, some observers believe that the crime drop is only one of several positive consequences of an economy that was extremely healthy through the 1990s.

Contextual vs. Policy Factors

The most intelligent discussion of the crime drop is in an Urban Institute paper, *Reflections on the Crime Decline: Lessons for the Future?*[9] Jeremy Travis and Michelle Waul make an important distinction between contextual and policy factors that affect crime.

The *contextual factors* include demographic changes, the rise and fall of the crack cocaine epidemic, and changes in labor markets. While the shifting proportion of crime-prone young people in the population explains a lot of the crime wave of the 1960s, the influence of this factor has been far more complicated in the last 20 years. A demographic analysis failed to predict the great increase in violent crime in the mid–1980s, as well as the sharp decline after 1993. The changing popularity of crack provides a much better explanation. The rise in violent crime coincided with the arrival of crack, and the crime drop has coincided with its waning popularity. Travis and Waul suggest that a younger generation saw the devastating effects of crack and decided that the drug was just not cool. With respect to changing labor markets, the Urban Institute paper cites data showing that the real wages (actual wages adjusted for inflation) of low-skilled workers declined by almost 25 percent from the early 1980s to 1993, when it bottomed out (from $9.00/hr to $6.74). The economic prosperity of the 1990s included a rise in real wages, and this coincided with the great crime drop.

The criminal justice policies the Urban Institute paper considers most relevant include several gun control policies (which we will examine in detail in Chapter 10), the increase in incarceration and consequent incapacitation of offenders (Chapter 7), and innovations in policing (Chapters 5 and 15).

After considering all these, the Urban Institute paper concludes that no single factor can explain the great crime drop. Instead, it is probably the *interplay* of different factors, including both contextual factors and criminal justice policies, that best explains it. If so, it is important for us to identify which of those factors contributed (and which ones did not) and to determine the relative importance of each one.

THE PURPOSE OF THIS BOOK

This book is a search for effective crime policies. It attempts to answer one basic question: *What works?* What criminal justice policies are effective in reducing serious crime? We will review some of the major crime control proposals and evaluate their effectiveness in light of what we know about crime and justice. Previous editions of this book, written when crime rates were high, sought to determine what *might* work. Now, in the face of the great crime drop, we have to turn the question around: What *did* work? Did certain crime policies contribute to the reduction in crime? If so, which ones? Why exactly were they effective? And can the lessons from one success story be transferred to other programs in other parts of the criminal justice system?

THE NEW STANDARD:
EVIDENCE-BASED CRIME POLICY

A new and higher standard has emerged for evaluating the effectiveness of crime policies. Evidence-based policymaking is extensively used in health care policy and has become one of the most important developments in criminology. This approach requires policies to be based on a solid foundation of evidence drawn from the best research. The relevant questions are: What is the evidence? Does the evidence indicate that the policy works? Does the research meet the highest scientific standards? Have the findings been replicated in other studies?

Evidence-based policy originated in England with the Cochrane Collaboration, which examined the effectiveness of health care policies. It has spread to health care policy in this country. There is now, for example, the Vanderbilt University Center for Evidence-Based Medicine and the Center for Evidence-Based Practice of the State University of New York; a program in evidence-based mental health; the Evidence-Based Medicine Resource Center; a program in evidence-based pediatrics at the University of Michigan; and the Coalition for Evidence-Based Policy, supported by the U.S. Department of Education.[10]

Governments are adapting the principles of evidence-based policy to crime control. In England, the Home Office (the equivalent of our Department of Justice) is aggressively promoting evidence-based crime reduction and has published a report, *Working Out What to Do: Evidence-Based Crime Reduction*.[11] In the United States, the state of Oregon has debated a bill—SB 267: Evidence-Based Prevention Programs—requiring that "programs intended to reduce the propensity of a person to commit crime, reduce anti-social behavior leading to juvenile crime, or improve the mental health of a person to reduce the need for emergency mental health services be evidence-based." The Center for Evidence-Based Policy is based at Oregon Health and Science University.

In January 2003, the Justice Department and the Coalition for Evidence-Based Policy initiated a joint effort to promote evidence-based crime and substance abuse policy.[12] The main recommendations of this effort are: "That the federal agencies develop a concise, uniform, user-friendly set of principles on what constitutes 'rigorous evidence' of an intervention's effectiveness" and "That agency crime/substance-abuse grant programs, where appropriate, require applicants to provide a concrete strategy for implementation of evidence-backed interventions with fidelity."[13] One result of this effort was a National Forum on Evidence-Based Crime and Substance Abuse Policy.

The movement for evidence-based crime policy was formally launched in the United States with the founding in February 2000 of the Campbell Collaboration in Philadelphia (named for the psychologist Donald Campbell, whose work is familiar to many criminal justice students through their research methods class). Over 80 people from 12 countries attended. Professor Robert Boruch of the University of Pennsylvania was appointed chair of the steering group, and a Crime and Justice Coordinating Group was established.[14] One of the leaders of the evidence-based criminology movement is Lawrence W. Sherman at the University of Pennsylvania, which now supports the Coalition for Evidence-Based Policy and offers a course, in cooperation with the university's Government Department, on evidence-based government.

Why the Need for Evidence-Based Crime Policy?

The Traditional Lack of Evidence-Based Policymaking The movement for evidence-based crime policy has added a refreshing, demanding—and over-due—element of scientific rigor to policy debates. The former director of the Office of Justice Programs, Deborah Daniels, declared: "In the past, criminal justice practitioners operated on instinct and assumption, not science. They tried new approaches, if they did so at all, because they sounded as though they should be effective. But it did not occur to the practitioners to examine the research before they instituted a particular practice, or to measure its effectiveness as they deployed it."[15] In short, good intentions are not enough; sound policies require solid evidence.

Even worse than the lack of evidence, many policies have been continued—at great expense—despite the fact that good research has found them to be ineffective. Daniels cites the example of the Drug Abuse Resistance Education program, or DARE, the highly popular school-based drug prevention initiative. It has operated in as many as 75 percent of all school districts in some years at a cost of about $200 million a year. Evaluations have found that DARE has little or no effect on drug use. But the program continues. DARE officials themselves did not begin to change their curriculum until 2001, 17 years after the program began.

Not Just Ineffective, But Actually Harmful   Some crime reduction policies are not merely ineffective, but actually cause harm. Can this be possible? Can it be that programs designed to help people actually leave them worse off? Sadly, the answer is yes. The noted criminologist Joan McCord identified several examples of programs where the outcomes were harmful.[16]

The first was the famous Cambridge-Somerville (Massachusetts) Youth Study begun in the 1930s and which officially ended in 1945 but involved follow-up reports on the original subjects through the early 1980s. Boys under the age of ten who received treatment were matched with control group boys. The treatment consisted of professional counselors who provided "friendly guidance," advised the boys' parents, and referred boys to specialists for particular problems. The boys were also tutored, taken to sports events, and encouraged to participate in various activities. Many were sent to summer camps.

McCord, who conducted the later evaluations, found that for the majority of the paired treatment and control groups, the treatment had no effect on their subsequent criminal behavior. But for the 103 pairs of youths who had different outcomes, those in the treatment group were actually *more likely* to have been convicted of Index crimes (those classifications of crimes reported in the UCR), to have died at a younger age, or to have been diagnosed as alcoholic, schizophrenic, or manic depressive. Even worse, the adverse effects were greater among those boys who received longer and more intensive treatment. Also, adverse effects appeared only among boys whose families participated in the program. McCord speculated that the summer camps exposed the boys to bad peer influences during unsupervised time, particularly from boys who bragged about their deviant behavior.[17]

McCord also found a Michigan Volunteers in Probation (VIP) program that involved volunteers who counseled probationers in juvenile court. The VIP program, of course, sounds wonderful: eager volunteers providing additional assistance to young delinquents, and at no cost to the state. What could be better? Unfortunately, delinquents who received the VIP counseling did *worse* than those who did not. In short, the kids would have done better with no treatment at all.

Another example given by McCord was the case of Scared Straight, a popular program designed to frighten kids out of criminal behavior by exposing them to the terrible conditions in prison. The Scared Straight idea was popularized by a 1979 television documentary and was eventually adopted in 38 states. And, finally, the San Quentin (California) Squires program was evaluated with treatment and control groups. Twelve months after being exposed to the prison, 81 percent of the treatment group had been arrested, compared with only 67 percent of the control group (this program is discussed in more detail in Chapter 6).[18]

The disturbing news is that well-intentioned treatment can sometimes harm. To guard against this possibility we need solid research evidence of effectiveness.

The New Standards of Evidence-Based Crime Policy

The evidence-based policy movement defines very specific standards. First, it demands empirical evidence of the effectiveness of a policy. This rules out hope, wishful thinking, good intentions, and even policies whose assumptions are extrapolated from other evidence (e.g., since we know that X works in the context of Y, we can assume that it will also work in the context of Z).

Second, it sets a very high requirement of experimental or quasi-experimental research design in which subjects are randomly assigned to treatment and control groups. This includes an assessment of the quality of the research design of studies. The 1997 University of Maryland report *What Works?* was probably the first to use the method in American criminal justice, rating studies on a scale of 1 to 5. Thus, when we ask whether or not there is any evidence of effectiveness in a program or policy, it makes a difference whether a study gives it a rating of 2 or 5. A rating of 2 may mean that the research design was so weak that we can't be sure of the findings.[19]

A third element of evidence-based policy is the requirement of replication. It is not sufficient that the effectiveness of a policy be validated by one study; the findings need to be confirmed by similar studies replicating it. This is a serious problem for criminal justice policymaking. Many policies have been based on only one study. The Kansas City Preventive Patrol Experiment (see Chapter 5) has been enormously influential in developing policy, but it was never replicated. Similarly, the Minneapolis Domestic Violence Experiment had a huge influence on the growth of mandatory arrest policies for domestic violence. It was replicated, but only later, and when the replications found mixed support for mandatory arrest, they were largely ignored.[20] Part of the problem is that experiments such as the one in Kansas City are enormously expensive, to the point where replications are almost impossible.

Closely related to the replication requirement is the use of systematic reviews of studies, or what are called *meta-analyses.* To determine whether or not a policy is effective, policy analysts should systematically review *all* of the available studies. It is no longer sufficient that a policy be based on one study that finds it effective.

Not everyone is completely happy with the movement for evidence-based crime policy. Its aggressive insistence on experimental designs with random assignment tends to devalue other important forms of criminological research. But with respect to policy-related research—which is only one part of the larger field of criminology—it has injected a necessary and healthy element of scientific rigor.

Our Approach to Evaluating Crime Policies

As the evidence-based policy movement argues, there are many policies that are either unsupported by any evidence of effectiveness or that have been found to be either ineffective or actually harmful. One of the major obstacles to finding sensible crime policies is that there are so many *bad* ideas. Especially when crime rates were high and rising even higher, people grasped desperately at any idea that seemed to offer hope. Politicians have eagerly obliged public opinion, offering simplistic solutions that promise quick and dramatic results. One of the most recent examples is the so-called "three strikes" law, providing mandatory life prison sentences to persons convicted of a third felony, enacted by 15 states between 1993 and 1994 alone. It was enormously popular when first proposed and was widely adopted across the country. But as we shall see in Chapter 7, there is no evidence that it has been effective in reducing crime, and some evidence that it has simply created new problems.

As we proceed through our examination of crime policy, we will frame our conclusion in terms of a series of propositions. Our first proposition is this:

PROPOSITION 1
Most current crime control proposals are nonsense.

UNDERSTANDING THE AMERICAN
CRIME PROBLEM

The main reason why most crime policies are nonsense is because people do not correctly understand the nature of the crime problem in this country. They also do not understand how the criminal justice system works (a subject that Chapters 2 and 3 address). One of the main goals of this book is to help people understand crime and criminal justice so that we can begin to think clearly about crime policy. In a review of public opinion surveys, the Sentencing Project found that the public "consistently misjudges" trends in crime; in the 1990s people continued to believe that crime was rising, even though it was actually falling dramatically. The Sentencing Project also found that people consistently believed that the justice system was far more lenient than it really was.[21] This is an important point that will arise throughout this book.

America's Two Crime Problems

Your risk of being a crime victim depends a lot on who you are. Most important are your race or ethnicity and your income. The victimization rate for robbery in 2003 was 1.9 per 1,000 for white Americans and 5.9 for African Americans. The burglary rate was 58 per 1,000 for the poorest Americans (annual income of less than $7,500), compared with 20.8 for the wealthiest (income of $75,000 or more).[22] Data on homicides provide especially dramatic evidence of the racial disparity in victimization. The number of murders nationally reached an all-time high of 26,250 in 1992. While the national homicide rate has fallen about 40 percent since the early 1990s (from 9.8 per 100,000 in 1991 to 5.6 in 2002), African Americans in 2002 were still six times more likely to be murdered than whites.[23]

In short, many analysts believe that the United States has *two* crime problems: one that affects most white, middle-class Americans and another that affects people of color, the poor, and young people of color in particular.

Very poor neighborhoods have been overwhelmed by crime and drugs. For their residents, whom some analysts call the *underclass,* the quality of daily life worsened significantly in the 1980s. In some neighborhoods the drug trade completely takes over the streets, with open drug use and selling. And despite the crime drop, many of these neighborhoods are still filled with unacceptable levels of violent crime, disorder, and community breakdown.

Elliott Currie, citing the evidence from two different surveys of drug use, extends this point by arguing that we have two drug problems: one involving the majority of the population and the other concentrated in the inner cities.[24] The 2003 National Survey on Drug Use and Health (formerly called the National Household Survey on Drug Abuse) reports some decreases in drug use since the 1970s. But the Drug Abuse Warning Network (DAWN), which surveys hospital emergency room admissions, reported soaring "mentions" of cocaine use in the late 1980s and persistently high rates in recent years.[25] These data suggest a very serious drug problem for one segment of the population but not for the nation as a whole. (In Chapter 13 we will discuss the different sources of data on drug use in more detail.)

Criminologists Franklin Zimring and Gordon Hawkins argue that the American crime problem is primarily one of violent crime, particularly *lethal* crime.[26] Comparative victimization surveys consistently indicate that the victimization rates for property crimes in most European and other English-speaking countries are not that different than those in the United States. Poland's rate is even higher, while the rates in New Zealand, the Netherlands, Australia, the Czech Republic, Spain, Canada, Italy, England, France, and Sweden are within 30 percent of the U.S. rate. The United States is not even that much worse in terms of overall violent crime rate (mainly robbery and assaults). The real difference is with lethal violence. In 1990, the U.S. homicide rate was more than 4 times that of Canada, 9 times the rate of France and Germany, and about 14 times the rate of England and Japan.[27] And despite the recent crime drop, the United States still has extremely high rates of lethal violence. Zimring and Hawkins argue that we need to focus our attention on murder rather than burglary, drug use, or other crimes.

The Bait and Switch Problem

Zimring and Hawkins also argue that the failure to understand the specific aspects of the American crime problem results in "bait and switch" crime policies. Many policies are simply unrelated to the most serious parts of the crime problem. They are advertised as solutions to the most serious crimes (meaning murder, armed robbery, and rape) but in practice have their most serious impact on less serious crimes (particularly burglary and assaults). The term *bait and switch* comes from the area of consumer fraud, where a retailer advertises a low-priced item to draw customers, but then will not sell the item to them, usually claiming that it is "sold out," and tries to steer them toward buying a higher-priced item. The National Criminal Justice Commission agrees with the bait and switch criticism, pointing out that the war on crime has promised to attack *violent* crime but has mainly resulted in the imprisonment of more nonviolent offenders.[28] In California, for example, 73 percent of the increase in the prison population between 1980 and 1993 involved persons convicted of nonviolent crimes. As we examine different crime policies in the chapters ahead, we want to make sure that they have an impact on their intended target. This consideration has important implications for incapacitation as a crime control policy, which we will examine in Chapter 7.

WAGING WAR ON CRIME

For 40 years, we have waged a "war on crime." President Lyndon Johnson first declared war on crime in 1965. President Richard Nixon then announced his own war in 1969, and President George Bush declared war on drugs on September 5, 1989.[29] Other politicians and policymakers have followed their lead and used the rhetoric of "war" to characterize our crime policy. In the 2000 and 2004 elections, presidential candidates from both major parties were still promising to get tough on crime.

The consequences of the war on crime and drugs have been enormous. The number of prisoners has increased sevenfold, from 196,429 in 1970 to 1,380,776 by mid-2003. With another 691,301 people in local jails, we have a total of 2 million behind bars. The United States has been on an imprisonment orgy, and as Figure 1.2 indicates, the last 30 years represent a radical break with the past. The incarceration rate rose from 96 per 100,000 in 1970 to 714 in 2003 (state and federal prisoners). This compares with incarceration rates of 111 per 100,000 in Canada, 79 in Australia, and 42 in Japan.[30]

FIGURE 1.2 Sentenced prisoners in state and federal institutions on December 31, 1995

SOURCE: Bureau of Justice Statistics, *Sourcebook of Criminal Justice Statistics—1995* (Washington, DC: Government Printing Office, 1996), p. 554.

Prisons are only part of the story. The national jail population more than doubled between 1979 and 2003, rising from 153,394 to 691,301 inmates. The number of people on probation grew from 1,079,258 adults in 1976 to 4,073,987 by the end of 2003, and the number of adults on parole soared from 156,194 to 774,558 by the end of 2003. Thus, the total number of people "under correctional supervision" by 2003 was almost 7 million.[31]

The imprisonment boom is the product of several forces, including some major crime policies that we will look at in this book. Public attitudes about crime and criminals became increasingly punitive, particularly with respect to drugs. These attitudes have been translated into laws producing more and longer prison sentences, particularly for drug offenses. Most of the growth in prison populations is the result of an increase in drug arrests.[32]

The impact of the war on crime on society, and on racial and ethnic minority communities in particular, is one of the main themes of this book. Is it responsible for the recent decline in crime? Has it contributed to the recent reduction in crime rates? Or has it made things worse, increasing the alienation of African American young men in particular? Conservatives such as John J. DiIulio, Jr., and the Council on Crime in America argue that a punitive policy is necessary, morally justified, and if used properly, effective. As the council puts it, prison is "socially beneficial and cost-effective."[33] We will take a close look at this argument.

Race, Ethnicity, and the War on Crime

Elliott Currie, Jerome Miller, the Sentencing Project, the Clark Foundation, and the National Criminal Justice Commission believe that the war on crime has made things worse: that it has not deterred crime, that it is racially biased, and that it has contributed to the destruction of inner-city communities, and as a consequence has increased the likelihood of juvenile violence. The war on crime has also weighed heavily on the Latino community, with young Latino men being stereotyped as gang members, drug dealers, and illegal immigrants.

Currie and others argue that the war on drugs has been waged primarily against young African American men. The Sentencing Project found that African Americans represented 13 percent of the population, but 35 percent of all people arrested for drug offenses, 55 percent of those convicted, and 74 percent of those sentenced to prison for drug offenses.[34] Yet, the National Survey of Drug Use and Health found only modest differences in reported illicit drug use by race and ethnicity. In 2002, for example, 8.5 percent of whites reported using drugs in the past month compared with 9.7 percent of African Americans. This small difference is far out of line with the huge disparities in arrests and convictions. Meanwhile, only 7.2 percent of Latinos reported using drugs in the past month.[35]

Jerome Miller characterizes the war on crime as a case of "search and destroy" directed at young African American men.[36] The National Center on Institutions and Alternatives estimates that on any given day, 42 percent of the young black men (ages 18 to 35) in Washington, DC, are under the control of the justice system: either in prison or jail or on probation or parole. The figure for Baltimore was 56 percent. About 75 percent of the Washington, DC, black men were likely to be arrested before they reached age 35.[37] A study by the California legislature painted a similar picture: one-sixth of the African American men over the age of 16 are arrested every year. Many of these arrests are for drug offenses. Yet the same study found that 92 percent of African American men arrested for drugs were subsequently released for lack of evidence.[38] In short, a huge number of African American men are acquiring arrest records as a result of the war on drugs. By 1990, more black men were in prison than in college.

One of the most profound consequences of the war on crime is the loss of the right to vote. Virtually every state strips a convicted felon of the right to vote. The impact on the African American community is enormous, considering that an estimated 10 percent of the adult African American population is under correctional supervision at any given moment. The Sentencing Project estimates that in 2000 about 4.7 million Americans could not vote because of a felony conviction at some point in their lives. In the city of Atlanta, to take just one example, one in seven African American men, or 14 percent, were disenfranchised.[39] We will take a closer look at disenfranchisement and other restrictions imposed on ex-offenders in Chapter 14. The disparate impact of the war on crime has been profound on attitudes toward the justice system. One survey found that 80 percent of whites believed that O. J. Simpson was guilty of murdering his ex-wife Nicole Brown Simpson and her friend Ronald Goldman.

But 80 percent of African Americans thought he was innocent.[40] The war on crime has contributed to deep distrust of the justice system among minorities.

Discrimination and the *sense* of unfairness contributes to the crime problem. As we will see in Chapter 12, Tom Tyler and other experts on procedural justice argue that people are more inclined to obey the law if they feel that the law and legal institutions are fair and treat them with respect. The sense of unfairness and alienation from the justice system, meanwhile, leads to disrespect for the law and a greater likelihood of lawbreaking.[41]

The War on Crime and the Criminal Justice System

The war on crime has also overloaded the criminal justice system so that in some instances it cannot perform some of its basic functions. In Philadelphia, the police commissioner described the criminal courts as being "on the verge of collapse" in 1990. The massive increase in arrests created a backlog of 12,129 cases, with the result that many more defendants failed to make their scheduled court dates. The number of defendants who did not appear soared from 13,807 in January 1987 to a whopping 32,880 by July 1990. The system was incapable of tracking them down and bringing them into court. Law professor Gerald Caplan described it as "a kind of amnesty for some criminals."[42]

"Getting tough" has actually backfired in many states. As prisons become overcrowded, correctional officials are forced to release many offenders earlier than they normally would just to make room for the new arrivals. The percentage of sentences served in Texas dropped from 30–35 percent during 1977–1980 to approximately 20 percent in 1990.[43] This process undermines the original intent of the tough sentencing law—to reduce crime through deterrence and incapacitation.

A very basic lesson is apparent here: The justice system can handle only so much business. It does not "collapse" like a building. It keeps on going, but only through adjustments that are often undesirable. We will discuss these adjustments in more detail in Chapter 3.

Finally, the enormous cost of the war on crime has drained tax dollars from other social needs, such as education, public health, and the economic infrastructure of roads and bridges. In California, for example, state expenditures for corrections were only half the amount spent on higher education in the early 1980s; by 1994, they were equal, at $3.8 billion. Prison budgets had risen dramatically, whereas the state colleges and universities had suffered drastic cuts.[44] If education has historically been an investment in the future of society, then the cuts in education to finance prison represent a *dis*investment in the future.

The Futility of Waging "War" on Crime

"War" is the wrong metaphor for crime policies. First, it raises unrealistic expectations, promising a "victory" and an end to the "war." In fact, we will never completely eliminate crime. At best, we will succeed in reducing it, hopefully to the point where it does not destroy entire communities. For the same reason, many medical experts do not like the idea of declaring "war" on cancer or other diseases. Whether the problem is crime or cancer, a realistic and sensible goal is to get it down to some tolerable level.[45]

The war metaphor is also wrong because it suggests that we are fighting a foreign enemy. This leads people to demonize criminals as people apart from the rest of us. To a great extent, this tendency to demonize has encouraged racial and ethnic stereotypes and aggravated the racial polarization of American society. Additionally, the "us versus them" attitude encourages police officers to regard suspects as people who do not have the same rights as other American citizens. Community policing, which emphasizes close working relations between police and citizens, is a far more appropriate approach for a democratic society. Finally, as we have already seen, the current war on crime has had a terrible effect on American society, particularly on racial and ethnic minority communities. These facts lead us to the following proposition:

PROPOSITION 2
Waging "war" is the wrong way to fight crime.

The truth is, we do not face a foreign enemy. We are up against ourselves. We need to deal with our own social institutions, our own values, our own habits, and our own crime control policies. Criminologists Steven F. Messner and Richard Rosenfeld argue that "the sources of crime" in this country lie "in the very same values and behaviors that are conventionally viewed as part of the American success story." The values of material success and individual advancement work for many people; but for others the opportunity to achieve the "American Dream" are blocked. They argue that to deal effectively and responsibly with the crime problem we cannot demonize criminals as "others," but instead need to reexamine how well our institutions serve all people.[46]

The American response to the crime problem resembles the way many people deal with being overweight—by "diet binging." Just as people go on crash diets, lose weight, put it all back on, and then take up another diet fad a year later, so we tend to "binge" on crime control fads. In the 1980s it was "selective incapacitation"; in the 1990s boot camps and "three strikes" laws; today it is offender reentry programs (see Chapter 14). And so it goes. Typically, everyone forgets yesterday's fad without examining whether it really worked. The solution to a weight loss problem does not lie in a miracle cure; instead, it involves difficult long-term changes in one's own behavior: eating less, eating less fattening food, and exercising more. By the same token, we will reduce crime when we make basic changes in all of our social policies that affect families, employment, and neighborhoods. There is no quick, easy, "miracle" cure for crime.

CRIME POLICY: A PLAGUE OF NONSENSE

Americans have trouble thinking clearly about crime. The result is a lot of crime control proposals that are nonsense. Why? The main reason is that we have been overwhelmed by violent crime. Even with the great crime drop, we still have far more violent crime than any other industrialized country.[47]

Fear of crime pervades our daily lives like a plague, affecting the way we think, the way we act, the way we respond to one another. It has a corrosive effect on interpersonal relations, making us wary of small acts of friendliness toward strangers. It also distorts the political process, with politicians offering quick-fix solutions that have no realistic hope of reducing crime. Fear and frustration about crime produce irrational thinking. Almost every year some new proposal promises to reduce crime by 30–50 percent.

Even some of the most informed experts on criminal justice are overwhelmed by the problem. When Jerome Miller first sent the manuscript of his book *Search and Destroy* to the publisher, his editor wrote back that it was "too pessimistic," with no optimistic recommendations on how to solve the crime problem. Miller admitted that his editor was right; he did not "have many suggestions—and those I do have, aren't likely to be taken."[48] Many other people have had the same problem: an inability to formulate sensible, realistic proposals for reducing crime.

We need to make an important distinction regarding the goals of different reform proposals. Many sensible proposals involve reducing the *harm* done by the criminal justice system. The Sentencing Project, the Edna McConnell Clark Foundation, and the National Criminal Justice Commission have all made proposals for reducing the harm done by our current sentencing practices. In *Malign Neglect,* Michael Tonry offers a specific proposal for reducing racial disparities in sentencing.[49] Harm reduction, meaning reducing the harm done by the criminal justice system, is a very important and laudable goal. After all, we shouldn't make a bad criminal justice problem worse. The focus in this book, however, is on policies that will reduce *crime,* particularly serious crime.

The Ground Rules

The goal of this book is to identify sensible and effective crime policies. Let us begin by establishing the ground rules for our inquiry. First, we will focus on crime control. We are concerned with policies that will reduce the level of serious crime. We will consider questions of justice and fairness as a basic constraint on crime policy. Effectiveness—defined as reduction in crime—is not the only criterion for a sensible crime control policy. We have limits to what we can do. A democratic society respects the rule of law and standards of justice and fairness, unlike totalitarian societies, which are based on the principle of unlimited government power. It might reduce crime if we just shot all robbers and drug dealers on sight. When an Islamic rebel group took power in Kabul, the capital of Afghanistan, in 1996, the group restored punishments such as stoning to death people guilty of adultery and cutting off the hands of thieves.

One criminal was driven through the streets on a truck with an amputated hand and heavy weights holding his jaw open. Such practices, however, violate our standards of decency and due process.

Second, we will focus primarily on the crimes of robbery and burglary. This limited focus helps impose some discipline on our thinking. Too many people evade the hard questions about crime by changing the subject. Liberals often find it difficult to talk about robbery and burglary, changing the subject to victimless crimes such as gambling, marijuana use, and unconventional sexual behavior. Conservatives, meanwhile, focus on celebrated cases (particularly mass murders or extremely vicious crimes) that have little to do with the routine felonies of robbery and burglary. We will discuss the celebrated case phenomenon in Chapter 2.

At several points along the way, we will consider other crimes to illustrate certain points. An entire section is devoted to drunk driving because this subject provides very useful insights into such issues as police crackdowns, sentencing reform, and deterrence. Domestic violence also illustrates some issues related to deterrence. Chapter 13 covers drugs because it is impossible to talk about crime policy today without addressing the drug issue.

Third, this book concentrates on crimes committed by adults. Juvenile crime and delinquency are serious problems that warrant attention, but the world of juvenile justice is a special realm that deserves a separate critical inquiry.

Thinking Clearly about Crime Prevention

As the 1997 University of Maryland report on *Preventing Crime* argues, many people are confused about the term *crime prevention*. The report points out that "the national debate over crime often treats 'prevention' and 'punishment' as mutually exclusive concepts, polar opposites on a continuum of 'soft' versus 'tough' responses to crime."[50] As we explain shortly, this dichotomy generally defines conservatives as the advocates of "tough" policies and liberals as the advocates of "soft" policies.

The Maryland report persuasively argues that this is a false dichotomy. Regardless of their label, all crime policies are designed to prevent crime. Particular policies are simply different means to that end. An allegedly soft treatment program (e.g., outpatient drug abuse counseling) is intended to prevent crime no less than is an allegedly tough sentencing policy (e.g., a three–strikes law). From the standpoint of effective crime prevention, the real issue is not one of intentions or methods but consequences. Which policies reduce crime?

The Question of Reasonable Goals

Our search for sensible and effective crime policies raises a difficult question of criteria. What do we mean by *effective*? Let us say we find a policy that would reduce crime by 5 percent without doing any serious harm. Is that a goal worth pursuing? A 5 percent reduction is not much, given the size of our crime problem. We would still be swamped by murder, robbery, rape, and drug abuse. It would be easy to dismiss that policy as hardly worth the effort.

The issue here is one of reasonable goals. In his discussion of gun crimes, Gary Kleck makes a persuasive case in favor of modest goals. We should not expect quick and dramatic changes. Unreasonable expectations lead to disappointment and frustration. Kleck advises thinking in terms of modest goals that can be achieved.[51] In the long run, a sensible approach to crime will probably include a series of different policies, each one focusing on a different aspect of the larger problem and each one producing a modest reduction in crime.

The New Focus on Communities and Crime

The most important new development related to thinking about crime policy is a focus on the community context. Community policing obviously emphasizes community, as do most problem-oriented policing programs. They are now joined by community prosecution programs that stress the impact of crime on the quality of life in neighborhoods. In the field of corrections, offender reentry programs focus on the community factors that influence ex-offenders' reintegration into society. Finally, all of these programs are supported by new perspectives in theoretical criminology that examine the collective efficacy of communities to deal with crime through informal means and through partnerships between neighborhood groups and criminal justice agencies.

Because the new community-focused programs share common elements, we will examine them together in Chapter 14. These common elements include undertaking careful planning and bringing in outside experts, working closely with community groups, developing partnerships with other criminal justice and non–criminal justice agencies, using nontraditional and often non–criminal justice responses (such as civil law remedies), and conducting rigorous evaluations to determine effectiveness. Keep these elements in mind as we examine traditional crime policies in Chapters 5 through 13. The new community-focused programs learn from the weaknesses and failures of those traditional approaches.

Contextual Factors: Recent Social Trends

In their Urban Institute paper on the crime drop, Travis and Waul examine the contextual factors affecting crime.[52] The importance of these factors is highlighted by recent trends in a number of social indicators, concerning not only the drop in crime, but also other aspects of the well-being of American society that have been moving in a positive direction. Unemployment in the late 1990s was the lowest since the 1960s. Welfare caseloads dropped significantly in the 1990s and had begun dropping even before enactment of the 1994 Welfare Reform Law. New AIDS cases were also down. Births to teenage women declined sharply between 1992 and 1998. And the divorce rate dropped slowly but steadily in the 1990s.[53] In short, the evidence does not support those who claim that American society is in a state of moral and social collapse. What is particularly striking is that all of these social trends closely parallel the trends in the crime rate. They moved in the same direction and in most cases turned in a positive direction at *almost exactly the same time* in the early 1990s. This points to an important hypothesis: Crime is down because of the general social and economic health of the country, not because of any particular crime policy or policies.

GUILTY: LIBERALS AND CONSERVATIVES

Nonsense about crime is politically nonpartisan. Both liberals and conservatives have been guilty of making extravagant promises about crime reduction. In 1967, the President's Crime Commission, representing a liberal perspective, promised "a significant reduction in crime" if its recommendations were "vigorously pursued."[54] In 1975, the conservative James Q. Wilson offered a program that he claimed would reduce serious crime by 30 percent.[55] Neither of these promises were realistic. And over the years other liberals and conservatives have made equally ridiculous promises. Consequently, our third proposition is as follows:

PROPOSITION 3
Both liberals and conservatives are guilty of peddling nonsense about crime.

Crime policies are guided by certain underlying assumptions. Liberals and conservatives begin with different assumptions about crime, the administration of justice, and human nature. To make sense of different crime control proposals, it is helpful to analyze the underlying assumptions of each side.

CRIME CONTROL THEOLOGY

A serious problem with the debate over crime policy is that faith usually triumphs over facts. Both liberals and conservatives begin with certain assumptions that are almost like religious beliefs. Too often, these assumptions are not supported by empirical evidence. We call this phenomenon *crime control theology.*[56]

Most conservatives, for example, believe that the death penalty deters crime. This view persists despite the fact that no evidence conclusively supports it. Most liberals, meanwhile, believe that "treatment" works as a cure for crime and drug abuse, despite considerable evidence on the limited effectiveness of treatment programs.

In *Point Blank,* Gary Kleck points out how people switch sides on the deterrence question to suit their beliefs. Conservatives believe that the death penalty deters crime but then argue that the exclusionary rule will not deter police misconduct. Liberals switch sides in the opposite direction, arguing that the death penalty does not deter crime but that the exclusionary rule does work.[57] This leads us to the following proposition.

PROPOSITION 4
Most crime control ideas rest on faith rather than facts.

Conservative Theology

Crime control theologies represent idealized worlds that express people's highest hopes and deepest fears. Conservative crime control theology envisions a world of discipline and self-control in which people exercise self-restraint and subordinate their personal passions to the common good. It is a world of limits and clear rules about human behavior.

Conservative crime control theology emphasizes personal responsibility. The problem is that criminals lack self-control. They succumb to their passions and break the rules. They kill because they cannot control their anger. They steal because they want something now and are unable to defer gratification. Poverty or other social conditions are no excuse for crime, in the conservative view. People remain poor because they lack the self-discipline to get an education, find a job, and steadily try to improve themselves. Conservatives are fond of pointing to the many individuals who were born in poverty but worked hard and became rich and successful.

Free will, rational choice, and moral responsibility reign supreme in conservative crime control theology. People are responsible for their own fate; they *choose* to commit crime. James Q. Wilson and Richard J. Herrnstein argue: "At any given moment, a person can choose between committing a crime and not committing it."[58] A good example of a policy based on rational choice theory is the Just Say No antidrug campaign. It assumes that all we have to do is persuade people to make the decision not to use drugs.

Rational choice theory holds that people weigh the relative risks and rewards of committing crime. If the risk of punishment is low or the punishments are relatively light, more people will tend to commit crime. If the chance of being caught and punished is high and the punishments are relatively severe, fewer people will choose to commit crime. Thus, the certainty and severity of punishment directly affect the crime rate.[59]

In conservative crime control theology, punishment has both a moral and a practical element. Because criminals choose to offend, they deserve punishment. They are morally responsible for their actions. Rules are the basis of a civil society, and rule breaking should be punished. This is called *retribution,* or *desert.* James Q. Wilson summed it up in a frequently quoted statement: "Wicked people exist. Nothing avails except to set them apart from innocent people."[60] Conservatives also believe that punishment shapes future behavior through the process of *deterrence. Specific* deterrence is directed at the individual offender, teaching him or her that bad actions have unpleasant consequences. *General* deterrence is directed at the general population, teaching by example.

Conservatives are deeply ambivalent about the role of government in controlling crime. William J. Bennett, John J. DiIulio, Jr., and John P. Walters argue that the "root cause" of crime is "moral poverty" (as opposed to material poverty). Too many children grow up not learning right from wrong. Moral health, they argue, is nurtured primarily by strong, two-parent families, religious training, and social institutions that reinforce the right values. "Can government supply manner and morals?" they ask. "Of course it cannot," they answer. People are socialized into law-abiding behavior primarily by private institutions, beginning with the family. But, these conservatives argue, government does have an important role to play in providing effective examples of holding people responsible for their behavior. Thus, the swift, certain punishment of offenders helps breed moral health. Moral poverty is fostered by the failure of the criminal justice system to punish criminals. Thus, while government cannot do everything, it can do something.[61]

Underlying conservative crime control theology is an idealized image of the patriarchal family. Punishment resembles parental discipline. Minor misbehavior is greeted with a gentle warning, a second misstep earns a sterner reprimand, and serious wrongdoing receives a severe punishment. The point is to teach the wisdom of correct behavior by handing out progressively harsher sanctions and threatening even more unpleasant punishment if the behavior continues.

The real world of crime and justice, unfortunately, does not work like the family. It is filled with some very incorrigible children. Some are so deeply alienated from society that they do not respect the overall structure of authority. Punishment, in fact, may only distance them further. Some observers believe, for example, that arrest and imprisonment are such common experiences in some poor racial and ethnic minority neighborhoods that they have lost whatever deterrent threat they might have once had.[62]

John Braithwaite's provocative book *Crime, Shame, and Reintegration* offers a useful perspective on this problem. Braithwaite describes the process of "reintegrative shaming" as being very much like the way a family handles someone who breaks the rules. But his theory also clearly indicates that informal sanctions work when close social bonds link the sanctioner and the sanctioned, and where no great differences in values exist in the community—that is, when the relationship more closely resembles a family.[63]

This is the heart of the problem. The family analogy breaks down in the real world because we have a highly fragmented society, characterized by great differences in wealth, race, religion, and lifestyles. Our society is anything but a tightly knit community with shared values. Braithwaite's theory, in fact, is a good explanation of why informal, family-style sanctions do not work in our society. His description of the conditions under which a system of reintegrative shaming can work is actually a very accurate description of a seventeenth-century New England village, where that approach to crime control was used very effectively.[64]

The limits of reintegrative shaming lend further support to the importance of a community orientation and the interdependency of institutions and policies emphasized by the University of Maryland *Preventing Crime* report. Effective reintegration requires a reasonably healthy community. Achieving a healthy community, in turn, probably requires a series of crime prevention programs directed toward a number of different institutions: families, schools, the local labor market, and so on.

Conservatives explain the failure of punishment to work by focusing on problems in the criminal justice system. Punishment, they say, is not certain or severe enough. Too many loopholes allow criminals to beat the system: the exclusionary rule, the Miranda warning, the insanity defense, plea bargaining, and so on. The idea that many criminals "beat the system" and "get off easy" is an article of faith in conservative crime control theology. Close these loopholes, ensure certainty of punishment, and we can reduce crime. Longer prison terms and the death penalty, meanwhile, will increase the deterrent effect and reduce crime. We will take a close look at this idea in several of the chapters ahead.

Liberal Theology

Liberal crime control theology has emphasized the social context of crime. According to liberals, criminal behavior is largely the result of social influences such as the family, the peer group, the neighborhood, economic opportunities, and discrimination. Much criminological theory, such as Shaw and McKay's social disorganization theory, reflects this view.

Liberal crime policy seeks to alter social influences that are associated with crime. Rehabilitation programs, for example, are designed to provide a structured set of influences—job counseling, substance abuse treatment—designed to encourage law-abiding behavior. Liberals favor community-based alternatives to imprisonment because they represent a normal social environment compared with the abnormal environment of prison.

Liberals are as guilty of wishful thinking as are conservatives. A fundamental article of faith in liberal crime control theology is the optimistic belief that people's behavior *can* be reshaped through some kind of formal treatment program. The history of prison and correctional reform is the story of a continuing search for the Holy Grail of rehabilitation: a program that will truly reform offenders. The people who invented the prison in the nineteenth century thought that that institution would do the job.[65] When it had obviously failed, reformers invented parole and the indeterminate sentence, advertising them as the magic keys to rehabilitation. When these measures did not solve the problem of crime, reformers came up with new variations (group counseling, intensive supervision, and so forth). None of these programs has demonstrated consistent effectiveness.

If conservatives refuse to face the facts about the failure of punishment, liberals refuse to look at the sad history of the failure of rehabilitation. Faith continues to survive in the face of repeated failure. It is also an article of faith among liberals that the United States is the most punitive country in the world. We do, in fact, lock up more people than any other country. Our current incarceration rate of 452 per 100,000 leads the world (keep in mind that this figure represents only the prison population; a higher figure is often cited that includes both prison and jail populations). James Lynch's research offers a valuable comparative perspective on this figure. Using arrests as a baseline, he notes that the probabilities of an offender's going to prison are only slightly different in the United States, Canada, England, and West Germany. In this regard, we are no more punitive than most other countries. We do, however, give much longer prison sentences. Our incarceration rate is greater primarily because we have more serious crime than these other countries.[66]

If conservatives believe that most of our problems are the result of loopholes that let too many people off easy, liberals are guilty of blaming everything on overly harsh punishments.

Liberals are ambivalent on the question of individual responsibility. Although they emphasize the importance of social conditions in causing crime and reject the conservative preoccupation with individual responsibility, they cannot completely ignore the role of individual choice. Rehabilitation programs, in fact, are designed to influence individuals to make different (and better) choices. In the realm of the public policy debate, however, liberals tend to downplay the element of individual responsibility.

Applying the New Evidence-Based Policy Standard This book will bring to bear the new standards of evidence-based crime policy on the recommendations of both conservatives and liberals. Wishful thinking and unverified assumptions are no longer sufficient. Each and every policy or recommended policy should be supported by solid evidence based on high-quality research.

A Word about Rules

One way to distinguish between conservatives and liberals with respect to crime policy is their attitude toward *rules*. Everyone believes in rules and their application in a consistent fashion. This is what people mean when they refer to the "rule of law."

Conservatives and liberals mainly disagree over which set of rules to emphasize. In criminal justice, we have two basic sets: criminal law and criminal procedure. The substantive *criminal law* is a set of rules governing everyone's behavior. It defines certain behavior as criminal and specifies the penalty for breaking the rules. *Criminal procedure,* on the other hand, is a set of rules governing criminal justice officials. It tells them what they may not do (e.g., conduct unreasonable searches and seizures) and what they must do (e.g., bring the suspect before a magistrate without unnecessary delay).[67]

Conservatives emphasize the rules of the criminal law. Harming a person or taking someone else's property violates the basic standards of a decent society. Anyone who violates these rules should be punished. Liberals tend to emphasize the rules of criminal procedure. A free society is one that strictly limits the potentially awesome power of government officials.

One way to understand the difference between liberal and conservative attitudes toward rules is to recognize what each side sees as its worst nightmare. For conservatives, unchecked criminality leads to anarchy and the death of freedom. For liberals, unchecked government power leads to tyranny and the death of freedom. The difference is really a question of what represents the greatest threat to freedom. Both sides are ambivalent about rule breaking. Conservatives tend to be willing to excuse violations of the rules of procedure to control crime. They will overlook the unreasonable search if it helps convict a criminal. Liberals, on the other hand, are more concerned about official rule breaking. They are willing to see a criminal suspect go free if a police officer or some other official has made a serious mistake. These differences are not absolute, of course. They are really matters of emphasis. Conservatives do not endorse gross abuses by the police, and liberals do not endorse crime.

The classic statement of the difference between conservatives and liberals on this issue is Herbert Packer's essay on the "two models of the criminal process."[68] Conservatives embrace the *crime control model,* which puts a high priority on the effective control of crime. To this end, they are willing to grant officials considerable leeway, not restricting them with a lot of rules. Liberals prefer the *due process model,* in which the highest priorities are fair treatment and the presumption of innocence. Formal rules (due process guarantees) are designed to achieve these goals.

Ideological Confusion: Switching Sides

The conservative/liberal dichotomy is a useful way to think about crime policy. It helps identify the basic assumptions that underlie different policies. In the last few years, however, this dichotomy is not quite as sharp as it was a few years ago. Strange things have been happening. Some conservatives have adopted traditional liberal policies, and many liberals have embraced traditional conservative ideas. Understanding the crime debate today requires sorting our way through this ideological confusion.

One major change involves the issue of legalizing drugs. Decriminalization has traditionally been a proposal by liberals. They have argued that we should not criminalize behavior that does not harm others. Moreover, criminalizing a lot of behavior often tends to make things worse, by overloading the criminal justice system, encouraging corruption, and failing to respond effectively to what are really social and medical problems. Surprisingly, many prominent conservatives endorse legalizing drugs. The most prominent is the writer and television talk show host William F. Buckley. We will examine the arguments in favor of drug legalization in Chapter 13. For the moment, it is important to note that some conservatives have switched sides and adopted a traditional liberal position.

Also, the conservative administration of George W. Bush has strongly supported offender reentry programs (see Chapter 14), which involve the traditional liberal idea of reintegrating offenders into society.

Meanwhile, many liberals have adopted some conservative crime control proposals. The best example is former President Bill Clinton. The 1994 Violent Crime Control Act, which he supported, calls for more police and longer prison sentences. In the 1996 presidential election campaign, political observers said that Clinton had moved to the right and embraced the traditional Republican position on crime. In short, the ideological lineup on crime control policies has become very muddled. Nonetheless, it is still possible to identify a set of crime policies that, because of their underlying assumptions, can be classified as conservative and another set that can be classified as liberal. These categories will help us analyze the different policies we will consider in this book.

CONCLUSION

Crime is a serious problem in the United States. The recent dramatic reductions in the crime rate still leave a problem of violent crime that is far higher than in other industrialized countries. Unfortunately, we do not have many good ideas about how to solve the crime problem. In this initial chapter, we have tried to sketch out some of the complexity of the U.S. crime problem. We have also indicated briefly why so many crime control policies are worthless. In the chapters that follow, we will develop these themes in more detail. The next two chapters take a closer look at how the criminal justice system actually works. Then we will turn our attention to specific crime control proposals. As we already indicated, our basic goal is to find some crime control policies that make sense and that are supported by persuasive evidence.

NOTES

1.   Bureau of Justice Statistics, *Criminal Victimization, 2003* (Washington, DC: Department of Justice, 2004). NCJ 205455. Available on the NCJRS website.

2.   Boston Police Department, *Annual Report 2004.* Available on the department's website. San Diego Police Department, *Annual Report 2004.* Available on the department's website.

3.   The best summary of these trends is Marc Miringoff and Marque-Luisa Miringoff, *The Social Health of the Nation: How America is Really Doing* (New York: Oxford University Press, 1999).

4.   "Camden's Streets Go From Mean to Meanest," *New York Times,* 29 December 2004.

5.   Alfred Blumstein and Joel Wallman, eds., *The Crime Drop in America* (New York: Cambridge University Press, 2000), p. 11.

6.   Ibid.

7.   George L. Kelling and Catherine M. Coles, *Fixing Broken Windows* (New York: Martin Kessler Books, 1996); William

Bratton and Peter Knoblach, *Turnaround* (New York: Random House, 1998).

8.   Substance Abuse and Mental Health Services Administration, Office of Applied Studies [SAMHSA-OAS]. *Emergency Department Trends From the Drug Abuse Warning Network, Final Estimates, 1995–2002,* DAWN Series: D-24, DHHS Publication No. (SMA) 03-3780, Rockville, MD, 2003. Available on the HHS website.

9.   Jeremy Travis and Michelle Waul, *Reflections on the Crime Decline: Lessons for the Future?* (Washington, DC: Urban Institute, 2002). Available on the Urban Institute website.

10.   Check the websites of these organizations for more details.

11.   Nick Tilley and Gloria Laycock, *Working Out What to Do: Evidence-Based Crime Reduction* (London: Home Office, 2002). Available on the Home Office website.

12.   Coalition for Evidence-Based Policy [CEBP], *Bringing Evidence-Driven Progress to*

Crime and Substance-Abuse Policy: A Recommended Federal Strategy (December 2003). Available on the CEBP website.

13. This material is found on the U.S. Department of Justice website.

14. David P. Farrington and Anthony Petrosino, "The Campbell Collaboration Crime and Justice Group," *The Annals* 578 (November 2001): 35–49.

15. *Remarks of the Honorable Deborah J. Daniels, Assistant Attorney General of Justice Programs, at the National Forum on Evidence-Based Crime and Substance Abuse Policy,* Washington, DC, June 14, 2004.

16. Joan McCord, "Cures That Harm: Unanticipated Outcomes of Crime Prevention Programs," in David Weisburd, Anthony Petrosino, and Cynthia Lum, eds., "Assessing Systematic Evidence in Crime and Justice: Methodological Concerns and Empirical Outcomes," special issue, *The Annals* 587 (May 2003): 16–30.

17. Ibid.

18. James O. Finckenauer, *Scared Straight and the Panacea Phenomenon* (Englewood Cliffs, NJ: Prentice-Hall, 1982).

19. Lawrence W. Sherman, Denise C. Gottfredson, Doris L. MacKenzie, et al., for the University of Maryland Department of Criminology and Criminal Justice, *Preventing Crime: What Works, What Doesn't, What's Promising* (Washington, DC: Government Printing Office, 1997), pp. 2. NCJ 171676.

20. Lawrence W. Sherman, *Policing Domestic Violence* (New York: The Free Press, 1992). Christopher D. Maxwell, Joel H. Garner and Jeffrey A Fagan, *The Effects of Arrest on Intimate Partner Violence: New Evidence from the Spouse Assault Replication Program* (Washington, DC: Justice Department, 2001). NCJ188199.

21. The Sentencing Project, *Crime, Punishment and Public Opinion: A Summary of Recent Studies and Their Implications for Sentencing Policy* (Washington, DC: The Sentencing Project, n.d.). Available on the Sentencing Project website.

22. Bureau of Justice Statistics, *Criminal Victimization, 2003.*

23. Bureau of Justice Statistics, *Homicide Trends in the United States: 2002 Update* (Washington, DC: Department of Justice, 2004). NCJ 204885.

24. Department of Health and Human Services [HHS], *2003 National Survey on Drug Use and Health* (Washington, DC: Author, 2004). Available on the HHS website.

25. SAMHSA-OAS. *Emergency Department Trends from the Drug Abuse Warning Network, Final Estimates, 1995–2002.*

26. Franklin E. Zimring and Gordon Hawkins, *Crime Is Not the Problem: Lethal Violence in America* (New York: Oxford University Press, 1997); James Lynch, "Crime In International Perspective," in James Q. Wilson and Joan Petersilia, eds., *Crime* (San Francisco: ICS Press, 1995), pp. 11–38.

27. Zimring and Hawkins, *Crime Is Not the Problem,* chapter 4.

28. Stephen R. Donziger, ed., *The Real War on Crime: The Report of the National Criminal Justice Commission* (New York: HarperCollins, 1996).

29. Samuel Walker, *Popular Justice: A History of American Criminal Justice,* 2nd ed. (New York: Oxford University Press, 1998).

30. Bureau of Justice Statistics, *Sourcebook of Criminal Justice Statistics,* online edition, available on the SUNY Albany web site. Table 6.12.

31. Bureau of Justice Statistics, *Probation and Parole in the United States, 2003* (Washington, DC: Department of Justice, 2004). NCJ 205336.

32. Edna McConnell Clark Foundation, *Americans Behind Bars* (New York: Author, 1994), p. 8.

33. William J. Bennett, John J. DiIulio, Jr., and John P. Walters, *Body Count* (New York: Simon and Schuster, 1996).

34. Elliott Currie, *Reckoning: Drugs, the Cities, and the American Future* (New York: Hill and Wang, 1992).

35. Department of Health and Human Services, *National Survey of Drug Use and Health, 2002* (Washington, DC: Author, 2003). Available on the SAMSHA website.

36. Jerome G. Miller, *Search and Destroy: African American Males in the Criminal Justice System* (New York: Cambridge University Press, 1996).

37. National Center on Institutions and Alternatives, *Hobbling a Generation: African American Males in the District of Columbia's Criminal Justice System* (Alexandria, VA: National Center on Institutions and Alternatives, 1992); Miller, *Search and Destroy*, p. 7.

38. Miller, *Search and Destroy*, p. 8.

39. Ryan S. King and Marc Mauer, *The Vanishing Black Electorate: Felony Disenfranchisement in Atlanta, Georgia* (Washington, DC: The Sentencing Project, 2004). Available on the Sentencing Project website.

40. Donziger, ed., *The Real War on Crime*, pp. 169–170.

41. Tom R. Tyler, *Why People Obey the Law* (New Haven: Yale University Press, 1990).

42. Michael de Courcy Hinds, "Philadelphia Justice System Overwhelmed," *New York Times*, 15 August 1990: 1, 13.

43. Sheldon Ekland-Olson, "Crime and Incarceration: Some Comparative Findings From the 1980s," *Crime and Delinquency* 38 (July 1992): 392–416.

44. Edna McConnell Clark Foundation, *Americans Behind Bars*.

45. One of the best early discussions of this point is Egon Bittner, "The Police and the 'War on Crime,'" in *The Functions of the Police in Modern Society* (Washington, DC: Government Printing Office, 1970), pp. 48–51.

46. Steven F. Messner and Richard Rosenfeld, *Crime and the American Dream*, 3rd ed. (Belmont, CA: Wadsworth, 2001).

47. Ineke Haen Marshall, "How Exceptional Is the United States? Crime Trends in Europe and the US," *European Journal on Criminal Policy and Research* 4: 7–35.

48. Miller, *Search and Destroy*, p. 235.

49. Michael Tonry, *Malign Neglect* (New York: Oxford University Press, 1995).

50. Sherman et al., *Preventing Crime*.

51. Gary Kleck, *Point Blank: Guns and Violence in America* (New York: Aldine de Gruyter, 1991), pp. 432–433.

52. Travis and Waul, *Reflections on the Crime Decline*.

53. A particularly valuable source is Miringoff and Miringoff, *The Social Health of the Nation: How America is Really Doing*.

54. President's Commission on Law Enforcement and Administration of Justice, *The Challenge of Crime in a Free Society* (Washington, DC: Government Printing Office, 1967), p. vi.

55. James Q. Wilson, *Thinking About Crime* (New York: Basic Books, 1975).

56. George C. Thomas and David Edelman, "An Evaluation of Conservative Crime Control Theology," *Notre Dame Law Review* 63 (1988): 123–160.

57. Kleck, *Point Blank*.

58. James Q. Wilson and Richard J. Herrnstein, *Crime and Human Nature: The Definitive Study of the Causes of Crime* (New York: Simon and Schuster, 1985), p. 44.

59. But everyone should read the article Wilson coauthored with Allen Abrahamse, "Does Crime Pay?" *Justice Quarterly* 9 (September 1992): 359–377.

60. Wilson, *Thinking About Crime*, p. 209.

61. Bennett et al., *Body Count*, p. 205.

62. See the discussion of this point in Daniel S. Nagin, "Criminal Deterrence Research at the Outset of the Twenty-First Century," in Michael Tonry, ed., *Crime and Justice: A Review of Research*, vol. 23 (Chicago: University of Chicago Press, 1998), pp. 4–5.

63. John Braithwaite, *Crime, Shame, and Reintegration* (New York: Cambridge University Press, 1989); John Braithwaite, "Restorative Justice: Assessing Optimistic and Pessimistic Accounts," in Michael Tonry, ed., *Crime and Justice: A Review of Research*, vol. 25 (Chicago: University of Chicago Press, 1999), pp. 1–127.

64. Lawrence M. Friedman, *Crime and Punishment in American History* (New York: Basic Books, 1993). Walker, *Popular Justice*, chap. 1.

65. David Rothman, *The Discovery of the Asylum* (Boston: Little, Brown, 1971).

66. Lynch, "Crime in International Perspective."

67. On the subject of rules and discretion, see Samuel Walker, *Taming the System: The Control of Discretion in American Criminal Justice, 1950–1990* (New York: Oxford University Press, 1993).

68. Herbert L. Packer, "Two Models of the Criminal Process," in *The Limits of the Criminal Sanction* (Stanford, CA: Stanford University Press, 1968), chap. 8.

2

Models of Criminal Justice

The triumph of faith over facts requires a willful disregard of the realities of crime and criminal justice. Many people believe what they want to believe about how the justice system works, disregarding any and all evidence to the contrary. This problem partly results from the fact that the American criminal justice system is so complex. We actually have 51 separate criminal justice systems (50 states plus the federal system), which include 18,769 separate state and local law enforcement agencies. To get a sense of the bewildering variety of only the formal structure of different court systems, take a look at the Bureau of Justice Statistics (BJS) report *State Court Organization*.[1] In addition, the criminal codes and the rules of criminal procedure vary in all of these systems.

The day-to-day administration of justice is even more complex than the formal machinery of the justice system. To the casual observer, things often seem chaotic. Many important decisions are made in informal, "low-visibility" settings—the arrest on the street, the plea bargain negotiated in the court hallway. Even many experts are mystified by some of the important features of our criminal justice system. We now have a general sense of what occurs in the hidden realms of police discretion and plea bargaining, but many other important decisions have not been researched. In this context, misunderstanding and myth prevail. Consequently, our next proposition is as follows:

PROPOSITION 5

Most crime control ideas are based on false assumptions about how the criminal justice system works.

Two attitudes dominate thinking about the administration of criminal justice: the Old Idealism and the New Cynicism. Neither is very helpful in explaining how the system works.

The Old Idealism is the civics-book picture of justice. This view holds that diligent and hardworking officials enforce the law as it is written in the statutes; a person who commits a crime is duly arrested and prosecuted for that offense; if convicted, he or she receives the prescribed punishment. It is an adversarial system of justice that determines the truth of guilt or innocence through a public contest between prosecution and defense, overseen by an impartial judge. Although inspiring, this version of the criminal process does not describe the reality of our justice system.

The New Cynicism is a mirror image of the Old Idealism. It portrays a chaotic criminal justice system in which there is neither law, order, nor justice. Police discretion is completely out of control: Officers arrest whomever they want, use force without provocation, and so on. Prosecutors plea-bargain wildly: Guilty people get off, and innocent people are railroaded into prison. Defense attorneys are friends of the prosecutors and cut deals to suit each other's needs.[2] Sentencing is totally arbitrary: There is no rhyme or reason why some people go to prison and others get probation. Parole boards grant or deny release without any rational or scientific basis for their decisions. Finally, the New Cynicism holds that the entire criminal justice system is pervaded with discrimination against people of color.[3]

The New Cynicism comes in two versions. Conservative cynics see irrational decision making undermining effective crime control. Criminals are not punished for their crimes: Either they are not arrested, they get their charges dropped, or they obtain early parole release. Crafty defense lawyers manipulate the rules of criminal procedure to beat the system. Liberal cynics, on the other hand, believe that the apparent chaos of the system produces systematic discrimination. The poor are punished while "respectable" offenders get off easy; African Americans and Hispanic Americans are the victims of systematic discrimination.

The challenge facing us in our search for effective crime policies is to find the truth about the justice system. It is undeniable that much criminal justice decision making *is* irrational. Many offenders *do* escape punishment: The risk of being arrested even for drunk driving, for example, is extremely low. There *is* racial discrimination in the system: The African American who murders a white person is far more likely to be sentenced to death than the white person who murders an African American.

But neither version of the New Cynicism adequately explains how the justice system handles *routine cases on a day-to-day basis*—and that is the focus of our inquiry. This chapter argues that most of the time, the system operates in a fairly consistent and predictable manner. The social science evidence supports this view. Donald Black and subsequent researchers have found predictable patterns in police arrest discretion.[4] Studies of plea bargaining found that about 80 percent of the outcomes were predictable with knowledge of the offense and the defendant's prior record.[5]

Despite a high degree of predictability, the justice system is filled with paradoxes and inconsistencies. There is much truth in the comment that "the problem is not that our system is too lenient, or too severe; sadly, it is both."[6] Norval Morris and Michael Tonry argue that we simultaneously send too many people to prison and give others meaningless forms of probation with little supervision: "We are both too lenient and too severe."[7] This paradox is a key to understanding how our criminal justice system really works.

Policing offers a concrete example of the contradictions in the administration of justice. In the same city, in the same precinct, on the same night, within the space of an hour, a pair of police officers will both *over*enforce and *under*enforce the law: They will be overly aggressive toward young African American men hanging out on a street corner and then within an hour not make an arrest in a domestic violence incident a few blocks away, denying the victim the protection of the law.[8] Sentencing offers additional examples. Some people with multiple drunk driving convictions manage to avoid long mandatory prison terms while someone arrested for possession of a small amount of drugs is sentenced to 25 years in prison. In terms of the harm to society, this inconsistency makes no sense.

THE CRIME COMMISSION'S MODEL

To help understand the administration of justice, social scientists have constructed models of the system. The first and most famous model (Figure 2.1) was developed 35 years ago by the President's Crime Commission (officially the President's Commission on Law Enforcement and Administration of Justice).[9] This commission introduced the "systems" approach to the administration of criminal justice, which has shaped thinking about the subject since it first appeared. Prior to that, people thought in terms of separate justice agencies that had little relationship to each other.

The Crime Commission's model was a great leap forward in our understanding of criminal justice. It accomplished exactly what models are designed to do: provide a conceptual framework, or paradigm, that helps identify general patterns, define problems, and focus research and policy planning. The systems model focuses attention on the flow of cases among agencies, the interrelationships among agencies (or "components"), and the pervasiveness of discretionary decision making in controlling the flow of cases.[10] It focuses attention on discretion and the factors that influence decision making. It also emphasizes the dynamic relationship among components of the system and how decisions at one point (say, the prosecutor) affect decisions "upstream" (the police) and "downstream" (the judge).

The Crime Commission's model has its limitations, however. Based on the growing body of criminal justice research, we offer an alternative model.

THE CRIMINAL JUSTICE WEDDING CAKE

The major shortcoming of the Crime Commission's model is that it portrays a single justice system that handles all cases alike. Our alternative model is a four-layer wedding cake that focuses attention on important variations in how cases are handled (Figure 2.2). The wedding cake model was first developed by Lawrence Friedman and Robert V. Percival in *The Roots of Justice,* a history of criminal justice in Alameda County, California, between 1870 and 1910.[11] Additional support, based on contemporary evidence, is found in Michael and Don Gottfredson's *Decision Making in Criminal Justice.*[12]

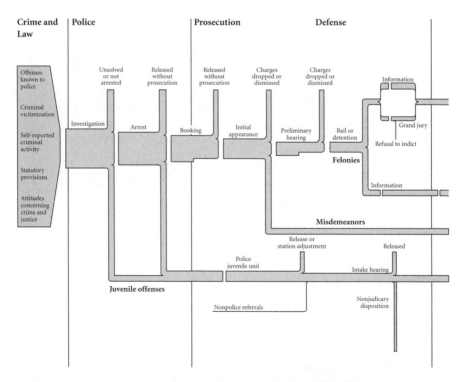

FIGURE 2.1 The Crime Commission's model of the criminal justice system

SOURCE: President's Commission on Law Enforcement and Administration of Justice, *Task Force Report: Science and Technology* (Washington, DC: Government Printing Office, 1967), pp. 58–59.

The wedding cake model emphasizes two points. First, there are significant differences *between* types of cases, based on seriousness and other factors. Second, there are fairly consistent patterns of disposition *within* each category.

Celebrated Cases: The Top Layer

At the top of the wedding cake is a very small layer of "celebrated cases." Every year the news is dominated by a celebrated case involving either a famous person or a particularly gruesome crime. In 2003–4 it was the case of Scott Peterson, who was convicted of murdering his pregnant wife, Laci. At the same time the faded television and movie star Robert Blake was charged with shooting and killing his girlfriend. The all-time celebrated case, of course, was the O. J. Simpson trial. Because of Simpson's fame as an athlete and movie star, the viciousness of the crime, the money involved and high-powered legal defense team, and the volatile mix of race and sex, probably no other case like this has appeared in American history.[13]

FIGURE 2.2 The criminal justice wedding cake

An excellent example of the impact of celebrated cases on public perceptions involves violence in public schools. The shocking Columbine High School massacre on April 20, 1999, in which 2 students shot and killed 13 students and faculty, left a deep imprint on public consciousness. Many people believe that schools are violent and dangerous places and that violence is increasing. The BJS study of school crime presents a very different picture. Between 1995 and 2001 the total victimization rate in schools declined 40 percent. About two-thirds of all victimizations involved theft. Between mid-1999 and 2000 only 16 students in the entire country died as a result of school-related violence (this is out of a total of 53 million public school children).[14]

Celebrated cases are different from other cases in several respects. First, they usually involve the *full criminal process,* including that rare event, the criminal trial. We get to see fundamental issues contested in public view: the sanity of the defendant; the admissibility of the evidence; the credibility of the witnesses; and the competence of prosecutor, defense attorney, and judge. Trials are dramatic events, filled with suspense about the outcome. Day-to-day, however, most cases never go to trial, and in fact many are dismissed without prosecution.

Second, celebrated cases receive an enormous amount of *publicity,* usually because of the nature of the crime itself (typically something ghastly) or the fame of the person involved (as either victim or defendant). A few cases become celebrated because they result in landmark Supreme Court rulings. The *Miranda* case is an excellent example.

Third, because of all the publicity, celebrated cases *distort public perceptions* about criminal justice. People mistakenly assume that they are typical of all cases. This fosters the belief that people like Ernesto Miranda (whose case gave us the *Miranda* warning) are "beating the system" every day through "technicalities."

The O. J. Simpson trial, for example, has led many people to conclude that spouse murderers beat the system all the time. Even worse, it has led many whites to believe that African American jurors will not convict an African American defendant. Both of these perceptions are grossly wrong. In response to the Simpson trial outcome, the BJS analyzed its data on spouse murders from the 75 largest counties in the country for 1988. This included a total of 540 cases.[15] As Figure 2.3 indicates, very few accused spouse murderers beat the system. In fact, only 2 percent of the husbands were acquitted. Wives were more likely to win acquittal (14 percent) because there were more likely to be mitigating circumstances, such as killing in self-defense. The system was tough on spouse murder defendants at every stage. Only 13 percent were not prosecuted. And of those who were convicted, 71 percent were sentenced to prison (81 percent of the husbands and 57 percent of the wives).

Unfortunately, the BJS data set does not include the racial composition of juries. Because the data come from the 75 largest urban counties in the country, however, it is a safe assumption that racial minorities were well represented. Thus, there is probably no truth to the idea that minority jurors refuse to convict minority defendants. These data, in fact, indicate no real difference in the conviction rates between whites (81 percent) and African Americans (79 percent).

FIGURE 2.3 Dispositions of spouse murder defendants

The great value of the BJS data set is that it reflects the routine, day-in, day-out administration of justice. It gives us a far more accurate picture of how the system operates than celebrated cases such as the O. J. Simpson trial. To understand how routine robberies and burglaries are handled, we need to turn our attention to the second and third layers of the wedding cake.

Serious Felonies: The Second and Third Layers

In their original version of the wedding cake, Friedman and Percival put all felony cases in one layer. The Gottfredsons made an extremely important refinement by dividing felonies into two categories based on perceived seriousness. In our wedding cake, the more serious felonies go into the second layer and the less serious felonies go into the third.

A large body of research supports the view that criminal justice officials consistently classify cases on the basis of three factors related to seriousness: (1) the nature of the crime, (2) the suspect's prior record, and (3) the relationship between the victim and the offender. In a study of violent felony cases in Detroit, Spohn and Cederblom identified five different factors that distinguished the more serious from the less serious cases: (1) the seriousness of the charge, (2) the defendant's prior record, (3) whether the victim and the offender were strangers, (4) whether the victim was injured, and (5) whether the offender used a gun.[16] Jeffrey T. Ulmer's study of sentencing under the Pennsylvania sentencing guidelines found that while the guidelines were designed to limit sentencing discretion, there were some departures from prescribed sentences and that considerations of seriousness (prior record, offense type, severity) accounted for most of those departures.[17]

The process of classifying cases is *informal;* there is no actual checklist of factors (although some prosecutors' offices have formal limits on plea-bargaining certain kinds of cases, such as those that involve drugs, weapons, or rape).[18] Essentially, officials ask themselves, "How much is this case worth?" or "How bad is this offender?"[19] The everyday language of police and prosecutors reveals a lot about how cases are handled. They refer to "heavy" cases and "real" crimes as opposed to the "garbage" or "bullshit" cases.[20] A study of California probation officers found that they used the same definitions of "heavy-duty" and "lightweight" cases that judges and prosecutors used.[21]

These judgments about seriousness are shared by all the members of the *courtroom work group.* As we will see in Chapter 3, the courtroom work group is one of the most important factors in determining how the system works. The work group consists of criminal justice officials who work together day in and day out. For the sake of efficiency, they develop shared understandings about how to handle routine cases. This approach has two important consequences. First, it means that individual discretion is controlled *informally,* through understandings and expectations (as opposed to formal rules). Second, it produces a high degree of consistency *within* each layer of the wedding cake. The shared definition of seriousness facilitates rapid disposition of a high volume of cases. Prosecutors and defense attorneys do not spend a lot of time arguing over particular cases. (We will discuss this effect in more detail in Chapter 8.) Actually, the idea of plea "bargaining" is misleading. The criminal court is not like a Middle Eastern bazaar, where people haggle over the price of each item. Instead, as Malcolm Feeley argues, it resembles a modern supermarket, with set prices and high volume.[22] The "fixed prices" reflect the shared assumptions about how much cases are "worth."

Ulmer's study of sentencing in three Pennsylvania counties also found, however, that the degree of shared understandings can vary. One county court system had a high degree of stability among its members (prosecution, defense, judges), and as a consequence their relations were characterized by a high degree of collegiality and agreement. A large urban county, on the other hand, had a high degree of turnover in the district attorney's office, which resulted in conflict between prosecution and defense and a high degree of collegiality and understanding between defense attorneys and judges.[23] In short, while *most* court systems operate under shared understandings, there are important *variations* depending on the composition and culture of the local courtroom work group. We will discuss the work group in more detail in Chapter 3.

Robbery illustrates how officials distribute cases between the second and third layers. Because robbery is generally considered a very serious crime, most such cases end up in the second layer. About one-third of all robberies, however, are between acquaintances. These are often private disputes: a disagreement over borrowed money or tools where the "offender" takes back his or her property by force.[24] These robbery cases tend to end up in the third layer because they are not considered as serious as robberies by strangers. If, however, the offender has a long prior record of arrests and convictions, the case might remain in the second layer.

The Impact of Prior Record

The BJS report on *Felony Defendants in Large Urban Counties, 2000* provides powerful evidence on the impact of prior record in the disposition of cases.[25] As Table 2.1 indicates, the percentage of defendants convicted of a violent offense sentenced to prison dropped from 75 percent for those with two or more prior felony convictions to only 40 percent for those with no prior convictions (felony or misdemeanor). A similar pattern exists for persons convicted of a property offense.

The Impact of the Victim/Offender Relationship

A Vera Institute study of felony arrests in New York City illustrates the tremendous impact of the relationship between the offender and the victim.[26] Figure 2.4 indicates that 88 percent of the stranger robberies resulted in conviction. Moreover, prosecutors were not lenient in plea bargaining: 77 percent of those convictions (68 percent of the original arrests) were on felony charges. Nearly three-quarters (74 percent) of those convicted were incarcerated, and half of them did time of a year or more. This is hardly the picture of a system "soft" on crime.

Table 2.1 Impact of prior record on sentencing: Percentage of offenders convicted of a violent offense sentenced to prison

Prior record	Percentage sentenced to prison
More than 1 felony conviction	75%
1 felony conviction	55
Prior misdemeanor conviction only	36
No prior convictions	40

SOURCE: Bureau of Justice Statistics, *Felony Defendants in Large Urban Counties, 2000* (Washington, DC: Department of Justice, 2003). NCJ 202021.

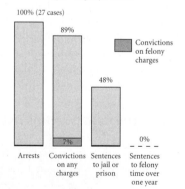

FIGURE 2.4 Outcomes of stranger and nonstranger robberies and burglaries, New York City

SOURCE: Vera Institute, *Felony Arrests,* rev. ed. (New York: Longman, 1981), pp. 68, 86. Reprinted with permission.

The prior-relationship robberies are a completely different story. Only about a third (37 percent) of the suspects were convicted, and only 13 percent of them (5 percent of the number originally arrested) were convicted on felony charges. Slightly more than half (56 percent) of those convicted were incarcerated, but none did a year or more.

The powerful effect of prior relationships is also evident in rape cases. About half of the sexual assaults in the Vera Institute study were committed by men who knew the victim. Sixty percent of these cases were dismissed; another 20 percent ended in a guilty plea with only minor punishment. All of the stranger-rape cases, however, went to trial. Three-quarters of these resulted in conviction and imprisonment, and two-thirds of the prison terms exceeded 25 years.[27]

The most important point that emerges from this analysis is that the criminal justice system is very tough on second-layer felonies. Offenders who have committed a serious crime, committed it against a stranger, and have a long prior record are very likely to be (1) prosecuted on the top charge, (2) convicted, and (3) given a relatively severe sentence (usually prison). As Spohn and Cederblom found, the use of a weapon and/or injury to the victim, factors that raise the seriousness of the offense, increases the severity of the disposition.

The third layer is a different story altogether. The less serious cases are regularly dismissed; defendants are often allowed to plead guilty to lesser offenses; and, if convicted, defendants are placed on probation. Outcomes are less predictable in the third layer because less consensus prevails about seriousness and the appropriate response than in the second layer.

In their classic study of the jury, Harry Kalven and Hans Zeisel explain this lack of consensus in terms of a "liberation" hypothesis. Under certain circumstances, they argue, jurors are "liberated" from normal constraints.[28] Applying this hypothesis to the wedding cake, we can say that in the third layer the lack of consensus about the seriousness of the crime or the offender's prior record liberates prosecutors and judges from the conventional shared understandings of seriousness. This allows them to base their decision on other factors. In some instances, the defendant's race or other personal attribute becomes a factor.

Spohn and Cederblom explored the liberation hypothesis in a study of 4,655 violent felony cases in Detroit from 1976 to 1978.[29] They found that African Americans were more likely to be incarcerated than whites. But this was true only in the less serious crimes: in assaults rather than more serious felonies, in acquaintance crimes, and in cases in which there were no prior violent felony convictions or no gun was involved. The outcomes in the more serious crimes (that is, the second-layer cases) were more consistent, with whites and African Americans treated equally harshly. In the less serious (e.g., third-layer) cases, there was less consensus about how much these cases were "worth," and this allowed extralegal factors such as race to come into play.

We might note that crime *victims* make the same distinctions about seriousness as do criminal justice officials. The National Criminal Victimization Survey consistently finds that victims report the more serious crimes at a higher rate than less serious ones. In 2003, victims reported 60.5 percent of all robberies but only 31.8 percent of all thefts. Moreover, victims have always reported completed robberies at a higher rate than attempted robberies. For all crimes, the more serious the crime, the higher the reporting rate.[30]

Prior Relationship: A Policy Dilemma

The role of the prior relationship between victim and offender presents a major policy dilemma. At issue is whether it is legitimate to use this role as a factor in decision making.

In the area of domestic violence, research has found that police traditionally have taken into account the nature of the relationship. The more intimate the relationship, the less likely the police are to make an arrest.[31] Thus, they are less likely to arrest the abusive husband than the abusive boyfriend or lover. In response to protests from women's groups, many police departments have adopted mandatory arrest or arrest-preferred policies that either require an arrest in a felonious domestic assault or advise officers that arrest is the preferred disposition. The intent is to ensure equal enforcement of the law and to eliminate discrimination based on marital status.

Along the same lines, Susan Estrich argues that all sexual assaults should be prosecuted with equal vigor. Rapes between acquaintances should not be treated less seriously than stranger rapes. Estrich describes her conversation with a local prosecutor who explained that he used the prior-relationship criterion in *all* criminal cases, not just rape. He was accurately describing how officials generally handle criminal cases.[32]

What would happen if we did eliminate prior relationship as a decision-making factor in all criminal cases? At the arrest stage, it would produce more domestic violence arrests. (In fact, some evidence suggests that the police have been making more domestic violence arrests in recent years. The FBI's arrest data indicate that aggravated-assault arrests have been increasing since the 1970s compared with other felony arrests.)[33] At the prosecution stage, it would move a large number of cases from the third to the second layer of the wedding cake. This would, in turn, result in more offenders being sentenced to prison.

This outcome presents us with a policy dilemma. Eliminating prior relationship as a decision-making factor would produce greater equality in the administration of justice—a desirable outcome. At the same time, however, it would increase the overall punitiveness of the justice system. Is that a desirable result?

A general lesson can be learned here. Significant changes in criminal justice policy often involve major trade-offs. The gains on one side of the equation need to be considered in light of the consequences on the other side.

Hard or Soft on Crime? Unraveling the Paradox

Is the criminal justice system hard or soft on crime? Our wedding cake illuminates the paradox noted by Zimring, Morris, and Tonry: The system is simultaneously harsh and lenient. A great deal depends on the seriousness of the case. The system is very hard on second-layer cases, such as robberies committed by people with long prior records. But it is relatively soft on assaults by offenders with no prior records. It is hard on stranger rapes but more lenient on acquaintance assaults.

Additional support for the distinction between the second and third layers of the wedding cake is found in some career-criminal prosecution programs. We will look at these in detail in Chapter 8. These programs are designed to concentrate prosecutorial resources on a special class of cases involving career criminals to make sure they are convicted and sentenced to prison. The San Diego Major Violator Unit succeeded in convicting 91.5 percent of the career criminals it handled. But 89.5 percent of the career criminals were being convicted before the program began. Under the program, 100 percent of the convicted career criminals were incarcerated, but the rate had been 95.3 percent beforehand. In short, criminals deemed "serious" by commonsense criteria were already being taken very seriously. As Diana Gordon, former director of the National Council on Crime and Delinquency, put it, "Being tough doesn't work because being lenient is not the source of the problem."[34]

The idea that our criminal justice system is tough on serious crime comes as a surprise to many people. A Sentencing Project report found that most people believed the system was much softer than in fact it was.[35] There are two reasons for this misperception. First, as we have already explained, celebrated cases that are not typical of general patterns have a powerful impact on public attitudes. Second, because official data usually aggregate sentences into general categories, they obscure the important distinctions between serious and less serious crimes. Aggregate data give the *appearance* of softness because relatively few cases end up in the second layer. Violent crimes represent only 10 percent of all felonies reported to the police. Larceny, the least serious felony, accounts for 54 percent of the total.[36] The wedding cake model allows us to focus on how the system responds to the most serious crimes, those in the second layer.

The Lower Depths: The Fourth Layer

The fourth layer of the wedding cake is a world unto itself. The lower criminal courts handle all of the misdemeanors in most jurisdictions. The volume of cases is staggering, far outnumbering felonies. The eight Part I Index crimes accounted for only 17 percent of the nearly 14 million arrests in 2003. About half of the Part II Index-crime arrests involved "public order" offenses: disorderly conduct, breach of the peace, drunkenness, and so on. In fact, the largest arrest category in 1998 was "All other offenses (except traffic)," with a total of 3.6 million.[37] Under the criterion of seriousness, these cases are not considered to be "worth" much at all. Few of the defendants are regarded as real threats to public safety.

Because of the huge volume of cases and their relative lack of seriousness, relatively little concern is shown for the formalities of the felony process. In an excellent study of the lower courts of New Haven, Connecticut, Malcolm Feeley concludes that these institutions remain virtually untouched by the due process revolution.[38] To enter these courts is to step back in time 80 years. None of the defendants in the 1,640 cases he examined insisted on a jury trial. Half never had an attorney. Even for those that did, the lawyer's contribution was minimal. Even more shocking, by our standards of due process, defendants were arraigned en masse, in assembly-line fashion. Sentences were extremely light. Half of the defendants received a fine of $50 or less, and only 4.9 percent were sentenced to jail.

Feeley concludes that the "process is the punishment": Simply being brought into the lower courts is the real punishment, quite apart from the eventual outcome of the case. Insisting on your "rights" only increases the "punishment." A private attorney, for example, would charge $200 to handle a case (about $800 at today's rates). This is four times the fine were you simply to cop a plea at the earliest possible moment. Moreover, because most defendants in the lower courts are hourly wage earners rather than salaried professionals, the lost wages involved in fighting a case would generally exceed the potential fine. (Each case in Feeley's study averaged three court appearances. Fighting the case would only increase the number and length of court dates.)

The closer we look, however, the more complicated the picture becomes. A study of the Philadelphia lower courts offers a different view and illustrates the hazards of generalizing about American criminal justice. Stephen J. Schulhofer found that in Philadelphia's two lower courts—Municipal Court and the Court of Common Pleas—about half (48 percent) of all cases went to trial, virtually all defendants had legal counsel, and the punishments meted out to the guilty were relatively significant. Nearly a quarter (22 percent) of the convicted offenders received a jail sentence, and 17.4 percent received fines (which ranged as high as several hundred dollars). Schulhofer argues that Feeley overstated the "process" costs of contesting a case in the lower courts. The price of the likely penalty, at least in Philadelphia, makes the case worth fighting. The main reason appears to be that penalties are significantly stiffer in Philadelphia than in New Haven.[39]

We do not need to resolve the differences between Feeley's and Schulhofer's findings here. The basic points are that (1) the lower courts are very different from the upper courts and (2) there are significant differences between courts in different jurisdictions.

CONCLUSION

Our wedding cake model of the criminal justice system is designed to help us make sense of the administration of justice in action. As we go along, the most important thing to keep in mind is that we should not be distracted by celebrated cases. They make great stories for the tabloids, but they interfere with our understanding of routine operations in criminal justice. In particular, we want to be very skeptical of any policies that are based on celebrated cases. And because we are primarily concerned with the control of serious crime—robbery and burglary in particular—we need to keep our eyes focused on the second layer of the wedding cake.

NOTES

1. Bureau of Justice Statistics, *State Court Organization, 1998* (Washington, DC: Department of Justice, 2000). NCJ 178932.

2. This interpretation is vividly captured in "The Practice of Law as a Confidence Game," in Abraham Blumberg, *Criminal Justice,* 2d ed. (New York: New Viewpoints, 1979), pp. 242–243.

3. For a reasonable review of the evidence, see Samuel Walker, Cassia Spohn, and Miriam DeLone, *The Color of Justice: Race, Ethnicity, and Crime in America,* 3rd ed. (Belmont, CA: Wadsworth, 2004).

4. Donald Black, *The Manners and Customs of the Police* (New York: Academic Press, 1980).

5. Peter F. Nardulli, James Eisenstein, and Roy B. Flemming, *The Tenor of Justice: Criminal Courts and the Guilty Plea Process* (Urbana: University of Illinois Press, 1988).

6. Franklin Zimring, Sheila O'Malley, and Joel Eigen, "Punishing Homicide in Philadelphia: Perspectives on the Death Penalty," *University of Chicago Law Review* 43 (Winter 1976): 252.

7. Norval Morris and Michael H. Tonry, *Between Prison and Probation: Intermediate Punishments in a Rational Sentencing System* (New York: Oxford University Press, 1990), p. 3.

8. Walker et al., *The Color of Justice,* chap. 4.

9. President's Commission on Law Enforcement and Administration of Justice, *Task Force Report: Science and Technology* (Washington, DC: Government Printing Office, 1967), pp. 58–59.

10. On the origins of the systems perspective, see Samuel Walker, "Origins of the Contemporary Criminal Justice Paradigm: The American Bar Foundation Survey, 1953–1969," *Justice Quarterly* 9 (March 1992): 201–229.

11. Lawrence M. Friedman and Robert V. Percival, *The Roots of Justice: Crime and Punishment in Alameda County, California, 1870–1910* (Chapel Hill: University of North Carolina Press, 1981).

12. Michael R. Gottfredson and Don M. Gottfredson, *Decision Making in Criminal Justice: Toward the Rational Exercise of Discretion,* 2d ed. (New York: Plenum, 1988).

13. Jeffrey Toobin, *The Run of His Life: The People vs. O.J. Simpson* (New York: Random House, 1996).

14. Bureau of Justice Statistics, *Indicators of School Crime and Safety: 2003* (Washington, DC: Department of Justice, 2003). NCJ 201257.

15. Bureau of Justice Statistics, *Spouse Murder Defendants in Large Urban Counties* (Washington, DC: Department of Justice, 1995). NCJ 153256.

16. Cassia Spohn and Jerry Cederblom, "Race and Disparities in Sentencing: A Test of the Liberation Hypothesis," *Justice Quarterly* 8 (September 1991): 306.

17. Jeffrey T. Ulmer, *Social Worlds of Sentencing* (Albany: State University of New York Press, 1997), pp. 60–62.

18. William F. McDonald, *Plea Bargaining: Critical Issues and Common Practices* (Washington, DC: Government Printing Office, 1985).

19. Lynn Mather, "Some Determinants of the Method of Case Disposition: Decision Making by Public Defenders in Los Angeles," *Law and Society Review* 8 (Winter 1974): 187–216.

20. David Sudnow, "Normal Crimes: Sociological Features of the Penal Code in a Public Defender Office," *Social Problems* 12 (Winter 1965): 255–276.

21. John Rosecrance, "Maintaining the Myth of Individualized Justice: Probation Presentence Reports," *Justice Quarterly* 5 (June 1988): 235–256.

22. Malcolm M. Feeley, "Perspectives on Plea Bargaining," *Law and Society Review* 13 (Winter 1979): 199.

23. Ulmer, *Social Worlds of Sentencing.*

24. Donald Black, *Toward a General Theory of Social Control,* vol. 2 (Orlando, FL: Academic Press, 1984), pp. 1–28.

25. Bureau of Justice Statistics, *Felony Defendants in Large Urban Counties, 2000* (Washington, DC: Department of Justice, 2003). NCJ 202021.

26. Vera Institute, *Felony Arrests,* rev. ed. (New York: Longman, 1981).

27. Vera Institute, *Felony Arrests,* pp. 42–43.

28. Harry Kalven, Jr., and Hans Zeisel, *The American Jury* (Boston: Little, Brown, 1966), pp. 164–166.

29. Spohn and Cederblom, "Race and Disparities in Sentencing."

30. Bureau of Justice Statistics, *Criminal Victimization, 2003* (Washington, DC: Department of Justice, 2004). NCJ 205455.

31. Black, *The Manners and Customs of the Police.*

32. Susan Estrich, *Real Rape* (Cambridge, MA: Harvard University Press, 1987).

33. See the arrest trends in Bureau of Justice Statistics, *Sourcebook of Criminal Justice Statistics, Online edition,* available on the SUNY Albany webster.

34. Diana R. Gordon, *Towards Realistic Reform: A Commentary on Proposals for Change in New York City's Criminal Justice System* (Hackensack, NJ: National Council on Crime and Delinquency, 1981), p. 16.

35. The Sentencing Project, *Crime, Punishment, and Public Opinion: A Summary of Recent Studies and Their Implications for Sentencing Policy* (Washington, DC: The Sentencing Project, n.d.). Available on the Sentencing Project website.

36. Federal Bureau of Investigation, *Crime in the United States, 2003.*

37. Ibid.

38. Malcolm M. Feeley, *The Process Is the Punishment* (New York: Russell Sage Foundation, 1979).

39. Stephen J. Schulhofer, "No Job Too Small: Justice Without Bargaining in the Lower Criminal Courts," *American Bar Foundation Research Journal* (Summer 1985): 519–598.

3

The Going Rate

EVALUATING THE SYSTEM

We now turn our attention to the question of how the criminal justice system works on a day-to-day basis. How effectively does it control crime? How successful is it in catching, prosecuting, and punishing dangerous criminals? Is the system fair? Is there a pattern of discrimination against people of color?

Great controversy surrounds these questions. In a book subtitled *The Collapse of Criminal Justice,* Judge Harold Rothwax bluntly declares, "The long arm of the law is somewhat fractured these days."[1] Rothwax describes case after case of criminals who committed serious crimes not being punished because of some loophole in the system. Other experts see a different problem. Jerome G. Miller argues in *Search and Destroy* that the system is "highly influenced by race," that there is systematic discrimination against African Americans, and that the criminal process "is an alienating and socially destabilizing exercise that usually creates more problems than it solves."[2]

Where does the truth lie? Is the system too weak or too harsh? Is the system completely out of control or are there understandable patterns in how decisions are made? Evaluating the performance of our criminal justice system is a difficult task. On some questions we do not have good data. Even where reasonably good data are available, experts disagree over what they mean. Is a three-year prison sentence for burglary "tough" or "lenient"? Where racial or ethnic disparities exist in traffic stops or sentencing, does that represent discrimination? Some experts say yes, others say no.[3]

The debate is complicated by the fact that we have over 50 separate criminal justice systems: those of the 50 states, the federal system, tribal police and courts on some Native American reservations, and the military justice system. Each one has its own distinct local legal culture, with slightly different traditions about how cases are handled. The Bureau of Justice Statistics (BJS) report *The Prosecution of Felony Arrests, 1988* illustrates some of the differences. In Los Angeles, 36 percent of all arrests were rejected by the prosecutor, compared with only 18 percent in Washington, DC. In Portland, Oregon, 10 percent of all cases went to trial, compared with a national average of 3 percent.[4] Even though these data are 15 years old, similar variations still exist. Research on federal courts, meanwhile, has found significant variations among local district courts, in particular on the important question of downward departures from the federal sentencing guidelines (which result in more lenient sentences for convicted offenders).[5]

Despite local variations, we can identify some general features of the criminal process in this country. In virtually every local jurisdiction, there is a *going rate* for crime.[6] Some scholars argue that if you know the offense and the defendant's prior criminal record, you can probably predict the outcome of about 80 percent of all cases. Plea "bargaining," in the sense of haggling over the final result as you would at a flea market, actually has very little impact on case outcomes.[7]

THE FUNNEL

To understand the going rate, a good place to begin is the analysis by the President's Crime Commission of the flow of cases through the system (Figure 3.1). These data are from the 1960s, but they are still relevant in terms of some general patterns in the administration of justice. The Crime Commission found that despite 6 million reported and unreported crimes, only 63,000 offenders were sentenced to prison. This led to the conclusion that only 1 percent of all criminals go to prison—a figure that many people have cited as evidence that the criminal justice system fails to punish offenders. We argue that it is a very misleading figure, based on a serious misunderstanding of how the system works.

Charles Silberman argued that the Crime Commission's analysis was "grossly misleading."[8] Reanalyzing the same data (Figure 3.2), he pointed out that about 260,000 (35.7 percent) of the original 727,000 arrests involved juveniles whose cases were transferred to juvenile court. What happens to those juveniles is, of course, extremely important but not our concern here. To remain consistent with our ground rules, however, we will concentrate on the adults.

Subtracting the juveniles leaves 467,000 adult arrests. Silberman argued that this was the proper baseline for assessing the performance of the adult criminal justice system. About 27 percent of these arrests (128,000) were dismissed, leaving 339,000 prosecuted adults. A prosecution rate of 73 percent is hardly a sign of softness on crime. Then, about half (48 percent) of these defendants pled guilty to a misdemeanor. These cases were not "lost"; the defendants were convicted and acquired a criminal record. We might disagree about severity of punishment, but the fact is that they were convicted of a crime.

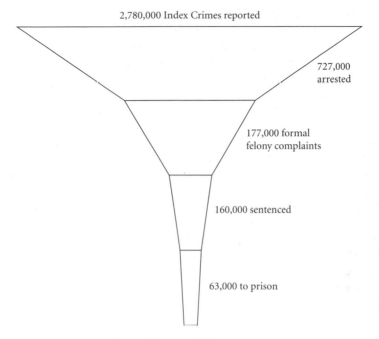

2,780,000 Index Crimes reported

727,000
arrested

177,000 formal
felony complaints

160,000 sentenced

63,000 to prison

FIGURE 3.1 The funneling effect of the criminial justice system

SOURCE: President's Commission on Law Enforcement and Administration of Justice, *Task Force Report: Science and Technology* (Washington, DC: Government Printing Office, 1967), p. 61.

Subtracting the misdemeanor convictions leaves 177,000 adult felony complaints. Of these, 90 percent were convicted: 130,000 by a guilty plea and 30,000 by trial. This is an extremely impressive conviction rate. When we combine the 177,000 felony convictions with the 162,000 misdemeanor convictions, we have a total of 332,000 adults convicted. This represents 69 percent of the adults arrested and 95 percent of those prosecuted. This is a picture of a fairly tough criminal justice system.

The Crime Commission and Silberman both used 1960s data. Have things changed in the past 40 years? The BJS report *Felony Defendants in Large Urban Counties, 2000* indicates that 64 percent of all felony arrests resulted in a conviction; 52 percent, or about half, were convicted of a felony and 12 percent were convicted of a misdemeanor. These patterns are not radically different from the 1960s.[9]

Conviction rates vary by the type of crime. In 2000, 64 percent of all murder defendants were convicted of a felony, compared with only 50 percent of both rape and robbery defendants. The lowest felony conviction rate was for assault defendants (35 percent). But the highest rate of convictions was for misdemeanors, suggesting a high rate of pleas to a lesser offense. Surprisingly, burglary had one of the highest felony conviction rates (59 percent), while larceny had only a 49 percent felony conviction rate.

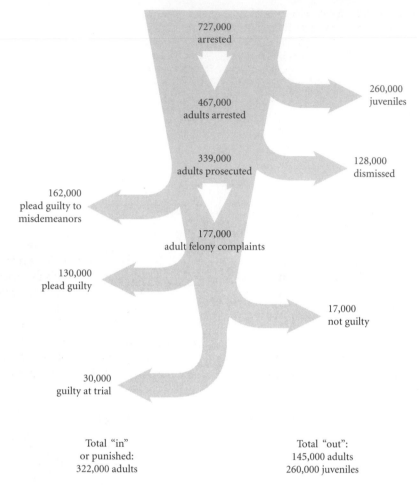

727,000
arrested

467,000
adults arrested

260,000
juveniles

339,000
adults prosecuted

128,000
dismissed

162,000
plead guilty to
misdemeanors

177,000
adult felony complaints

130,000
plead guilty

17,000
not guilty

30,000
guilty at trial

Total "in"
or punished:
322,000 adults

Total "out":
145,000 adults
260,000 juveniles

FIGURE 3.2 Silberman's recalculation of the Crime Commission's funnel

SOURCE: Charles Silberman, *Criminal Violence, Criminal Justice* (New York: Random House, 1978), pp. 257–261.

What happens to people convicted of a felony? The BJS report indicates that in 2000, 40 percent of all convicted felony defendants were sentenced to prison, 33 percent to jail, and 27 percent were placed on probation. In short, 73 percent were incarcerated (prison or jail) in one form or another. This represents an increase in punitiveness since the days of the President's Crime Commission.

In trying to make sense of the going rate, it is important to understand how aggregate data mask the severe treatment of people convicted of serious offenses. An amazing 96 percent of people convicted of murder were sentenced to prison. That is hardly being soft on crime. Meanwhile, 73 percent of convicted robbers were sentenced to prison (and another 12 percent sentenced to jail, for an overall incarceration rate of 86 percent).

**Table 3.1 Probable outcomes of felony arrests
and felony convictions, 2002**

	Likelihood of felony arrest leading to felony conviction	Likelihood of felony conviction resulting in prison sentence
Murder	41%	91%
Robbery	47	71
Aggravated assault	23	42
Burglary	50	46
Drug trafficking	80	42

SOURCE: Bureau of Justice Statistics, *Felony Sentences in State Courts* (Washington, DC: Department of Justice, 2004). NCJ 206916.

As we learned in Chapter 2, seriousness of the offense has a major impact on the severity of the system. Only 49 percent of people convicted of a burglary were sent to prison, along with only 33 percent of those convicted of larceny/theft. Most of these are third-layer cases in the wedding cake model.

Another measure of the going rate is the overall probability of an arrested person going to prison. For a person arrested for murder, the probability is 54 percent. A person arrested for robbery has a 32 percent probability, while someone charged with burglary has a 27 percent probability of going to prison[10] (see Table 3.1).

Rejections and Dismissals: Loophole?

The percentage of felony arrests that do not result in prosecution and conviction needs some further analysis. The BJS report on felony defendants in 2000 indicated that 27 percent were not convicted and that almost all of those were listed as dismissals (26 percent of the total, with only 1 percent acquitted). We need to look closely at the reasons for dismissal. Are cases being dismissed because of "loopholes" in the system? Many conservatives believe that this is the case, and we will look at some of their proposals for closing loopholes in Chapter 8. Alternatively, are cases dismissed because of understandable factors? For reasons that are explained shortly, the BJS data do not take into account arrests that are rejected by prosecutors (that is, not accepted for prosecution).

This issue leads us into some additional complexities of the criminal justice system. The data in the BJS report do not accurately represent all the people who were actually arrested. A Police Foundation report found that police departments did not report arrests in a comparable fashion, with the result that many cases in which a person was taken into custody were not officially recorded as an arrest.[11] If you are stopped and detained on the street by a police officer, you are legally under arrest (in the sense that you are not free to go). Some departments record these incidents as an arrest, but many do not. If you are taken to police headquarters, questioned, and then released, you were legally arrested. But not all of these cases are recorded. In some cases an arrest is made and officially recorded but then dismissed by the police themselves (because of insufficient evidence, the arrest of a different suspect, etc.). Joan Petersilia found that about 11 percent of all arrests in California were dropped by the police.[12] These cases never reach a prosecutor's desk, and consequently are not reported in many data sets, including the BJS felony defendant report. In short, the "true" number of persons arrested in any given year is much larger than official data indicate.

After a case reaches the prosecutor's desk, it can either be *rejected* by the prosecutor or *dismissed* by a judge. These are two distinct stages in the process. We need to inquire into why cases are rejected or dismissed. Table 3.2 on pages 54–55 presents BJS data on the reasons for rejections and dismissals in New York and San Diego. Evidence problems—either insufficient evidence or lack of any evidence—account for most of the rejections by prosecutors: 61 percent in New York and 51 percent in San Diego. Witness problems are the second most important reason: 18 percent of the rejections in New York and 19 percent in San Diego. For most crimes against persons (robbery, rape, assault), the testimony of the victim or a witness is the primary evidence. These data indicate that evidence and witness problems account for about 70 to 80 percent of all rejections. (These data are from the 1988 BJS report; subsequent reports on prosecution and sentencing do not include the reasons for case attrition.)

Evidence and witness problems are also important factors in the dismissal of cases, accounting for 33 percent of the dismissals in New York City and 20 percent in San Diego. The lack of evidence or witnesses is a legitimate reason for dropping a case. A prosecutor cannot win a case without them. Dismissing cases for this reason does not mean that the system is soft on crime. Officials are simply doing what circumstances force them to do. In short, rejections and dismissals are not a loophole.

A closer look reveals that the term *dismissal* is misleading. Many of these cases are not really "lost," as some critics of the system argue. In San Diego, for example, almost half of the "dismissals" involved some form of action by the system: 11 percent were diverted, 27 percent were referred for other prosecution, and 10 percent were covered by another case. In short, these defendants were still in the hands of the criminal justice system and were liable for some kind of sanction.

The data on rejections and dismissals have very important policy implications. Most important, they clearly indicate that due process problems—illegal searches or coerced confessions—are not a major reason why cases are not prosecuted. They accounted for only 15 percent of the rejections and none of the dismissals in San Diego. Equally important, due process problems arose primarily in drug and weapons cases. They accounted for only 1 percent of the rejections of robbery cases and 8 percent of the burglary rejections. In short, thousands of criminals are not "beating the system" in the early stages of prosecution because of legal "technicalities" or loopholes. Judge Harold Rothwax's attack on the rights of criminal suspects in his book *Guilty* is a classic example of using only celebrated cases and ignoring the general patterns in the administration of justice.[13] We will look more closely at some other alleged loopholes in the system in Chapter 8.

One unresolved question remains, however. The BJS data indicate that many cases are dismissed in the "interest of justice." What exactly does this mean? It may mean that the offense is not that serious, or that the victim and offender know each other, or that some form of private settlement has been worked out. Until more detailed research is done on this question, we do not know whether these dismissals are appropriate or represent a covert pattern of bias in the system.

The decision to reject or dismiss a case is a highly discretionary one. Most of these decisions are made very quietly, and the prosecutor does not really have to account to anyone for them. An important question is whether a pattern of racial and ethnic bias is apparent in these decisions. Cassie Spohn and her colleagues found that women and white defendants were more likely to have their cases rejected than males and minorities. The racial and ethnic disparities were strongest at the rejection stage only. This may result from the fact that the decision to reject is much less visible than the decision to dismiss. Once a case has been accepted for prosecution, it becomes known to a wider range of people, and this visibility may act as a constraint on prosecutors and judges.[14]

Joan Petersilia's analysis of racial disparities found that African American defendants in California were more likely to have their cases rejected and dismissed than whites. This apparent favored treatment, however, may be a result of discrimination at the arrest stage. Some research suggests that police arrest African Americans on weaker evidence than whites. When these weak evidence cases reach the prosecutor, they are more likely to be dismissed or rejected. In short, discrimination takes place, but at an earlier point than that identified by Spohn and her colleagues.[15]

Punishing Offenders

Once the weak cases have been weeded out, the criminal justice system becomes extremely punitive. Almost all of those offenders indicted are convicted, and the majority of those convicted are incarcerated, in either prison or jail.[16] To make sense of what actually happens to convicted offenders in terms of punishment, it is necessary to specify the categories carefully. There are important differences between the percentage of convicted offenders incarcerated, the percentage sentenced to prison, the length of the formal sentence, and the amount of time served.

The term *incarcerated* applies to people sent to prison and jail. Many people conclude that the system is soft on crime because they look at the data only on felons sent to prison. In practice, however, there are many "split sentences," involving a jail term followed by probation. In 2000, 40 percent of convicted felons were sentenced to prison, 33 percent went to jail (under a split sentence), and 27 percent got probation.[17]

Table 3.2 Why felony arrests are declined for prosecution

Manhattan, New York 1988

Most serious charge	Diversion	Other prosecution	Arrests declined due to:					
			Evidence	Witness	Due process	Interest of justice	Covered by other case	Other
Percentage of declinations	0%	3%	61%	18%	2%	10%	0%	6%
Murder and manslaughter	0	0	75	25	0	0	0	0
Rape	0	0	30	40	0	30	0	0
Robbery	0	8	63	22	0	3	0	4
Aggravated assault	0	3	33	40	0	13	0	11
Burglary	0	0	79	21	0	0	0	0

San Diego, California 1988

Most serious charge	Diversion	Other prosecution	Arrests declined due to:					
			Evidence	Witness	Due process	Interest of justice	Covered by other case	Other
Percentage of declinations	0%	0%	51%	19%	13%	11%	3%	4%
Murder and manslaughter	0	0	50	3	0	30	0	17
Rape	0	0	30	60	0	8	1	2
Robbery	0	0	49	36	1	6	0	7
Aggravated assault	0	0	39	46	2	9	1	3
Burglary	0	0	59	15	8	8	5	5

Table 3.2 continued Why felony arrests are declined for prosecution

Manhattan, New York 1988

Most serious charge	Diversion	Other prosecution	Evidence	Witness	Due process	Interest of justice	Covered by other case	Other
				Cases dismissed due to:				
Percentage of declinations	0%	0%	19%	14%	0%	10%	6%	51%
Murder and manslaughter	11	1	17	15	0	2	14	39
Rape	0	0	13	33	0	4	3	47
Robbery	0	0	18	21	0	4	4	53
Aggravated assault	1	0	10	26	0	13	3	48
Burglary	0	0	15	11	0	13	6	54

San Diego, California 1988

Most serious charge	Diversion	Other prosecution	Evidence	Witness	Due process	Interest of justice	Covered by other case	Other
				Cases dismissed due to:				
Percentage of declinations	11%	27%	14%	6%	0%	7%	10%	25%
Murder and manslaughter	0	20	20	0	0	30	0	30
Rape	0	4	22	22	0	31	4	18
Robbery	0	17	27	27	1	4	3	22
Aggravated assault	2	26	21	17	0	5	5	23
Burglary	2							

Source: Bureau of Justice Statistics, The Prosecution of Felony Arrests, 1988 (Washington, DC: Government Printing Office, 1992).

BJS has estimated the average maximum length of sentences imposed in 2000 (note carefully: these data represent the *average maximum* sentence). Convicted murderers received an average maximum of 248 months (or about 22 years), robbers got an average of 94 months, and burglars got an average of 52 months (or 4 years and 4 months).[18]

The time served by a convicted offender is the most realistic estimate of how punitive the criminal justice system is. Most offenders sentenced to prison are released early as a result of good-time reductions and parole. And in a particularly significant development, the system has become steadily more punitive. The percentage of sentences actually served increased from 32 percent in 1988 to 45 percent in 1996 and 55 percent in 2000. The estimated time served by robbers increased from 38 months in 1988 to 48 months in 1996 and 55 months in 2000. The time served by burglars increased from 22 to 25 to 29 months in the same period. These increases were the result of several developments: the abolition of discretionary parole in some states; mandatory sentencing laws that have increased sentences; sentencing laws that deny good-time reductions for some offenses; and a general attitude of punitiveness that has led judges to hand out longer prison sentences.

An International Perspective on the Going Rate

How does the going rate for crime in the United States compare with its counterpart in other countries? One of the standard liberal criticisms is that our criminal justice system is far more punitive than that of any other country. Conservatives, meanwhile, argue that we are too lenient and fail to punish criminals. James Lynch's careful analysis of comparative data suggests that both liberals and conservatives are clinging to their favorite myths on this question.[19]

On one hand, we do lock up a lot of people. We already have the highest incarceration rate in the world (350 per 100,000, representing the prison population only; a higher figure that is frequently used includes both jail and prison populations), and current sentencing trends suggest that this will continue.[20] And as our previous discussion indicates, we are fairly tough on those offenders we manage to arrest. From this perspective, it is hard to say that we are soft on crime.

At the same time, however, our high incarceration rate is mainly the result of our high rates of violent crime. At one point, the American murder rate was four times higher than Canada's and ten times higher than England's and West Germany's. Our robbery rate was five times higher than those of England and West Germany. These differences have narrowed in recent years because of the great crime drop, but our rates of violent crimes are still much higher than those of other industrialized societies. Violent crimes, moreover, were more likely to result in prison sentences, and armed robbery was more likely to result in a prison sentence than unarmed robbery. Lynch points out that a far higher proportion of robberies in the United States are armed than in other countries. In other words, we have a high incarceration rate in large part because we have such high rates of those crimes that typically send an offender to prison.[21]

The relevant question becomes: Is the going rate for particular crimes significantly higher in the United States than it is in other countries? Lynch estimated the chances of going to prison for a person arrested for murder, robbery, burglary, and larceny/theft in the United States, England, Canada, and West Germany. He found that a robber's chance of going to prison was 36 percent in the United States, 41 percent in Canada, and 39 percent in the United Kingdom. The odds were lower only in West Germany.

The odds of going to prison were also roughly the same for murder, burglary, and larceny in the three English-speaking countries. In terms of the tendency to send convicted offenders to prison, then, the United States is not that much more punitive than other countries.[22]

In terms of time served, however, the United States is significantly more punitive, especially for property crimes. Lynch found that the average number of months served in prison for murder in the United States (50.5) was slightly higher than in England and Wales (43) but lower than in Canada (57). (Because of different methodologies, these estimates for the United States vary slightly from the ones cited earlier in this section.) Average time served for robbery was somewhat higher in the United States and substantially higher for both burglary and theft. Burglars in the United States, for example, served an average of 16.06 months, compared with 5.23 in Canada and 6.72 in England and Wales. The gap was even greater for theft. Convicted thieves in America served an average of 12 months, compared with only 2 in Canada and 4.65 in England and Wales.

A separate BJS report comparing crime and punishment in the United States and in England and Wales between 1981 and 1996 found that the United States and England incarcerated an equally high percentage of convicted murderers, robbers, and rapists but that the United States imprisoned a far higher percentage of burglars, assaulters, and auto thieves. The BJS data also indicate that American incarceration rates have risen dramatically since the 1960s, particularly in the late 1980s, and these trends hardly indicate that the American criminal justice system is "collapsing" in the sense of failing to punish convicted offenders.[23]

Lynch's comparative research highlights the fact that the going rate consists of two components. The first is the tendency to imprison serious offenders. On this point, the American going rate is very similar to other industrialized countries'. The second is the amount of prison time actually served. Here, the United States is more punitive—but primarily for property, not violent, crimes. Lynch did not study drug offenses, but the United States is likely comparatively very punitive, in terms of both incarceration and length of sentences.

THE COURTROOM WORK GROUP

The going rate is established and maintained by the people who work in the criminal justice system. The phrase "the system" implies some impersonal entity, but in fact it is a *process* involving people who make a series of discretionary decisions day in and day out.[24] A police officer decides to make an arrest; a prosecutor rejects a case; a judge sentences an offender to prison, and so on. Prosecutors, defense attorneys, judges, and to some extent police officers make up the *courtroom work group,* or what some refer to as the *local legal culture.* To understand how the system works, we need to examine how they go about their work: the decisions they make, the reasons why they make them, how they adjust to changes in the law or the workload, how they respond to people who challenge their established going rate.

In perhaps the best study of this phenomenon, Nardulli, Eisenstein, and Flemming characterized local courthouses as communities. "After spending an enormous number of hours in various county courts," they observed, "we became convinced that the concept of a courthouse community can be an immensely useful tool in trying to understand them."[25] In this context, "community" means that a group of people work together and have a mutual interest in getting the job done as efficiently as possible.

The bureaucratic setting of the courtroom work group exerts a major influence on the decisions of individual officials. All criminal justice officials exercise enormous discretion, but there are important differences in the settings in which they work. Police officers generally work alone or in pairs, often with no witnesses. For this reason, police work has been characterized as a "low-visibility" activity. To be sure, if an officer makes an arrest, it will be reviewed by others: a supervisor will sign off on it and prosecutors and defense attorneys will review it. But if the officer does not make an arrest, that decision is not reviewed by anyone. Prosecutors, defense attorneys, and judges, on the other hand, work in the highly visible setting of the courthouse. Their actions also leave a paper trail that enhances accountability. The news media and the public are potential witnesses to decisions that occur in open court. Finally, other members of the work group constrain the decisions of individual members. A truly outrageous decision by a prosecutor is likely to be challenged by a defense attorney or judge. Bail amounts and plea agreements are, in fact, negotiated among work group members. As a result, the actions of courtroom officials are constrained by other officials.

Working together every day, members of the courtroom work group reach a general consensus about how different kinds of cases should be handled. This involves a shared understanding about how much cases are "worth." There are "heavy" cases (that is, serious violent crimes) and "garbage" cases (relatively minor theft). This valuation allows them to move cases along quickly.

An Administrative System of Justice

Conflict between prosecution and defense is the exception rather than the rule. In theory we have an *adversarial* system of justice. The bedrock principle of the Anglo-American system of justice is that a person is innocent until proven guilty and that the state has to prove guilt beyond a reasonable doubt. Additionally, the defendant has a right to challenge the prosecutor's case, with the assistance of counsel, in a public trial overseen by a neutral judge. This is different from the *inquisitorial* system of justice, where there is a presumption of guilt and the rights of defendants are not protected the way they are in the American system.

The reality of American criminal justice, however, is that we have an *administrative* system of justice. Few cases (about 10 percent) are settled through a public trial. There is no public clash between prosecution and defense. That occurs only in the few celebrated cases. In our administrative system of justice, decisions are negotiated among members of the courtroom work group, with a high degree of consensus and cooperation. A study of nine courts by the National Center for State Courts found that work group members in each court shared a "norm of proportionality," that is, of how much different cases are worth.[26] Experts on plea bargaining describe the process as a "supermarket": with set prices and a high volume of business.[27] (We will discuss plea bargaining in detail in Chapter 8.)

Frederic Suffet's study of bail setting offers an excellent illustration of the consensus and cooperation that prevail in the courtroom work group. Only 3 percent of the cases he examined involved any conflict over the bail decision; some disagreement arose in another 9 percent.[28] Over the years, the members of this work group had developed a shared understanding about how much bail to set for different kinds of cases—in other words, how much each case was worth. In her study of plea bargaining, Alissa Pollitz Worden found a high degree of judicial agreement with prosecutorial sentence recommendations. She speculated that going rates "may be so predictable that a prosecutor need not make a formal recommendation in order to ensure that a sentence bargain will be honored by the court."[29]

Another example is John Rosecrance's study of presentence investigation (PSI) reports by probation officers. In theory, the PSI is an independent evaluation of a convicted offender's social history, taking into account criminal record, employment history, family status, and so on. Yet Rosecrance found that probation officers (POs) classified offenders very quickly on the basis of their offense and prior record. Even more important, they based their recommendations on what they thought judges and prosecutors wanted. The California POs he studied were in regular contact with prosecutors and discussed their cases with them. They rarely challenged plea agreements, which often included an understanding about the sentence. As one PO put it, "It's stupid to try and bust a deal. . . . Who needs the hassle? . . . Everyone, including the defendant, has already agreed."[30]

Nardulli, Eisenstein, and Flemming add the important point that courtroom work groups vary from jurisdiction to jurisdiction. Each courtroom community has its own "distinctive character." Typically, one person plays "a dominant role . . . by virtue of personality, professional skills (or reputation), political power, longevity, or some other attribute."[31] Ulmer's study of three Pennsylvania courts found important differences related to the stability of the membership in local work groups. In the wealthy suburban court system ("Rich County"), there was a high degree of membership stability and a culture of understanding and collegiality. In the large urban court ("Metro County"), on the other hand, there was considerable turnover in the prosecutor's office, which resulted in conflict between prosecutors and defense attorneys and close relations between the defense attorneys and judges. The Metro County example illustrates the extent to which other members of a courtroom work group adjust to some kind of disruption arising from one member of the group.[32]

Interestingly, the National Center for State Courts study found that the ability of local criminal courts to process cases efficiently was not necessarily related to caseloads and resources. The courts that handled cases faster than other courts were characterized by a sense of mutual respect among work group members. That is, prosecutors and defense attorneys regarded each other as competent and well prepared. Even when they challenged each other over issues related to evidence they respected the other side's professionalism. In the slower courts, work group members regarded each other as not fully competent. The lack of respect led to questions and misunderstandings that slowed down the processing of cases. The respect that work group members have for each other, in short, is a major part of the local work group culture.[33]

The Limits of Reform

The courtroom work group has enormous power to limit, frustrate, or even block reforms in the justice system. A state legislature might pass a new law, or the Supreme Court might issue a landmark ruling, but that does not guarantee that the process will really change. Our capacity to make significant changes in how the system works is extremely important. Remember, we are searching for policies that will help to reduce crime. Assuming we find some policies that do work, we have to be able to implement them and change how the system works. A few examples illustrate the power of the courtroom work group to frustrate reforms.

- The Supreme Court ruled in 1967 that defendants in juvenile court have a constitutional right to an attorney (*In re Gault*). Barry Feld, however, found that only half (47.7 percent) of the kids in Minnesota juvenile courts in 1984 actually had legal counsel. State officials simply did not comply with the law.[34]

- Congress passed a "speedy trial" law in 1974, and several states enacted similar laws. Malcolm Feeley, however, found that these laws had almost no effect on the flow of cases. All members of the courtroom work group—judges, prosecutors, and defense attorneys—had their own reasons for delaying cases. The laws permit exceptions to the requirement, and officials take advantage of them. As one judge explained, "Our court has figured out ways to deal with the [speedy trial] act that don't cause us to change our practices at all."[35]

- Many states passed "three strikes" laws in the 1990s, but with the exception of California, prosecutors in most states were simply not using the law. Wisconsin had used it only once in a year and a half, whereas five other states had not used it at all. Even in California, the law was frequently used by prosecutors in Los Angeles but hardly at all in San Francisco.[36] Prosecutors in San Francisco and most other states, in short, used their discretion essentially to nullify the law.

We should not be completely cynical about the prospects for change. Some reforms have been implemented. A few examples illustrate this point.

- The "defense of life" rule was designed to reduce police use of deadly force. As a result, the number of persons shot and killed by the police fell from 559 in 1975 to 300 in 1987, and the racial disparity between African Americans and whites shot and killed was cut in half.[37]

- The Minnesota Sentencing Guidelines enacted in 1980 had the explicit goal of limiting the use of imprisonment. To a great extent this strategy has worked, and Minnesota has maintained the lowest incarceration rate of any state (with the possible exception of South Dakota).[38]

- The federal Sentencing Guidelines imposed harsher sentences and limited the discretion of judges. While some judges have found ways to get around the guidelines' strict requirements, there has been a significant increase in imprisonment for federal crimes.

The Dynamics of Reform

In short, some reforms are successfully implemented and some are not. What makes the difference? A great deal depends on the nature of the reform itself. Some experts believe that modest reforms, which require only slight changes in how the courtroom work group operates, are more likely to succeed than sweeping changes. Raymond T. Nimmer argues that "the probability of system change is inversely related to the degree of change sought by a reform."[39] Eisenstein, Flemming, and Nardulli agree, concluding that "the more radical a proposed change the less likely is its adoption."[40] The three-strikes laws represent radical disruptions of established going rates and probably for that reason have been ignored in most jurisdictions.

In their study of rape law reform, on the other hand, Cassia Spohn and Julie Horney found significant changes in only one of six jurisdictions. They speculated that the new Michigan rape law was so comprehensive that it forced changes in the attitudes and behavior of courtroom work group officials, whereas the minor reforms in the other five jurisdictions had little impact.[41]

In the conclusion of their study of courts and their communities, Eisenstein, Flemming, and Nardulli offer some other sobering conclusions about the possibilities for reform. On one hand, changes mandated from *outside* the courtroom work groups face serious obstacles. They agree with Feeley that work groups have enormous ability to resist change. At the same time, however, change initiated from *within,* by the work group itself, also faces major obstacles. Efforts by judges to speed up trials may be blocked by prosecution and defense attorneys.[42]

In short, *some* things work. We should not adopt the cynical view that *nothing* works, or the naive view that *everything* works. The important point here is that the power of the courtroom work group to frustrate reform is extremely relevant to our search for sensible and effective crime policies. Even if we found a good policy, officials could not implement it.

An evaluation of the implementation of three-strikes laws explained that "[t]o some degree, sentencing policies and reforms involve a tug-of-war between the judicial, executive, and legislative branches of government for control over criminal justice matters."[43] The courtroom work group has enormous power to limit or frustrate reforms, but it does not have total control. When the legislature directs a major change—as in the case with sentencing guidelines—the courtroom work group can adapt and offset some of the intended change but cannot completely nullify it.

The going rate can change over time, however. Change can be the result of two factors. The first is a conscious change in *policy*. The new three-strikes laws, which dramatically increase the penalties for certain repeat offenders, is a good example. A second kind of change is the result of *unplanned* developments. The impact of the post–World War II baby boom on crime was not planned by anyone. A significant increase in the workload of the justice system, meanwhile, produces adaptations. Arrests for public order offenses, for example, declined significantly between the 1960s and the 1990s.[44] As serious crime increased, police simply shifted their priorities and gave less attention to relatively minor crimes.

Criminal Justice Thermodynamics

The systems perspective on the administration of justice helps us see how changes in one part of the system affect decisions in other parts. Malcolm Feeley suggests that a major change may set off a "chain reaction throughout the entire system," forcing other officials to adapt and in some cases creating new and unanticipated problems.[45] We explain this chain reaction effect in terms of "criminal justice thermodynamics." You may remember from a physics class that the law of thermodynamics says that every action has an equal and opposite reaction. The justice system works in much the same way: actions produce reactions.

Our law of criminal justice thermodynamics states:

An increase in the severity of the penalty will result in less frequent application of that penalty.

Our law has an important corollary:

The less often a severe penalty is applied, the more arbitrary will be the occasions when it is applied.

The death penalty is an excellent example of the law of criminal justice thermodynamics. Because it is the ultimate penalty, it exerts enormous pressure on the courtroom work group. Many devices are used to evade its application (plea bargaining to a second-degree murder charge, demanding a jury trial, using the insanity defense, appealing on every potential issue, requesting pardon or commutation, and so forth). Thus, the action of the prosecutor in filing first-degree murder charges (making the case eligible for the death penalty) causes a reaction by the defense.

Because the death penalty is rarely used, its application is very arbitrary. In the landmark case of *Furman v. Georgia* (1972), the Supreme Court characterized the application of the death penalty as being so rare that it is "freakish" and akin to being "struck by lightning."[46]

Three-strikes laws are another excellent example. These laws provide very severe sentences for people convicted of a third felony (part of the California law also applies to people with certain kinds of second felonies)—typically, life or a very long mandatory prison term. Every study, however, has found that prosecutors rarely if ever use the law. And even in California, where it is used most often, it is primarily used by prosecutors only in certain counties.[47]

Pamala L. Griset's study of correctional practices in New York illustrates how an increase in severity can produce adaptations that, in many respects, undermine the original intent of getting tougher with criminals. New York adopted a series of mandatory sentencing laws in 1973 and 1978, followed by several early release programs in 1987 and 1989. The result was an odd mix of indeterminate and mandatory sentencing policies. The prison population began to increase, but because of financial constraints, the state did not build all of the planned new prisons.[48]

The three new early release programs—shock incarceration, "earned eligibility" for parole, and CASAT (Comprehensive Alcohol and Substance Abuse Treatment)—gave correctional officials enormous discretion over offenders' eligibility for early release. They began using these programs to reduce prison populations. Under earned eligibility, inmates gained a "presumption of release" for merely participating in a treatment, educational, or work program. Thus, they received a reward for what in the past had been considered minimal good conduct. The net effect was to release them early and to undercut the intent of mandatory minimum sentencing laws. Meanwhile, many offenders released under work release programs were allowed to live at home and report in twice a week. Over one-third of the participants in this "day reporting" program had been convicted of violent crimes. Here, also, correctional officials gained a vast amount of hidden discretion and used it to undercut the supposedly tough sentencing laws.

WRONGFUL CONVICTIONS:
HOW MANY MISTAKES?

Since the administration of justice is a human process, involving day-in, day-out decisions by members of the courtroom work group, it is inevitable that there will be mistakes. The question is, How frequent are they? How often are innocent people wrongfully convicted? The issue of wrongful convictions has received a lot of publicity recently because of advances in DNA technology, which makes it possible to positively link a suspect with a crime and also to positively clear someone.

In 1992 Barry Scheck and Peter Neufeld established the Innocence Project at Cardozo Law School in New York City to provide legal assistance to convicted offenders on DNA issues. By May 2005, 158 convicted offenders had been exonerated and released. Some had been sentenced to death; others were serving sentences of life in prison. Larry Mayes, for example, served 18 and a half years in prison in Indiana after being wrongfully convicted of rape and robbery and sentenced to 80 years in prison. Local Innocence Projects have been established in 41 states and the District of Columbia.[49]

How can an innocent person be convicted of murder and sentenced to death or life in prison? The Innocence Project has identified several causes. The most important are false identification, police or prosecutor misconduct, bad lawyering by defense counsel, and incorrect scientific analysis of evidence.

Errors such as these raise disturbing questions about the courtroom work group. If the police or prosecutor engaged in misconduct, why didn't the defense attorney or judge notice and blow the whistle? If a defense attorney was grossly incompetent, why didn't the judge intervene? The answer to these questions goes to the very nature of the courtroom work group. The basic norms of the group emphasize cooperation and not challenging other members of the group. While this facilitates efficient handling of cases in the vast majority, the cases handled by the Innocence Project indicate that it can also cover up willful misconduct or incompetence—and send an innocent person to death row.

Most of the Innocence Project cases were celebrated cases to begin with: usually gruesome murders or rape and robbery crimes. Exoneration through DNA evidence automatically moved all of them into the celebrated case category. The question for us is, How often do mistakes happen in routine cases? How often do they occur in run-of-the-mill burglary and robbery cases? What is the overall error rate? Are there just a few celebrated cases, or do miscarriages of justice happen all the time?

C. Ronald Huff and his colleagues developed an ingenious method for estimating the number of wrongful convictions. They surveyed 229 Ohio criminal justice officials (judges, prosecutors, public defenders, police), along with attorneys general from all states, and asked for *their* estimate of the frequency of wrongful convictions. After eliminating the extremely high and low estimates, they concluded that errors occur in slightly less than 1 percent of all felony cases.[50]

What are we to make of this estimate? From one perspective, an error rate of less than 1 percent is very good. We should all be so successful in whatever we do. It compares very favorably with the false positive and false negative rates we will encounter with the prediction problem in Chapter 4. But Huff and his associates projected this error rate to the national level and estimated 5,729 wrongful convictions in 1981 (one-half of 1 percent of the total of 1,145,780 convictions). Six thousand innocent people convicted of a felony every year is a shocking fact to contemplate.

As for the death penalty, Hugo Bedau and Michael Radelet estimated that for every 20 persons executed in this country since 1900, at least 1 innocent person was convicted of a capital crime. They found a total of 343 persons mistakenly convicted of capital crimes; 25 were actually executed, while many of the others served prison terms of up to 25 years.[51]

In short, serious mistakes do occur in the criminal justice system. Some innocent people are in fact convicted and sent to prison—in some cases for long prison terms. We need to be ever-vigilant to guard against such mistakes and develop appropriate policies that will help to prevent them. Nonetheless, if Huff's 1 percent estimate is correct, mistakes are extremely rare. The focus of this book is on the routine processing of cases in the 99 percent of cases free of serious error.

CONCLUSION

A going rate for crime exists in the United States. If you are convicted of a certain crime and have a certain prior record, it is possible to predict the outcome of your case with a high degree of accuracy. The going rate does vary between jurisdictions but is fairly stable within each one. It is established and maintained by the members of the courtroom work group, who work together daily.

The concept of the going rate is extremely important for our search for sensible and effective crime policies for two reasons. First, many proposed policies are based on mistaken assumptions about how the system works. They do not take into account the fact that the administration of justice is very stable, consistent, and predictable and that it is relatively tough on those offenders who are caught and prosecuted. Second, many proposed reforms would have trouble being implemented. The going rate is determined by the courtroom work group, which has tremendous power to adapt and either ignore or evade the intent of a new law or policy. Simply passing a new law does not necessarily mean that the intended changes will occur.

NOTES

1.   Judge Harold J. Rothwax, *Guilty: The Collapse of Criminal Justice* (New York: Random House, 1996), p. 25.

2.   Jerome G. Miller, *Search and Destroy: African-American Males in the Criminal Justice System* (Cambridge: Cambridge University Press, 1996), p. xii.

3.   Samuel Walker, Cassia Spohn, and Miriam DeLone, *The Color of Justice: Race, Ethnicity, and Crime in America,* 3rd ed. (Belmont, CA: Wadsworth, 2004).

4.   Bureau of Justice Statistics, *Prosecution of Felony Arrests, 1998* (Washington, DC: Department of Justice, 1999).

5. Information about the Federal Sentencing Guidelines, including research reports, can be found on the website of the U.S. Sentencing Commission.

6. Excellent discussions of the going rate are in James Eisenstein, Roy B. Flemming, and Peter F. Nardulli, *The Contours of Justice: Communities and Their Courts* (Boston: Little, Brown, 1988), and Peter F. Nardulli, Roy B. Flemming, and James Eisenstein, *The Tenor of Justice* (Urbana: University of Illinois Press, 1988). Also see Jeffrey T. Ulmer, *Social Worlds of Sentencing* (Albany: State University of New York Press, 1997).

7. Nardulli et al., *The Tenor of Justice,* p. 246.

8. Charles Silberman, *Criminal Violence, Criminal Justice* (New York: Random House, 1978), p. 258.

9. Bureau of Justice Statistics, *Felony Defendants in Large Urban Counties, 2000* (Washington, DC: Department of Justice, 2003), Figure 30, p. 31. NCJ 20201.

10. Ibid.

11. Lawrence W. Sherman and Barry Glick, *The Quality of Police Arrest Statistics* (Washington: The Police Foundation, 1984).

12. Joan Petersilia, *Racial Disparities in the Criminal Justice System* (Santa Monica, CA: Rand, 1983), p. 21.

13. Rothwax, *Guilty.*

14. Cassia Spohn, John Gruhl, and Susan Welch, "The Impact of the Ethnicity and Gender of Defendants on the Decision to Reject or Dismiss Felony Charges," *Criminology* 25 (1987): 175–191. For a provocative discussion on whether sentencing guidelines achieve their designed result of increasing the visibility or "transparency" of the sentencing process, see Ulmer, *Social Worlds of Sentencing.*

15. Petersilia, *Racial Disparities in the Criminal Justice System,* pp. 20–30.

16. Bureau of Justice Statistics, *Felony Sentences in State Courts, 2000* (Washington, DC: Government Printing Office, 2003). NCJ 198821.

17. Bureau of Justice Statistics, *Felony Defendants in Large Urban Counties, 2000,* Table 30.

18. Bureau of Justice Statistics, *Felony Sentences in State Courts, 2000,* Table 3.

19. James Lynch, "Crime in International Perspective," in James Q. Wilson and Joan Petersilia, eds., *Crime* (San Francisco: ICS Press, 1995), pp. 11–38

20. Marc Mauer, *Americans Behind Bars: A Comparison of International Rates of Incarceration* (Washington, DC: The Sentencing Project, 1991). Available on the Sentencing Project website.

21. Lynch, "Crime in International Perspective."

22. Ibid. A more recent and more thorough analysis is Bureau of Justice Statistics, *Cross-National Studies in Crime and Justice* (Washington, DC: Department of Justice, 2004). NCJ 200988.

23. Bureau of Justice Statistics, *Crime and Justice in the United States and in England and Wales, 1981–1996* (Washington, DC: Department of Justice, 1998). NCJ 169284.

24. Samuel Walker, *Taming the System: The Control of Discretion in Criminal Justice, 1950–1990* (New York: Oxford University Press, 1993); Michael R. Gottfredson and Don M. Gottfredson, *Decision Making in Criminal Justice,* 2d ed. (New York: Plenum, 1988).

25. Nardulli et al., *Tenor of Justice.*

26. Brian J. Ostrom and Roger A. Hanson, *Efficiency, Timeliness, and Quality: A New Perspective From Nine State Criminal Trial Courts* (Williamsburg, VA: National Center for State Courts, 1999). Available on the National Center for State Courts website.

27. Malcolm Feeley, "Perspectives on Plea Bargaining," *Law and Society Review* 13 (Winter 1979): 199.

28. Frederic Suffet, "Bail-Setting: A Study in Courtroom Interaction," *Crime and Delinquency* 12 (1966): 318–331.

29. Alissa Pollitz Worden, "The Judge's Role in Plea Bargaining: An Analysis of Judges' Agreement with Prosecutors' Sentencing Recommendations," *Justice Quarterly* 12 (June 1995): 273.

30. John Rosecrance, "Maintaining the Myth of Individualized Justice: Probation Presentence Reports," *Justice Quarterly* 5 (June 1988): 235–256.

31. Nardulli et al., *Tenor of Justice,* p. 41.

32. Ulmer, *Social Worlds of Sentencing,* especially Table 8.1.

33. Ostrom and Hanson, *Efficiency, Timeliness, and Quality.*

34. Barry C. Feld, *Justice for Children: The Right to Counsel and the Juvenile Courts* (Boston: Northeastern University Press, 1993), p. 55.

35. Malcolm Feeley, *Court Reform on Trial* (New York: Basic Books, 1983), p. 173.

36. Campaign for an Effective Crime Policy, *The Impact of "Three Strikes and You're Out" Laws: What Have We Learned?* (Washington, DC: Author, 1996). Vincent Schiraldi, Jason Colburn, and Eric Lotke, *3 Strikes & You're Out: An Examination of 3-Strike Laws 10 Years after Their Enactment* (Washington, DC: Justice Policy Institute, 2004). Available on the Justice Policy Institute website.

37. William A. Geller and Michael S. Scott, *Deadly Force: What We Know* (Washington, DC: Police Executive Research Forum, 1992), p. 503; Bureau of Justice Statistics, *Policing and Homicide, 1976–98: Justifiable Homicide of Felons by Police and Murder of Police by Felons.* (Washington, DC: Department of Justice, 2001). NCJ 180987.

38. Terance D. Miethe and Charles A. Moore, *Sentencing Guidelines: Their Effect in Minnesota* (Washington, DC: Department of Justice, 1989); Bureau of Justice Statistics, *Sourcebook of Criminal Justice Statistics Online,* available on the SUNY Albany website. Information about the Minnesota Sentencing Guidelines is available on the Minnesota Sentencing Guidelines Commission website.

39. Raymond T. Nimmer, *The Nature of System Change* (Chicago: American Bar Foundation, 1978), p. 181.

40. Eisenstein et al., *Contours of Justice,* p. 294.

41. Cassia Spohn and Julie Horney, *Rape Law Reform: A Grassroots Revolution and Its Impact* (New York: Plenum, 1992), pp. 171–173.

42. Ibid., pp. 291–305.

43. Peter W. Greenwood, Susan S. Everingham, Elsa Chen, Allan F. Abrahamse, Nancy Merritt, and James Chiesa, *Three Strikes Revisited: An Early Assessment of Implementation and Effects* (Santa Monica, CA: Rand, 1998). Schiraldi, Colburn, and Lotke, *3 Strikes & You're Out: An Examination of 3-Strike Laws 10 Years after Their Enactment.* Available on the Justice Policy Institute website.

44. See the annual arrest data reported by the Uniform Crime Reports; go to the FBI website for the most recent reports. The best compilation is *The Sourcebook of Criminal Justice Statistics,* available on the SUNY Albany website.

45. Malcolm Feeley, *Court Reform on Trial,* p. 184.

46. *Furman v. Georgia,* 408 U.S. 238 (1972); Raymond Paternoster, *Capital Punishment in America* (Lexington, MA: Lexington Books, 1991).

47. Schiraldi, Colburn, and Lotke, *3 Strikes & You're Out: An Examination of 3-Strike Laws 10 Years after Their Enactment.* Available on the Justice Policy Institute website.

48. Pamala L. Griset, "The Politics and Economics of Increased Correctional Discretion over Time Served: A New York Case Study," *Justice Quarterly* 12 (June 1995): 307–323.

49. For more information about the Innocence Project, and current data on cases, go to the organization's website.

50. C. Ronald Huff, Arye Rattner, and Edward Sagarin, "Guilty Until Proven Innocent: Wrongful Convictions and Public Policy," *Crime and Delinquency* 32 (October 1986): 518–544; C. Ronald Huff, Arye Rattner, and Edward Sagarin, *Convicted but Innocent* (Beverly Hills, CA: Sage, 1996).

51. Hugo Adam Bedau and Michael L. Radelet, "Miscarriages of Justice in Potentially Capital Cases," *Stanford Law Review* 40 (November 1987): 21–179.

4

❖

The Career Criminal

The career criminal has been a major focus of crime control policy for 30 years. Several important crime control policies that we will examine in this book—preventive detention, major-offender prosecution programs, selective incapacitation—are aimed at the so-called career criminal. All of these programs assume that if we could identify and effectively respond to these offenders—through incapacitation, treatment, whatever—we could make significant reductions in crime. After three decades of research, experimentation, and program evaluation, we have a reasonably good idea of whether targeting the career criminal actually works. This chapter reviews that evidence.

WOLFGANG'S BIRTH COHORT

In the past, people have always talked about "hard-core" criminals, "repeaters," or "chronic recidivists," but these terms were based largely on myth and stereotypes. We are indebted to Marvin Wolfgang, Robert Figlio, and Thorsten Sellin for giving us a detailed profile of these people. Wolfgang and his colleagues' landmark study, *Delinquency in a Birth Cohort,* one of the most important pieces of criminal justice research in the last 30 years, has had a profound influence on thinking about crime policy.[1]

Wolfgang's birth cohort included all the males born in Philadelphia in 1945 and traced their careers through their eighteenth birthday in 1963. Using official records, such as police and school records, the study reconstructed the criminal careers of a sample of 9,945 juveniles. The principal finding was that a small percentage of delinquents were responsible for a majority of all crimes and for about two-thirds of all violent crimes.

As Table 4.1 indicates, 35 percent of the cohort had at least one *officially recorded contact* with the police. Of that group, 46 percent had no more contacts. Wolfgang labeled them "one-time offenders." He divided the remaining 1,862 juveniles into two groups. The 1,235 with two, three, or four contacts were labeled the "nonchronic recidivists." The remaining 627 with five or more contacts were the "chronic delinquents." They represented 6 percent of the original cohort and 18 percent of the 3,475 delinquents. These 627 are the so-called career criminals.

Several comments about Wolfgang's data are in order. Most important, he measured delinquency in terms of officially recorded police contacts. Obviously, many delinquents were never caught, and the actual prevalence of criminal behavior was undoubtedly higher than 35 percent. Some of those with a recorded police contact, meanwhile, may have been picked up by mistake and should not be considered "offenders." Also, many of the "one-time delinquents" committed other illegal acts but were never caught. And, finally, some "nonchronic delinquents" committed more than four crimes.

Despite these limitations, however, the cohort study highlighted some important patterns in delinquency. It gave us the first clear picture of the prevalence of delinquency: that is, what percentage of any group of males commit crime. Second, it gave us a good picture of the percentage we can consider "career criminals." Finally, it documented the fact that most delinquents stop committing illegal acts at some point, and most of them stop relatively early. We do not know what makes them stop. Some "mature out." Others may be deterred by their contact with the police. Still others may be helped by the treatment program included in their juvenile court disposition. All we know for sure is that most eventually stop.

Wolfgang's most important finding, and the one that excited policymakers, was the small group of 627 chronic recidivists that was responsible for more than half (52 percent) of all the crimes committed by the entire cohort and 63 percent of all the Index crimes (71 percent of the murders, 73 percent of the rapes, and 82 percent of all the robberies). The one-time offenders committed only 16 percent of the total; the nonchronic recidivists, the remaining 32 percent.

The policy implications of these data are obvious: If we could successfully identify and effectively respond to that 6 percent, we could achieve a major reduction in serious crime. And the point is relevant for both liberal and conservative crime policies. If you are a liberal who believes in rehabilitation, identifying and successfully treating that 6 percent would achieve a huge reduction in crime. If you are conservative, you will get a tremendous crime reduction by successfully incapacitating in prison that same 6 percent.

Table 4.1 Wolfgang's birth cohort

	Number	Percentage of original sample	Total criminal offenses	Percentage of total offenses
Original sample	9,945			
Delinquents	3,475	34.9%	10,214	
One officially recorded contact with police	1,613	16.2	1,613	15.8%
Two to four contacts	1,235	12.4	3,296	32.3
Five or more contacts	627	6.3	5,305	51.9

SOURCE: Marvin Wolfgang, Robert M. Figlio, and Thorsten Sellin, *Delinquency in a Birth Cohort* (Chicago: University of Chicago Press, 1972).

OTHER COHORT STUDIES

Wolfgang's original findings have been confirmed by other cohort studies. He and his associates conducted a follow-up study of males and females born in Philadelphia in 1958. This was a larger cohort (28,338 subjects) and more representative in terms of race and sex. Following their criminal careers between 1968 and 1974 (ages 10 to 18), they found a similar pattern in criminal behavior: 33 percent had at least one recorded contact with the police, whereas the chronic recidivists represented 7.5 percent of the total cohort (compared with 6.3 percent in the original study).[2]

The 1958 cohort did commit more crimes. Remember, this study covered the late 1960s, when the crime rate soared. The murder rate was three times higher and the robbery rate five times higher than for the 1945 cohort. Thus, about the same percentage of cohort members became delinquent, but those who did committed more crimes and far more serious ones.

Some people might question whether Philadelphia is representative of the rest of the country. Lyle Shannon studied three cohorts in Racine, Wisconsin, tracing the careers of 6,127 persons born in 1942, 1949, and 1955. Unlike Wolfgang, he followed his subjects into adulthood. Members of the 1942 cohort were 33 years old when the study ended. Shannon found that most of his subjects had at least one contact with the police: 68 percent of the 1942 group, 69 percent of the 1949 cohort, and 59 percent of the 1955 cohort (but the members of this last cohort were only 22 years old when the data collection ended, so it missed part of their high-crime years). These figures may seem frightening until we learn that most of the arrests were for relatively minor crimes. Part I Index crimes represented only 12.7 percent of all the arrests for the 1942 cohort and 15.9 and 24.6 percent for the 1949 and 1955 cohorts, respectively. These data confirm what criminologists have long known: that most males in this country break the law at some point in their lives but that most of the lawbreaking involves minor crimes such as vandalism.[3]

The career criminal patterns in Racine closely resembled those in Philadelphia. Shannon found that 9.5 percent of the 1942 cohort had 51 percent of the police contacts, 8 percent of the 1949 group had 50.8 percent of the contacts, and 5.8 percent of the 1955 group had 50.8 percent of that group's police contacts. Looking at felony arrests only, he found that people with four or more contacts represented 0.6 percent of the 1942 cohort but accounted for 27.1 percent of the felony arrests. For the 1949 group, 1.7 percent of the cohort had four or more contacts and were responsible for 44.1 percent of the felony contacts; for the 1955 group, 3.5 percent of the cohort had four or more and accounted for 63.8 percent of the felony contacts.

The fact that the Racine findings parallel those from Philadelphia is very significant. Racine is a relatively small midwestern community, with a population of only 71,000 in 1950 and 95,000 in 1970. Racial minorities constituted only 11 percent of the population in 1970. Philadelphia in 1970 was the third largest city in the country, with a minority population of 33.6 percent. The Racine study suggests that Wolfgang's most important finding holds true for other communities. Additional support comes from David Farrington's study of young men in London. Farrington found that 6 percent of his sample accounted for 49 percent of all the criminal convictions in the cohort.[4] In short, there appears to be a near universal pattern in which a small group of offenders account for a very high proportion of all the crimes committed by their cohort.

DEFINING OUR TERMS AND CONCEPTS

Before going any further, it is useful to clarify some of the terminology used in career criminal research.[5] First, we can distinguish *criminal careers* from *career criminals*. Every offender has a criminal career. Some have short ones; others have long ones. Everyone who goes to school has an academic career. If you drop this and every other course tomorrow and never return to school, you have had an academic career—a very short one. The kid who commits one act of minor vandalism has a criminal career—a short one. The career criminal is the person with a long criminal career.

Another basic concept is the *prevalence* of criminality. We define this in terms of *participation,* which distinguishes between those who commit at least one crime and those who do not commit any. As we mentioned previously, the Philadelphia cohort study found that 35 of the original cohort had a contact with the police. To identify the real career criminals, we need to know the *frequency* of offending—that is, the rate at which active criminals commit crimes. As we will learn later, this issue has extremely important implications for crime policy. If the frequency is about five felonies a year, imprisoning offenders will have a certain crime reduction effect through incapacitation. But if the frequency is 144 felonies per year, the crime reduction effect will be much greater. Obtaining an accurate estimate of the frequency, then, is extremely important for assessing the impact of incapacitation. Determining the *seriousness* of offending is also important, because we want to identify those who commit the more serious crimes. The beginning of a criminal career is referred to as the *onset*. Do career criminals begin earlier than one-time offenders? If they do, we might be able to spot them that way. *Persistence* refers to continuing criminal activity and *desistance* to stopping. The amount of time between onset and desistance is the *career length*.

FROM RESEARCH TO POLICY

Wolfgang's original birth cohort study generated an enormous amount of excitement, stimulating further research and influencing the development of crime policies. The study was published at a politically opportune moment. By 1972, crime rates had been rising dramatically for a decade. The public was disillusioned with the liberal rehabilitation-oriented policies of the 1960s and was ready for programs that promised to "get tough" with hard-core criminals.[6] Wolfgang's data suggested that it might be possible to identify that small group.

This book examines some of the specific policies inspired by the career criminal research. They include police programs that target suspected career criminals for intensive surveillance (Chapter 5), pretrial detention of allegedly "dangerous" offenders (Chapter 7), career criminal prosecution programs (Chapter 8), and selective incapacitation for repeat offenders (Chapter 7). Many of the treatment-oriented crime control policies proposed by liberals are also designed to deal with particular classes of offenders. Intensive probation programs (Chapter 11) are designed for "high-risk" offenders, whereas boot camps are designed for special categories of offenders.

The data in Table 4.1 make it look simple: Spot the chronic recidivists, and either treat or punish them accordingly. The problem, however, is that nothing is simple in the real world of criminal justice. Ideas that sound good in theory do not necessarily work out in practice. Let us look at some of the problems that arise when we try to translate Wolfgang's birth cohort research into crime control policy.

APPLICATION PROBLEMS

As is so often the case with path-breaking research, *Delinquency in a Birth Cohort* raised more questions than it answered. It was a major breakthrough to learn that we needed to focus on 6 percent of a cohort, but it was only the beginning. Criminologists have devoted an enormous amount of time and energy to answering some basic questions. First, exactly who are the career criminals? Second, when do they begin their criminal careers, and can we identify them early in their careers before they commit most of their crimes? Third, how much crime does each one commit? (As we will see shortly, this question is particularly important.) Fourth, what kinds of crime do they commit? Fifth, how long do they remain active criminals? Sixth, when do they stop? Seventh, why do they stop? Is it the result of some criminal justice policy or do they simply mature out? All of these issues are related to the bottom line question: Are there criminal justice programs or interventions that cause them to stop earlier than they otherwise would?

The basic challenge confronting any policy directed toward career criminals is to identify and control these offenders *and only them*. It is a waste of time and money to imprison one-time offenders who do not commit more crimes. Traditionally, criminal justice officials believed that they could identify the repeat offenders or the truly dangerous criminals. Judges denied bail to defendants they "knew" were dangerous. Judges granted some convicted offenders probation because they "knew" they were not going to commit more crimes. Most of these decisions were based on hunch, guesswork, or just plain bias. At best, they relied on the seriousness of the immediate offense and the offender's prior record.

This issue is illustrated by the famous story about how one Supreme Court justice defined pornography. In the *Jacobellis* case (1964), Justice Potter Stewart admitted that he could not define "hard-core pornography" but said, "I know it when I see it."[7] Many criminal justice officials believe they know a career criminal when they see one.

In the real world of criminal justice, career criminal programs run into two serious problems. The first is correctly identifying the career criminal and not mistakenly identifying low-rate offenders. We call this the *prediction problem*. The second is accurately estimating how much crime these career criminals actually do (the frequency of offending)—and thus how much crime we will prevent by either imprisoning or treating them. Let us look at both of these problems in detail.

THE PREDICTION PROBLEM

Identifying someone as a career criminal is essentially a prediction. We are predicting that they will commit many crimes in the future. We can use three basic methods for predicting criminal behavior. The first is an *actuarial* approach that relies on patterns of behavior among individuals with similar characteristics. Insurance companies use this method. The data indicate that young drivers have more accidents than middle-age drivers and that young men have much worse records than young women. Thus, insurance companies charge higher insurance rates for young people.

A second approach uses the *prior history* of the individual. Someone has committed many crimes in the past, and so we predict that this behavior will continue in the future. Or, in education we say that you flunked the first test in this course and, therefore, we predict that you will flunk the next one. As we learned in Chapter 3, criminal justice officials typically use prior criminal record to assess offenders. Sentencing guidelines build prior record into the matrix, assigning more points for each offense.

A third approach is *clinical evaluation*. Here, predictions about future behavior are based on the assessments of trained experts. A psychologist or social worker, for example, might conduct a personal interview, review the individual's social history (family, employment record, and so forth), and possibly administer a psychological test. Presentence investigations by probation officers are an example of clinical evaluations based on an offender's social history.

The Wenk Study

The question is, Can these techniques be used to successfully predict future criminal behavior? A good test was conducted on behalf of the National Council on Crime and Delinquency by Ernst A. Wenk, James O. Robison, and Gerald W. Smith. The results were not reassuring. Wenk and his colleagues began with a sample of 4,146 youths committed to the California Youth Authority (CYA). Of this group, 104 subsequently became "violent recidivists." Wenk and his colleagues sought to develop a prediction instrument that would have identified these 104 individuals if it had been used in advance. Their instrument involved a combination of prior record and clinical assessment, using each juvenile's prior criminal record and history of violence and substance abuse, among other factors. Clinical assessments were based on psychological tests and interviews.[8]

Table 4.2 indicates the results. As is obvious, the method successfully identified only half (52) of the 104 who subsequently committed a violent act. This group, referred to as the *true positives,* were correctly and positively identified as likely to commit a violent act. The other 52 slipped through the net, however. We call them the *false negatives.* They were falsely (or incorrectly) predicted not to be violent. From this perspective, the prediction instrument was only 50 percent accurate; it missed half of those who actually became violent.

There is an additional problem, however. As Table 4.2 indicates, 404 people were incorrectly predicted as likely to become violent. These are referred to as the *false positives.* What this means is that the method used by Wenk and his associates incorrectly identified about eight people for every one who was successfully identified as likely to become violent. From this perspective, the prediction instrument is accurate only about 12 percent of the time (52 out of the total of 456 predicted to be violent). To translate this figure into real-world terms, it would mean imprisoning eight nonrecidivists for every violent recidivist correctly identified. Obviously, the costs in terms of dollars and unnecessary deprivation of liberty would be enormous.

The Wenk study reveals the difficulty in predicting human behavior. Even with the extensive data available, the study's method produced large numbers of both false positives and false negatives. Even though many people think

Table 4.2 Number of youths predicted to be violent and nonviolent who proved to be violent and nonviolent, California,1972

	Predicted violent	Predicted nonviolent
Actual violent	True positives: Violent persons correctly identified as violent and incarcerated 52	False negatives: Violent persons incorrectly identified as nonviolent and not incarcerated 52
Actual nonviolent	False positives: Nonviolent persons incorrectly identified as violent and needlessly incarcerated 404	True negatives: Nonviolent persons correctly identified as nonviolent 3,638

SOURCE: Ernst A. Wenk, James O. Robison, and Gerald W. Smith, "Can Violence Be Predicted?" *Crime and Delinquency* 18 (October 1972): 393–402.

they "know" career criminals "when they see one," in fact it is very difficult to predict future behavior accurately.

We can illustrate the prediction problem by applying it to Wolfgang's birth cohort. If juvenile court officials used the same prediction instrument to identify the 627 chronic recidivists, they would miss half of them (313) and then needlessly lock up 2,500 juveniles who would not become chronic recidivists. The same problem bedevils all prediction schemes, and as we shall see that it affects both conservative-oriented incapacitation policies and liberal-oriented rehabilitation programs.

The Texas Death Row Inmate Study

A more recent test of predicting dangerousness was conducted by the Texas Defender Service, the agency that represents death row inmates. It reviewed 155 cases in which prosecutors in recommending the death penalty had used experts to predict a defendant's future dangerousness. It then examined the prison disciplinary records of these inmates with respect to violent behavior. The predictions of dangerousness were *wrong in 95 percent of the cases.* Only 8 of the 155 predicted dangerous inmates had records of "seriously assaultive behavior." In fact, 20 percent of the inmates ($n = 31$) had no disciplinary violations of any sort. The remaining 75 percent had some record of disciplinary actions, but none involved serious assaults. Sixty-seven of the 155 inmates had been executed and had spent an average of 12 years on death row. Forty currently reside on death row and have been incarcerated an average of 8 years. Forty-eight inmates had their sentences reduced and had served an average of nearly 22 years.[9]

The Federal Sentencing Guidelines

The 1987 law creating the federal sentencing guidelines also established the U.S. Sentencing Commission with a staff and a mandate to evaluate the implementation and impact of the guidelines. Since one of the goals of the guidelines is to reduce crime through incapacitation, the commission attempted to evaluate whether they were accurately predicting future criminal behavior. In a 2004 report, the commission found that the guidelines system of criminal history scores was positively correlated with recidivism rates. As offender criminal history scores increased, so did recidivism rates. Only 13.6 percent of the offenders with the lowest scores (Criminal History Category [CHC] I) recidivated in the first two years, compared with 55.2 percent of those with the highest scores (CHC VI). The Sentencing Commission concluded that the guidelines were accurately predicting future criminal behavior.[10]

The problem with the Sentencing Commission approach is that its prediction system relies on very broad categories based on prior record and does not attempt to predict the future behavior of individuals within a particular criminal history category. And in fact, the federal sentencing guidelines were intended to severely limit the discretion of judges in sentencing and prevent them from sentencing on the basis of individual factors (that is, making predictions about individual offenders). The sentencing guidelines can be properly seen as a "justice model" of sentencing, in which sentences are based on the seriousness of the offense and prior record. All the Sentencing Commission report tells us is that in general, people with longer criminal histories are more likely to commit more crime in the future than people with less serious criminal histories.

In the end, the evidence clearly indicates that the prediction problem is a recurring issue in criminal justice. We will encounter it again in Chapter 7 with regard to bail setting and incarceration, and in Chapter 11 with respect to probation and parole decision making.

The Rand Selective Incapacitation Study

A second exercise in prediction was conducted by the Rand Corporation in its report *Selective Incapacitation*.[11] The Rand Inmate Survey (RIS) involved self-report interviews in California, Texas, and Michigan in which prison inmates were asked how many crimes they had committed between arrests. While far from perfect, this self-report method yields a reasonably good estimate of the undetected crime committed by these offenders.

Then, using the actuarial method of prediction, the Rand researchers correlated the self-reported criminal activity with the social histories of the 2,190 inmates. They identified thirteen characteristics that were correlated with high rates of criminal activity. Only those characteristics that were legally relevant and appropriate were used. An offender's race is not a legally appropriate factor, for example. Rand then used these data to develop a seven-point prediction scale (Table 4.3). Offenders with four or more points were then predicted to be high-rate offenders; those with two to three points were

Table 4.3 Seven-point scale of factors affecting prediction of offense rates

1. Prior conviction for the instant offense type
2. Incarcerated more than 50 percent of preceding two years
3. Conviction before age 16
4. Served time in a state juvenile facility
5. Drug use in preceding two years
6. Drug use as a juvenile
7. Employed less than 50 percent of the preceding two years

SOURCE: Peter W. Greenwood, *Selective Incapacitation* (Santa Monica, CA: Rand, 1982), p. 50.

Table 4.4 Predicted versus self-reported offense ratio for robbery and burglary

	Self-reported offense rates (%)			
Score on prediction scale	Low	Medium	High	Total
Low (0–1)	14	10	3	27
Medium (2–3)	12	22	10	44
High (4–7)	4	10	15	29
Total	30	42	28	100

SOURCE: Peter W. Greenwood, *Selective Incapacitation* (Santa Monica, CA: Rand, 1982). p. 59.

predicted to be medium rate, and those with only one or no points were low-rate offenders.

In the next stage, Rand retrospectively correlated the prediction scores with inmates' actual reported criminal activity. The results appear in Table 4.4. The prediction device was correct only 51 percent of the time. This represents the combination of the predicted low-risk offenders who proved to be low risks (14 percent), the predicted medium risks who proved to be medium risks (22 percent), and the predicted high risks who actually proved to be high risks (15 percent). A 51 percent accuracy rate is not very good. You could do as well flipping a coin.

At the same time, the prediction device was *grossly* wrong in 7 percent of the cases: the 4 percent who were predicted to be high risks but who turned out to be low risks (false positives) and the 3 percent who were predicted to be low risks but proved to be high risks (false negatives). The prediction device was only *moderately* wrong in the remaining 42 percent of the cases. (Consider for a moment the real-world implications of the 4 percent error rate for those incorrectly predicted to be high risks. Given our current prison population, that translates into about 50,000 people needlessly imprisoned.)

We can hardly expect any system to be perfect. The relevant question is whether the Rand prediction device is *better than existing sentencing practices.* (Recall our discussion of goals in Chapter 1. We should not seek perfection, only an improvement over what we have been doing.) If it leads to a substantial improvement, even though less than perfect, it would be useful. Peter Greenwood took his sample of offenders and categorized them as low, medium, or high risks according to the sentences they had actually received. These sentences were "correct" 42 percent of the time. That is, in 42 percent of the cases, the sentencing judges had correctly identified the high-rate offenders and sentenced them to long prison terms and correctly identified low-rate offenders and sentenced them to short terms. Meanwhile, the judges were grossly wrong 12 percent of the time. In short, the extremely sophisticated Rand prediction device was only slightly better than what judges had in fact already done with these offenders (51 percent versus 42 percent).

Several years later, Rand researchers made another attempt at predicting career criminals. They used two samples. One group included 2,700 men who had been committed to the CYA as juveniles between 1966 and 1971. The second group included 200 RIS inmates who had been incarcerated for either burglary or robbery and had been released at least two years before the new study. Rand used the original seven-point prediction scale for the RIS group and a modified five-point scale for the CYA group.[12]

The results of this study are expressed in the subtitle of the Rand report: *Why the High-Rate Offenders Are Hard to Predict.* The authors concluded that "high rate offenders cannot be accurately identified, either prospectively or retrospectively, on the basis of their arrest rates alone,"[13] and they conceded that the earlier Rand conclusions about the ability to identify high-rate offenders and reduce crime by selectively incapacitating them were "overly optimistic."[14]

HOW MUCH CRIME DO THEY COMMIT?

A critically important problem in translating career criminal research into crime policy involves estimating how many crimes the average high-rate offender commits. The estimate has important practical ramifications. How many crimes will we prevent if we lock up an armed robber for five years? How much safer will we be compared with the robber's doing a three-year sentence? Criminologists have devoted considerable energy to developing estimates of the *annual offending rate* for career criminals.

The RIS attempted to estimate annual offending rates through interviews with inmates in three states. It was one of the most influential studies, and its findings have been widely used. The self-report method was a major advance because official records (e.g., arrest reports) do not provide a complete picture of a criminal's criminal behavior. Many crimes are not reported, and obviously, most crimes do not result in an arrest.

The RIS estimated high rates of criminal activity, but with some important variations. California robbers averaged 53 robberies per year, compared with 77 for Michigan robbers but only 9 a year for those in Texas. The RIS also found that criminals did not specialize in one type of crime. California robbers also averaged 90 burglaries, 163 thefts or frauds, and 646 drug offenses each year. Texas robbers, meanwhile, averaged 24 burglaries and 98 thefts each year.[15]

The variations in annual offending rates among the three states are striking. Why were the rates so much higher for Michigan and California compared with Texas? The best explanation is that Texas judges sent more robbers to prison, regardless of their actual criminal histories. As a result, the Texas sample included a higher proportion of low-rate offenders than the Michigan and California samples did, thereby dragging down the group's average. California judges were being more selective, incarcerating only the worst robbers, with the result that the inmates in that state had much higher annual crime rates.

The difference in the annual offending rates may seem like a minor technical point, but it has tremendous practical consequences. We need a precise estimate of the annual offending rate to calculate the amount of crime reduction we will get. The annual offending rate is expressed as *lambda*. If the lambda is large, then we can expect a substantial reduction in crime for every career criminal who is imprisoned or rehabilitated. But if the lambda is low (that is, if the average career criminal commits relatively few crimes each year), then the payoff will be much lower.

Estimates of lambda by respected scholars vary enormously. Alfred Blumstein and Jacqueline Cohen estimated that adult arrestees committed an annual average of 3.4 robberies and 5.7 burglaries in Washington and 4.7 robberies and 5.3 burglaries in Detroit. The National Youth Survey estimated that active offenders committed an average of 8.4 robberies and 7.1 burglaries per year.[16] At the other end of the scale, Edwin W. Zedlewski, in *Making Confinement Decisions,* used an estimate of 187 felonies per year.[17] The practical implications of these different estimates are obvious. If we accept Zedlewski's figure, we could expect a great reduction in crime. But if we accept Blumstein and Cohen's figure, we will get a much smaller payoff for locking up each offender. When we discuss incapacitation as sentencing policy in Chapter 7, we will take a critical look at Zedlewski's use of his 187 figure.

A major part of the problem here is the concept of *average* offending rates. The RIS data clearly indicate that there is no such thing as an "average" career criminal. The median annual robbery rate for the RIS inmates was 5 per year. The top 10 percent, however, averaged 87 robberies per year. It is important to remember that the RIS inmates were a pretty select group: They got caught and were sent to prison because judges regarded them as dangerous offenders. The top 10 percent of the RIS sample, then, were the worst of the worst.

From a practical standpoint, to get some real payoff in terms of crime reduction, it is necessary to identify this small group from among all the other "serious" offenders. Say, for example, that you wanted to send most robbers (5 robberies per year) to 5-year prison terms and give the really high rate robbers (87 per year) 15 years. You would have to make very precise predictions.

We will examine this subject again in Chapter 7 when we discuss incapacitation as a crime control strategy. It is worth pointing out, however, that despite all the initial excitement about the possibilities of applying career criminal research through *selective* incapacitation, we have in practice abandoned that goal and adopted a policy of *gross* incapacitation. The prison population has soared because we are locking up lots of people without making fine distinctions.

CONCLUSION

The subject of career criminals is an excellent example of the difficulties of translating research into policy. No one seriously questions Wolfgang's original finding about the fact that a small group of offenders is responsible for a huge percentage of all crime. Subsequent research has tended to confirm it. Nor does anyone seriously question the argument that we could make a substantial reduction in crime *if* we could correctly identify those people and keep them from committing more crime.

The key word here, of course, is *if.* Research on the prediction problem indicates that it is difficult, if not impossible, to precisely identify in advance the small group of high-rate offenders. This difficulty is compounded by the fact that estimates conflict on how much crime these high-rate offenders actually do. If the averages are in fact low, we will not get that much payoff in terms of crime reduction.

The problems we have identified here have a direct impact on many of the crime control policies we will examine in the chapters ahead. As we mentioned earlier, the administration of justice consists of a series of discretionary decision points. Many of those decisions involve predictions about who is and who is not dangerous.

NOTES

1.   Marvin Wolfgang, Robert M. Figlio, and Thorsten Sellin, *Delinquency in a Birth Cohort* (Chicago: University of Chicago Press, 1972).

2.   Paul E. Tracy, Marvin E. Wolfgang, and Robert M. Figlio, *Delinquency in Two Birth Cohorts* (Chicago: University of Chicago Press, 1985).

3.   Lyle W. Shannon, Judith L. McKim, James P. Curry, and Lawrence J. Haffner, *Criminal Career Continuity: Its Social Context* (New York: Human Sciences Press, 1988).

4. The findings of all the longitudinal studies are reviewed in David P. Farrington, Lloyd E. Ohlin, and James Q. Wilson, *Understanding and Controlling Crime: Toward a New Research Strategy* (New York: Springer, 1986), see especially pp. 50–52.

5. Alfred Blumstein, Jacqueline Cohen, Jeffrey Roth, and Christy A. Visher, eds., *Criminal Careers and "Career Criminals"* (Washington, DC: National Academy Press, 1986).

6. Samuel Walker, *Popular Justice: A History of American Criminal Justice,* 2nd ed. (New York: Oxford University Press, 1998).

7. *Jacobellis v. Ohio,* 378 U.S. 184, 197 (1964).

8. Ernest A. Wenk, James O. Robison, and Gerald W. Smith, "Can Violence Be Predicted?" *Crime and Delinquency* 18 (October 1972): 339–402.

9 Texas Defender Service, *Deadly Speculation: Misleading Texas Capital Juries with False Predictions of Future Dangerousness* (Austin: Texas Defender Service, 2004). Available on the Texas Defender Service website.

10. U.S. Sentencing Commission, *Measuring Recidivism: The Criminal History Computation of the Federal Sentencing Guidelines* (Washington, DC: Author, 2004).

11. Peter W. Greenwood and Allan Abrahamse, *Selective Incapacitation* (Santa Monica, CA: Rand, 1982).

12. Peter W. Greenwood and Susan Turner, *Selective Incapacitation Revisited: Why the High-Rate Offenders Are Hard to Predict* (Santa Monica, CA: Rand, 1987).

13. Ibid., p. x.

14. Ibid., p. 49.

15. The data are in Greenwood and Abrahamse, *Selective Incapacitation.* The original report is Joan Petersilia, Peter W. Greenwood, and Marvin Lavin, *Criminal Careers of Habitual Felons* (Santa Monica, CA: Rand, 1977).

16. Alfred Blumstein and Jacqueline Cohen, "Estimating Individual Crime Rates from Arrest Records," *Journal of Criminal Law and Criminology* 70 (1979): 561–585; Blumstein et al., *Criminal Careers and "Career Criminals."*

17. Edwin W. Zedlewski, *Making Confinement Decisions* (Washington, DC: Government Printing Office, 1987).

PART II

"Get Tough":
The Conservative
Attack on Crime

Conservatives argue that we can reduce serious crime if we just "get tough" with criminals. Their crime control agenda, which has not changed in 40 years, includes the following items. First, we can reduce crime if we would just unleash the cops and give them more power and resources. We will look at several strategies for unleashing the cops in Chapter 5. Second, we can deter crime through swifter, more certain, and more severe punishments. We will take a close look at the theory of deterrence and some deterrence-oriented programs in Chapter 6. Third, we should lock up more criminals by sending more to prison and for longer prison terms. This represents a strategy of incapacitation. We will look at several incapacitation programs in Chapter 7. Fourth, conservatives believe that too many criminals "get off" through loopholes in the criminal justice system. We will examine four proposals designed to close loopholes in Chapter 8. Conservatives and some policy analysts believe that the recent reduction in crime is a result of these policies.

5

Unleash the Cops!

Conservatives believe we can reduce crime if we just "unleash" the cops. Give them more officers and expanded powers, they argue, and the police will deter crime more effectively and arrest more criminals. The two basic strategies include putting more police officers on the street and removing constitutional restraints on obtaining evidence and confessions. Let us look at these and some other proposals to see whether they are likely to reduce crime.

In recent years the traditional approaches to improving the effectiveness of the police have been supplemented by some innovative programs: community-oriented policing, problem-oriented policing, and zero-tolerance policing. The full scope of new ideas and innovative programs is truly astonishing. David Bayley characterized the last years of the twentieth century as perhaps the most innovative period in the history of policing.[1] These new programs have been characterized as "working smarter" because they apply important research findings to police operations. In this chapter we will examine the impact on crime of all these approaches to improving policing.

MORE COPS ON THE STREET

The idea of putting more police on the street is very popular with the public. Most people want more cops in their neighborhood. When the National Crime Victimization Survey asked people what improvement in policing they would

Table 5.1 Police/population ratios, major cities, 2000

	Sworn officers per 1,000 population
Washington, DC	6.3
New York City	5.0
Philadelphia	4.6
Detroit	4.4
Los Angeles	2.5
Denver	2.7
San Diego	1.7
San Jose	1.6

SOURCE: Bureau of Justice Statistics, *Local Police Departments, 2000* (Washington, DC: Government Printing Office, 2003).

like, both whites and African Americans said they wanted more police.[2] The idea that police patrol deters crime has been the bedrock principle of policing since Robert Peel created the London Metropolitan Police in 1829. There are two separate questions for us to consider. First, does adding more cops increase the deterrent effect of policing? There is a certain commonsense logic to this idea: If police patrol prevents crime, shouldn't more police reduce crime even further? The second question is, Do different police strategies and tactics improve the crime-fighting capacity of the police?

The Police and Crime

There is a lot of mythology about the relationship between the police and crime rates. Simply hiring more police officers does not necessarily mean that more patrol officers will be on the street or that they will be used effectively in fighting crime.

The standard measure of the level of police protection is the police/population ratio: the number of officers per 1,000 people. (Current data on police/population ratios for individual cities and the nation are available in the FBI's annual Uniform Crime Reports (UCRs) and the Bureau of Justice Statistics' periodic LEMAS (Law Enforcement Management and Administrative Statistics) report. Nationally, there are 2.3 sworn officers per 1,000 people in the United States. Table 5.1, however, indicates that police/population ratios vary enormously. In the largest cities the ratio is 2.9 per 1,000, but in medium-sized cities (population 100,000 to 249,999) it is only 1.9. The variations are even more striking when we look at particular cities. Washington, DC, has more than twice as much police protection as Los Angeles and almost four times as much as San Diego. This does not make Washington a safer city, however.

In practice, the police/population ratio is a virtually meaningless figure because it does not tell us how police departments *utilize* their officers. If a department

Table 5.2 Deployment of patrol officers in two hypothetical cities

	City X	City Y
Population	500,000	500,000
Sworn officers	900	600
Percentage of officers assigned to patrol	50	70
Officers assigned to patrol	450	420
Percentage of patrol officers assigned to 4 P.M.–12 A.M. shift	33	50
Patrol officers, 4 P.M.–12 A.M. shift	148	210
One-officer patrols	20	190
Two-officer patrols	64	10
Total patrols, 4 P.M.–12 A.M.	84	200

does not put those officers on the street, or if it uses inefficient two-officer patrols, additional officers will not have any real impact. Table 5.2 illustrates the point by comparing two hypothetical police departments, one that is very efficiently operated and one that is not. Both are in cities with populations of 500,000. One has 900 sworn officers, the other 600. The department with 900 officers, however, assigns a lower percentage to patrol. Many officers are probably assigned to desk jobs. The department also does not assign its patrol officers according to a rational workload formula, leaving the busy evening shift understaffed. Finally, it employs two-officer patrol units, which are much less efficient than one-officer units. The net result is that the city with the higher police/population ratio actually has fewer patrol units on the street during the high-crime evening shift. The citizens are paying more for police protection but getting less.

The important question, of course, is what police officers actually *do* when they are on the street. A department may put a lot of officers on patrol, but if they do little active police work—initiate contacts with citizens, intensively patrol known high-crime areas, for example—the public will not get much in the way of actual crime fighting. In short, simply adding more police to an already inefficient department is throwing money—or cops, in this case—at the problem. Conservatives are fond of attacking liberals for throwing money at social problems. This criticism also applies to the idea of hiring more police.

In the most systematic review of the evidence, Eck and Maguire reviewed 27 studies of the relationship between the number of police officers and the crime rate and found very mixed results. Only 20 percent of them found that more police was correlated with lower crime rates, while 30 percent found just the reverse: more police was correlated with more crime. By the standards of evidence-based crime policy, this is not persuasive evidence that increasing the number of police reduces crime.[3]

Hiring More Police: The COPS Program

The largest and most expensive crime-fighting program in recent memory has been the federal Community-Oriented Policing Services (COPS) program, which has spent over $7 billion since 1994 to put more officers on the street. Because of its cost and national scope, we need to take a close look at it. The 1994 Violent Crime Control Act provided federal funds to pay for 75 percent of the cost of a new officer for three years. One analysis called the COPS program "the largest federal anti-crime supplemental investment in U.S. history." (It is supplemental in the sense of expenditures over and above the normal budget for local police.)[4] What did we get for that huge expenditure? Did all those new officers hired under the COPS program help to reduce crime?

There is a lot of controversy over the COPS program, and it is important to sort out the issues. First we have to specify exactly what the program funded and how many new officers were added. The COPS office made three different kinds of grants. The Universal Hiring Program funded the hiring of new officers. Technology grants, meanwhile, funded equipment designed to free officers from administrative duties and make them available for street duty. Finally, Innovative grants supported community-oriented policing programs. By mid-2001, it was estimated that 60,012 new COPS-funded officers were hired and on the street. An additional 23,012 officers were counted as "redeployed" through COPS-funded technology grants. Thus, the combined total was 83,024 additional police officers on the street as a result of the COPS program.

A second question is, What did the new officers actually do? Did they engage in new and different kinds of community policing programs through the Innovative grants, or did they simply supplement existing officers in traditional policing? This is an important question. If there was any impact on crime, what exactly was the "treatment": new and innovative approaches to crime fighting or simply adding more cops?

Zhao, Scheider, and Thurman conducted a national evaluation of the impact of the COPS program.[5] They studied 7,179 city police agencies that received COPS funding between 1994 and 1998 (omitting state police, county sheriffs, and other special purpose agencies, as well as 535 cities with populations of less than 1,000). They separately evaluated the three types of COPS grants. The grant data were lagged by one or more years (depending on the type of grant) to allow for implementation. Common sense tells us that it takes time for new officers to be recruited, trained, and placed on the street, so the effect, if any, will be delayed by a year or more.

Analyzing official UCR data from 1994 to 1999, Zhao and his colleagues found that in cities with 10,000 or more people the hiring grants and the Innovative grants did reduce crime. They estimated that *one dollar in grant funding per city resident* for hiring (that is, $350,000 in a city of 350,000 people) resulted in a decline in 5.26 violent crimes per 100,000 people (e.g., about 18 violent crimes in a city of 350,000 people). Innovative grants, meanwhile, were associated with even greater reductions in violent crimes. No crime reductions were associated with the technology grants, however.

At the same time, COPS funding had just the opposite effect in smaller cities (less than 10,000) and was associated with an increase in crime. What explains this paradoxical finding? Why opposite effects in cities of different sizes? Zhao and his colleagues speculated that in very small police departments the addition of even one officer makes a huge difference in their capacity to serve the public. In a department with only five officers—and there are a lot of them—one additional cop represents a 20 percent increase in the force. This increase in the number of officers may significantly facilitate citizen reporting of crime (e.g., the department can keep the office open more hours, particularly at night; officers will be more available to take calls, etc.).

Cost-Effective?

The finding that the addition of COPS-funded officers reduces crime in large cities is extremely important but does not answer all of the questions surrounding the COPS program. A cost-benefit analysis puts this issue in a different perspective. Let's take a hypothetical city of 350,000 people. COPS funding of $350,000 ($1 per resident in the Zhao analysis) would result in a reduction of about 18 violent crimes (at the rate of 5 per 100,000). This comes to about $19,400 per violent crime. Let's assume that the city is Omaha, Nebraska (2000 population: 390,000). In 2003 Omaha had 2,627 reported violent crimes. The $350,000 would have purchased less than a 1 percent reduction in violent crime (0.68 percent, to be exact).

These data raise serious questions about the cost-effectiveness of the COPS program. It would require an expenditure of an additional $4 million dollars to achieve a 10 percent reduction in violent crime in a city of 350,000. Consider the implications of this for other cities. An additional expenditure of $1.3 million in Phoenix would produce a slightly less than 1 percent reduction in violent crime; and it would take more than an extra $13 million to approach a 10 percent reduction.

Remember that the ground rules for our inquiry require that a program not just be effective but that it be consistent with our legal standards (e.g., not violate constitutional law) *and that it be practical*. This includes considerations of cost. The program has to be something we can realistically afford. It is not clear that the COPS formula meets the cost-effectiveness test.

The evidence on the COPS program leads to the following conclusion:

PROPOSITION 6

Adding police officers, in combination with community policing programs, can produce modest reductions in crime but is not cost-effective.

The Deterrent Effect of Patrol: Lessons of Kansas City

The idea that a *visible police presence* deters crime has been the core principle of modern policing since the days of Peel in London. For nearly 150 years everyone accepted this idea on faith, without any scientific evidence to back it up. The Kansas City Preventive Patrol Experiment (1972–73), one of the most important research projects in police history, finally tested the deterrent effect of policing.[6]

The design of the experiment divided the South Patrol District into three groups of patrol beats. *Proactive* beats received two or three times the normal level of patrol. *Reactive* beats received no routine patrol: Police cars entered those areas only in response to a citizen's call for service; officers handled the call and then left the beat area. *Control* beats kept the normal level of patrol. Using a victimization survey, the experiment examined the effect of different levels of patrol on criminal activity and citizen perceptions of police protection. Unlike earlier experiments, they controlled for other variables that might affect the level of criminal activity: temporary or random changes in criminal activity, unreported crime, the possible displacement of crime into neighboring areas, and the reactions of both police officers and citizens to changes in police activity.

The Kansas City experiment found that the *level of patrol had no effect on either crime or citizen perceptions and fear of crime.* Crime did not increase in the reactive beats where there was less patrol and did not decline in the proactive beats where there was more patrol. Moreover, people did not seem to notice the differences in the level of patrol. Fear of crime did not go up in the reactive beats and did not go down in the proactive beats.[7]

It is important to emphasize that the experiment did *not* prove that patrol has absolutely no effect on crime. At no time were there beats with no police presence whatsoever. Patrol cars entered reactive beats to handle 911 calls, and officers in other units (e.g., juvenile, criminal investigation) entered them to handle their own assignments. Law-abiding citizens and potential criminals alike saw a marked police car and assumed that the police were patrolling the area. This phenomenon has been described as the *phantom effect* or *residual deterrence.* Even if there are no police around, patrol works if people believe they are. Residual deterrence works in several ways. People who saw patrol cars in proactive beats probably assumed that there were patrol cars in reactive beats. Moreover, as a practical matter we all pass through different police beats as we go about our lives (from home to job, school, the store, and so on). When we see a patrol car in one beat, that impression stays with us as we move through other beats. Most important for our purposes, the experiment found that *more* police patrols did not *reduce* the criminal activity.

The Kansas City findings were partly confirmed by the subsequent Newark (New Jersey) Foot Patrol Experiment (1978–79), which found that different levels of foot patrol had no effect on the crime rate. Interestingly, it found that additional foot patrol officers reduced citizen fear of crime and improved attitudes toward the police department. While important, that effect is a different subject than the one we are concerned with in this book.[8]

Understanding Deterrence

Why did adding patrol officers not reduce crime in either Kansas City or Newark? A major part of the answer lies in the underlying theory of deterrence. It assumes that the "treatment" (in this case, more patrol officers) communicates a threat of apprehension. As deterrence theorists explain, deterrence is really a matter of social psychology. The target audience has to *perceive* the threat (in this case, more police patrol), *calculate* the increased risk (of arrest), *understand* that the consequences are unpleasant (prosecution and possible conviction and imprisonment), and then make a *rational decision* not to commit a crime.[9] (We will discuss the theory of deterrence in more detail in Chapter 6 when we look at other deterrence-oriented policies.)

In the real world of policing, deterrence theory breaks down. First, police patrol is spread very thin even in the best of circumstances. A patrol car actually passes each point in its assigned beat very few times in any seven-day period. Doubling the number of patrol units (increasing the "dose") may not represent a difference that people are likely to perceive.

Second, many actual or potential offenders do not perceive police patrol as a meaningful threat. They simply don't think they will be caught. Remember, the official clearance rate for burglary was only 13 percent in 2002 according to UCR data.[10] Teenagers, for example, have a sense of invincibility. Much crime is impulsive, with offenders not rationally calculating. Experienced criminals, meanwhile, are fatalistic and assume that sooner or later they will be caught. Analyzing the Rand Inmate Survey, James Q. Wilson and Alan Abrahamse found that most inmates were fatalistic and thought there was a good chance they would be arrested, convicted, or even injured as a result of doing crime.[11]

Third, many crimes are inherently not suppressible by patrol. The majority of murders and assaults, and about half of all rapes, occur between people who know each other. Because they usually occur indoors and in the heat of passion, the amount of police patrol out on the street is not going to affect them. Robbery, burglary, and auto theft, which do occur outside, are at least theoretically suppressible through patrol.

By the standards of evidence-based crime policy, both the Kansas City and Newark experiments provide persuasive evidence that simply adding additional patrol officers (and not changing how they patrol or what they do) does not increase the deterrent effect of patrol. The evidence leads us to the following proposition:

PROPOSITION 7
Increasing the level of traditional police patrol will not reduce crime.

Traditional Police Crime-Fighting Strategies

So far we have discussed proposals to hire and place more officers on the street. This has involved simply the number of officers and not what they actually do. Now let's examine different police strategies and tactics for reducing crime.

Crackdowns Traditional police "crackdowns" are a classic example of the "get tough" approach to policing. Essentially, a *crackdown* is a short burst of intensive law enforcement, involving many arrests, directed toward a particular area or a particular crime.[12]

One well-known antidrug crackdown was Operation Pressure Point (OPP) in New York City. In the early 1980s, OPP targeted an open-air drug market on the city's Lower East Side that had been described as a "drug buyer's paradise." An additional 240 officers flooded the area, dispersing crowds, stopping and questioning suspected drug buyers and sellers, writing traffic tickets, and making a high volume of arrests (more than 2,000 in the first month alone). Also, the police department ended its Desk Appearance Ticket (DAT) policy, which allowed persons charged with misdemeanors to be released immediately, and the U.S. attorney's office agreed to process many of the drug arrests in federal court, where the defendants would face harsher sentences.[13]

There are a number of serious questions about the process and impact of OPP, however. The evaluation did not control for the possible displacement of drug trafficking into other neighborhoods. Moreover, drug dealers adapted to the crackdown with more sophisticated techniques, such as using lookouts and "steerers" to insulate the actual dealers from the police. The cost-effectiveness of the large number of arrests was not evaluated. Finally, the evaluation mentioned but did not discuss in detail the implications of the police misconduct that the program encouraged. Officers disrupted drug dealing, for example, by harassing potential buyers and scaring them off.

Even more significant, the drug problem in the area and the city worsened dramatically after OPP. The arrival of crack in the mid-1980s overwhelmed entire neighborhoods with even more serious open drug dealing than had existed before. Police officers in those neighborhoods have conceded that large numbers of arrests do little good. As one put it, for every person arrested "there is always a replacement."

One of the major problems with traditional crackdowns is that they are unfocused. They do not have a specific strategy for targeting particular offenders or problems. In Chapter 14, we will examine how some focused strategies have proven effective. Another problem is that traditional crackdowns rely completely on the police. In Chapter 14, we will see how a variety of innovative crime control strategies rely on partnerships among criminal justice agencies, other government services, and community organizations.

FASTER RESPONSE TIME

Many people believe that we could reduce crime if the police got to crime scenes faster. This idea has a basic, commonsense logic to it: The faster the police get there, the greater the likelihood they will arrest the offender. More arrests, meanwhile, will deter or incapacitate more criminals and lower the crime rate. Let us take a look at this idea.

In practice, however, faster response time does not produce more arrests. The police are called to very few crimes in progress. At most, only about 30 percent of all patrol dispatches involve criminal activity. Some studies put the figure as low as 17 percent. Moreover, about 75 percent of these crime-related calls involve "cold" crimes: typically, a burglary that occurred many hours earlier. The offender is long gone, and it makes no difference whether the police get there in three minutes or three hours.[14]

The remaining crime-related calls are "involvement" crimes, meaning that a confrontation exists between the victim and a suspect. At most, they represent only 25 percent of crime-related calls and only 7.5 percent of all dispatches. Response time rarely makes a difference in these crimes, either. In many cases, the victim and offender are acquaintances. The victim can identify the suspect no matter when the police arrive. Also, victims usually do not call the police immediately. Traumatized and confused, they often try to compose themselves, decide whether to even call the police, and often call a friend or family member first. This delay in calling the police renders the police travel time irrelevant in terms of catching the offender. Faster police response might make a difference in a very small number of crime calls: about 3 percent, according to a study by the Police Executive Research Forum. Commercial robberies are the best example. If someone calls the police while the crime is in progress, a very quick response time might improve the chances of catching the offender at the scene. But these kinds of crime are rare events.[15]

The National Academy of Sciences report concluded that increasing police response time does not reduce crime.[16] We agree.

PROPOSITION 8
Faster response time will not produce more arrests or lower the crime rate.

Innovations in Policing

Most police experts agree that the traditional approaches of adding more police, engaging in crackdowns, and emphasizing faster response times will not reduce crime. But they also agree that certain police innovations, such as problem-oriented policing (POP), which involves carefully planned and focused police activities, can be effective. The National Academy of Sciences report on policing concluded that while still preliminary, there is "a strong body of evidence suggesting that taking a focused geographic approach to crime problems can increase the effectiveness of policing."[17] Let's look at some of the programs that were the cause of the National Academy's optimism.

Problem-Oriented Policing POP programs represent a more sophisticated kind of focused police activity. Most draw upon four important new developments in policing.

First, the POP approach involves careful *planning* utilizing the SARA model (scanning, analysis, response, assessment).[18] Second, many programs draw heavily on the concept of "hot spots." Lawrence W. Sherman's analysis of 911 calls in Minneapolis found the astonishing fact that 5 percent of the addresses in the city accounted for 64 percent of all 911 calls. A very few places, which he labeled hot spots, were consuming the vast majority of police time and effort.[19] The concept of hot spots has since become a major focus of research and policy development in policing. Third, they involve *partnerships* with other government agencies and private groups to address social problems that are associated with criminal activity. Police departments, for example, have developed working partnerships with local housing officials to help fix up deteriorated buildings. Fourth, some programs use *civil remedies,* such as restraining orders against known offenders or legal actions against landlords or other community nuisances.

Case Study: SMART in Oakland

The Specialized Multi-Agency Response Team (SMART) program was directed toward specific drug hot spots in Oakland, California. The police were, as the acronym spells out, part of a multiagency task force. In addition to increased law enforcement activity by the police (more patrol, field interrogations, arrests), SMART mobilized officials from the housing, fire, and public works departments to enforce local building codes and clean up the physical appearance of the neighborhoods. A training program for landlords was designed to help them screen prospective tenants and evict existing tenants for rules violations. Lorraine Green's evaluation of SMART found that it reduced the level of drug activity in the target areas. Moreover, it not only did not displace crime to nearby areas, but had a "diffusion" effect of improving surrounding areas.[20]

Three key factors, working in combination, distinguish the SMART program from the traditional police crime-fighting approaches. First, it represents a change in police *activity,* as opposed to the mere number of police officers. Second, it focuses narrowly on specific hot spots, as opposed to unfocused patrol of the entire community. Third, it enlists other agencies (e.g., the city housing agency) and uses non–criminal justice tactics (code enforcement) to address problems associated with crime.

The emerging consensus among crime policy experts is that not only must the police engage themselves with non–criminal justice agencies, but they also need to work closely with other criminal justice agencies and focus on the full range of problems in specific neighborhoods. We will discuss the community-focused approach to crime in more detail in Chapter 14.

The evidence so far supports the conclusions of the National Academy of Sciences report, and our position is:

PROPOSITION 9
Carefully planned and focused problem-oriented policing
strategies can be successful in reducing crime and disorder.

Zero-Tolerance in New York City

No single city has received more publicity about crime reduction than New York City. By 2000 violent crime had fallen to a level not seen since the mid-1960s. Inevitably, the NYPD claimed credit for this tremendous development. In particular, they claimed that the policy of "zero tolerance" policing (sometimes called "disorder policing") was the main factor. Exactly what produced the reduction of crime in New York City is a matter of some dispute, however.[21]

There were three major developments just within the police department that might have had some effect on crime. First, the number of sworn officers increased by more than a third between 1990 and 1995, from about 25,000 to 40,000. Second, zero-tolerance policing focused on quality-of-life offenses such as public urination and failure to pay subway fares. NYPD officials claim that tough enforcement relating to small offenses had a direct payoff in terms of serious crime. People arrested for minor offenses, they claim, were often found to be illegally carrying a weapon. Third, the NYPD adopted COMPSTAT, a management tool that provides immediate data on crime by precinct and involves regular meetings where precinct commanders are held accountable for crime trends in their areas.[22]

Did these developments, independently or in combination, contribute to the reduction in crime? The National Academy of Sciences report expressed considerable skepticism.[23] First, most cities have enjoyed comparable reductions in major crimes without any of the changes that the NYPD made. San Diego, for example, also experienced a return to the levels of crime of the 1960s, with only a modest increase in the number of officers, only one-third the police/population ratio, and no aggressive zero-tolerance policy.[24]

Second, as the Urban Institute report on the crime drop argues, the decline in the popularity of crack was particularly important in terms of reducing violent gun crimes among young men. Crack was a particular problem in New York City, and the decline in its popularity coincided with the great crime drop.[25] The National Academy also pointed out that, in practice, zero-tolerance policing in New York was implemented in selected neighborhoods. As a result, it was really a geographically focused approach to crime (similar to the approach we discussed and endorsed above) and not a generalized, citywide policy.

The Urban Institute cautiously warns us that no single factor can explain fluctuations in the crime rate.[26] It would be wise to be skeptical about the claims made for zero-tolerance policing and instead we should think in terms of multiple factors acting in combination: a national decline in crime, an improving economy, the declining popularity of crack, and, finally, innovations in policing.

MORE DETECTIVES

Some people believe that adding more detectives, or making other improvements to detective work, will result in more arrests and thereby lower the crime rate. Let's look at the evidence.

Myths and Realities of Detective Work

Detective work is surrounded by myths that are perpetuated by the media and the police themselves. Movies and television cop shows portray criminal investigation as fast-paced, exciting, and dangerous work, with frequent shootings, car chases, and confrontations with dangerous criminals. In the classic television show from the 1950s, *Dragnet,* Sgt. Joe Friday (Jack Webb) always caught the offender. Today, the highly popular television show *CSI* emphasizes the forensic aspects of detective work. From *Dragnet* to *CSI,* however, the media image of detectives is pure mythology.

The reality of criminal investigation is very different from the myth. Most detective work is boring, unglamorous, and highly unproductive. Instead of kicking in doors, ducking bullets, and wrestling with dangerous sociopaths, detectives spend most of their time writing reports. The clearance rate (the percentage of crimes solved by arrest) for Part I Index crimes was 20 percent in 2002. It was highest for acquaintance crimes (homicide: 64 percent) and lowest for property crimes (burglary: 13 percent). A Rand study of criminal investigation found that the typical case gets an average of about four hours' work, and most of that involves paperwork.[27]

When the police do solve a crime, it is generally because the victim or a witness knows the offender or can provide a good lead to the first police officer who arrives on the scene.[28] In many acquaintance crimes (e.g., assaults, rapes) the offender is still there when the police arrive, so that no real "detective" work is required. This explains why between 60 and 80 percent of all arrests are made by patrol officers instead of detectives.[29]

The importance of having a good lead at the very beginning was documented almost 40 years ago by the President's Crime Commission. It analyzed 1,905 cases handled by the Los Angeles Police. As Figure 5.1 indicates, the LAPD cleared 86 percent of the 349 cases in which a suspect was immediately identified by the victim or witness. But they cleared only 12 percent of the remaining 1,556 cases in which no suspect was immediately identified.[30]

The key to solving crimes and making arrests, in short, is *information about a suspect.* When the police begin with little or no information to work with, the chances of clearing the crime are very low. In other words, the odds of solving a crime depend primarily on the characteristics of the crime rather than the number of detectives or the amount of hours they devote to a case. Increasing the number of detectives is not going to help if there is not a good lead at the outset. Detectives always complain about being overworked, and it is true that they are swamped with cases. Information rather than time is the critical factor.[31]

It is indeed true that detectives solve some crimes through exhaustive detective work. But these are rare events and not typical of most cases. They are in fact good examples of the celebrated cases we discussed in Chapter 2.

Better training for detectives is not likely to increase the clearance rate. Even the smartest and best-trained detective is not likely to solve a "cold" crime for which there are no leads. The Rand study of criminal investigation found that the quality of training made little difference in clearance rates between departments.[32] Training is not completely irrelevant, of course. An incompetent detective can easily lose a case by bungling the interrogation or mishandling the evidence. Skill does make a difference and training can improve skills. But this assumes that there is some evidence to begin with.

A Word about Fingerprints A great deal of mythology surrounds fingerprints. The FBI has elevated fingerprints to near-mythical status in the solving

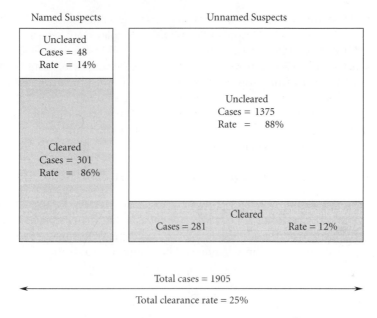

FIGURE 5.1 Clearance of crimes with named and unnamed suspects, Los Angeles
Police Department, 1966

SOURCE: President's Commission on Law Enforcement and Administration of Justice, *Task
Force Report: Science and Technology* (Washington, DC: Government Printing Office, 1967),
p. 8.

of crimes. The Bureau now has over 200 million fingerprint cards on file, representing about 79 million individuals. The mystique of fingerprints was designed
to project an image of the Bureau as an incredibly efficient agency—efficient
because it was backed by the massive weight of "science."

In reality, fingerprints are rarely the critical factor in solving crimes. It is
extremely difficult to get usable prints from a crime scene. The New York City
police obtain usable prints in only about 10 percent of all burglaries. And in
only 3 percent of those cases do the prints help with the arrest. In Long Beach,
California, a suspect was identified through fingerprints in only 1.5 percent of
all cases.[33] The TV show *CSI* is great entertainment, but it seriously distorts the
reality of police work. Fingerprints, blood samples, and hair specimens are not
what solve most crimes. Information about a suspect does.

And a Word about DNA   Some police departments have also tried to use
DNA testing to identify criminal suspects. The science of DNA testing offers
great opportunities in criminal justice, but only if it is used correctly. The greatest
successes have involved exonerating mistakenly convicted offenders. In these cases, DNA evidence from the crime scene (even cases many years in the past) have
proven that the convicted person was not the offender. Some police departments,
however, have engaged in DNA "sweeps": taking samples from as many as 1,000

or even 2,000 people. The most celebrated case involved the so-called "BTK Killer" in Wichita, where the police took DNA samples from several hundred people. But in this and other cases, there was no individualized suspicion about those tested. Consequently, there was much controversy over violations of the 4th Amendment rights of the people tested. Even more important, a national survey found that DNA "sweeps" were extremely ineffective in solving cases. DNA evidence identified the perpetrator in only 1 out of the 18 cases that were located. DNA testing can clinch a case where there is a clear suspicion about a suspect, but it cannot identify a perpetrator where there is no individualized suspicion.[34]

Targeting Career Criminals

One of the hot ideas of the 1980s called for the police to target a small number of suspected career criminals. Like selective incapacitation and major-offender prosecution programs, these programs were based on Wolfgang's birth cohort study, which we examined in Chapter 4. The assumption was that if detectives succeeded in arresting this small group of high-rate offenders, a significant reduction in crime would follow.

The Repeat Offender Project (ROP, pronounced "rope") in the Washington, DC, police department involved a special unit of 60 officers targeting suspects they believed were committing five or more Index crimes a week. The list of suspects was developed by cross-indexing information from other units in the department, such as Investigation Services, the Career Criminal Unit, the Warrant Squad, the Court Liaison Division, the district commanders, and the Youth Division. ROP officers surveilled these suspects to arrest them for felonies.[35]

An evaluation of Washington's ROP program revealed mixed results. Around-the-clock surveillance of suspects quickly proved to be "time-consuming, frustrating, and unproductive." ROP officers got bored waiting and watching. As a result, ROP shifted its emphasis to suspects with arrest warrants on file. Eventually, half of the unit's time was devoted to this activity. In this respect, then, ROP essentially became an intensified warrant enforcement unit. Like many other supposed innovations, it called for officers to do what they always said they were doing.

The ROP unit officers succeeded in arresting 58 percent of their targeted group, significantly more than the 8 percent arrested among a control group of potential suspects. Nonetheless, the overall arrest productivity of ROP officers was less than that of a comparison group of officers. The 62 ROP officers produced 66 convictions by the end of the first year, or a little more than 1 per officer. Whether this was money well spent is a good question. Even more disturbing is the 37.2 percent conviction rate for ROP arrests (66 of 177). This seems to defy the basic rationale of career-criminal programs that supposedly target people who are believed to be active, high-rate offenders. You would expect a high conviction rate for these suspects. Given the cost of the program and the reduction of nonarrest activities (such as order maintenance) by ROP officers, the evaluation raised serious questions about the cost-effectiveness of the program.[36]

To sum up this section, arrest is the weakest point in the criminal justice system. As we explained in Chapter 2, only 20 percent of crimes are cleared by arrest, compared with about 50 percent of all arrests being prosecuted and about 90 percent of prosecuted cases resulting in conviction. Unfortunately, there does not appear to be any way to increase the clearance rate significantly. The ability of the police to solve crimes is determined primarily by the nature of individual crimes, and in particular whether there is a good lead about a suspect. The evidence leads to our next proposition:

PROPOSITION 10
More detectives, or other changes in detective work,
will not raise clearance rates or lower the crime rate.

ELIMINATE THE "TECHNICALITIES"

Conservatives firmly believe that the courts have "handcuffed" the police with procedural rules that limit their power to investigate and solve crimes. According to this view, these "technicalities" of criminal procedure allow streetwise criminals to "beat the system" and avoid punishment. In a sweeping indictment of the criminal justice system, Judge Harold Rothwax of New York argues that the system is geared for "anything but the truth." Procedural rules designed to ensure "fairness" undermine the search for truth about guilt or innocence, with the result that "criminals go free."[37]

Conservatives direct their fire at the Supreme Court, particularly the Warren Court (1953–1969), which issued a series of decisions protecting the rights of suspects and limiting the powers of the police. The two most famous decisions, *Mapp* (1961) and *Miranda* (1966), coincided with the great increase in crime between the early 1960s and early 1970s. Consequently, many people blame the Court for our high rates of crime.[38]

Repeal the Exclusionary Rule

The Supreme Court established the exclusionary rule in the 1961 *Mapp v. Ohio* decision. The Court held that "all evidence obtained by searches and seizures in violation of the Constitution is, by that same authority, inadmissible in a state court."[39] Prosecutors cannot use evidence obtained in violation of the Fourth Amendment's guarantee of "the right of the people to be secure in their persons, houses, papers, and effects, against unreasonable searches and seizures." Evidence obtained illegally is "excluded," or inadmissible in court.

Mapp produced a storm of controversy that has continued for 40 years. Critics charge that the exclusionary rule has limited the ability of the police to gather evidence necessary to convict criminals. Actually, the exclusionary rule was nothing new in 1961. The Supreme Court had applied it to federal proceedings in 1914 (*Weeks v. United States*) and by 1961 it was already in effect in more than half of the states, mainly through decisions by state supreme courts. *Mapp* simply applied the exclusionary rule to all the states.

The exclusionary rule has three basic purposes: to protect the rights of individuals against police misconduct, to maintain the integrity of the judiciary, and to deter the police from misconduct. The rule has always evoked far more outrage than the equally famous *Miranda* warning. *Miranda* excludes confessions that have been obtained improperly. Even many law-and-order advocates concede that a coerced confession is wrong. But the *Mapp* exclusionary rule applies to physical evidence that speaks for itself, no matter how it was obtained. Therefore, they believe it should be allowed as evidence.

The Exclusionary Rule and Crime Fighting   Several studies indicate that the exclusionary rule has virtually no impact on the crime-fighting capacity of the police. James J. Fyfe argues that the impact is "minuscule" and "infinitesimal."[40] Very few cases are "lost" because the evidence is excluded as a result of an improper search. Drug cases are the only area where the rule has any noticeable impact, and even there the effect is fairly small. Take another look at the data in Table 3.2 in Chapter 3, which indicate that due process problems account for a very small percentage of all rejections and dismissals and that not all of those due process problems involve the exclusionary rule.

When we consider the realities of police work, we can understand why the exclusionary rule has such a limited impact. As we pointed out earlier, the police solve crimes when they immediately obtain a good lead about a suspect, from either the victim or a witness. Physical evidence, independent of some other kind of identification of the suspect, is rarely the primary factor in making an arrest and convicting an offender.

The limited impact of the exclusionary rule is mainly confined to drug possession, weapons possession, and gambling cases. It is not hard to see why. The most important element of a drug possession case is whether the defendant actually had the drugs and how the police obtained the evidence. Robbery cases, on the other hand, are more likely to depend on eyewitness identification of the suspect. Physical evidence is rarely the crucial factor.

Once in court, few defendants try to use the exclusionary rule, and even fewer succeed. Procedurally, the defense attorney asks the court to exclude or suppress the evidence. Judges have the discretion to grant or deny the motion. Peter F. Nardulli found that motions to suppress physical evidence were made in fewer than 5 percent of all cases and were successful in only 0.69 percent of the total. A General Accounting Office study of the federal courts found that motions to suppress evidence were filed in only 11 percent of all cases and that between 80 and 90 percent were denied. Finally, a study of search warrants by the National Center for State Courts showed that only 5 percent of all motions to suppress were successful.[41]

Defense lawyers file motions to suppress evidence because they have a professional obligation to represent their clients' interests. Not filing such motions might raise questions about their competence. Most of the time, however, they are just going through the motions, if you will pardon the expression. They are not the "crafty" lawyers of popular folklore. Most felony cases are handled by public defenders who are conscientious but extremely overworked. They have little time to devote to any one case, and in some jurisdictions they meet their clients only moments before entering the courtroom.

Even when a motion to exclude evidence succeeds, the defendant will not necessarily go free. He or she can still be convicted on other evidence. If an appeals court overturns a conviction under the exclusionary rule, the prosecutor can refile charges on the basis of the remaining evidence. A study of search warrant cases found that 12 of the 17 defendants (70 percent) who succeeded in having evidence suppressed were subsequently convicted on other charges.[42]

Judges vary greatly in their willingness to invoke the exclusionary rule. Sheldon Krantz and his colleagues found in their study of Boston that one judge granted 45.4 percent of the motions to suppress, whereas another granted only 22.2 percent. Three judges denied all motions presented to them. Motions to suppress were successful in only 2 percent of all the gambling and drug cases that Krantz et al. studied.[43]

A controversial 1982 study by the National Institute of Justice produced a much higher estimate of the rule's impact. It found that in 520,993 felony arrests in California between 1976 and 1979 prosecutors rejected a total of 86,033 cases for various reasons. Illegally obtained evidence accounted for 4,130 of those rejections. The Justice Department claimed that the 4,130 represented 4.8 percent of the 86,033 rejections.[44] In a pair of stinging critiques, Thomas Y. Davies and James J. Fyfe argued that it was more accurate to consider the 4,130 rejections as a percentage of the original 520,993 cases. This produces a rejection rate of only 0.8 percent (a figure that is very close to some of the other studies).[45]

In short, the exclusionary rule does not let "thousands" of dangerous criminals loose on the streets, and it has almost no effect on violent crime. Judge Rothwax and other critics of the exclusionary rule are guilty of reacting to a few celebrated cases. Yes, some convictions are overturned, and some of those defendants who are factually guilty are released, but these are rare events. Research on the exclusionary rule has so conclusively found that it does not impede professional law enforcement that there has hardly been any new research in the last 20 years.

The evidence leads us to the following proposition:

PROPOSITION 11

Repeal or modification of the exclusionary rule will not help the police reduce serious crime.

The Positive Impact of the Exclusionary Rule Far from impairing police work, the exclusionary rule has played a major role in improving the professionalism of police work. Myron Orfield's study of narcotics officers in Chicago found that the exclusionary rule produced a number of significant reforms. The Chicago police and the Illinois state attorney's office developed a closer working relationship, the state attorney scrutinized applications for warrants more closely, and the police department improved its own training and supervision. The result was better police work. Interviews with Chicago narcotics detectives found that they supported the rule and were very concerned that weakening it would open the door to police abuse. Officers said that the experience of having evidence excluded in court was a valuable learning experience—the best on-the-job training they ever got.[46]

Response to the exclusionary rule depends on the professionalism of a police department. Craig Uchida and Tim Bynum studied the impact of the 1984 *Leon* decision, which allowed a "good faith" exception to the exclusionary rule. Like the earlier studies, they found that the overall impact of the exclusionary rule in seven jurisdictions was "slight." Less than 1 percent (0.9) of all motions to suppress evidence obtained by search warrants were successful. In three of the seven jurisdictions, no motions to suppress evidence were successful. Those sites had a high degree of cooperation between police and prosecutors that included training of police officers and supervision of warrants. In "River City," however, the police were less professional and had an antagonistic relationship with prosecutors. Motions to suppress were filed in 57 percent of all cases, and 14 percent of them were successful.[47]

Many thoughtful law enforcement executives now accept and even welcome the rule. Former FBI Director William Sessions said that "protections that are afforded by the exclusionary rule are extremely important to fair play and the proper carrying out of the law enforcement responsibility."[48] Most law enforcement experts believe that the exclusionary rule forces law enforcement agencies to be more professional, and that weakening the rule would permit lazy and unprofessional work. Because of the rule, law-abiding citizens do not have to fear overzealous and intrusive action by a cop, and so the police enjoy greater public respect.

Instead of abolishing the exclusionary rule altogether, some critics propose modifying it to permit good-faith searches: cases in which the officer made an honest mistake (as in getting a number wrong on a street address). As noted previously, the Supreme Court adopted the good-faith exception in *United States v. Leon* (1984), ruling that evidence could be admitted if it were obtained under a valid search warrant even though it was later found that there was not probable cause to issue the warrant.[49]

The good-faith exception, however, presents several problems. First, it complicates rather than simplifies search-and-seizure cases by opening the door to appeals based on whether the search was in good or bad faith and whether the officer made an honest mistake or a deliberate one. Fyfe argues that this makes the judge's job even harder. Second, the good-faith exception encourages police incompetence. It gives officers an incentive to claim that they made a minor mistake instead of prodding them to do a professional job in the first place. One of the main effects of the exclusionary rule has been to stimulate police professionalism.[50]

Finally, and the most important in terms of crime fighting, the good-faith search is not going to significantly increase the number of convictions because few convictions are being "lost" owing to the exclusionary rule's existence.

Abolish *Miranda*

The *Miranda* warning is the second major so-called technicality that conservatives believe handcuffs the police. The 1966 *Miranda v. Arizona* decision held that to ensure a suspect's Fifth Amendment protection against self-incrimination, the police must advise a criminal suspect of certain rights: Prior to any questioning, the person must be warned that he has a right to remain silent, that any statement he does make may be used against him, and that he has a right to the presence of an attorney, either retained or appointed.[51]

Conservatives have been angry about *Miranda* ever since. In the original decision, Justice Byron White dissented on the grounds that it "return[s] a killer, a rapist or other criminal to the streets and to the environment which produced him, to repeat his crime whenever it pleases him." Other opponents have repeated this criticism for 30 years.[52]

Almost 35 years later, the *Miranda* warning is the most widely known and probably most misunderstood element of police procedure. Hollywood and television writers love it. The warning adds a special dramatic complication to the plot. In one movie, a narcotics detective wrestles the suspect to the ground with one arm while reading from the *Miranda* warning card he holds in the other hand. Get it? The police have one hand tied behind their backs. A 1991 public opinion poll on the two-hundredth anniversary of the Bill of Rights found that while only 10 percent knew why it was originally adopted, 80 percent knew about their right to remain silent if arrested.[53] A recent book observed that "School children are more likely to recognize the *Miranda* warnings than the Gettysburg Address."[54]

***Miranda* in Operation**   Does the *Miranda* warning really handcuff the police? Let us look at it in operation. First, let us clear up a few myths about the decision. The *Miranda* warning does not have to be given at the moment of arrest but only before questioning. If a suspect blurts out a confession ("Why did I do it?"), the confession is admissible. Also, a suspect can waive his or her rights by agreeing to talk and agreeing to do so without a lawyer. In fact, many suspects do waive their rights.

Paul G. Cassell, a strong critic of *Miranda,* and Bret S. Hayman properly raise the question of how we should measure the impact (or the "cost") of *Miranda.* They make a persuasive argument that we should not look at the number of convictions overturned because of a *Miranda* violation but the number of confessions the police do not get. Surveying all of the studies done to date, they estimate that the rate of confessions has declined by 16 percent because of *Miranda.* But that is not the whole story, because some offenders are convicted even without a confession. The authors estimate that confessions are needed in about 24 percent of all cases. Thus, the net effect is that *Miranda* results in a "loss" of convictions in 3.8 percent of all cases (16 percent of 24 percent = 3.8 percent). Despite Cassell and Hayman's own claims, this is not a very significant impact.[55]

Stephen J. Schulhofer, moreover, argues that Cassell and Hayman's study suffers from a number of methodological flaws. One of the more serious is their failure to take into account the fact that confession rates were dropping in the years before *Miranda,* for reasons unrelated to the decision. Factoring in a continuation of this trend and adding in the effect of other methodological problems, Schulhofer estimates that the "loss" due to *Miranda* is not 3.8 percent but less than 1 percent (0.78). "For all practical purposes," he concludes, "*Miranda's* empirically detectable net damage to law enforcement is zero."[56]

The best study of *Miranda* in operation is Richard Leo's "Inside the Interrogation Room," in which he directly observed a total of 182 police interrogations in three police departments. Leo found that 78 of the suspects waived their *Miranda* rights and cooperated with the police. (Cassell found that 84 percent of the suspects in Salt Lake City waived their *Miranda* rights).[57] As a result, two-thirds (64 percent) made a full confession, a partial confession, or some incriminating statement. What tactics did the police use to get them to cooperate? In over 80 percent of the cases, the police either confronted them with evidence of their guilt or appealed to their self-interest (it will help you if you talk), or both.[58]

In short, the *Miranda* warning was no barrier to successful police work. In the vast majority of the cases, the police got suspects to waive their rights and confess or make an incriminating statement, and they did so through lawful means. It should be noted, however, that in 30 percent of the cases, the police lied by confronting the suspects with false information about their guilt, as in falsely telling them that their partner had confessed. This evidence supports keeping the *Miranda* warning.

Why do so many suspects waive their rights and confess? Why do only about 20 percent of suspects take advantage of their right to remain silent? The first point is that the police do not arrest very many suspects. They clear only about 26 percent of all robberies and 14 percent of all burglaries. Thus, they usually have some evidence against the few suspects they do arrest. This leaves a small group of cases in which there is reasonably strong evidence. And as Leo discovered, detectives confront 85 percent of all suspects with evidence of their guilt. The suspects in these remaining cases have powerful incentives to cooperate and confess. They know that they committed the crime, and they realize that the police have some fairly good evidence against them. A lot of them feel guilty about it. Leo found that detectives appealed to suspects' consciences in 23 percent of all cases. Some suspects who confess hope to get a better deal in a plea bargaining. The detectives in Leo's study appealed to the suspects' self-interest in 88 percent of the cases.[59]

The image of the tough, streetwise criminal who is skilled at manipulating the rules is another myth. Some suspects do invoke their *Miranda* rights, but the majority cooperate with the police. Felony suspects are typically young, poorly educated, and in many instances functionally illiterate. Most failed to learn how to manipulate the public school bureaucracy to their advantage, and they are not much more successful in the criminal justice system. The typical robber or burglar is so disorganized and impulsive that he does not even plan his crimes very well. The Rand Inmate Survey found that 40 percent of the juvenile robbers and 25 percent of the adults had not even intended to rob anyone when they left home. As one kid put it, "It was just a sudden thing. I didn't really mean to do it. I didn't plan nothing; it just happened." Among the adult career criminals, only 40 percent bothered to visit the sites of their crimes in advance, and as few as 22 percent made an effort to check on police patrol in the area.[60]

In custody, young offenders may strike a tough pose, but it is usually nothing more than that—a pose, an act. A skilled professional detective can get most suspects to talk.

Modifying *Miranda* In 1984, the Supreme Court finally accepted the conservative argument and created a "public safety" exception to the *Miranda* warning. In *New York v. Quarles,* the Court held that when the safety of an officer or a citizen is threatened, as by the presence of a gun, the officer may ask questions before advising a suspect of his or her rights.[61] The decision represents a major victory in the conservatives' 30-year campaign to reverse the rules laid down by the Warren Court. Given the limited impact of the *Miranda* warning on confessions, however, it is hard to imagine that this limited exception would result in many more arrests or any significant crime reduction. Consequently, the evidence leads to this proposition:

> **PROPOSITION 12**
>
> Repeal or modification of the *Miranda* warning
> will not result in more convictions.

CONCLUSION

The police are the front line of the criminal justice system. Patrol is the primary strategy for preventing crime, and arrest is the "gatekeeping" point for all criminal cases. Many people believe we could reduce crime significantly if we would just "unleash" the cops: give them more resources and more powers. We have found that these ideas are not likely to reduce crime. The promising strategies involve focused police programs, such as hot spots and problem-oriented policing programs. We will examine them, and the reasons why they can be effective, in Chapter 14.

NOTES

1.   David Bayley, *Police For the Future* (New York: Oxford University Press, 1994), p. 101.

2.   Department of Justice, *The Police and Public Opinion* (Washington, DC: Department of Justice, 1977).

3.   John Eck and Edward Maguire, "Have Changes in Policing Reduced Violent Crime? An Assessment of the Evidence," in Alfred Blumstein and Joel Wallman, eds., *The Crime Drop in America* (New York: Cambridge University Press, 2000), pp. 210–214, especially Table 7.1.

4. Jihong "Solomon" Zhao, Matthew C. Scheider, and Quint Thurman, "Funding Community Policing to Reduce Crime: Have COPS Grants Made a Difference?" *Criminology and Public Policy* 2 (2002): 11.

5. Ibid. Other criticisms of the COPS program are in Peter Eisler and Kevin Johnson, "10 Years and $10B Later, COPS Drawing Scrutiny," *USA Today,* 11 April 2005, p. 1.

6. George L. Kelling, Tony Pate, Duane Diekman, and Charles E. Brown, *The Kansas City Preventive Patrol Experiment: A Summary Report* (Washington, DC: The Police Foundation, 1974).

7. Ibid.

8. The Police Foundation, *The Newark Foot Patrol Experiment* (Washington, DC: The Police Foundation, 1981).

9. Franklin E. Zimring and Gordon J. Hawkins, *Deterrence: The Legal Threat in Crime Control* (Chicago: University of Chicago Press, 1973).

10. Federal Bureau of Investigation, *Crime in the United States, 2002* (Washington, DC: Department of Justice, 2003), Figure 3.1.

11. James Q. Wilson and Alan Abrahamse, "Does Crime Pay?" *Justice Quarterly* 9 (September 1992): 372–373.

12. Lawrence W. Sherman, "Police Crackdowns," in Michael Tonry and Norval Morris, eds., *Crime and Justice: An Annual Review of Research,* vol. 12 (Chicago: University of Chicago Press, 1990), pp. 1–48.

13. Lynn Zimmer, "Proactive Policing against Street-Level Drug Trafficking," *American Journal of Police* 9.1 (1990): 43–74.

14. William Spelman and Dale K. Brown, *Calling the Police: Citizen Reporting of Serious Crime* (Washington, DC: Department of Justice, 1984).

15. Ibid.

16. National Academy of Sciences, *Fairness and Effectiveness in Policing: The Evidence* (Washington, DC: National Academy Press, 2004), pp. 226–227.

17. Ibid., p. 235.

18. Herman Goldstein, *Problem-Oriented Policing* (New York: McGraw-Hill, 1990);

Michael S. Scott, *Problem-Oriented Policing: Reflections on the First Twenty Years* (Washington, DC: Department of Justice, 2000).

19. Lawrence W. Sherman, Patrick R. Gartin, and Michael E. Buerger, "Hot Spots of Predatory Crime: Routine Activities and the Criminology of Place," *Criminology* 27 (1989): 27–55.

20. Lorraine Green, "Cleaning Up Drug Hot Spots in Oakland, California: The Displacement and Diffusion Effects," *Justice Quarterly* 12 (December 1995): 737–754.

21. Bernard Harcourt, *Illusion of Order: The False Promise of Broken Windows Policing* (Cambridge, MA: Harvard University Press, 2001); George L. Kelling and Catherine M. Coles, *Fixing Broken Windows* (New York: Free Press, 1996); William J. Bratton and Peter Knoblach, *Turnaround* (New York: Random House, 1998).

22. Eli Silverman, *NYPD Battles Crime* (Boston: Northeastern, 1999); David Weisburd, Stephen Mastrofski, Ann Marie McNally, Rosann Greenspan, and James Willis, "Reforming to Preserve: COMPSTAT and Strategic Problem Solving in American Policing," *Criminology and Public Policy* 2 (July 2003): 421–456.

23. National Academy of Sciences, *Fairness and Effectiveness,* pp. 228–230.

24. Gary Cordner, "Problem-Oriented Policing vs. Zero Tolerance," in Tara O'Connor Shelley and Anne C. Grant, eds., *Problem-Oriented Policing: Crime-Specific Problems, Critical Issues and Making POP Work* (Washington, DC: Police Executive Research Forum, 1998), pp. 303–314.

25. K. Jack Riley, *Crack, Powder Cocaine, and Heroin: Drug Purchase and Use Patterns in Six U.S. Cities.* NCJ 167265 (Washington, DC: Department of Justice, 1997); For an examination of the declining appeal of crack cocaine, see R. Terry Furst, Bruce D. Johnson, Eloise Dunlap, and Richard Curtis, "The Stigmatized Image of the 'Crack Head': A Sociocultural Exploration of a Barrier to Cocaine Smoking Among a Cohort of Youth in New York City," *Deviant Behavior,* 20 (1999): 153–181.

26. Jeremy Travis and Michelle Waul, *Reflections on the Crime Decline: Lessons for the*

Future? (Washington, DC: Urban Institute, 2002). Available on the Urban Institute website.

27. Peter Greenwood, *The Criminal Investigation Process* (Santa Monica, CA: Rand, 1975).

28. Wesley Skogan and George Antunes, "Information, Apprehension, and Deterrence: Exploring the Limits of Police Productivity," *Journal of Criminal Justice* 7 (Fall 1979): 217–241.

29. Albert J. Reiss, *The Police and the Public* (New Haven, CT: Yale University Press, 1971), p. 104.

30. President's Commission on Law Enforcement and Administration of Justice, *Task Force Report: Science and Technology* (Washington, DC: Government Printing Office, 1967), p. 8.

31. John E. Eck, *Solving Crimes: The Investigation of Burglary and Robbery* (Washington, DC: Police Executive Research Forum, 1983).

32. Greenwood, *Criminal Investigation Process.*

33. Joan Petersilia, "Processing Latent Fingerprints—What Are the Payoffs?" *Journal of Police Science and Administration* 6 (June 1978): 157–167.

34. Police Professionalism Initiative, *Police DNA Sweeps Extremely Unproductive: A National Survey of Police DNA "Sweeps"* (Omaha: University of Nebraska at Omaha, 2004). Available on the Police Professionalism Initiative website.

35. Susan E. Martin and Lawrence W. Sherman, "Selective Apprehension: A Police Strategy for Repeat Offenders," *Criminology* 24 (February 1986): 155–173; Susan E. Martin, "Policing Career Criminals: An Examination of an Innovative Crime Control Program," *Journal of Criminal Law and Criminology* 77 (Winter 1986): 1159–1182.

36. Martin and Sherman, "Selective Apprehension."

37. Harold J. Rothwax, *Guilty: The Collapse of Criminal Justice* (New York: Random House, 1996), p. 15.

38. Samuel Walker, *Popular Justice: A History of American Criminal Justice,* 2nd ed. (New York: Oxford University Press, 1998).

39. *Mapp v. Ohio,* 367 U.S. 643 (1961).

40. James J. Fyfe, "The NIJ Study of the Exclusionary Rule," *Criminal Law Bulletin* 19 (May–June 1983): 253–260.

41. Peter F. Nardulli, "The Societal Costs of the Exclusionary Rule: An Empirical Assessment," *American Bar Foundation Research Journal* 1983 (Summer 1983): 585–690; Comptroller General of the United States, *Impact of the Exclusionary Rule on Federal Criminal Prosecutions,* Report #GGD-79-45 (April 19, 1979); National Center for State Courts, *The Search Warrant Process* (Williamsburg, VA: National Center for State Courts, 1986).

42. National Center for State Courts, *Search Warrant Process.*

43. Sheldon Krantz, Bernard Gilman, Charles G. Benda, Carol Rogoff Hallstrom, and Gail J. Nadworny, *Police Policymaking* (Lexington, MA: Lexington Books, 1979), pp. 189–192.

44. National Institute of Justice, *The Effects of the Exclusionary Rule: A Study in California* (Washington, DC: Government Printing Office, 1982).

45. Fyfe, "The NIJ Study of the Exclusionary Rule"; Thomas Y. Davies, "A Hard Look at What We Know (and Still Need to Learn) about the 'Costs' of the Exclusionary Rule: The NIJ Study and Other Studies of 'Lost' Arrests," *American Bar Foundation Research Journal* 3 (Summer 1983): 611–690.

46. Myron W. Orfield, Jr., "The Exclusionary Rule and Deterrence: An Empirical Study of Chicago Narcotics Officers," *University of Chicago Law Review* 54 (Summer 1987): 1016–1055.

47. Craig Uchida and Tim Bynum, "Search Warrants, Motions to Suppress and 'Lost Cases': The Effects of the Exclusionary Rule in Seven Jurisdictions," *Journal of Criminal Law and Criminology* 81 (Winter 1991): 1034–1066.

48. Sessions quoted in *New York Times,* 5 November 1987.

49. *United States v. Leon,* 468 U.S. 897 (1984).

50. James J. Fyfe, "In Search of the 'Bad Faith' Search," *Criminal Law Bulletin* 18 (May–June 1982): 260–264.

51. *Miranda v. Arizona,* 384 U.S. 436 (1966).

52. An invaluable collection of articles on the subject is Richard Leo and George C. Thomas, III, eds., *The Miranda Debate: Law, Justice, and Policing* (Boston: Northeastern University Press, 1998).

53. "Poll Finds Only 33% Can Identify Bill of Rights," *New York Times,* 15 December 1991.

54. Leo and Thomas, eds., *Miranda Debate,* p. xv.

55. Paul G. Cassell and Bret S. Hayman, "Police Interrogation in the 1990s: An Empirical Study of the Effects of Miranda," *UCLA Law Review* 43 (February 1996): 860.

56. Stephen J. Schulhofer, "Miranda's Practical Effect: Substantial Benefits and Vanishingly Small Social Costs," in Leo and Thomas, eds., *Miranda Debate,* p. 205.

57. Paul G. Cassell, "Miranda's Social Costs: An Empirical Reassessment," *Northwestern University Law Review* 90 (Winter 1996): 387–499.

58. Richard A. Leo, "Inside the Interrogation Room," *Journal of Criminal Law and Criminology* 86 (1996): 266–303.

59. Ibid.

60. Joan Petersilia, Peter W. Greenwood, and Martin Lavin, *The Criminal Careers of Habitual Felons* (Washington, DC: Government Printing Office, 1978).

61. *New York v. Quarles,* 467 U.S. 649 (1984).

6

Deter the Criminals

eterrence is an article of faith among conservatives: Punishment deters
crime; swifter, more certain, and more severe punishments will reduce
crime even further. In Chapter 5 we discussed why routine police patrol
does not deter crime as Robert Peel imagined it would. In this chapter we will
look at deterrence in theory and practice. We are going to violate our own
ground rules and discuss some issues that fall outside the scope of our inquiry:
the death penalty, drunk driving crackdowns, and domestic violence. They are
not directly related to robbery and burglary, but they offer some important
evidence about deterrence.

DETERRENCE THEORY

The theory of deterrence has a simple, intuitive appeal. People want to avoid
unpleasant experiences; if we make the punishment for crime more unpleasant,
fewer people will commit crime. The basic theory is simple, but in actual
practice it is very complex, resting on a number of related assumptions that
may not work in the real world of criminal justice.[1]

First, it is important to distinguish between the deterrent effect of the
criminal law and the criminal justice system on one hand and the more limited
deterrent effect of particular policies or programs on the other.

The criminal law and the criminal justice system have some general deterrent effects. The law defines the boundaries of acceptable behavior and specifies the consequences of crossing those boundaries. To a certain extent, this deterrent effect works; the threat of punishment contributes to law-abiding behavior. Most of us do *not* commit serious crimes. We are not murderers, robbers, or burglars. In the most comprehensive review of the subject, Daniel Nagin concludes that "the collective actions of the criminal justice system exert a very substantial deterrent effect."[2] The law and the justice system, however, are only two of the factors at work in shaping our behavior. Families, religious training, schools, and peers also exert powerful influences. In this broad social context, it is difficult to specify the independent effect of the law and the justice system. (Of course, as we learned in Chapter 4, there is a small group of offenders for whom the conventional forms of socialization have failed.)

Nagin explains that the real issue of deterrence is "whether a specific policy, grafted onto the existing structure, will materially add to the preventive effect."[3] That is the main point of this book: Are there policies that will reduce serious crime from its current level? On this issue, Nagin is very cautious. There is a lack of clear and convincing evidence of policies that, from a deterrence perspective, produce real, long-term reductions in crime. To understand why we should be skeptical about the added deterrent effect of any criminal justice policy, let's examine the assumptions underlying deterrence.

Assumptions Underlying Deterrence

The theory of deterrence involves a number of basic assumptions. As we noted in Chapter 5, deterrence theory operates in the realm of social psychology. It assumes the existence of an information loop involving potential offenders' knowledge and perception of the potential punishment. First, offenders have to be *aware* of the penalty for particular crimes. They have to know, for example, that a new law imposes a mandatory jail term for a first-offense drunk driving conviction, or that a new law requires a mandatory ten-year prison term for a drug possession conviction.

Second, potential offenders have to *perceive* the consequences of lawbreaking as *unpleasant* and therefore something to be avoided.

Third, they have to *believe* a real *risk* of arrest, conviction, and punishment is present. As Scott Decker and his colleagues point out, "Deterrence is essentially a psychological process that involves the balancing of personally held beliefs about possible punishment and anticipated gain."[4] Certainty and swiftness of punishment are regarded as essential to this process in order to heighten the connection between the crime and its consequences.

Finally, and perhaps most important, deterrence theory assumes that people are *rational actors* who weigh the relative costs and benefits of their actions and make conscious decisions about the best course. On this point, deterrence-oriented policymakers assume that we can influence behavior by altering the perceived costs and benefits. Thus, if we raise the costs by making punishment more certain and/or more severe, we will influence people not to commit crime. Or, if we educate kids about the personal costs of doing drugs, they will choose not to use illegal drugs.

Deterrence operates in two ways, depending on the target audience. *Specific* deterrence is directed at the individual offender. The punishment is intended to teach that person right and wrong, that criminal activity leads to unpleasant consequences. *General* deterrence is directed at the society as a whole. Punishing a few criminals is designed to communicate a message to the larger audience.[5]

With respect to designing crime policies, an important distinction must also be made between *absolute* and *marginal* deterrence. The idea of absolute deterrence posits that a particular punishment will deter crime, or a particular crime, completely. No one realistically expects that to happen. Instead, we think in terms of marginal deterrence, which involves some relative improvement over what we are currently doing.[6] In this book we will be looking for crime policies that represent an improvement over those currently in effect.

After being out of favor among criminologists for decades, deterrence theory enjoyed a tremendous revival in the 1980s. The revival was not confined to criminal justice policy. Ronald L. Akers points out that the underlying theory of rational choice became a "hot topic" in many of the social sciences in the 1980s.[7] It was especially influential in economic theory and many aspects of social policy. Recent welfare reform, for example, rests on the assumption that traditional welfare programs provided too few incentives for finding employment. Cutting welfare benefits and putting a cap on the number of years of welfare eligibility, conservatives argue, encourages people to find employment and get off welfare.[8]

While deterrence theory is generally associated with conservatives, on certain issues many liberals also believe in deterrence. Some liberals, for example, believe that the exclusionary rule will deter illegal searches and seizures by police officers, or that citizen review of complaints against the police will deter police misconduct. Many liberals also support mandatory arrest for domestic violence in the belief that it will deter that crime.[9]

From Theory to Practice: Four Problems

Nagin gives four reasons for being skeptical about how effectively deterrence-oriented policies are translated into practice.[10] First, we know little about the long-term effects of policies. In theory, part of the "cost" of crime is the resulting social stigma. But if arrest and imprisonment are common experiences in a particular social group, they begin to lose their stigmatizing effect. Many observers believe that this is precisely what has happened with young and poor African American males as a result of the war on crime. So many people in their neighborhoods are arrested and convicted that it is simply a "normal" life experience, with little deterrent effect. Obviously, the career criminals we discussed in Chapter 4 are not deterred by their frequent arrests and convictions.

Second, Nagin points out that we know relatively little about the process of how perceptions of risk are formed. How do young people develop their understanding of the risk of a drunk driving arrest or an arrest for drug possession, for example? Research on this subject is relatively recent, and little has been done with regard to serious offenders.

Third, the impact of particular policies depends upon how they are implemented. As we learned in Chapter 5, two police departments may add the same number of new police officers, but one may use them far more efficiently and effectively in terms of crime fighting. In an inefficiently run department, the potential deterrent effect of additional officers is lost. In California, the state's "three strikes" law has been used extensively in Los Angeles but to a very limited extent in San Francisco. There can be little if any deterrent effect in the latter city.

Fourth, laws and policies are not always implemented as intended. As we learned in Chapter 3, the courtroom work group has a tremendous ability to undermine new laws or policies that disrupt the established going rate. The case of three-strikes laws is an excellent example. Prosecutors in San Francisco and some other cities simply do not file the necessary charges to make the law applicable in many cases. With respect to domestic violence, we are not absolutely certain that police officers faithfully carry out mandatory arrest laws or policies.

SCARE THE *%!#@ OUT OF THEM!

A Famous but Failed Program

One of the most publicized treatment programs of the late 1970s was Scared Straight, which involved exposing juveniles to prison conditions as a way of scaring them out of criminal behavior. Scared Straight was the subject of a 1978 television documentary, loosely based on an actual program in the Rahway prison in New Jersey. (There is also a more recent version available on DVD, following up on the story 20 years later.) The program was begun by inmates serving life sentences. On the surface it seemed like a great idea. Who better to give kids a realistic idea of where crime leads than a group of lifers?[11]

The underlying theory of Scared Straight–type programs is deterrence: Provide direct evidence of the unpleasant consequences of criminal behavior and cause juveniles to not commit crimes. Education and public awareness programs in many other areas of life are based on the same theory. Many "drug awareness" programs, for example, try to convince people that drug use will cause permanent damage. The most famous, of course, is the "This is your brain on drugs" advertisement (we will discuss this in Chapter 13). Many antismoking ads take the same approach. There are some ads involving warnings about the hazards of smoking by people who subsequently died of lung cancer. And there are many versions of warnings about the dangers of drinking and driving.

Taking an evidence-based policy approach, one study located all the evaluations of Scared Straight–type programs that had been subject to evaluation using randomized or quasi-randomized assignment to treatment and control groups. They found a total of nine studies over 25 years that involved over 1,000 participants.[12]

None of the programs effectively reduced crime, and some had adverse outcomes. A Michigan program in the 1960s resulted in a 43 percent recidivism rate for those "scared" compared with only 17 percent for the control group. Several studies had results that were statistically insignificant, but with more negative than positive results. Finckenauer's evaluation of the highly publicized New Jersey Scared Straight program found recidivism rates of 41 percent for those in the program and only 11 percent for the controls. Only one of the nine evaluations found positive results, but they were not statistically significant.

Despite these depressing findings, Scared Straight and similar programs continue to be popular. This represents another triumph of faith over facts. In fact, when the negative results of the Squires program in California were released, officials abolished the evaluation and kept the program.

One key question is why these programs tended to have criminogenic effects, that is, tended to produce higher rates among the treatment group compared with the control group. What is it about these programs that is harmful? Some people have argued that fear-based antidrug campaigns only heighten the allure of drugs and may actually lead to higher drug usage.

PROPOSITION 13
Fear-based deterrence programs do not reduce crime.

The Risk of Arrest: Some Preliminary Evidence

Because deterrence theory rests on the actual and perceived risk of crime, it is useful to review what we learned in Chapters 2 and 3 about the administration of justice. While the criminal law and the justice system may have some general deterrent effect, the fact is that the risk of apprehension and punishment for most crimes is very low. Only 37 percent of all Index crimes are reported to the police (Check the latest NCVS data on the NCJRS website), who clear only 20 percent of these crimes (Check the Uniform Crime Report data on the FBI website). Thus, only 8 percent of all Index crimes result in arrest. Since about half of all felony arrests are dismissed, only 4 percent of all crimes are prosecuted. In short, the overall risk of punishment (defined as conviction) is extremely low.

The risks are somewhat higher for particular crimes. Virtually all murders are reported, and the police clear about 68 percent of them. A Justice Department report found that 87 percent of all husbands tried for murdering their wives were convicted, and 81 percent of them were sentenced to prison.[13] Only about 54 percent of all robberies are reported, however, and the police clear only about 26 percent of them. This yields an overall apprehension risk of 14 percent.

Looking at the risks of crime from the perspective of individual offenders, particularly career criminals, creates some additional problems for deterrence theory. The Rand Inmate Survey (RIS) found that offenders were extremely fatalistic about their chances of being arrested and punished. Unfortunately, neither the perceived risk nor the actual experience of imprisonment seemed to deter them from criminal activity. James Q. Wilson and Allan Abrahamse concluded that the RIS offenders did not act rationally, as deterrence theory requires.[14] And in a study of 1,000 Nebraska prisoners, Julie Horney and Ineke Marshall found that offenders with higher arrest rates relative to self-reported crime also reported higher perceptions of the risk of arrest and punishment.[15]

Now let us turn our attention to some policies designed to deter crime and see what we can learn about deterrence theory in practice.

THE DEATH PENALTY

The death penalty is a good subject for examining deterrence theory for two reasons. First, many people believe that capital punishment deters crime; second, considerable research has been done on the subject.

Sorting Out the Issues

We can debate the merits of the death penalty in terms of three separate issues.[16] First is the moral question of whether it is a just form of punishment. Some people firmly believe that the death penalty is a morally justifiable form of punishment for murder, whereas others believe it is morally wrong. This debate involves basic conceptions of morality and justice and is not subject to empirical proof one way or the other.

The question of whether the death penalty is constitutional is the second issue. Constitutional challenges began in the 1960s and eventually led to the 1972 *Furman v. Georgia* decision, in which the U.S. Supreme Court ruled that the death penalty had been applied in an unconstitutionally arbitrary and capricious fashion.[17] It rejected the argument that capital punishment was inherently cruel and unusual. Four years later, in *Gregg v. Georgia,* the Court upheld the constitutionality of the death penalty where there were guidelines to control its application.[18]

The third issue is whether the death penalty deters crime. This is the focus of our discussion here. The moral and constitutional questions are extremely important, but as we explained in Chapter 1, this book focuses on issues of crime policy.

Executions and Crime: Sellin's Studies

Some of the first attempts to study the deterrent effect of capital punishment were relatively simple comparative and longitudinal studies. The noted criminologist Thorsten Sellin compared neighboring states, two with and one without the death penalty. As Table 6.1 indicates, Ohio and Indiana, two death penalty states, did not have lower crime rates than Michigan, which does not have the death penalty. Murder rates in all three states changed in roughly

Table 6.1 Homicide rates in death penalty states (Ohio, Indiana) and in a state without the death penalty (Michigan), 1920–1974 (homicides per 100,000 population)

Five-year periods	Michigan	Ohio		Indiana	
	Rates	Rates	Number of executions	Rates	Number of executions
1920–1924	5.5	7.4	45	6.1	5
1925–1929	8.2	8.4	40	6.6	7
1930–1934	5.6	8.5	43	6.5	11
1935–1939	3.9	5.9	29	4.5	22
1940–1944	3.2	4.3	15	3.0	2
1945–1949	3.5	4.8	36	3.8	5
1950–1954	3.8	3.8	20	3.7	2
1955–1959	3.0	3.4	12	3.0	0
1960–1964	3.6	3.2	7	3.2	1
1965–1969	6.6	5.1	0	4.7	0
1970–1974	11.3	7.8	0	6.4	0

SOURCES: National Office of Vital Statistics, *Vital Statistics of the United States;* William J. Bowers, *Executions in America* (Lexington, MA: Heath, 1974), Appendix A; Thorsten Sellin, *The Penalty of Death* (Beverly Hills, CA: Sage, 1980), p. 144.

the same direction, decreasing from the 1930s to the early 1960s and then rising sharply. This suggests that broad social factors common to all states, rather than executions, were the primary causal factors in homicide rates.[19] Sellin also examined individual states over time. Kansas, which had earlier abolished the death penalty, restored it in 1935. Its homicide trends were nearly identical to those in Missouri and Colorado, which had kept the death penalty throughout the period.

Sellin's research did not conclusively demonstrate the absence of a deterrent effect. His fairly simple methodology did not control for all the variables that might influence homicide rates. Now let us turn our attention to one controversial study that did attempt to control these variables.

Dr. Ehrlich's Magic Bullet

The debate over the deterrent effect of the death penalty entered a new phase in 1975, when economist Isaac Ehrlich produced a study of crime and executions between 1930 and 1969 purporting to prove that each execution deterred seven or eight murders.[20] If Ehrlich's analysis is correct, the death penalty has a powerful deterrent effect.

Did Ehrlich prove his case? His major contribution to death penalty research was his sophisticated formula that attempted to control for all of the variables that might have affected the murder rate. This included the probability of apprehension, the probability of conviction for murder, the probability of execution, the unemployment rate, the labor force participation of adults, the real per capita income, and the proportion of the population between the ages of 14 and 24. He explicitly embraced the rational choice theory of human behavior, explaining that the "propensity" to commit crimes "is influenced by the prospective gains and losses associated with their commission."[21]

Critics, however, quickly found flaws in Ehrlich's analysis. His sophisticated mathematical formula, which appeared to be the strongest part of his approach, also turned out to be his greatest weakness. The formula is highly sensitive to problems with the reliability of the data. Critics focused on the 1960s, when executions stopped and violent crime increased. As we already noted, this pattern leads many people to believe that the death penalty does deter crime. In their respective analyses, Brian Forst, Peter Passell, and William Bowers and Glenn Pierce all argue that when you exclude the years from 1962 to 1969, the deterrent effect claimed by Ehrlich vanishes.[22] His formula does not explain the trends between the 1930s and the early 1960s, when executions declined while the crime rate either declined or remained stable.

We might add that the murder rate increased dramatically in the late 1980s at the same time that executions increased. The number of homicides increased from 18,980 in 1985 to 24,530 in 1993, despite an average of almost 20 executions per year in that period, with a peak of 31 in 1992.[23] The lesson here is that it is often easy—but inappropriate—to try to prove an argument by selecting a certain time period when the trends favor your position.

Ehrlich's critics also found serious problems with the official Uniform Crime Report data he used. The data on crime and arrests indicate that the certainty of apprehension declined from the 1930s through the 1960s. We have good reason to believe, however, that because of the lack of professionalism in most departments, these data seriously undercount the amount of crime. In New York City alone, for example, at least two well-documented episodes (in 1955 and 1965) occurred in which administrative changes in the police department produced huge increases in officially reported crime. In Chicago, meanwhile, reporters in 1983 caught the Chicago police unfounding a substantial number of crimes. In other words, the apparent risk of apprehension was higher in the pre-1960 years because police record keeping kept the number of reported crimes artificially low.[24] Consequently, the real risk of apprehension had not declined as much between 1930 and 1969 as Ehrlich asserted.

Research on the deterrent effect of the death penalty continues. The safest conclusion we can draw at this point is that no convincing evidence has surfaced indicating that the death penalty deters crime. This point leads us to the following proposition:

PROPOSITION 14
The death penalty does not deter crime.

Delays and Deterrence

Death penalty advocates reply to the critics by arguing that the deterrent effect is undermined by long delays in carrying out executions. In fact, the average time between conviction and execution is over 8 years. Appeals in some cases take 15 years or more. Also, many death sentences are vacated, through appeal, executive clemency, or death by natural causes. In 2003, 65 offenders were executed while four times as many (265) were removed from death row by other causes.[25] Death penalty advocates argue that these factors undermine both the certainty and the swiftness of the death penalty. If we would eliminate these obstacles, the argument continues, the deterrent effect would work.

Long delays in death penalty cases are to be expected. Someone sentenced to die is going to explore every possible avenue of appeal. The process of appeal is an essential part of the criminal justice system, designed to protect against errors in the process. And mistakes do happen. Hugo Bedau and Michael Radelet identified a total of 350 miscarriages of justice in potentially capital cases since 1900. They define *miscarriage of justice* as a case in which "the defendant was erroneously convicted of a capital crime." Of the 350 cases they identified, 139 were given death sentences, and 23 were actually executed.[26] In January 2000, the governor of Illinois suspended all executions after 13 people were released from death row because they had been wrongly convicted. The Innocence Project, established by Barry Scheck and Peter Neufeld in 1992, has exonerated over 150 convicted offenders through the use of DNA technology. Facts on individual cases can be found at the Innocence Project's website.

"Brutalization" and "Resetting"

Some research suggests that capital punishment, instead of deterring crime, actually leads to more criminal activity. This idea was first suggested by Bowers and Pierce, who found that executions were followed by a two- to threefold increase in the number of homicides the next month. In three California counties, there was a "slight but discernible" increase in the number of murders in the ten days following an execution (0.25 per execution). Bowers and Pierce labeled this effect *brutalization* and speculated that among a limited group of people who have already "reached a state of 'readiness to kill,'" an execution conveys the message that vengeance is justified.[27]

Other scholars have found a similar effect in non–capital crime cases and label it a "resetting" process. As we explained earlier, deterrence theory operates in the realm of social psychology. Potential offenders calculate their risk of being caught and punished. Pogarsky and Piquero suggest that offenders who have been arrested "reset" their estimate of the likelihood of being caught again, figuring that the odds are very low that they will be. (This is sometimes referred to as the "gambler's fallacy," i.e., because I haven't won so far, the odds are good that I will win the next time.) Like much deterrence research, this study was based on hypothetical scenarios given to college students, and we do not know whether the resetting process works among actual offenders.[28]

Summary

Research on the effect of the death penalty on crime is extremely mixed. Because so many different factors influence criminal behavior, it may never be possible to determine the extent of any deterrent effect. For the moment, then, we can say that the advocates of capital punishment have not persuasively established the existence of a deterrent effect.

DETERRING THE DRUNK DRIVER

In the 1980s, a crusade against drunk driving arose and swept the country. Spurred by a wave of public outrage, virtually every state enacted new laws and policies, most of which were designed to deter drunk driving through tougher punishment.[29] Leading the national crusade was an organization called MADD (Mothers Against Drunk Driving), founded by Candi Lightner, whose 13-year-old daughter, Cari, was killed in a crash involving Clarence Busch, who had two previous drunk driving convictions and was out on bail on a third drunk driving charge. Cari Lightner's death confirmed the belief of many people that repeat drunk drivers beat the system.

The "Killer Drunk" and Other Myths

Like so many aspects of criminal justice, the subject of drunk driving is dominated by myths that inhibit the development of sound and effective policies. It is widely believed, for example, that drunk drivers are responsible for half of all traffic fatalities. One Justice Department report repeated the widely publicized claim that drunk driving kills 50,000 people every two years—"almost as many American lives as were lost in the entire ten years of the Vietnam war."[30] This grossly exaggerated estimate originated in a 1968 report by the U.S. Department of Transportation (DOT) and has been widely repeated ever since.

Current data indicate that 40 percent of all traffic fatalities in 2003 were "alcohol related."[31] Alcohol was not necessarily the *cause* of each of those accidents, however. The term *related* includes many different situations. There is an important distinction between drivers who have been drinking and those whose driving is *impaired* by drinking. James B. Jacobs argues that only 30 percent of all traffic deaths are associated with drunk driving, and H. Laurence Ross estimates that it is about 25 percent.[32]

Another myth is that many "killer drunks," people with a serious drinking problem and many arrests, frequently beat the system.[33] The myth of the killer drunk has several aspects. First, it places the blame on a small number of dangerous people. Second, it emphasizes the killing of innocent people. Third, it puts much of the blame on the criminal justice system for not punishing these offenders and keeping them off the road. Fourth, it makes criminal punishment the primary focus of efforts to reduce traffic fatalities.

Ross argues that each of these aspects distorts the reality of alcohol-related fatalities. First, the problem is not confined to a few dangerous people. Driving after drinking is fairly common. Ross estimates that every year about 20 percent of all drivers, or 33 million people, drive after drinking. That is a lot of people. Moreover, because about 20 to 30 percent of the population do not drink at all, the percentage of drinkers who drive after drinking is higher than 20 percent. Ross's point is that drinking and driving is a routine part of a society where driving is nearly universal (and practically necessary in terms of work) and drinking is an acceptable social custom. In short, we cannot address the problem by assuming that only a handful of people are responsible for it.[34]

Second, innocent drivers or bystanders are not the typical victims of alcohol-related crashes. About half (57 percent) of all the people killed are the drunk drivers themselves, and another 21 percent are passengers in their cars. Only 7 percent are the drivers in other cars. In 2003, 11 percent of those killed were pedestrians, some of whom were themselves impaired by alcohol.[35]

Third, the argument that the criminal justice system is "soft" on drunk drivers is one part of a general view of the criminal justice system which we have already discussed in Chapters 2 and 3. We will take a close look at the alleged loopholes in the criminal justice system in Chapter 8. Later in this chapter, we will look specifically at the handling of drunk driving cases.

In fact, most of the drivers killed in alcohol-related crashes do not have a history of drunk driving. It is not possible, therefore, to spot them in advance on the basis of their driving records. Once again, we are up against the prediction problem we discussed in Chapter 4. The crash that killed Cari Lightner, involving an innocent victim and a driver with a long record, is the classic "celebrated case" at the top of our criminal justice wedding cake.

Fourth, and perhaps most important in terms of reducing drinking and driving, both Ross and Jacobs argue that many different kinds of policies can contribute to reducing alcohol-related traffic fatalities.[36] Most do not involve deterrence-oriented enforcement. We will examine some of these policies in the "Alternative Strategies for Dealing with Traffic Fatalities" section below.

Deterrence and Drunk Driving

Deterrence-oriented efforts to reduce drunk driving involve both short-term enforcement crackdowns and long-term changes in sentencing policy.[37] There are several reasons for thinking that tougher punishment is more likely to work with drunk driving than, for example, with robbery or burglary. Because people who drink and drive are more representative of the general population, more of them will have a stake in society and therefore feel threatened by the stigma of arrest and the impact on their jobs and families. Reasons also abound for thinking that the probability of arrest is higher for drunk driving: It is a public crime, occurring in plain view and readily observable to the police, over an extended period of time. The evidence, however, suggests that these assumptions do not work in practice and that deterring the drunk driver is extremely difficult.

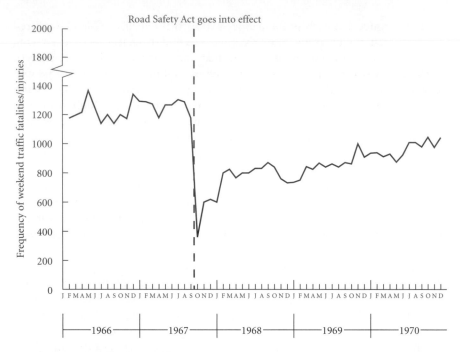

FIGURE 6.1   The effect on traffic fatalities and serious injuries of a crackdown on drunk driving, United Kingdom, 1966–1970

SOURCE: Reprinted by permission of the publisher, from *Deterring the Drinking Driver: Legal Policy and Social Control,* by H. Laurence Ross (Lexington, MA: Lexington Books, D. C. Heath and Company). Originally appeared in Ross, 1973, Journal of Legal Studies, University of Chicago Press.

One of the most famous drunk driving crackdowns involved the 1967 Road Safety Act in England. The law empowered the police to require a breath test of any driver and specified that refusal to submit to the test was punishable as an actual failure. It attempted to increase the certainty of apprehension, without changing the severity of punishment.[38]

As Figure 6.1 indicates, weekend traffic fatalities and serious injuries dropped to one-third of their previous levels after the law went into effect. Some observers saw this as evidence of a deterrent effect. But it is also obvious that the effect gradually wore off. Within three years, fatalities returned to their previous level. This decay appears to be a general phenomenon in enforcement crackdowns. A 1984 Justice Department evaluation of four anti–drunk driving campaigns found similar results and concluded that the deterrent effects of an enforcement effort, even when it exists, "appear to diminish over time."[39]

Lawrence Sherman characterizes the decline in deterrent effect as "initial deterrence decay." Some deterrent effect does remain, and he calls this "residual deterrence."[40] The challenge for policymakers is to increase the amount of residual deterrence over the long term. Unfortunately, the evidence indicates that short-term crackdowns do not achieve this effect.

The British crackdown illustrates a phenomenon known as the *announcement effect*. The publicity surrounding a crackdown causes people to alter their behavior: People decide not to have another drink, or they ask someone else to drive them home; a bartender refuses to serve a drink, or friends tell someone that he or she has had enough to drink. In short, people do perceive the threat of punishment and make rational decisions to alter their behavior. In some instances, these changes occur before the law actually goes into effect, as people's awareness of the potential penalty rises.

The announcement effect may also change the behavior of police officers, causing them to become more active in stopping drunk drivers in the early months of a new law. A Justice Department evaluation of four anti–drunk driving campaigns, for example, found that arrests went up in three of them but not in the one in which "relatively little publicity" was made about the mandatory imprisonment law.[41]

As the publicity surrounding an enforcement effort diminishes, however, the effect wears off. Drinkers become less conscious of the risks and revert to their normal behavior. Police officers return to their normal levels of enforcement activity.

One of the main problems with drunk driving crackdowns is that the risk of arrest is extremely low. In his evaluation of the British experiments, H. Laurence Ross estimated that the probability of being asked to submit to a breath test was 1 per million vehicle miles driven. (Consider this figure in terms of the mileage on your odometer.) The risk was higher for drinking drivers because their behavior attracted the attention of the police, but it was still "low by any reasonable criterion." The U.S. Department of Transportation estimates that someone would have to drive drunk between 200 and 2,000 times to be apprehended—and even then would face only a 50 percent chance of being punished.[42]

Most people, moreover, believe that the risk is low. A survey of Minneapolis and St. Paul residents found that 75 percent thought their chances of being arrested if they drove drunk were "unlikely" or "very unlikely."[43] And according to deterrence theory, the deterrent effect is weak or nonexistent if the perceived risk is low.

Looking at enforcement from the perspective of the police officer helps to explain why the risk is low. Both regular patrol officers and traffic unit officers are theoretically on the lookout for drunk drivers. Regular patrol officers, however, have many responsibilities—law enforcement, order maintenance, and service—and are concerned primarily with answering calls for service. Moreover, as we learned in the previous chapter, they are spread very thin and are responsible for patrolling streets that are not prime "hunting grounds" for drunk drivers. Traffic unit officers, meanwhile, represent no more than about 10 percent of the sworn officers in a department. They also have other responsibilities, such as watching for speeders. Drunk driving is heaviest at those hours when the police are busiest with other assignments. In short, not that many police officers are concentrating exclusively on drunk driving.

Certain disincentives affect aggressive traffic enforcement. Traffic stops are unpleasant and occasionally dangerous experiences for police officers. Citizens resent them and sometimes let the officer know it. Traffic situations are the fourth most hazardous situation for police officers in terms of officers killed on duty (and these situations include accidents resulting from pursuits).[44] In the absence of any strong incentives, such as ticket quotas, most cops prefer to avoid traffic stops except in the most serious cases.

When officers do make arrests, the law of diminishing returns comes into play. Processing an arrest may take up to two hours (or more, depending on local procedures). Thus, each arrest removes the police officer from the street and lowers the level of enforcement. While there may be some gain in specific deterrence related to the person arrested, there is an offsetting loss in general deterrence.

If the hunters are few, the hunted are many and well hidden among law-abiding drivers. Experts estimate that even during the peak drunk driving hours (Friday and Saturday nights), only about 3 to 4 percent of all drivers are legally drunk.[45] Perhaps another 5 percent have some detectable level of alcohol in their blood. But some drivers who are legally drunk may not be impaired, and their driving may not attract the attention of the police. The drive home from a neighborhood bar may be very short, leaving a small window of opportunity for detection.

Drunk Drivers in Court

Another factor undermining the deterrent effect of a crackdown is the fate of drunk driving cases in court. James B. Jacobs estimates that about 90 percent of all arrested drunk drivers are convicted through guilty pleas.[46] In this respect, the prosecution of drunk driving offenses closely resembles the handling of other criminal cases. Those data, however, reflect only convictions. The main purpose of crackdowns is to deter drunk driving by increasing the severity of punishment, usually through a mandatory jail or prison sentence.

Mandatory sentencing provisions can be evaded through dismissal, plea bargaining, or blatant disregard for the law. H. Laurence Ross and James P. Foley examined the implementation of new mandatory sentencing laws enacted in New Mexico and Indiana in the 1980s. The New Mexico law required a jail term of not less than 48 hours for offenders with a prior drunk driving conviction, and prohibited suspended sentences. Ross and Foley found that in 238 cases the mandated sentence was imposed and served in only 106, or 45 percent of the total. In another 60 cases (25 percent) the mandatory sentences were imposed but there was no documented proof that the offenders served them. In 10 percent of the cases, the judge suspended the sentence, and in another 20 percent the offender served no jail sentence. The Indiana law mandated five days in jail, with at least 48 consecutive hours, or a minimum of 80 hours of community service for offenders with a prior drunk driving conviction. Yet 30 percent of the convicted offenders did not serve the mandated sentence. Of 753 cases, 64 percent served the 48 consecutive hours, and another 6 percent did the required 80 hours of community service.[47]

Ross and Foley offer several possible explanations for this evasion of mandatory sentences. In some cases, the judges may have been ignorant of the offender's prior record. We might ask whether they chose not to find out as a deliberate strategy for evading the mandatory sentencing provision. It is possible that some jurisdictions do not have data systems that accurately record all prior convictions. Or, it is possible that prosecutors do not file evidence of prior convictions (This is one of the methods prosecutors use to evade "three strikes" laws). In others, judges may have chosen to interpret the law as covering only certain kinds of prior convictions (for example, felonies and not misdemeanors). Judges may have simply ignored the law in some cases. For some sentenced offenders, the term "48 hours" may not have been interpreted literally. Correctional officials may have counted a few hours a day as representing the entire day; if the offender spent a few hours in jail spanning midnight, he might have been credited with having served both days. Similar evasions of mandatory sentencing have been found in studies of other crackdowns.

Evasion of the law by justice officials is not universal by any means. The Justice Department's evaluation of enforcement efforts in Seattle found that the incarceration rate for convicted drunk drivers went from 9 to 97 percent as a result of new procedures. In Memphis, it went from 29 to almost 100 percent.[48] A 1982 California law increased the statewide jail incarceration rate for second-time offenders from 83 percent in 1980 to 97.5 percent in 1984. In Sacramento County, the percentage of first-time drunk drivers sent to jail went from 10 percent to more than 50 percent. These data make it clear that second-offense drunk drivers were not getting off easy before passage of the new law. The most significant effect of the California law was on first-time offenders; the percentage going to jail increased from about 10 percent to over 50 percent.[49]

Nonetheless, as the Ross and Foley study suggests, a certain amount of evasion of mandatory sentencing persists in some jurisdictions that undermines both the certainty and the severity of punishment. This compounds the low perceived and actual risk of arrest. In the end, most experts believe that enforcement crackdowns are not likely to deter drunk driving. After reviewing all the evidence, Ross concludes that "deterrence-based policies are questionable in the long run. No such policies have been scientifically demonstrated to work over time."[50] Jacobs agrees but adds that deterrence-based laws play a symbolic role in expressing society's moral condemnation of drunk driving.[51] Our conclusion can be stated as follows:

PROPOSITION 15
Enforcement crackdowns do not deter drunk driving over the long term.

Crackdown Costs

When a drunk driving crackdown does result in more punishment, it imposes significant costs on the criminal justice system. The most direct impact is on local jails and courts. Additional judges were needed in Seattle to handle the

Table 6.2 Motor vehicle deaths per 100,000 vehicle miles

Year	Death Rate
1927	16.33
1937	14.68
1947	8.82
1957	5.98
1967	5.50
1977	3.35
1987	2.51
1997	1.71
2003	1.75

SOURCE: *U.S. Department of Transportation Facts 2003* (Washington, DC: US Department of Transportation, 2004).

increase in cases. Cincinnati had to add an additional daily traffic court. In Sacramento County, California, more defendants insisted on going to trial, with the result that convictions at trial decreased. In Seattle, the county had to open a new jail facility just to handle the drunk drivers. In Memphis, some offenders had to wait six or seven months to serve their jail sentences. In two California counties, the jails became so overcrowded that courts found jail conditions unconstitutional.[52]

In short, as with other "get tough" policies, drunk driving crackdowns not only may fail to achieve their intended goals but may also impose unintended costs on the justice system.

Alternative Strategies for Dealing with Traffic Fatalities

Actually, there is considerable good news about traffic fatality trends. As Table 6.2 indicates, the motor vehicle death rate per 100,000 vehicle miles dropped from 16.33 in 1927 to 3.35 in 1977 to 1.75 in 2003 (this includes all fatalities and not just alcohol-related).[53] The long-term decline since 1930 is substantial, and the nearly 50 percent reduction since 1980 is a particularly significant achievement. How do we explain this success, especially in light of our conclusion that enforcement crackdowns do not work? The answer is that *some things do work*. Tougher enforcement by the criminal justice system may have contributed to this decline, but both Ross and Jacobs argue that at best it was only one factor. Other social policies also played important roles.

First, cars have become safer. Steering wheels, for example, are less likely to impale a driver than they were in the 1950s. Dashboards and door handles have been redesigned over the years to reduce potential harm in accidents.

Second, seat belts are required on all new cars, and their use is mandatory in every state except New Hampshire. The National Highway Traffic Safety

Administration estimates that seat belts reduce the risk of death in an accident by 45 percent and the risk of moderate to critical injury by 50 percent. Child restraints, meanwhile, reduce the risk of death by 71 percent for infants (one year old) and by 54 percent for toddlers (one to four years old). In 2004 it was estimated that air bags saved 15,000 lives in the previous 20 years, or about 750 a year.[54]

Third, federal law has forced states to raise the legal age for drinking to 21 (by withholding federal highway funds if they do not). Although this law has not necessarily curbed teenage drinking, it may have helped to reduce drunk driving by teenagers, and the DOT estimates that it saved 16,513 lives between 1975 and 1996.[55]

Fourth, the policy of administrative license revocation (ALR) has resulted in speedier loss of driver's licenses. In this procedure, a police officer can revoke a license on the spot if the driver fails a breath test. Forty-one states have ALR laws. It is important to point out that this is a *civil* law rather than a criminal law approach. It rests on the theory that a driver's license is essentially a privilege that can be withdrawn without resort to the full criminal process. Ross argues that it is both swift and certain, resulting in the immediate incapacitation of the offender (in the sense that the person cannot drive legally, although obviously some people drive without a license). He cites studies indicating that this approach has been effective in reducing alcohol-related accidents and fatalities.[56]

Fifth, socialization may have contributed to some of the long-term reduction in traffic fatalities. The national anti–drunk driving crusade, with all of the attendant publicity, may have helped to change attitudes and behavior about drinking and driving. Public opinion surveys have found that the percentage of people saying that they "sometimes" drove after drinking fell from 25 percent in 1983 to 16 percent in 1995. The percentage indicating that they "never" did rose correspondingly.[57] We have good reason to assume that these attitudes reflect real changes in behavior. Not only has the number of traffic fatalities fallen, but the percentage that are alcohol related fell from 57.3 in 1982 to 40.9 in 1996 and remained at that level in 2003.[58]

Sixth, the National Safety Council's policy of Graduated Driver Licensing (GDL) allows limited driving privileges to teenagers and then gradually expands them. (For additional information go to the National Safety Council web site.) It is well known that teenagers, and young men in particular, engage in the riskiest driving behavior. Reducing their driving, and/or introducing them to driving gradually, is likely to reduce traffic accidents and fatalities. Although almost all states always had provisions for temporary licenses, the idea of a comprehensive system emerged only in the 1980s, first in New Zealand and then in Canada. It finally began to spread in the United States in the 1990s. Evaluations have found reductions in the number of crashes ranging from a high of 60 percent to a low of 4 percent among teenage drivers.[59]

Seventh, ignition "interlock" systems serve as in-car breathalyzers that prevent an alcohol-impaired driver from starting the car. They may have also contributed to a decline in driving by seriously drunk people.

PROPOSITION 16

Multipronged strategies that do not rely completely on the criminal law can effectively reduce drunk driving and traffic fatalities.

Summary

There are some important lessons in our success in substantially reducing traffic fatalities. Most important, it is clear that relying solely on criminal law enforcement is not likely to produce significant results. In Chapter 13 we will discuss the limits of the criminal law with regard to drugs and other types of behavior (e.g., drinking). Second, it appears that a variety of policies operating in combination is likely to get results. Third, some of these policies involve noncriminal strategies (e.g., interlock systems). These points are at the heart of the community-focused crime prevention strategies that we will examine in Chapter 14.

DETERRING BURGLARS AND ROBBERS

So far, we have discussed deterrence in relation to the death penalty and drunk driving. But what about burglars and robbers? Are they deterred by a perceived higher risk of arrest, greater certainty of conviction, and probability of harsher punishment? As we indicated at the beginning of this chapter, the criminal law and the criminal justice system have some general deterrent effect. The real question is whether any particular change in policy will increase the deterrent effect and reduce crime.

As Nagin points out, until recently there has been little research on the crucial element of deterrence theory: how particular groups of people perceive the deterrent.[60] Moreover, most of the social psychological research involves college undergraduates and relatively minor offenses. One critic derides this body of literature as "the science of sophomores."[61] Horney and Marshall's study of 1,000 prison inmates is one of the few that investigates the perceived risk of apprehension and punishment by serious offenders.[62]

In an imaginative study, Scott Decker and his colleagues interviewed a group of 48 active residential burglars and a control group of 40 nonoffenders drawn from two job training and recreation centers in the same city. Procedures were taken to ensure the anonymity of the active burglars (unlike subjects in most of the career criminal research, these individuals were not currently prison inmates). Both groups were given hypothetical situations that altered the risk of apprehension, the reward from doing the burglary, and the penalty if caught.[63]

Including the expected reward in the equation added an important element. As we already noted, deterrence theory assumes a rational choice between the relative costs *and* gains from doing crime. Virtually all of the deterrence research has focused only on the cost side: the effect of different punishments. Because the theory assumes a choice between alternatives, it is necessary to include the expected gains as well.

Decker and his colleagues found a "clear and highly significant difference" between the burglars and the control group.[64] The active burglars were much more likely to commit a crime than were members of the control group. Increasing the risk of apprehension lowered the willingness to commit a burglary for both groups. But only 10 percent of the controls indicated a willingness to commit a burglary when told that the risk of apprehension was only 1 percent. Meanwhile, even with a 50 percent chance of apprehension, slightly more than half (55.2 percent) of the active burglars would still commit a burglary.

For the active burglars, an increase in the severity of the penalty had some effect on their willingness to commit a burglary, but it was surprisingly modest. When the punishment was described as two years' probation, 61.5 percent said they would commit a burglary; increasing the penalty to five years in prison reduced it to only 52.5 percent. The burglars were more influenced by changes in the relative gain from the burglary; that is, they indicated a greater willingness to commit crime when the expected gain was higher than they had previously believed it to be.

The study provides little support for traditional deterrence theory. Decker and his colleagues concluded that neither the burglars nor the control group "were significantly affected by the severity of the threatened penalty on its own."[65] Certainty of apprehension did have some effect, but, as we learned in the previous chapter, the prospects for increasing clearance rates are not good.

The Rand Inmate Survey

The RIS asked prisoners in three states (California, Michigan, and Texas) to estimate the probable results of doing crime. In their responses, well over 80 percent believed that they had an "even chance" of being arrested, imprisoned, injured, or killed. Over 60 percent believed they had a "high chance" of arrest and imprisonment or that it was "certain." In short, the prisoners were extremely fatalistic about the consequences of criminal activity. Significantly, they were only half as likely to expect a high chance or certainty of enjoying the good outcomes of crime (the responses of "high living," having "expensive things," or "being own man").[66]

In their analysis of these data, James Q. Wilson and Allan Abrahamse posed the obvious question: If their estimate of bad consequences is so high and their estimate of good consequences so much lower, why do they commit crime? (Remember, these were imprisoned offenders, some of whom were classified as high rate.) The answer is that they do not act on the basis of a rational calculation of costs and benefits. Wilson and Abrahamse, for example, found that they consistently overestimated the financial rewards of crime. They acted impulsively, overestimating the immediate, short-term gains of crime and underestimating unpleasant consequences, such as imprisonment, which lay in the future.[67] They also may have felt that they had no alternatives in terms of legitimate work—in other words, they perceived no positive rewards for a law-abiding lifestyle.

Like Decker's study of active burglars, the RIS provides little support for traditional deterrence theory. Actual offenders do not appear to make their decisions about criminal activity on the basis of a rational and carefully calculated assessment of the costs and benefits.

DETERRING DOMESTIC VIOLENCE

Another area that has seen considerable research on the deterrent effect of punishment is arrest for domestic violence. Traditionally, police officers avoided arrest in domestic violence situations, especially when married couples were involved. In the 1970s, the women's movement challenged this practice, arguing that failure to arrest left the female victim vulnerable to further violence. Women's groups successfully sued the New York City and Oakland police departments on equal protection grounds and won settlements that included mandatory arrest policies. By the 1980s, a national movement was under way toward mandatory arrest or arrest-preferred policies. These have been implemented through either police department policy or state law.[68]

Most advocates of mandatory arrest for domestic violence believe that it deters future violence. The first study of this issue, the Minneapolis Domestic Violence Experiment, became one of the most publicized and influential experiments in criminal justice history. The experiment tested the effect of three different police actions: arrest, separation, and mediation. Through official police records and interviews with victims, it found lower rates of repeat violence over the following six months as a result of arrest compared with either of the other two alternatives. The experiment seemed to indicate that arrest deterred domestic violence. The authors of the experiment were careful to point out that the persons arrested were rarely prosecuted or incarcerated; the "punishment" was usually nothing more than arrest, or at most a night in jail.[69]

These findings had an enormous impact on public policy. Over the next few years, most police departments adopted mandatory arrest policies. By 1988, 60 percent of all big-city police departments mandated arrest, and another 30 percent specifically encouraged it.[70]

Replications of the Minneapolis experiment in Omaha, Charlotte, Miami, and Milwaukee, however, found no consistent evidence that arrest deters future violence. Moreover, the Milwaukee experiment found that arrest had different effects on different kinds of offenders. It seemed to increase the level of repeat violence among unemployed men compared with employed. It is probable that employed men have a greater stake in social conformity and are more likely to be deterred by the sanction of arrest than are unemployed men, who have less of a stake in conformity.[71]

Lawrence Sherman, a principal investigator in the original Minneapolis experiment, now argues that the impact of arrest in domestic violence situations is an extremely complicated matter and that we cannot assert conclusively that arrest deters violence.

CONCLUSION

The evidence on the death penalty, drunk driving, burglary and robbery, and domestic violence leads us to the following general conclusion:

PROPOSITION 17

Deterrence-oriented policies that rely exclusively on criminal law enforcement do not enhance the inherent deterrent effect of the criminal justice system.

The commonsense notion that people will avoid unpleasant things and that we can influence their decisions by increasing the unpleasantness does not necessarily work in the real world of criminal justice. Let us be careful about exactly what we are saying. As in so many other areas, it is not true that "nothing works." The criminal law does have some deterrent effect. Most of us, after all, do not become career criminals. The threat of punishment, however, probably plays a relatively minor role in influencing the behavior of law-abiding people. The threat works, but it just is not the major factor. In terms of controlling behavior, the broader processes of socialization are the primary factors. As Leslie Wilkins put it, there are "those of us who have never needed a deterrent."[72] When these processes have broken down, we should not expect the criminal justice system—and deterrence-oriented policies in particular—to fix the problem. We will return to this issue in Chapter 12 when we discuss procedural justice. Experts in this field argue that we need to put more emphasis on building voluntary compliance with the law and less effort on trying to scare people into being law abiding.

NOTES

1. The best treatment of the subject is still Franklin E. Zimring and Gordon J. Hawkins, *Deterrence: The Legal Threat in Crime Control* (Chicago: University of Chicago Press, 1973).

2. Daniel S. Nagin, "Criminal Deterrence Research at the Outset of the Twenty-First Century," in Michael Tonry, ed., *Crime and Justice: A Review of Research,* vol. 23 (Chicago: University of Chicago Press, 1998), p. 3.

3. Ibid.

4. Scott Decker, Richard Wright, and Robert Logie, "Perceptual Deterrence among Active Residential Burglars: A Research Note," *Criminology* 31 (February 1993): 135.

5. Zimring and Hawkins, *Deterrence,* pp. 92–248.

6. Ibid., pp. 13–14.

7. Ronald L. Akers, "Rational Choice, Deterrence, and Social Learning Theory in Criminology: The Path Not Taken," *Journal of Criminal Law and Criminology* 81 (Fall 1990): 653–676.

8. See, for example, the extremely influential conservative argument in Charles Murray, *Losing Ground: American Social Policy, 1950–1980* (New York: Basic Books, 1984).

9. Dallin Oaks, "Studying the Exclusionary Rule in Search and Seizure," *University of Chicago Law Review* 37 (Summer 1970): 665–757.

10. Nagin, "Criminal Deterrence Research," pp. 4–6.

11. James O. Finckenauer, *Scared Straight and the Panacea Phenomenon* (Englewood Cliffs, NJ: Prentice-Hall, 1982).

12. Anthony Petrosino, Carolyn Turpin-Petrosino, and John Buehler, "Scared Straight and Other Juvenile Awareness Programs for Preventing Juvenile Delinquency: A Systematic Review of the Randomized Experimental Evidence," *The Annals of the American Academy of Political and Social Science* 589 (September 2003): 41–62.

13. Bureau of Justice Statistics, *Spouse Murder Defendants in Large Urban Counties* (Washington, DC: Department of Justice, 1995). NCJ 156831.

14. James Q. Wilson and Allan Abrahamse, "Does Crime Pay?" *Justice Quarterly* 9 (September 1992): 359–377.

15. Julie Horney and Ineke Haen Marshall, "Risk Perception among Serious Offenders: The Role of Crime and Punishment," *Criminology* 30 (1992): 575–594; Nagin, "Criminal Deterrence Research," p. 16.

16. Raymond Paternoster, *Capital Punishment in America* (Lexington, MA: Lexington Books, 1991), part IV, "Arguments for and against the Death Penalty," pp. 185–270.

17. *Furman v. Georgia,* 408 U.S. 238 (1972).

18. *Gregg v. Georgia,* 428 U.S. 153 (1976).

19. Thorsten Sellin, *The Penalty of Death* (Beverly Hills, CA: Sage, 1980).

20. Isaac Ehrlich, "The Deterrent Effect of Capital Punishment: A Question of Life and Death," *American Economic Review* 65 (1975): 397–417.

21. Isaac Ehrlich, "Participation in Illegitimate Activities: A Theoretical and Empirical Investigation," *Journal of Political Economy* 81 (1973): 521.

22. Brian Forst, "Capital Punishment and Deterrence: Conflicting Evidence," *Journal of Criminal Law and Criminology* 74 (Fall 1983): 927–942; Peter Passell, "The Deterrent Effect of the Death Penalty: A Statistical Test," *Stanford Law Review* 28 (November 1975): 61–80; William J. Bowers and Glenn Pierce, "The Illusion of Deterrence in Isaac Ehrlich's Research on Capital Punishment," *Yale Law Review* 85 (1975): 187–208.

23. Bureau of Justice Statistics, *Homicide Trends in the United States: 2002 Update* (Washington, DC: Department of Justice, 2004). NCJ 204885.

24. Robert Hood and Richard Sparks, *Key Issues in Criminology* (New York: McGraw-Hill, 1980), pp. 40–41; Zimring and Hawkins, *Deterrence,* p. 334; Philip Wattley, "City Hit on Crime Data," *Chicago Tribune,* 28 April 1983: 1–2.

25. Bureau of Justice Statistics, *Capital Punishment, 2003* (Washington, DC: Department of Justice, 2004). NCJ 206627.

26. Hugo Adam Bedau and Michael L. Radelet, "Miscarriages of Justice in Potentially Capital Cases," *Stanford Law Review* 40 (November 1987): 21–179.

27. William J. Bowers and Glenn L. Pierce, "Deterrence or Brutalization? What Is the Effect of Executions?" *Crime and Delinquency* 26 (October 1980): 453–484. Brian Forst reached a similar conclusion in his study "Capital Punishment and Deterrence."

28. Greg Pogarsky and Alex R. Piquero, "Can Punishment Encourage Offending? Investigating the Resetting Effect," *Journal of Research in Crime and Delinquency* 40 (2003): 95–120.

29. The two best surveys of the subject are H. Laurence Ross, *Confronting Drunk Driving: Social Policy for Saving Lives* (New Haven, CT: Yale University Press, 1992), and James B. Jacobs, *Drunk Driving: An American Dilemma* (Chicago: University of Chicago Press, 1989).

30. Bureau of Justice Statistics, *Jailing Drunk Drivers: Impact on the Criminal Justice System* (Washington, DC: Government Printing Office, 1984).

31. National Highway Traffic Safety Administration, *Traffic Safety Facts 2003* (Washington, DC: National Safety Council, 1998), p. 86.

32. Jacobs, *Drunk Driving,* pp. 27–28; Ross, *Confronting Drunk Driving.*

33. Ross, *Confronting Drunk Driving,* pp. 21–22, 168–170.

34. Ross, *Confronting Drunk Driving.*

35. National Safety Council, Injury Facts 2003 (Washington, DC: National Safety Council, 2003).

36. Jacobs, *Drunk Driving;* Ross, *Confronting Drunk Driving.*

37. Lawrence W. Sherman, "Police Crackdowns: Initial and Residual Deterrence," in Michael W. Tonry and Norval Morris, eds., *Crime and Justice: An Annual Review of Research,* vol. 12 (Chicago: University of Chicago Press, 1990), pp. 1–48.

38. H. Laurence Ross, *Deterring the Drinking Driver: Legal Policy and Social Control,* rev. ed. (Lexington, MA: Lexington Books, 1984), pp. 24–34.

39. Bureau of Justice Statistics, *Jailing Drunk Drivers,* p. 2.

40. Sherman, "Police Crackdowns: Initial and Residual Deterrence."

41. Ibid.

42. Ross, *Deterring the Drinking Driver,* pp. 33, 105

43. Donald E. Green, "Past Behavior as a Measure of Actual Future Behavior: An Unresolved Issue in Perceptual Deterrence Research," *Journal of Criminal Law and Criminology* 80 (1989): 781–804.

44. Federal Bureau of Investigation, *Law Enforcement Officers Killed and Assaulted, 2003.* Report issued annually.

45. Jacobs, *Drunk Driving,* p. 47.

46. Jacobs, *Drunk Driving,* pp. 98–100.

47. H. Laurence Ross and James P. Foley, "Judicial Disobedience of the Mandate to Imprison Drunk Drivers," *Law and Society Review* 21.2 (1987): 315–323.

48. Bureau of Justice Statistics, *Jailing Drunk Drivers,* p. 2.

49. Rodney Kingsworth and Michael Jungsten, "Driving under the Influence: The Impact of Legislative Reform on Court Sentencing Practices in Drunk Driving Cases," *Crime and Delinquency* 34 (January 1988): 3–28.

50. Ross, *Deterring the Drinking Driver,* p. 111.

51. Jacobs, *Drunk Driving,* p. 126.

52. Bureau of Justice Statistics, *Jailing Drunk Drivers;* Kingsworth and Jungsten, "Driving under the Influence."

53. National Safety Council, *Injury Facts* (Washington, DC: National Safety Council, 2003). [Formerly published as Accident Facts.].

54. Ibid.

55. Ibid.; "15,000 saved by air bags in past 20 years," *USA Today,* 12 July 2004.

56. U. S. Department of Transportation, *Reducing Highway Crashes Through Administrative License Revocation* (Washington, DC: Government Printing Office, 1986); Ross, *Confronting Drunk Driving,* pp. 63–67.

57. Bureau of Justice Statistics, *Sourcebook of Criminal Justice Statistics Online.*

58. National Safety Council, *Injury Facts,* 2003.

59. Herb M. Simpson, "The Evolution and Effectiveness of Graduated Licensing," *Journal of Safety Research* 34 (2003): 25–34.

60. Nagin, "Criminal Deterrence Research."

61. Raymond Paternoster, "The Deterrent Effect of the Perceived Certainty and Severity of Punishment: A Review of the Evidence and Issues," *Justice Quarterly* 4 (June 1987): 173–217.

62. Horney and Marshall, "Risk Perceptions among Serious Offenders."

63. Decker et al., "Perceptual Deterrence," pp. 135–147.

64. Ibid., p. 139.

65. Ibid., p. 145.

66. Wilson and Abrahamse, "Does Crime Pay?" p. 373.

67. Ibid., pp. 372–373.

68. Lawrence W. Sherman, *Policing Domestic Violence: Experiments and Dilemmas* (New York: Free Press, 1992).

69. Ibid.

70. Ibid.

71. Ibid. Christopher D. Mexwell, Joel H. Garner, and Jeffrey A. Fagan, *Effects of Arrest on Intimate Partner Violence: New Evidence from the Spouse Assault Replication Program* (Washington, DC: Department of Justice, 2001). NCJ 188199.

72. Quoted in Zimring and Hawkins, *Deterrence,* p. 97.

7

Lock 'Em Up

GETTING CRIMINALS OFF THE STREET

The main conservative crime control strategy is to get criminals off the street. This includes three "lock 'em up" proposals: preventive detention, incapacitation, and mandatory sentencing. All three are based on the assumption that the criminal justice system turns dangerous criminals loose on society, where they prey on law-abiding citizens. The new "three strikes" laws are the ultimate lock 'em up policy.

All of the lock 'em up strategies seek to limit the discretion of judges.[1] The underlying assumption is that judges have too much discretion to release dangerous criminals on bail, grant them probation, or sentence them to inappropriately short prison terms. Conservatives believe that the misuse of judicial discretion is the result of two factors. First, too many judges are "bleeding hearts" who are too lenient with convicted offenders. Second, many of our policies encourage not locking people up. American law has traditionally embodied the principle of a right to bail. The philosophy of rehabilitation, meanwhile, encourages alternatives to prison for convicted felons. Conservative proposals attack these laws and policies as soft on crime.

PREVENTIVE DETENTION

Conservatives believe that people released on bail commit a large number of crimes. President Ronald Reagan's Task Force on Victims of Crime declared in 1982, "A substantial proportion of the crimes committed in this country are committed by defendants who have been released on bail or on their own recognizance."[2] Preventive detention, a policy that allows judges to deny bail to high-risk criminal defendants, is the conservative policy on this issue.

Preventive detention raises both *constitutional* and *empirical* questions. The constitutional question is whether the Eighth Amendment to the U.S. Constitution prohibits detaining someone solely for the purpose of preventing crime. The Eighth Amendment guarantees that "excessive bail shall not be required." As with many other parts of the Bill of Rights, the exact meaning of the Eighth Amendment is ambiguous. Traditionally, it has meant that all criminal defendants have a right to bail, with the exception of persons accused of "capital" crimes, or those crimes punishable by the death penalty. The original purpose of bail in Anglo-American law was to ensure the defendant's appearance at trial. Preventive detention, then, represents a fundamental change in the purpose of bail.[3]

The Supreme Court answered the constitutional question in 1987, when it upheld the preventive detention provision of the 1984 federal Bail Reform Act. In *United States v. Salerno,* the Court ruled that there is no absolute right to bail and that preventive detention is a legitimate "regulatory" measure.[4] In this context, *regulatory measure* refers to a crime control policy.

The empirical question we are interested in is whether preventive detention will reduce serious crime. How much crime do offenders do while on bail? And will preventive detention significantly reduce the crime rate?

A Short History of Bail Reform

The demand for preventive detention is a backlash against the first bail reform movement of the 1960s. The civil rights movement focused public attention on the plight of the poor in the criminal justice system. The President's Crime Commission found that 52 percent of all people in jail were awaiting trial (in 2002 it was only 28.2 percent). Critics labeled America's jails the "new poorhouses." Wealthy organized crime figures easily raised large bail amounts, while poor people stayed in jail.[5] Caleb Foote's pioneering studies of bail in the 1950s found that defendants not released on bail were more likely to be convicted and imprisoned, thereby compounding the injustice of denying them a constitutional right.[6] In addition, the money bail system raises the cost of operating the jails and often contributes to jail overcrowding.

Current data support Foote's earlier finding about the impact of pretrial detention. In 1992, 79 percent of those detained before trial were convicted, compared with only 61 percent who were released. Additionally, 70 percent of those detained were convicted of a felony, compared with only 45 percent of those released. Finally, among those who were convicted, 89 percent of the detained were sentenced to incarceration, compared with only 59 percent of those who were released.[7]

The bail reform movement sought to correct these problems by facilitating pretrial release. The major innovation was *release on recognizance* (ROR), which allowed a defendant to be released without any financial considerations. Evidence of a job, family ties, or other roots in the community was used to evaluate whether the defendant was likely to appear for scheduled court dates. The 1966 federal Bail Reform Act directed federal courts to develop ROR procedures. Many states, meanwhile, developed their own ROR programs and/or adopted 10 percent plans that allowed defendants to post 10 percent of the dollar bail amount.[8]

The bail reform movement achieved many of its goals. The percentage of people in jail who were being held for trial dropped from 52 percent in 1967 to 33 percent in 1971 to 28.2 percent in 2002.[9] In 2000, 30 percent of all felony defendants in large urban counties were released on nonfinancial conditions, and 32 percent were released on financial conditions. The first bail reform movement did not achieve all of its goals, however. Because employment status is a major criterion for ROR, it discriminates against the unemployed and the marginally employed. Nearly three-quarters (72 percent) of employed defendants were released in 1990 compared with 46 percent of those who were unemployed.[10] (Data on this point was not reported for 2000.) Nor did bail reform eliminate the practice of keeping defendants in jail simply by setting high bail. In 2000 less than 20 percent of those defendants facing bail of $50,000 or more obtained their release, compared with almost 80 percent of those with bail of $5,000 or less.[11]

Seriousness of the offense and prior record, which we discussed in Chapter 2, has a major influence on pretrial release decisions. Only 13 percent of defendants charged with murder in 2000 obtained pretrial release. Only 44 percent of robbers were released, compared with 68 percent of defendants charged with larceny/theft. With respect to prior record, 77 percent of those with no previous arrests obtained their release, compared with 63 percent of those with one arrest and only 44 percent of those with five or more.

The first bail reform movement coincided with the great rise in serious crime. Between 1963 and 1973, the robbery rate tripled, while the burglary rate went up two and a half times. Conservatives argue that bail reform contributed to this by releasing many dangerous offenders. This section examines the evidence on that argument.

The focus of the backlash was Washington, DC. Because of rising crime rates, Congress passed a preventive detention law for the District of Columbia in 1970. By the 1980s, public support for preventive detention was widespread, and nearly all states had adopted it. Some states amended their state constitutions to limit the right to bail. The Michigan constitution allows preventive detention in four kinds of crimes when the judge finds a possibility of danger were the defendant to be released.[12] Let us take a look at how preventive detention works in practice.

An Early Test: Preventive Detention in Washington, DC

The 1970 District of Columbia law offered the first evidence of how preventive detention might work. The law allowed a judge to hold without bail for 60 days a defendant charged with a crime of violence or a dangerous crime. Several procedures were designed to protect defendants' rights. A formal hearing was required to determine that substantial probability of guilt existed and that no other release procedure could guarantee public safety. The defendant must have been convicted of a crime in the preceding ten years, been a narcotics addict, or on pretrial release, probation, or parole. Finally, if the trial were not held within 60 days, the defendant had a right to release on bail.

Something funny happened in Washington, however: The law was hardly ever used. (As we will see later in this chapter, the same thing happened with "three strikes" laws.) Judges detained very few defendants without bail. A study by Georgetown University and the Vera Institute found that in the first six months, prosecutors filed detention motions against only 20 of 6,000 felony defendants (or less than one-third of 1 percent!). These motions resulted in nine formal hearings and eight actual detentions. Another two defendants were detained through judicial initiative. Thus, only ten defendants were detained in six months.[13]

This is not the end of the story, however. Five of the ten detentions were reversed on appeal or reconsideration. Another was dismissed when the grand jury refused to indict the suspect. Thus, a grand total of four people were fully detained during the entire ten-month period.

What happened? Federal prosecutors in the District of Columbia had full discretion to use or not use the law. (As we will see later in this chapter, prosecutors' decisions not to use recent "three strikes" laws have nullified those laws in a similar fashion.) It is easy to explain why they chose not to. They could detain someone simply by setting bail at a level beyond his or her financial means. Because most robbers are poor, unemployed, or marginally employed, setting a higher bail amount than a defendant can afford is easy to do. This is the courtroom work group's traditional method of covertly undermining the nominal right to bail. In effect, it says, "Sure you have a right to bail—how much *can't* you afford?" And remember from our discussion of the courtroom work group in Chapter 3 that disagreements rarely erupt over bail.[14]

This practice continues today. In 2000, the median bail for all robbery defendants was $25,000 (up from $10,000 in 1992). Those who succeeded in obtaining release faced a median bail of only $10,000. Under a 10 percent plan, they would need to post only $1,000. But those who did not obtain their release faced a median bail of $50,000. In short, robbery defendants fall into two categories: those who get relatively low bail and those who get high bail because the courtroom work group wants to detain them.[15]

The 1984 Federal Bail Reform Act

The 1984 Bail Reform Act allows federal judges to detain a defendant without bail if "no condition or combination of conditions . . . will reasonably assure . . . the safety of any other person and the community." The law has had a very different impact than the 1970 District of Columbia law. Federal judges have used it extensively, reflecting the "get tough" mood of the last twenty years. The number of defendants detained by federal judges increased from 2,733 in the first six months of 1987 (before the Supreme Court upheld the law) to 4,470 in the last six months of 1988. The war on drugs accounted for much of this increase: More people were arrested for drug offenses, and prosecutors requested detention for drug defendants far more often than for defendants of other crimes. Between 70 and 75 percent of the prosecutors' requests for detention were granted.[16]

Close inspection, however, reveals that the *overall detention rate* did not increase that much. The percentage of all federal defendants detained before trial only increased from 24 to 29 percent (and to 34 percent by 1996). The major change was a shift in the *method* of detention. Before the 1984 law, virtually all of the detained defendants remained in jail because they could not raise bail. Of the 29 percent detained after the law went into effect, 19 percent were detained under the preventive detention law, and 10 percent were detained because they could not raise bail.[17] In short, the 1984 law gave judges legal authority to do what they had previously done covertly.

The important question, from our perspective, is whether preventive detention has helped reduce crime. Unfortunately, none of the studies of bail reform evaluates the impact on the overall crime rate. Evaluations have focused on crime by persons released on bail and have found no significant impact on pretrial crime. The percentage of federal defendants granted pretrial release who were rearrested for a felony increased from 1.2 percent in 1983 to 1.3 percent in 1985. The percentage arrested for misdemeanors went from 0.6 to 0.7 percent.[18] It is important to note how small a percentage of defendants were being rearrested before 1984. If anything, the percentage should have gone down, since judges were now able to detain suspected repeat offenders. These data force us to take a closer look at the whole question of crime by persons out on bail.

Crime on Bail: Myths and Reality

Contrary to popular belief, defendants out on bail do not commit that much crime. Let us take a look at the data on this issue. A defendant released on bail can "fail" in one of two ways: either by committing a crime or by failing to appear (FTA) at a scheduled court hearing. Let's first look at crime on bail. In 2000, 16 percent of all felony defendants in large urban counties released before trial were rearrested prior to the disposition of their case; 10 percent were rearrested for a felony and 6 percent for a misdemeanor (Table 7.1). Interestingly, persons originally charged with a violent crime were rearrested at a slightly lower rate (14 percent) than were persons charged with property (15 percent) or drug (19 percent) offenses. Contrary to public impression, defendants charged with the most violent crimes had the lowest rearrest rates for another felony (rape, 4 percent; murder, 6 percent). Robbers had one of the highest rates (21 percent). About 60 percent of all those rearrested are convicted on the new charge, but only about 45 percent are convicted of a felony. The net result is that only about 7 percent of all defendants released before trial are convicted of a new felony (45 percent of 16 percent).[19]

Turning now to FTAs, in 2002, 22 percent of all felony defendants failed to appear for a court date. Most FTAs are not intentional. Defendants forget their court date or are confused about the process (remember, felony defendants are

Table 7.1 Pretrial misconduct by released felony defendants, 2000

	Not rearrested	Felony arrest	Misdemeanor arrest
All Felony Defendants	84%	10%	6%
Murder	94	6	0
Rape	96	1	3
Robbery	79	14	7
Burglary	84	11	6
Drug trafficking	79	15	6

SOURCE: Bureau of Justice Statistics, *Felony Defendants in Large Urban Counties, 2000* (Washington, DC: Department of Justice, 2003). NCJ 202021.

not known for their self-discipline). The really serious FTAs, which we should be concerned about, are those in which the defendant flees and becomes a fugitive from justice. In 2000, 6 percent of all felony defendants absconded and remained at large.[20]

The Prediction Problem Revisited

The relatively low rearrest and reconviction rates bring us back to the prediction problem we discussed in Chapter 4. A judge faces the problem of spotting in advance the defendants likely to commit a crime on bail, especially those 10 percent who will be rearrested for a new felony. The point of preventive detention is to detain them and *only* them. Overpredicting dangerousness will result in many people needlessly being detained in jail. How successful are judges likely to be in this effort?

Predicting Dangerousness: Pretrial Drug Testing Many people believe that testing arrestees for drug use would be a reliable method of predicting whether or not a defendant is likely to commit a crime on bail. The assumption is that the combination of an arrest and illegal drug use indicates a lifestyle that includes crime.

A National Institute of Justice study of pretrial misconduct in six cities, however, found that "except for heroin use, pretrial drug testing did not appear to help predict rearrests." In fact, even those defendants who tested positive for more than one drug were not more likely to be rearrested than other defendants. Heroin use did predict rearrest, and was a particularly strong predictor in three of the six cities. Cocaine use was a predictor of only FTAs. In the end, the best predictor of rearrest was the number of prior arrests.[21] In short, testing for drug involvement does not help judges improve their decisions related to pretrial misconduct.

A Natural Experiment   A 1984 Supreme Court case on preventive detention for juveniles produced a natural experiment in predicting dangerousness.
(A natural experiment occurs when a change in policy or practice creates
comparable experimental and treatment groups.) A New York law authorized
preventive detention of juveniles who posed a "serious risk" of committing
another crime if released. In 1981, however, a federal judge declared it unconstitutional and enjoined its operation. New York appealed, and in 1984 (*Schall
v. Martin*) the U.S. Supreme Court ruled that preventive detention for juveniles
was unconstitutional.[22]

The district court decision had a quirk, however; the judge enjoined the
commissioner of corrections from detaining allegedly dangerous juveniles, but
judges were not so enjoined. Thus, judges continued to order some juveniles
detained. These kids were turned over to the commissioner of corrections, who
was forced to release them. This arrangement produced a natural experiment
that allowed an examination of how accurate the judges were in predicting
the dangerousness of a small group of juvenile defendants who were ordered
detained but promptly released.[23]

Jeffrey Fagan and Martin Guggenheim identified 69 "at risk" juveniles who
were ordered detained by judges but then released. They were compared with
a control group of 64 with similar backgrounds but who were not ordered
detained. After 90 days, 40 percent of the at-risk group had been rearrested,
compared with only 15.6 percent of the control group. In short, the judges
were reasonably accurate in identifying juveniles who posed a higher risk than
comparable offenders. This was achieved, however, at the cost of a high rate of
false positives: 60 percent of the at-risk group were not rearrested. Moreover,
only 19 percent were rearrested for a violent crime, meaning that the judges
were not very successful in predicting violent behavior.

Fagan and Guggenheim argue, as others have, that the goal of policy reform
is not to achieve perfection but to improve on current practice, to make some
marginal improvement in predictive accuracy. (Economists refer to this as the
marginal utility: How much do you gain through one investment strategy or
tax policy compared with another?) If you used an actuarial method for making
preventive detention decisions based on objective criteria and applied it to all
the juveniles in their study, you would detain members of the control group.
Remember that they were comparable to an at-risk group in terms of their
background characteristics (about 90 percent of both groups had some prior
criminal record, for example). Yet only 15.6 percent of the control group were
arrested within 90 days (think of them as false negatives). Applying the same
objective prediction formula to the control group would result in detaining
the 84.4 percent of the control group who were not rearrested. This outcome
translates into five false positives for every true positive. (Recall from Chapter 4
that the Wenk study produced eight false positives for every true positive.)

Fagan and Guggenheim concluded that "the accuracy of prediction of
dangerousness during the pretrial period remains questionable." And because of
the costs and limited marginal gains likely to be achieved, "preventive detention
appears to be unjustified."[24] As we will see shortly, the Rand Corporation

reached a similar conclusion regarding the prediction of high-rate criminal offenders.

Because the evidence clearly indicates that only a small percentage of people on bail are rearrested, and because we cannot predict which ones will commit more crime, we conclude:

PROPOSITION 18
Preventive detention will not reduce serious crime.

Speedy Trial: A Better Way

If we want to prevent both crime on bail and failure to appeal, speedy trial is a much better approach. Among the 1992 defendants who were rearrested prior to trial, 8 percent were rearrested in the first week and 37 percent within a month.[25] Disposing of all cases within five to six weeks would prevent about half of the crime committed by persons out on bail (this assumes that most will be convicted and sentenced to some confinement). Speedy disposition would also reduce the FTA rate and preserve two constitutional rights: the right to bail and the right to a speedy trial. Therefore, we can draw the following conclusion:

PROPOSITION 19
Speedy trials can reduce crime while preserving constitutional rights.

Actually, we have tried to require speedy trials. Congress and many states have enacted speedy-trial laws. Yet, as Malcolm Feeley found in his research on court reform, these laws were often evaded by the courtroom work group.[26] Thus, we face another dilemma: how to achieve a desired reform in the face of resistance by the courtroom work group. One possibility might be to expedite trials for only those offenders who are high risks. This policy would preserve their constitutional rights to both bail and a speedy trial as well as protecting the public.

INCAPACITATION

Incapacitation is a crime policy that seeks to reduce crime by imprisoning repeat offenders. It represents the same logic underlying preventive detention: Keep criminals off the street so that they cannot commit more crimes. Incapacitation further assumes that if we keep them in twice as long, we will prevent twice as many crimes. As a sentencing philosophy, incapacitation does not try to rehabilitate offenders; nor does it seek to deter them; it is intended only to get them off the street.[27]

There are actually two kinds of incapacitation. *Selective incapacitation* is designed to lock up only the few high-rate offenders, or career criminals. Like preventive detention, it builds on Wolfgang's career criminal research, which we discussed in Chapter 4. *Gross incapacitation,* on the other hand, involves locking up large numbers of offenders regardless of their criminal histories. Three-strikes laws are the ultimate form of gross incapacitation.

Selective Incapacitation: The Rand Formula

Selective incapacitation was one of the hot ideas in criminal justice in the 1970s and 1980s. James Q. Wilson endorsed it in his influential 1975 book, *Thinking about Crime,* claiming that serious crime could be reduced by *one-third* if each person convicted of a serious crime received a mandatory three-year prison sentence. He cited an earlier study claiming that selective incapacitation could reduce crime by an amazing 80 percent.[28]

These extravagant claims generated much excitement, and some criminologists tried to develop sophisticated selective incapacitation formulas. The most notable was a 1982 study, *Selective Incapacitation,* by Peter Greenwood and his associates at the Rand Corporation.[29] We have already discussed this work in Chapter 4; let's take another look at it in terms of sentencing policy.

Selective Incapacitation estimated that a fine-tuned sentencing policy could reduce robbery by 15 percent while also reducing prison populations by 5 percent. The reduction in the prison population (with the resulting cost savings) would be achieved because the longer prison terms for career criminals would be offset by reduced punishments for low-risk offenders (i.e., shorter prison terms or probation).[30] Like so many crime control proposals, the policy seems to offer the best of all possible worlds: more effective crime control at less cost.

The Rand sentencing proposal was based on the Rand Inmate Survey (RIS), discussed in Chapter 4. In the most important part of the RIS, interviews with 2,190 prison and jail inmates in California, Texas, and Michigan were used to develop estimates of the *average annual offending rates* for offenders.[31] These estimated rates allowed Rand to then estimate how much crime would be reduced by locking up particular types of offenders.

The Rand annual offending rate estimates have been the subject of considerable controversy. The estimate you choose has enormous policy implications. If you believe that the average career criminal commits more than a hundred crimes a year, incapacitation will achieve significant crime reduction. But if the average offending rate is only about five crimes a year, the payoff will be relatively small.[32]

Rand developed a prediction instrument by correlating inmates' background characteristics with their self-reported criminal behavior. The result is a seven-point scale of factors associated with high rates of criminal behavior (see Table 4.3, Chapter 4). Offenders were then classified as low risk (one point), medium risk (two to three points), and high risk (four to seven points).

Rand then correlated inmates' predicted offense category with their actual self-reported level of criminal activity (see Table 4.4). The prediction scale was correct 51 percent of the time. The 51 percent figure is calculated by adding the predicted low rate and actual low rate (14 percent), the predicted medium risk and actual medium risk (22 percent), and the predicted high risk and actual high risk (15 percent). The prediction device was grossly wrong 7 percent of the time (the 4 percent who were predicted high but actually low, and the 3 percent predicted low but actually high). In the remaining 42 percent of the cases, the prediction scale was only moderately accurate.[33]

Once again, the challenge is to improve on current practice (that is, to gain some marginal utility). When the Rand experts correlated their predictions with inmates' actual sentences, they found that the judges imposed a "correct" sentence (that is, a long sentence for a predicted high-rate offender) 42 percent of the time. In short, this figure is only a slight improvement over what judges are currently doing.[34]

Why such a small marginal improvement? The Rand system has several problems. Most important is our old friend the prediction problem. As other studies have found, prior criminal records and other indicators such as drug use are relatively weak predictors of future behavior. We consistently get significant numbers of false positives and false negatives. In fact, in the face of widespread criticism, Rand took another look at its own proposal five years later and admitted that its earlier estimates were "overly optimistic." It concluded that "there are no reliable methods for either measuring or predicting future offense rates."[35]

The attempt to estimate annual offending rates is a serious technical problem that has huge policy implications. The rates developed by Rand are *averages* that, like all averages, are inflated by the extremely high rates for the very worst offenders. The Rand report itself observes that "most offenders reported fairly low rates of crime." The median robbery rate was only 5 per year, but the worst 10 percent (or the 90th percentile) averaged 87 per year![36] Incapacitating a member of the 90th percentile will produce a significant crime reduction, but there will be very limited payoff for locking up any of the other offenders with low annual offending rates.

The most shocking aspect of the Rand prediction scale is the use of employment history as a criterion for sentencing. An offender acquires one point for having been unemployed for more than half of the two preceding years. It carries the same weight as a prior conviction for the same offense. Under the formula, an additional point might reclassify the offender from a low risk to a medium risk, and thus it would mean the difference between jail and prison.

When you take out any one of the seven factors in the prediction scale, the entire scheme begins to collapse. With only six factors, the success rate will fall below the 51 percent that Rand estimates. You would then be doing no better than judges currently do, using a combination of presentence investigations and pure hunch.

It is outrageous that imprisonment might be contingent on unemployment. The Rand formula takes us back 200 years to the days of imprisonment for debt. Even if such a policy were to become practice somewhere, it would immediately be challenged in court. The fact is that unemployment *is* highly correlated with criminal activity but that correlation is not something we should translate into crime policy. An alternative response to the problem would be not to punish people for being unemployed but to provide greater employment opportunities.

Finally, the Rand *Selective Incapacitation* proposal faces a major political obstacle. The idea of not imprisoning low-risk and medium-risk offenders is exactly what corrections experts advocated in the 1960s. The 1967 President's Crime Commission argued that we locked up too many people and for prison terms that were unnecessarily long, and recommended greater use of probation.[37] In 1980 the American Bar Association's *Standards for Criminal Justice* stated that "in many instances prison sentences which are now authorized, and sometimes required, are significantly higher than are needed in a vast majority of cases."[38] Because of the public demands to "get tough," however, these recommendations have been consistently rejected in favor of a policy of gross incapacitation.

If selective incapacitation seems too good to be true, that is because it is. The evidence indicates that because of the prediction problem and the political obstacles related to adopting the lower sentences that would make the Rand policy cost-effective, we have to conclude as follows:

PROPOSITION 20
Selective incapacitation is not a realistic strategy for reducing serious crime.

Gross Incapacitation: Zedlewski's New Math

Selective incapacitation is a fine-tuned surgical instrument that involves making careful distinctions among criminal offenders. The political reality is that we have completely ignored this approach and adopted instead a policy of gross incapacitation: locking up a lot of people and sending them to prison for long terms. This is the main reason that the prison population has soared since the 1970s. Let us take a look at the impact of gross incapacitation on the crime rate.

One of the most extraordinary endorsements of incapacitation is Edwin J. Zedlewski's report *Making Confinement Decisions.*[39] He reached the startling conclusion that imprisonment actually *saves* money. Challenging the liberal conventional wisdom about the high cost of imprisonment, he calculated that for every dollar we spend imprisoning a criminal, we save $17 in total social costs. Although he focused on the dollar costs of crime, his formula has important implications for crime reduction.

How did Zedlewski reach such an amazing conclusion? Let us take a close look at his figures. First, he estimated that in 1983 crime cost American society a total of about $100 billion. This included $33.8 billion for criminal justice system expenditures, $35 billion in victim losses (medical care, lost wages, property damage, and so on), $26.1 billion for private security expenses, and so forth. The National Crime Victimization Survey (NCVS), meanwhile, estimated that 42.5 million crimes were committed in 1983. Thus, Zedlewski calculated that each felony costs society $2,300 ($100 billion ÷ 42.5 million).

Using the RIS, Zedlewski then estimated that each criminal commits an average of 187 crimes a year. Locking up each offender for one year, therefore, "saves" society $430,000 per year ($2,300 × 187 = $430,000). After you subtract the cost of imprisonment ($25,000 per year), you get a net social "savings" of $405,000 a year for each offender imprisoned (or about 17 times the $25,000 cost of incarceration).

If this seems too good to be true, it is. Franklin Zimring and Gordon Hawkins demolished the key assumptions underlying Zedlewski's computations.[40] The most serious problem is the estimate of 187 crimes a year. They point out that Zedlewski does not mention the great disagreement among career-criminal specialists over annual offending rates. Many put the figure at about 18 crimes a year, and some use an even lower estimate. If the average is only 18, then locking up one criminal saves only $43,000 a year, according to Zedlewski's formula.

It was professionally dishonest of Zedlewski not to mention the debate over annual offending rates and to use one of the highest possible estimates. As we mentioned in Chapter 1, faith often triumphs over facts in discussions of crime policy. Here we have a case of someone deliberately misrepresenting the facts to make a point.

Zedlewski also did not take into account the problem of diminishing returns. As we lock up more people, we quickly skim off the really high rate offenders and begin incarcerating more of the less serious offenders. Because they average far fewer crimes per year (perhaps as few as five, according to the RIS), we get progressively lower returns in crime reduction and dollar savings.

The estimate of the dollar savings is also flawed. A reduction in crime does not produce a direct reduction in criminal justice system costs. If the crime rate goes down by 25 percent, we are not going to cut police department budgets by 25 percent. Also, because 80 to 90 percent of all department budgets involve personnel costs, which would really mean laying off one-quarter of all the officers. In fact, police departments have not reduced their size as a result of the great crime drop. Police officers do a lot more than fight crime. About 70 to 80 percent of patrol work involves order maintenance and service activities.[41] These are important tasks that people want the police to perform. The same is true for other criminal justice system costs. If crime drops by 25 percent, the cost of running the criminal courts will not automatically decline by the same percentage.

In the most devastating attack on Zedlewski, Zimring and Hawkins show that his own formula leads to absurd estimates of crime reduction. We have been running a natural experiment in gross incapacitation. They point out that between 1977 and 1987 the prison population increased by 230,000. If each criminal did an average of 187 crimes a year, that should have "prevented" 43 million crimes (230,000 × 187 = 43 million). Yet this figure is more than the number of crimes that the NCVS reported as occurring in 1987. In short, Zedlewski's formula predicts the complete elimination of all crime by 1986!

Of course that did not happen. First, criminals do not average 187 crimes a year, as Zedlewski estimated (a very small percentage of them do, but most average only a few crimes). And second, he did not consider the replacement factor: As some drug dealers are arrested, others take their place. You can do your own update of Zimring and Hawkins's critique with more recent data. Compute the increase in the prison population from the mid-1980s to the present and, using the estimated annual rate of 187 crimes per offender, estimate the amount of expected crime reduction. Compare that figure with the NCVS estimate of actual number of crimes committed. Crime has declined since the early 1990s.

Incapacitation: A Sober Estimate

Having demolished Zedlewski's fantastic estimates, Zimring and Hawkins undertook their own study of incapacitation, examining incarceration and crime trends in California. Using a variety of sophisticated models, they concluded that the incarceration of each offender in California in the 1980s prevented 3.5 crimes per year. We should note that this is one-fiftieth of the 187 figure used by Zedlewski and is even lower than the estimates of many experts on career criminals. The huge increase in the state prison population (115,000) reduced the crime rate by 15 percent.[42]

As Zimring and Hawkins pursued their analysis, however, some problems surfaced. For burglary, juvenile arrests declined significantly, but adult arrests increased. This is "exactly the opposite" of what the incapacitation model would predict, because most of those incarcerated were adults. A similar pattern appeared with larceny and rape, but not robbery. Consequently, Zimring and Hawkins concluded that it was not absolutely clear that incapacitation was the "primary cause" of the drop in crime.[43]

Zimring and Hawkins also did a cross-state comparison of changes in incarceration rates and crime rates in 17 states during the 1980s. California stood at one extreme, with the greatest increase in imprisonment and the greatest reduction in crime. Yet Georgia had a very high increase in imprisonment and one of the highest rises in crime. Minnesota, meanwhile, had almost no increase in incarceration and virtually no change in the crime rate. In short, Zimring and Hawkins could detect "no clear patterned relationship" between incarceration rates and crime rates.[44]

Serious crime declined in the 1990s, but we should be skeptical of claims that incapacitation was the sole or even the primary cause. Remember that we have been on an imprisonment binge for 25 years. Imagine going to a doctor, getting a prescription, taking the medicine (two pills a day), but not getting any better. You go back to the doctor, who increases the dosage (four pills a day). But you still do not get any better. The doctor then raises the dosage again (six a day). You repeat this process for 20 years. Finally, in about the nineteenth year, you begin to get better. Was it the medicine? Probably not. You cannot claim success for a prescription (pills/prisons) that failed for 19 years and then suddenly appeared to work in the twentieth year.

The evidence indicates no clear link between incarceration and crime rates. Moreover, gross incapacitation locks up many low-rate offenders at a great dollar cost to society. Consequently, the evidence leads us to the following conclusion:

PROPOSITION 21
Gross incapacitation does not reduce serious crime.

Let Them Out, but Keep Them Away from Us:
Megan's Laws

So-called Megan's Laws involve two procedures designed to control sex offenders: registration and community notification. A 1996 federal law requires sex offenders who are released to the community to register with state officials. The law then allows states some discretion in establishing procedures for notifying community residents about where convicted sex offenders are living. All 50 states currently have some law or laws to this effect. Such laws do not involve incapacitation by a strict definition, but the intent is somewhat the same: to keep criminals away from the rest of society. The original Megan's Law was named after seven-year-old Megan Kanka, who was raped and murdered in 1994.[45]

Advocates of registration and community notification believe that sex offenders pose a high risk of reoffending, that registration will assist law enforcement in surveilling and/or arresting them, that the knowledge of this surveillance will deter them from reoffending, and that notification will help residents take protective measures they feel are appropriate. (There are a number of advocacy groups that support these laws; do a Web search for "Megan's Laws" websites for their perspective on this issue.)

Are Megan's Laws effective? Do they successfully reduce sex offenses? First, it should be noted that research on recidivism consistently shows that parolees who had been convicted of rape do not reoffend at high rates. Many people believe they do because of a few "celebrated cases" every year. The rearrest rate for parolees who had been convicted of rape was 46 percent over the next three years after parole, signficantly lower than the rearrest rate for all felons paroled (67 percent); it was far lower than the rearrest rate for robbers (70 percent) and burglars (74 percent). In short, the danger of sex offenders reoffending has been greatly exaggerated.[46]

An evaluation of the Wisconsin community notification law found a number of different effects. Law enforcement officials had little difficulty carrying out their responsibilities in implementing the law. But probation and parole officials were faced with more work, especially when intensive supervision was part of the requirement. Communities were notified in part through public meetings, but an equal number of people attending those meetings left feeling more worried about being victimized than feeling reassured. Among the offenders interviewed, however, all but one said that notification adversely affected their readjustment to society. The problems included difficulty in finding housing and employment, threats or harassment, and ostracism. (When we examine offender reentry programs in Chapter 14 we will examine the many obstacles facing offenders returning to the community.) The Wisconsin study did not, however, attempt to evaluate the law's effect on recidivism.[47]

MANDATORY SENTENCING

The third lock 'em up strategy for preventing crime is mandatory sentencing. Actually, mandatory sentencing is a *means* to an end, either incapacitation or deterrence or both. Mandatory sentencing is operationalized in two ways: mandatory imprisonment for a certain crime and/or a mandatory minimum prison term.

Mandatory sentencing is an extremely popular crime policy. A Justice Department report on sentencing policies found that all 50 states had some form of mandatory sentencing by 1994. Most of these laws apply to specific offenses. Forty-one states have it for repeat offenders, 31 for certain drunk driving offenses, 32 for certain drug offenses, and 42 for some weapons offenses.[48] Meanwhile, by 1996, about 22 states had adopted three-strikes laws, which represent an extreme form of mandatory sentencing.[49]

The popularity of mandatory sentencing can be explained in part by the celebrated case syndrome we discussed in Chapter 2. Public opinion is heavily influenced by a few highly publicized cases. The O. J. Simpson trial has convinced many people that spouse murderers are frequently acquitted. But as the Bureau of Justice Statistics data on spouse murder indicate (see Chapter 2), most people who murder their spouse are convicted and imprisoned. Another good example is the Polly Klaas case. Twelve-year-old Polly was brutally murdered by Richard Allen Davis, who was out on parole and had been twice convicted of kidnaping. The public uproar over her case led to the California three-strikes law and similar ones in other states.

Two Case Studies

Let us review two case studies of mandatory sentencing laws in practice, one from the past and one current example.

Case 1: "The Nation's Toughest Drug Law" Most current mandatory minimum sentencing laws are modeled after a 1973 New York law, often referred to as the Rockefeller Drug Law and also the "nation's toughest drug law."[50] The law contained three major provisions designed to incapacitate drug offenders and deter future drug use: mandatory and long prison terms for heroin dealers, restrictions on plea bargaining for heroin dealers, and mandatory prison terms for certain categories of repeat offenders.

The prescribed prison terms were considered awesome at the time, but other states have since adopted similar laws. The law established three categories of heroin dealers. Class A–I offenders (major dealers, defined as people who either sold one ounce of heroin or possessed two ounces) would serve minimum prison terms of 15 or 25 years and a maximum of life imprisonment. Class A–II (middle-level dealers, defined as those who sold one-eighth of an ounce of heroin or possessed one to two ounces) would serve prison terms of at least 6 to 8⅓ years and a maximum of life. Class A–III offenders (minor street dealers, defined as anyone who sold less than one-eighth of an ounce of heroin or possessed up to one ounce) would serve a minimum prison term of at least 1 to 8⅓ years and a maximum term of life. In short, anyone caught selling heroin would definitely go to prison and would face the possibility of life imprisonment.

The law attempted to prevent abuse of plea bargaining. Anyone arrested for either an A–I or A–II offense could plead guilty to an A–III charge, but people originally charged with an A–III offense could not plead to anything lower. The result was a floor that meant at least some prison time and a potential life term. The law also included a habitual-criminal provision, imposing mandatory prison terms on anyone with a prior felony conviction. To cope with the anticipated increase in the criminal courts' workload as a result of the law, New York added 49 new judges, 31 of them in New York City.

In practice, the law was a paper tiger. An evaluation concluded that "the threat embodied in the words of the law proved to have teeth for relatively few offenders."[51] An enormous amount of slippage or leakage occurred between arrest and conviction. Between 1972 and 1976, the percentage of drug arrests leading to indictment declined from 39 to 25 percent. Meanwhile, the percentage of indictments resulting in a conviction fell from 86 to 80 percent. Thus, the overall percentage of arrests leading to conviction fell from 33.5 to 20 percent.

The law was not a total failure. For those who were convicted, the rate of incarceration went up from 33 to 55 percent. Nonetheless, if only 55 percent were going to prison, about half the defendants were evading the supposedly mandatory sentencing provisions. Overall, however, little changed. The percentage of people arrested for sale of heroin who went to prison was 11 percent in 1972–73, and it was 11 percent in 1976.

The law did produce longer prison terms. Among those sentenced to prison, the percentage receiving a sentence of three years or longer rose from 3 percent of all those convicted to 22 percent.

The slippage that occurred in the application of the New York law is consistent with the long history of mandatory sentencing laws. The process can be explained in terms of the thermodynamics of the criminal justice process, which we discussed in Chapter 3. An increase in the severity of the potential punishment creates pressure to avoid its actual application. In this case, the controls over plea bargaining did not prevent a rise in dismissals. The enormous increase in the potential prison terms, meanwhile, encouraged defense attorneys to go to trial. The percentage of defendants demanding a trial increased from 6 to 15 percent. Because a tried case takes 15 times as long to process as a case that is not tried, the addition of even a few trials significantly disrupts the process. Disposition time for all drug cases doubled under the new law despite the addition of the new judgeships (and for some unexplained reason, the new courts were noticeably less efficient than previously established courts were).

Finally, and most important, the law had no significant effect on crime or drug use. Heroin use in New York City was as widespread in 1976 as it had been in 1973. Serious property crime, the kind generally associated with heroin users, increased 15 percent between 1973 and 1975, but neighboring states had similar increases. Nor did the law appear to deter convicted felons from committing additional crimes. According to the National Household Survey, drug use did begin to decline in the late 1980s, but this trend was nationwide, and we cannot say that the New York law had any special impact in that state.[52]

Adaptation As we argued in Chapter 3, the criminal justice system adapts to major changes in the going rate. Our law of thermodynamics has been clearly at work in New York in the years since the 1973 drug laws were enacted. The state has taken one step backward, another step forward, and then another step backward again.

The "nation's toughest drug law" proved to be too much for the system. In 1976, the chief prosecutor of drug cases in New York City quietly announced that he would no longer enforce the law's prohibitions on plea bargaining. Three years later, the legislature formally eliminated these same prohibitions and permitted more flexibility in sentencing. It also allowed resentencing of some offenders given extremely long sentences under the original law.[53]

An important part of the slippage occurs after sentencing. As states have sent more offenders to prison and for longer terms, many prisons have become seriously overcrowded. In 2003 almost half of all states held more prisoners than the rated capacity of their institutions. Illinois was at least 38 percent and possibly 59 percent over capacity (there are two different methods for rating the capacity of a prison). The California prisons were anywhere from 3 to 101 percent over capacity.[54]

States have responded to overcrowding by releasing prisoners early through a variety of schemes. Some of them are overt emergency release procedures. But others are covert backdoor schemes embedded in changes in correctional practices. Pamala Griset's study of correctional trends in New York, which we discussed in Chapter 3, illustrates the extent to which this strategy involves both a hidden form of sentencing and a device for undermining the intent of mandatory sentencing laws.[55]

New York supplemented the 1973 drug law with two additional mandatory sentencing laws in 1978, covering juveniles and certain violent felonies. Prison overcrowding resulted, and because of the state's financial problems, the needed prison cells were not constructed. The state responded in 1987 and 1989 with laws creating three early release programs: shock incarceration, earned eligibility, and CASAT (Comprehensive Alcohol and Substance Abuse Treatment). These programs transfer enormous discretion to correctional officials over how much time offenders will actually serve.

Shock incarceration, like many boot camp programs we will examine in Chapter 11, involves early release after a short six-month program. Griset found that about 40 percent of those admitted to the program had been convicted of a second felony and that about 99 percent were immediately paroled upon completing the program. Many of these offenders were technically subject to the state's mandatory sentencing law regarding second offense felons. Yet on the basis of decisions by correctional staff—and not sentencing judges—they were released sooner than the law "mandated."

The second program, earned eligibility, speeds up an inmate's date of first eligibility for parole. Inmates who participate in treatment, educational, and work programs obtain a certificate of earned eligibility from correctional staff that grants them a virtual presumption of parole release (82 percent of those with certificates were paroled). As Griset explains, correctional staff have full discretion over whether to grant the certificate of earned eligibility.[56] Thus, control over the actual amount of time served passes from the legislature and judges to correctional officials.

Similarly, under the CASAT program, inmates with alcohol or drug histories may be released up to 18 months earlier than the expiration of their minimum sentence. As with the other two programs, correctional officials have full discretion to grant admission to CASAT.

The net result of these three programs, Griset explains, is that the reality of sentencing diverges from the rhetoric. New York politicians retained mandatory minimum sentencing but quietly authorized correctional officials to let prisoners out early.[57] On one hand, this is a cynical political maneuver: talking tough about crime while not facing up to paying the bill. At the same time, it is a classic example of how criminal justice thermodynamics often undermine the intent of "tough" sentencing laws.

Partial Repeal After years of campaigning by advocacy groups, New York significantly modified the Rockefeller Drug Law in December 2004 (although it did not completely repeal the law). Newly convicted drug offenders will now be given determinate rather than indeterminate sentences, which will result in generally shorter sentences. Additionally, offenders serving 15- or 25-year-to-life sentences under the old law can apply for resentencing. Other provisions of the law are also expected to reduce the length of prison terms. It is still too early to measure the impact of the 2004 law.[58]

Case 2: The Federal Sentencing Guidelines   The federal sentencing guidelines that went into effect in 1987 include a number of mandatory sentencing provisions, and they have contributed to the increase in the federal prison population. To achieve "truth in sentencing," the guidelines reduced the range of possible sentences and abolished discretionary parole release. The percentage of convicted federal offenders sentenced to prison increased from 51 percent in 1982 to 65 percent in 1994. Also, the average prison term increased 27 percent, from an average of 48 to 61 months.[59]

A basic question is whether prosecutors and judges are complying with the federal sentencing guidelines. There is mixed evidence on this issue. A study by the Federal Judicial Center found that slightly less than half of the offenders who were eligible under a mandatory minimum provision actually received it. This is a fairly high rate of slippage and leakage.[60]

Another problem is plea bargaining—specifically, charge bargaining that allows defendants to plea to a lesser offense and avoid a long mandatory minimum. Section 5K1.1 of the federal sentencing guidelines allows a departure from the presumptive sentence where the defendant "has provided substantial assistance in the investigation or prosecution of another person who has committed an offense."[61] In other words, a defendant can reduce his or her potential sentence by cooperating and naming other criminals.

Ilene H. Nagel and Stephen J. Schulhofer examined plea bargaining in three federal district courts and found that departures from the guidelines occurred in between 15 and 25 percent of all cases, with the national average about 17 percent. They concluded that circumvention of the guidelines was not the norm and that it was not necessarily unfair. They did, however, find some cases in which defendants won substantial sentence reductions: in one case, from 168 to 21 months; in another, from 69 months to 9.[62] These reductions may be excessive compared with what most defendants receive.

The point is that through prosecutorial discretion, "mandatory" sentences are not necessarily mandatory in practice. As we will see shortly, the mandatory provisions of three-strikes laws are ignored in most states. The various adaptations, moreover, because they are often hidden, increase the arbitrariness of decisions and the possibility of discrimination.

Mandatory Sentencing and Crime

The basic question, of course, is whether mandatory sentencing effectively reduces crime. A 1982 Justice Department report concluded that "it is difficult, perhaps fundamentally impossible, to substantiate the popular claim that mandatory sentencing is an effective tool for reducing crime."[63] By 15 years later, we had much more experience with mandatory sentencing. A 1996 report on structured sentencing in a variety of states found no correlation between incarceration rates and crime rates.[64] Zimring and Hawkins's multistate comparison of incapacitation, which we cited earlier, also did not find any clear correlation between incarceration rates and crime rates.[65]

After reviewing all of the evidence on mandatory sentencing, Michael Tonry, one of the leading experts on sentencing, declared, "Mandatory penalties do not work."[66] In his view, they are widely circumvented, tend to shift discretion from justices to prosecutors, and often result in punishments that are "unduly harsh." We agree. Our position is as follows:

PROPOSITION 22
Mandatory sentencing is not an effective means of reducing serious crime.

THREE STRIKES—WE ARE ALL OUT

The most popular new idea in mandatory sentencing is "three strikes and you're out." The basic concept is a mandatory life prison sentence for anyone convicted of a third felony, although in actual practice there are many variations. The state of Washington passed the first law, the Persistent Offender Accountability Act, in November 1993. The idea really caught fire after the brutal murder of Polly Klaas in California by Richard Allen Davis, a man with a long criminal record who had been paroled only three months earlier. California passed its three-strikes law in March 1994. Twenty-six states and the federal system have some kind of three-strikes law.[67]

The different state three-strikes laws vary considerably. The Washington law mandates life without parole for conviction to a "most serious offense" if the person had two prior convictions to "most serious offenses," which includes a wide range of felonies. The California law has separate two-strikes and three-strikes provisions. The second-strike provision doubles the sentence for a person convicted of a felony who has a prior felony conviction to a designated "strikeable" offense. The third-strike provision mandates life imprisonment, with no parole eligibility before 25 years, to someone convicted of a felony who has two prior convictions to designated strikeable offenses. The 1994 Georgia law mandates life without parole for a second conviction to a "serious violent felony."[68]

The three-strikes idea has been almost universally condemned by criminologists and other experts on sentencing. Franklin Zimring calls it "the voodoo economics of California crime." Jerome Skolnick says it represented the values of "the dark ages." A book labels it "Vengeance as Social Policy." Princeton's John J. DiIulio is one of the few to support it, arguing that "society has a right not only to protect itself from convicted criminals but to express its moral outrage at their acts by, among other things, keeping them behind bars."[69]

One of the major criticisms has been that three-strikes laws are crude instruments and do not focus on serious repeat offenders. The first California case, in fact, involved Jerry Williams, who stole a slice of pepperoni pizza. The first woman prosecuted under the law was arrested for a $20 cocaine purchase that occurred 14 years after her second strike. One of the first people sentenced to life in prison in the state of Washington had stolen $151 from a sandwich shop; his two previous strikes involved robberies totaling $460. In short, they violate the basic principle of selective incapacitation by failing to focus on the few offenders with the most serious criminal records.

Actually, the basic idea underlying three strikes is nothing new. Most states have had some kind of repeat offender law for many decades. The first such law in the United States was passed in 1797. A famous 1926 New York law mandated life in prison for conviction to a third felony. A national survey of repeat offender laws by William F. McDonald in the mid-1980s found that they were "rarely used" and widely regarded as a "dead letter."[70] Forty-one states had some kind of repeat offender or habitual offender law on the books in February 1994, before the three-strikes movement took off.[71] Three-strikes laws raise the same questions we have already considered in this book. First, will a law in fact be implemented or simply evaded by the courtroom work group? Second, assuming it is implemented, what impact will it have on the criminal justice system? Third, will it reduce serious crime?

Implementation

With the exception of California, and to a certain extent Georgia, states have not used their three-strikes laws. An early study found that Wisconsin used its law only once in the first year and a half, while Tennessee, New Mexico, and Colorado did not use theirs at all.[72] Local prosecutors simply do not file the necessary charges. In some instances, the law becomes a plea bargaining tool. Many cases can be filed either as felonies or misdemeanors (say, misdemeanor assault versus felonious assault). The law gives the prosecutor a powerful weapon to get a guilty plea to a misdemeanor; in Sacramento, California, there were charge reductions in 67 percent of all the eligible cases. Even in California, application of the law varied tremendously. Two-thirds of all cases under the law originated in Los Angeles County. Officials in San Francisco, meanwhile, have publicly stated that they will not use it in certain kinds of cases, including drug cases.[73]

Impact on Crime

The California law was far more punitive and more far-reaching than the laws in other states. While the laws in most other states applied only to serious or violent offenses, the California law doubled the sentence length for *any* felony conviction if the offender had one prior serious or violent felony conviction. Another provision mandated a 25-year-to-life sentence for any felony conviction if the offender had two prior serious or violent felony convictions. Finally, "strikers," people convicted under the law, are not eligible for parole until they have served 80 percent of their sentence.

What happened? Did the law reduce serious crime as its supporters promised? Did it cause huge backlogs in criminal courts as its opponents warned? What was the fiscal impact on the state? In 2004, to mark the tenth anniversary of the California law, the Justice Policy Institute (JPI) undertook an evaluation of the law's impact.[74]

First, the law did send a lot of people to prison for long terms. By 2004 over 42,000 strikers were serving terms in California prisons, about 25 percent of all prisoners.

Second, the law did not send as many people to prison as had been expected. The California Department of Corrections had projected an additional 80,000 prisoners by 1999. Nor did the dollar cost of the law reach the $4.5 to $6.5 billion level estimated by the Rand Corporation.

The law was simply not implemented in most counties. Across the state, prosecutors, with the obvious support of other members of their courtroom work groups, used their discretion to not invoke the law (see our discussion in Chapter 3).

Third, consistent with the "bait and switch" problem we discussed in Chapter 1, the law weighed most heavily on the less serious offenders. The number of third strikers grew from 254 in 1994 to 7,234 in September 2003, but the number of second strikers soared from 4,154 in 1994 to 35,211 in September 2003. The JPI concluded that "[t]he Three Strikes law has a disproportionate effect on people convicted of non-violent offenses." Almost two-thirds (64.5 percent) of second and third strikers were in prison for a nonviolent offense.[75]

The law also compounded the racial disparities in the California justice system. The JPI found that the African American incarceration rate for third strikes (143 per 100,000 African American residents) was 12 times higher than the third-strike incarceration rate for whites (12 per 100,000 white residents). Latinos were only moderately affected by the law.

Most important from our standpoint, the three-strikes law did not produce a reduction in crime. The JPI report summarized several other studies. Stolzenberg and D'Alessio (1997) found that the law did not reduce Index crimes in the California Crime Index below the level that would have been expected given the downward trend that had begun before the law was enacted.[76]

In their book *Punishment and Democracy: Three Strikes and You're Out in California*, Franklin Zimring and his colleagues argue that even if fully applied, the law would have only a modest impact on crime. They estimate that even if all the arrestees who were eligible under the law "were to disappear from the earth without a trace," the result would be only a 10.6 percent reduction in felonies.[77]

The failure of the law to reduce crime was also confirmed by cross-state comparisons. States without three-strikes laws experienced a greater average drop in violent crime in the 1990s than states with such laws.

Additionally, in 2000, California voters passed Proposition 36, the Substance Abuse and Crime Prevention Act, which required that drug possession offenders be eligible for drug treatment instead of prison. This included offenders who were three strikes–eligible and had been out of prison for five years.

Summary: Striking Out

Three-strikes laws represent all the worst aspects of the "get tough" approach to crime. First, they are a classic example of overreaction to celebrated cases. Second, they represent a crude, meat-ax policy that sweeps up many nondangerous criminals. Third, they are not consistently implemented and thus increase the arbitrariness of the administration of justice. Fourth, they upset the normal going rate and impose new costs on local criminal justice systems, including more trials, delays, and greater dollar costs. Finally, no clear evidence indicates that they will reduce serious crime (and some good evidence shows that they incarcerate a lot of people who will not commit any crimes at all).

Rereading today William F. McDonald's 1986 report on the old repeat offender laws is a sobering experience. In effect, McDonald predicted all of the problems associated with three-strikes laws. Surveying all of the states with such laws, he found: "Only a small fraction of eligible habitual offenders have been or are currently being sentenced as such." McDonald interviewed members of the courtroom work group (prosecutors, defense attorneys, judges) and found a general perception that "prior criminality is already being taken proper account of under the normal sentencing structure."[78] In short, as we argued in Chapter 3, the prevailing going rate did allow serious offenders to avoid significant punishment. For the most part, the old repeat offender laws were used as plea bargaining tools. Not surprisingly, prosecutors gave the laws generally favorable ratings, while defense attorneys and judges were highly critical.

McDonald's report also anticipated the conceptual confusion that surrounds three-strikes laws. The old repeat offender laws failed to distinguish among seriousness, repetitiveness, intensity, and dangerousness. *Seriousness* refers to gravity of the particular crimes, including both the immediate crime for which an offender is being prosecuted and past crimes. *Repetitiveness* refers to a defendant's prior record or criminal career. *Intensity* refers to the rate at which a defendant has committed crimes in the past, as in the annual offending rate. *Dangerousness,* meanwhile, represents a predictive assessment of the amount of harm an offender might do to the community. McDonald found that practitioners believed that the old laws often sentenced offenders who were "not truly dangerous predators but comparatively petty offenders."[79] As we have seen, three-strikes laws are blunt instruments that often result in the incarceration of persons convicted of relatively less serious offenses but whose records happen to fit a mechanical formula.

> ## PROPOSITION 23
> **Three strikes and you're out laws are a terrible crime policy.**

CONCLUSION

From a commonsense standpoint, lock 'em up strategies appear to be a simple and effective way to reduce crime. Unfortunately, it is not that simple in the real world of the criminal justice system. First, we cannot precisely identify the small group of high-rate offenders. Second, gross incapacitation policies create all sorts of problems in the justice system. Third, because of these problems, the courtroom work group often finds ways to evade extremely punitive laws. Fourth, no conclusive evidence indicates that locking up a lot of people actually produces the promised reductions in crime. Finally, even where some crime reduction does occur, it is not clear that it is worth the enormous dollar cost to society.

NOTES

1.   On the general subject of discretion, see Samuel Walker, *Taming the System: The Control of Discretion in Criminal Justice, 1950–1990* (New York: Oxford University Press, 1993).

2.   President's Task Force on Victims of Crime, *Final Report* (Washington, DC: Government Printing Office, 1982), p. 22.

3.   Caleb Foote, "The Coming Constitutional Crisis in Bail," *University of Pennsylvania Law Review* 113 (May 1965): 959–999 and (June 1965): 1125–185.

4.   *United States v. Salerno,* 481 U.S. 739 (1987).

5.   On the background of the bail issue, see Wayne Thomas, *Bail Reform in America* (Berkeley: University of California Press, 1976); Bureau of Justice Statistics, *Profile of Jail Inmates, 2002* (Washington, DC: Department of Justice, 2004). NCJ 201932.

6.   Caleb Foote, "Compelling Appearance in Court: Administration of Bail in Philadelphia," *University of Pennsylvania Law Review* 102 (1954): 1031–1079.

7.   Bureau of Justice Statistics, *Pretrial Release of Felony Defendants, 1992* (Washington, DC: Department of Justice, 1994).

8.   Thomas, *Bail Reform in America.*

9.   Ibid., p. 37; Bureau of Justice Statistics, *Profile of Jail Inmates, 2002.*

10. Bureau of Justice Statistics, *Pretrial Release of Felony Defendants, 1992* (Washington, DC: Department of Justice, 1994). NCJ 148818.

11. Bureau of Justice Statistics, *Felony Defendants in Large Urban Counties, 2000* (Washington, DC: Department of Justice, 2003). NCJ 202021.

12. John Goldkamp, "Danger and Detention: A Second Generation of Bail Reform," *Journal of Criminal Law and Criminology* 76 (Spring 1985): 1–74.

13. *Preventive Detention in the District of Columbia: The First Ten Months* (Washington, DC: Georgetown Institute of Criminal Law and Procedure, 1972); Thomas, *Bail Reform in America,* pp. 231–232.

14. Frederic Suffet, "Bail Setting: A Study of Courtroom Interaction," *Crime and Delinquency* 12 (1966): 318–331.

15. Bureau of Justice Statistics, *Felony Defendants in Large Urban Counties, 2000,* Table 16. 16. General Accounting Office, *Criminal Bail: How Bail Reform Is Working in Selected District Courts* (Washington, DC: Department of Justice, 1987); Bureau of Justice Statistics, *Pretrial Release and Detention: The Bail Reform Act of 1984* (Washington, DC: Department of Justice, 1988).

17. Thomas E. Scott, "Pretrial Detention under the Bail Reform Act of 1984: An Empirical Analysis," *American Criminal Law Review* 27.1 (1989): 1–51; Bureau of Justice Statistics, *Federal Pretrial Release and Detention, 1996* (Washington, DC: Department of Justice, 1999). NCJ 168635.

18. Bureau of Justice Statistics, *Pretrial Release and Detention,* Table 9; Bureau of Justice Statistics, *Sourcebook of Criminal Justice Statistics—1998* (Washington, DC: Department of Justice, 1996), p. 401.

19. Bureau of Justice Statistics, *Pretrial Release of Felony Defendants, 1992;* Bureau of Justice Statistics, *Felony Defendants in Large Urban Counties, 1994* (Washington, DC: Department of Justice, 1998). The 2000 report on felony defendants does not include these data.

20. Bureau of Justice Statistics, *Felony Defendants in Large Urban Counties, 2000,* Table 20.

21. William Rhodes, Raymond Hyatt, and Paul Scheiman, *Predicting Pretrial Misconduct with Drug Tests of Arrestees: Evidence from Six Sites* (Washington, DC: Department of Justice, 1996).

22. *Schall v. Martin,* 467 U.S. 253 (1984).

23. Jeffrey Fagan and Martin Guggenheim, "Preventive Detention and the Judicial Prediction of Dangerousness for Juveniles: A Natural Experiment," *Journal of Criminal Law and Criminology* 86.2 (1996): 415–448.

24. Ibid., pp. 445, 448.

25. Bureau of Justice Statistics, *Pretrial Release of Felony Defendants, 1992.*

26. Malcolm Feeley, *Court Reform on Trial* (New York: Basic Books, 1983).

27. Franklin E. Zimring and Gordon Hawkins, *Incapacitation: Penal Confinement and the Restraint of Crime* (New York: Oxford University Press, 1995).

28. James Q. Wilson, *Thinking about Crime* (New York: Basic Books, 1975), pp. 200–202

29. Peter Greenwood, *Selective Incapacitation* (Santa Monica, CA: Rand, 1982).

30. Ibid., xix.

31. Jan M. Chaiken and Marcia R. Chaiken, *Varieties of Criminal Behavior: Summary and Policy Implications* (Santa Monica, CA: Rand, 1982).

32. Alfred Blumstein, Jacqueline Cohen, Jeffrey Roth, and Christy Visher, eds., *Criminal Careers and "Career Criminals"* (Washington, DC: National Academy of Sciences, 1988).

33. Ibid., p. 59.

34. Ibid., p. 60.

35. Peter W. Greenwood and Susan Turner, *Selective Incapacitation Revisited: Why the High-Rate Offenders Are Hard to Predict* (Santa Monica, CA: Rand, 1987).

36. Ibid., Table 4.3.

37. Edna McConnell Clark Foundation, *Overcrowded Time* (New York: Author, 1982); Don C. Gibbons, *The Limits of Punishment as Social Policy* (San Francisco: National Council on Crime and Delinquency, 1988); Marc Mauer, *Americans Behind Bars: One Year Later* (Washington, DC: The Sentencing Project, 1992); Campaign for an Effective Crime Policy, *What Every Policymaker Should Know About Imprisonment and the Crime Rate* (Washington, DC: Author, 1995).

38. American Bar Association, *Standards for Criminal Justice,* "Sentencing Alternatives and Procedures," Standard 18–2.1 (Boston: Little, Brown, 1980), pp. 18–25.

39. Edwin W. Zedlewski, *Making Confinement Decisions* (Washington, DC: Department of Justice, 1987).

40. Franklin E. Zimring and Gordon E. Hawkins, "The New Mathematics of Imprisonment," *Crime and Delinquency* 34 (October 1988): 425–436. See also Zimring and Hawkins, *Incapacitation.*

41. Eric J. Scott, *Calls for Service* (Washington, DC: Department of Justice, 1981).

42. Zimring and Hawkins, *Incapacitation.*

43. Ibid., p. 126

44. Ibid., pp. 106–107.

45. Peter Finn, *Sex Offender Community Notification* (Washington, DC: Department of Justice, 1997). NCJ 162364.

46. Bureau of Justice Statistics, *Recidivism of Prisoners Released in 1994* (Washington, DC: Department of Justice, 2002), Table 9. NCJ 193427.

47. Richard G. Zevitz and Mary Ann Farkas, *Sex Offender Community Notification: Assessing the Impact in Wisconsin* (Washington, DC: Department of Justice, 2001). NCJ 179992.

48. Bureau of Justice Assistance, *National Assessment of Structured Sentencing* (Washington, DC: Department of Justice, 1996), pp. 24–25.

49. Campaign for an Effective Crime Policy, *The Impact of "Three Strikes and You're Out" Laws: What Have We Learned?* (Washington, DC: Author, 1996).

50. U.S. Department of Justice, *The Nation's Toughest Drug Law: Evaluating the New York Experience* (Washington, DC: Author, 1978).

51. Ibid., p. 18.

52. Bureau of Justice Statistics, *Drugs, Crime, and the Justice System* (Washington, DC: Department of Justice, 1992), p. 30.

53. Malcolm M. Feeley and Sam Hakim, "The Effect of 'Three Strikes and You're Out' on the Courts," in David Shichor and Dale K. Sechrest, eds., *Three Strikes and You're Out: Vengeance as Social Policy* (Thousand Oaks, CA: Sage, 1996), p. 141.

54. Bureau of Justice Statistics, *Prisoners in 2003* (Washington, DC: Department of Justice, 2004), Table 8. NCJ 205335.

55. Pamala Griset, "The Politics and Economics of Increased Correctional Discretion over Time Served: A New York Case Study," *Justice Quarterly* 12 (June 1995): 307–323.

56. Ibid., p. 316.

57. Ibid., p. 321.

58. Information on the 2004 changes in the Rockefeller Drug Law can be found on a number of websites. Excellent information can be found on the websites of the Drug Policy Alliance.

59. Bureau of Justice Statistics, *Sourcebook of Criminal Justice Statistics—1995* (Washington, DC: Department of Justice, 1996), pp. 472–473.

60. Barbara Meierhofer, *The General Effect of Mandatory Minimum Prison Terms* (Washington, DC: Department of Justice, 1992).

61. U.S. Sentencing Commission, *Federal Sentencing Guidelines Manual* (St. Paul, MN: West, 1990), p. 281.

62. Ilene H. Nagel and Stephen Schulhofer, "A Tale of Three Cities: An Empirical Study of Charging and Bargaining Practices Under the Federal Sentencing Guidelines," *Southern California Law Review* 66 (1992): 501–566.

63. U.S. Department of Justice, *Mandatory Sentencing: The Experience of Two States* (Washington, DC: Department of Justice, 1982).

64. Bureau of Justice Assistance, *National Assessment of Structure Sentencing,* p. 117.

65. Zimring and Hawkins, *Incapacitation.*

66. Michael Tonry, "Mandatory Penalties," in Michael Tonry, ed., *Crime and Justice: A Review of Research,* vol. 16 (Chicago: University of Chicago Press, 1992), p. 243.

67. A good collection of material on three-strikes laws is Shichor and Sechrest, eds., *Three Strikes and You're Out: Vengeance as Social Policy.*

68. Michael G. Turner, Jody Sundt, Brandon K. Applegate, and Francis T. Cullen, "'Three Strikes and You're Out'

Legislation: A National Assessment," *Federal Probation* 59 (September 1995): 16–35.

69. Jerome H. Skolnick, "Wild Pitch," *American Prospect* 17 (Spring 1994): 31–37; Shichor and Sechrest, *Three Strikes and You're Out;* John J. DiIulio, Jr., "Instant Replay," *American Prospect* 18 (Summer 1994): 12–18.

70. William F. McDonald, *Repeat Offender Laws in the United States: The Form, Use, and Perceived Value* (Washington, DC: Department of Justice, 1986), p. 5.

71. Bureau of Justice Assistance, *National Assessment of Structured Sentencing,* pp. 24–25; Turner et al., "'Three Strikes and You're Out' Legislation."

72. Campaign for an Effective Crime Policy, *Impact of "Three Strikes and You're Out" Laws.*

73. Ibid.

74. Scott Ehlers, Vincent Schiraldi, and Jason Ziedenberg, *Still Striking Out. Ten Years of California's Three Strikes* (Washington, DC: Justice Policy Institute, 2004). Available on the Justice Policy Institute website.

75. Ibid.

76. Lisa Stolzenberg and Stewart J. D'Alessio, "Three Strikes and You're Out: The Impact of California's New Mandatory Sentencing Law on Serious Crime Rates," *Crime and Delinquency* 43 (1997): 457–469.

77. Franklin E. Zimring, Gordon Hawkins, and Sam Hakim, *Punishment and Democracy: Three Strikes and You're Out in California* (New York: Oxford University Press, 2001).

78. McDonald, *Repeat Offender Laws in the United States,* abstract, n.p.

79. Ibid., pp. 7, 19.

8

Close the Loopholes

Conservatives believe that many dangerous criminals beat the system and escape punishment: Their cases are dismissed, they plead guilty to lesser offenses, or if convicted they are not sent to prison. As a result, they return to the streets and commit more crimes. A major part of the conservative crime control agenda, therefore, is to close these perceived loopholes in the criminal justice system.

PROSECUTE THE CAREER CRIMINAL

To make sure that the really dangerous criminals are punished, a number of prosecutors have created special *major-offender* or *career criminal programs*. The basic idea is to focus special attention on them to make sure they are prosecuted, convicted, and incarcerated. Like some of the other programs we have examined, this idea is based on Wolfgang's career criminal research (Chapter 4), which found that a very small group of career criminals are responsible for a high percentage of all serious crimes.

Getting Tough in San Diego

The San Diego Major Violator Unit targeted robbery and robbery-related homicide cases in which the defendant is charged with three or more separate robbery-related offenses or has been convicted of one or more serious offenses in the preceding ten years.[1] The individual prosecutor assigned a major-violator case follows it through to completion. This policy provides *continuity of prosecution,* which is designed to prevent mistakes that might result from passing a case from one prosecutor to another as it moves through the system from the initial charge to preliminary hearing and eventual disposition. It is also designed to help maintain close contact between the prosecutor and the victim and witnesses. (Witness problems are one of the main reasons that cases are dismissed.) Prosecutors are involved in the preparation of the presentence investigation (PSI) report, and they submit an independent sentence recommendation to the judge, often asking for a stiff sentence.

Like other career criminal programs, the San Diego Major Violator Unit includes restrictions on plea bargaining.[2] Prosecutors may not "charge bargain": they cannot accept a plea to a lesser offense but can accept a plea only to the top felony count. This is designed to prevent the defendant from avoiding prison by pleading to a misdemeanor or a lesser felony that would result in a sentence of probation or a short prison term.

Despite these special procedures, however, the San Diego Major Violator Unit had only a modest impact on the prosecution of career criminals. The reason is simple: Prosecutors were already very tough on serious crime. The Major Violator Unit won conviction in an impressive 91.5 percent of its cases. But San Diego prosecutors normally convicted 89.5 percent of all career criminals. The unit did increase the percentage of convicted offenders sent to prison, from 77.1 percent to 92.5 percent. But this change was less significant than it might appear. The percentage of convicted offenders who were incarcerated (either prison or jail) increased only slightly, from 95.3 percent to 100 percent.[3] These data illustrate the point we made in Chapters 2 and 3: The criminal justice system is very harsh on repeat offenders and offenders who have committed serious crimes.

The San Diego data illustrate another often misunderstood aspect of sentencing in America. The category of incarceration includes both sentences to prison and *split sentences,* in which the offender does some time in jail followed by release on probation. Split sentences are actually fairly common. In 2000, one-third of all convicted felons received a sentence of time in jail. In most jurisdictions these sentences are officially listed as probation (as opposed to prison). The net result is that in 2000, 73 percent of convicted felons were incarcerated (prison: 40 percent; jail: 33 percent; straight probation: 27 percent).[4]

These data on sentencing are extremely important in terms of public *perception* of how the system works. If you look only at the percentage of convicted offenders sentenced to prison (40 percent), the system looks somewhat weak. But when you include everyone who is incarcerated (73 percent), it looks a lot tougher. True, going to jail is not as serious as going to prison, but it is still an unpleasant experience, and these offenders are not beating the system.

The Major Violator Unit did double the average length of incarceration. In this respect it significantly increased the severity of punishment. But it is important to recall that the length of prison terms has been rising across the country (particularly for serious crimes), so some of the increase in San Diego probably would have occurred even without the Major Violator Unit.

The important question for us is whether the San Diego Major Violator Unit had any impact on the crime rate. The evaluation of the program did not address this question. Common sense, however, suggests that it could not have had any significant effect, because the changes in the percentage of offenders convicted and the percentage incarcerated were so small. True, there was an increase in incapacitation as a result of the longer prison terms. But as we learned in Chapter 7, there is no evidence that increasing incapacitation actually reduces crime.

Other Prosecution Programs

Special prosecution programs in other jurisdictions have produced results similar to those in San Diego. In Kalamazoo, Michigan, a special program raised conviction rates from 66.6 percent to 73.4; in New Orleans, they rose from 81.8 percent to 88.7 percent; and they went from 73.9 percent to 76.4 percent in Columbus, Ohio. Incarceration rates rose slightly in two of the cities but actually declined in New Orleans. Sentence lengths went up in two cities but went down in Kalamazoo.[5]

A Phoenix, Arizona, repeat offender program (ROP) involves police officers in the prosecution effort, working with prosecutors as a team. Detectives "walk" warrants or information about additional charges through the courts to ensure a high bond so that the defendant is not released before trial. They also attend trials inconspicuously and provide feedback to prosecutors about the reaction of jurors. ROP detectives also personally contact probation officers and provide information for the PSI report.

The results of the program were similar to those in San Diego. Over 98 percent of the ROP offenders were prosecuted, and 89.9 percent were convicted, but the figures for the control group were nearly identical: 98.9 percent prosecuted and 86.4 percent convicted. The percentage incarcerated was almost the same, although a slightly higher proportion were sent to prison rather than given a split sentence.[6]

These data on the prosecution of so-called career criminals confirm the points made in Chapters 2 and 3. First, the criminal justice system is generally tough on repeat offenders who have committed a serious crime. Second, these patterns of prosecution and sentencing reflect the going rate agreed upon informally by the local courtroom work group. In short, local prosecutors and judges, without the benefit of a special program, are generally very tough on major offenders.

Most people are surprised to find that the system is consistently tough on career criminals (a fact that a Sentencing Project report on public attitudes confirmed).[7] This misperception can be explained in terms of our criminal justice wedding cake (Chapter 2). Public perception is heavily influenced by a few celebrated cases in the top layer: the armed robber who got probation; the rapist who pled guilty to misdemeanor assault; the O. J. Simpson trial. The typical career criminal case, however, falls into the second layer: successful prosecution, conviction, and a prison term. Additional public misunderstanding arises from aggregating second- and third-layer felonies. The relatively softer treatment of third-layer cases masks the tough response to the career criminals in the second layer.

In the end, it turns out that the alleged loophole of being soft on dangerous offenders does not exist. The evidence does not support the widespread belief that there is a large loophole allowing major offenders to beat the system.

The evidence leads to the following proposition:

PROPOSITION 24
Career criminal prosecution programs do not produce either higher conviction rates or lower crime rates.

ABOLISH THE INSANITY DEFENSE

John W. Hinckley never succeeded at much in life, but he is singlehandedly responsible for some significant changes in American criminal justice. Hinckley's acquittal for the attempted assassination of President Ronald Reagan in 1981 sparked a national outcry over the insanity defense.[8] In the following years almost every state and the federal government changed its law on the insanity defense. Twelve states adopted a new "guilty but mentally ill" (GBMI) standard and five abolished the insanity defense altogether.[9] (A wealth of information about the Hinckley case, including a videotape of the shooting, materials from the trial, and a discussion of the impact of the case on the insanity defense is on the Web on the Famous American Trials project of the University of Missouri at Kansas City Law School.)

Hinckley's acquittal touched one of the raw nerves of public opinion: the sight of a guilty person "beating the rap" and "getting off" because of a "technicality." There was no question that John Hinckley shot and wounded the president; the videotape was broadcast on television all across the country. People were outraged over the Hinckley verdict of not guilty by reason of insanity (NGRI), which appeared to let him off. The fact is that he was institutionalized—in a hospital rather than a prison. He remains there today, although in 1999 he was granted the right to supervised visits to his parents, and in 2000 gained longer unsupervised visits. His notoriety has probably kept him there longer than if he had shot an ordinary person, pled guilty, and gone to prison.

For many people, the insanity defense is the classic loophole. It conjures up images of criminally insane persons roaming the streets in search of more victims. Insanity defense proceedings also anger many people. The parade of psychiatrists and expert witnesses on both sides of the case creates the impression that you can always find an expert somewhere to say what you want said. Like the O. J. Simpson trial, the Hinckley case supports the impression that the wealthy can buy lawyers and experts who will win them acquittal. In one public opinion survey, 87 percent of the respondents felt that the insanity defense was a loophole; about 40 percent called it the "rich person's defense."[10]

The conservative response is to try to close the loophole. Changes in the law over the past two decades fall into six categories: (1) abolishing the insanity defense altogether; (2) changing the test of insanity; (3) shifting the burden of proof to the defendant (instead of the state having to prove criminal intent, the defendant has to prove mental illness); (4) creating a new "guilty but mentally ill" verdict; (5) revising trial procedure for raising an insanity plea; raised; and (6) changing procedures for committing a person found not guilty by reason of insanity.[11]

Sorting Out the Issues

To make sense of changes in the law on the insanity defense we need to sort out four separate issues. The first concerns the extent of the use of the defense. How many criminal defendants successfully win verdicts of not guilty by reason of insanity? A second issue involves the fate of those who do win acquittal. Do they return to the streets? How soon? Do they endanger the public? The third issue is predicting dangerousness. If some offenders are dangerous, how can we identify them? How can we tell when it is safe to release them? The fourth issue is the effect of abolishing the insanity defense. What is the impact on crime and the criminal justice system?

The Reality of the Insanity Defense

Despite all the attention it receives, the insanity defense is very rarely used successfully. Very few defendants even try to use it, and not many of them succeed. Studies have consistently found that the insanity defense is raised in less than 1 percent of all criminal indictments, and only between 15 and 25 percent of those efforts are successful.[12] Henry J. Steadman and his colleagues, for example, found that in four states (California, Georgia, Montana, New York), the insanity defense was *raised* in slightly less than 1 percent (0.90 percent) of all felony indictments, and only about 23 percent of these *succeeded* in getting an NGRI verdict.[13] The American Psychiatric Association Insanity Defense Work Group concluded, "While philosophically important for the criminal law, the insanity defense is *empirically unimportant* (involving a fraction of 1 percent of all felony cases)".[14]

The extent of public misunderstanding about the frequency of the insanity defense is extraordinary. An Illinois poll found that people believed nearly 40 percent of all criminal defendants used the insanity defense. This misunderstanding explains the fact that nearly half of the respondents wanted the insanity defense abolished.[15]

Given how infrequently the insanity defense is successfully used, closing this alleged loophole would have no noticeable impact on the crime rate. Additionally, there would be absolutely no impact on robbery and burglary cases, since the insanity defense is most often raised in murder cases. The few successful insanity defense cases are the classic celebrated cases in the top layer of the criminal justice wedding cake. They are completely unrepresentative and tell us nothing about how most serious crimes are routinely handled.

When the insanity defense is successfully used, it is usually the result of a plea bargain or a stipulated finding. That is, the prosecutor, defense attorney, medical experts, and judge all agree that the defendant is indeed mentally ill. This is another example of the courtroom work group in operation: settling cases through mutual agreement. A study of 60,432 felony indictments in Baltimore, Maryland, in 1991 found that the insanity defense was raised in only 190 cases; it was eventually dropped in 182 cases, and the remaining eight defendants were stipulated mentally ill by both prosecution and defense.[16] This is not a picture of innumerable dangerous criminals beating the system.

Another popular myth about the insanity defense is that the people who use it are violent and dangerous. Not all of the defendants committed to mental health institutions by way of an insanity verdict have committed a violent offense, however. Of the 500 men in the Bridgewater (Massachusetts) State Hospital for the Criminally Insane, more than 100 had been charged with vagrancy.[17] These people are not dangerous sociopaths. Many are pathetic individuals who have serious mental health problems and cannot cope with their lives. Most sank through the various safety nets and ended up on skid row, where they finally were arrested.[18]

Aftermath of Acquittal

What happens to defendants who are committed to mental institutions after winning not guilty by reason of insanity verdicts is a matter of much controversy. Liberals generally contend that they are likely to spend more time in a mental hospital than if they had been found guilty of the crime and sent to prison. Conservatives argue that they get out too soon.

In the past, there was some truth to the liberal argument. Many allegedly mentally ill people were hospitalized for years, even decades, without any treatment or any evidence that they were really dangerous. Supreme Court decisions and new state laws, however, have led to greater protection of the rights of the confined.[19] One of the most important is a mental patient's right to periodic review of his or her condition to determine whether continued confinement is justified. The landmark case of *Baxstrom v. Herold* (1966) forced the release of persons held for long periods of time in the New York State Hospital for the Criminally Insane and necessitated the development of new procedures for continued confinement.[20]

Nonetheless, persons hospitalized after being found not guilty by reason of insanity still spend more time confined in hospitals than comparable offenders spend in prison after being found guilty of the crime. Henry Steadman and his associates found that in New York, 88 percent of all NGRIs were hospitalized; of the 12 percent immediately released, a disproportionate share were women. Those who were charged with murder but found not guilty by reason of insanity spent an average of 6.4 years in the hospital; those acquitted of other violent crimes were hospitalized for an average of 5.2 years; and for nonviolent crimes, hospital stays averaged 2.8 years. For all the crimes except murder, these terms of confinement were longer than for offenders found guilty of similar crimes.[21]

In an earlier study, Steadman studied a group of defendants found incompetent to stand trial to see whether they "beat the rap." A defendant who is too mentally ill to comprehend the nature of a criminal trial is committed to an institution until he or she is able to understand the proceedings, at which point the criminal process resumes. Steadman found that those defendants deemed "nondangerous" spent less than two years in mental institutions, whereas the "dangerous" were confined an average of two years and two months. If they were subsequently convicted at trial, they faced the possibility of additional prison time. Do you beat the rap by taking the mental health route? Steadman argues not: "Mental hospitals are simply an alternative place to do time."[22] In short, the system is not turning hordes of dangerous psychotics loose on society.

Danger to the Community

How dangerous are the criminally insane? We have had some natural experiments on this question as a result of court decisions that forced the release of criminal defendants. A 1971 decision forced the clinical reassessment of 586 inmates of Pennsylvania's Fairview State Hospital for the Criminally Insane. More than two-thirds were eventually released. Over the next four years, 27 percent were rearrested, but only 11 percent for a violent crime. Including some others who were rehospitalized for a violent act, a total of 14.5 percent of those released proved to be dangerous.[23] A recent review of the literature concluded that the recidivism rate for persons acquitted by reason of insanity was "no greater than that of felons.[24]

Once again we encounter our old friend the prediction problem from Chapter 4. A decision to release or confine a person alleged to be criminally insane involves a prediction about his or her future behavior. Do they pose a danger to the community? The success rate in predicting the dangerousness of the criminally insane is no better than in other areas of criminal justice. Because only 14.5 percent of the Fairview inmates committed another violent act, you could argue that the experts were wrong about the other 85.5 percent. This translates into six false positives (people unnecessarily locked up) for each true positive.

The Impact of Abolition

For many people, "abolishing" the insanity defense (like "abolishing" plea bargaining) is a slogan. As we have seen, changing the law on the insanity defense can be done six different ways. Each of these changes involves complex legal and practical problems.

Abolishing or modifying the insanity defense raises fundamental issues about the criminal law. Our justice system rests on the principle that the accused is innocent until proven guilty and that the prosecution must prove guilt beyond a reasonable doubt. To prove guilt, the prosecution must establish three things: The accused committed the act (*actus reus*), the accused had criminal intent (*mens rea*), and a connection exists between the two (that is, the accused did it and intended to do it).[25]

The key issue with the insanity defense is the *mens rea* requirement. The criminal law has long recognized different degrees of intent. The law distinguishes between a planned murder (first degree) and one committed in the heat of passion (second degree). It further recognizes that some homicides occur without any criminal intent (manslaughter). Differences in the degree of intent are reflected in the severity of the punishment. First-degree murder carries a potential death sentence in many states.

The law has historically recognized that some people lack full criminal intent because they do not understand what they are doing. We readily accept the idea that the 5-year-old who picks up the loaded handgun and accidentally kills his brother does not have criminal intent. He simply does not understand the nature and consequences of firing the gun. Another example is the truly deranged person who kills because he or she hears voices from another planet. Like the child, this person does not appreciate the criminal nature of her act.[26]

Unfortunately, not all cases are as simple as these examples. The legal system has struggled for 150 years to develop a formula for resolving questions about the accused's mental state. The principle of insanity first entered English law in 1843 with the famous *M'Naughton* case, which established the "right-wrong test": Did the accused understand the difference between right and wrong? Because this test is somewhat crude, legal scholars have attempted to develop alternatives, such as the "irresistible impulse" test. Laypersons are often mystified by the arcane distinctions among those alternatives, none of which resolves the basic problem created by the intersection of medical diagnoses, with their inevitable shades of gray, and the legal system, with its requirement of an absolute verdict of guilt or innocence.[27]

Attempts to abolish the insanity defense run up against the *mens rea* requirement. Suppose a state adopted a law that said "mental condition shall not be a defense to any charge of criminal conduct." This might be interpreted as abolishing the *mens rea* requirement altogether. The prosecution would not have to prove anything about the accused's mental state, only that he or she did the crime. Among other things, it would wipe out the distinction between first-degree murder, second-degree murder, and manslaughter. It is doubtful that even the most ardent opponents of the insanity defense seriously want to take this approach, which would probably be found unconstitutional. Wisconsin (1909) and Mississippi (1928) abolished the insanity defense early in this century. In both cases, the new laws were declared unconstitutional under the due process clauses of their state constitutions.[28]

A more limited interpretation of the law that mental condition shall not be a defense to any charge of criminal conduct would be that an affirmative plea of not guilty by reason of insanity could not be raised. The crucial distinction here is between affirmative and ordinary defenses. An *ordinary defense* is simply an attempt to show that the prosecution has failed to connect the accused with the crime. An *affirmative defense* is that, yes, the accused did kill the victim and intended to, but he or she does not have criminal responsibility for the act (because of self-defense, duress, insanity).

What would happen if we abolished insanity as an affirmative defense? As a recent review of the literature pointed out, we have little empirical evidence on this question, because so few states (five) have actually abolished the insanity defense and also because there are so few cases. Put yourself in the shoes of a defense attorney, and the answer is obvious. You would directly attack the prosecution's case on the basic *mens rea* requirement and argue that your client lacked the necessary criminal intent. You would not win every time, of course, but you might win some of the time, with the net result that your client would be fully acquitted. The people who oppose the insanity defense would find this outcome even more outrageous than our current situation. Even if you did not win, you would force the prosecution to address your client's mental state. In short, the basic issues underlying the insanity defense would reappear in a different form. There is no getting around it; the *mens rea* requirement is a bedrock principle of our legal system.

The GBMI alternative has three serious flaws. First, it strikes indirectly at the *mens rea* requirement, introducing the slippery notion that the accused had partial, but not complete, criminal intent. Second, it creates a lesser and included offense that judges and juries may choose simply as a compromise verdict. They may decide that the accused probably did something wrong and deserves some punishment, but they are unwilling to bring in a verdict of guilty on the top charge. The GBMI option would allow them to split the difference and choose the lesser verdict. Finally, the GBMI verdict does not guarantee treatment for the person who has been declared mentally ill.

Prisons and jails, many of which are overcrowded, cannot handle their current inmates with mental problems. A 2000 Bureau of Justice Statistics survey found that 16 percent of state prison inmates were receiving some treatment for mental illness; 10 percent were receiving some medication (in five states 20 percent were on medication).[29] State prison systems spend an average of only about 10 percent of their budgets on all forms of health care; obviously only a small part of those expenditures involve *mental* health care.[30]

For the GBMI offenders, we can imagine the sequence of events. The convicted offender is sentenced to prison, where his behavior becomes a problem. He is then transferred to the state mental hospital for treatment. After his behavior stabilizes, he is transferred back to prison, where because of the brutal conditions his behavior again deteriorates. The cycle then repeats itself. This is not to suggest that our mental hospitals are models of effective treatment and humane custody. They are not, and much of the "treatment" is meaningless. But sending an allegedly mentally ill person to prison is an even worse solution.

The GBMI option has already proved to be a bogus reform. A 1981 Illinois law added GBMI as an additional verdict, retaining the traditional insanity defense. In Cook County (Chicago), NGRI verdicts actually increased from 34 to 103 between 1981 and 1984. At the same time, GBMI verdicts went from

16 in 1982, the first year the option was available, to 87 in 1984. This represents a variation on the "bait and switch" problem that we discussed in Chapter 1, whereby a new law is advertised as affecting one category of crime but actually affects other less serious ones. GBMI verdicts appear to have involved people who would otherwise have been found guilty, not defendants who would have been found not guilty by reason of insanity.[31]

The Illinois GBMI law also failed to provide medical treatment for GBMI defendants. An evaluation found that "not a single GBMI offender has been transferred from the Department of Corrections to the Department of Mental Health" for treatment. The law only "complicated rather than resolved [the] fundamental issues surrounding the insanity defense."[32] A study of the GBMI verdict in another state reached similar conclusions: There was no reduction in the number of insanity pleas, jurors were more likely to be confused about the legal issues, many offenders receiving a GBMI verdict were placed on probation, and offenders had no assurance that they would receive any medical treatment.[33]

The real function of the guilty but mentally ill option is symbolic, to appease public opinion. The public has little concern for the details of what actually happens to a mentally ill criminal defendant. Basically, it wants a symbolic statement of guilty. In practice, as Richard Moran points out, the GBMI verdict has as much meaning as "guilty but brown eyes."[34]

In sum, the various proposals to abolish or modify the insanity defense fail on two counts. Not only do they fail to reduce crime, because the insanity defense is so rare, but they create new problems for the criminal justice system. The evidence is overwhelming that the insanity defense is not a loophole that allows thousands of dangerous offenders to beat the system. This leads us to conclude:

PROPOSITION 25

Abolishing or limiting the insanity defense
will have no impact on serious crime.

Richard Moran offers the best verdict on this issue: "The insanity defense has been misinterpreted and abused"—not by criminal defendants but "by politicians and journalists who mistakenly attack it as a major loophole in the law."[35] A review of attempts to revise or abolish the insanity defense over the past 20 years concluded that all of these changes have had "little effect," in large part because "there is no real evidence that it is broken."[36]

ABOLISH PLEA BARGAINING

Everyone seems to dislike plea bargaining. Conservatives believe it is a major loophole through which criminals beat the system and avoid punishment. Liberals, meanwhile, believe that it is the source of grave injustices: with prosecutors offering better deals to some types of defendants than others; with defense attorneys making private deals with prosecutors rather than fighting for their clients; and with defendants being coerced into waiving their right to a trial.[37]

In many instances, the process of plea bargaining makes a mockery of justice. In court the judge goes through the charade of asking the defendant whether any promises have been made in return for the guilty plea, and the defendant answers no. But, of course, a deal has been made.[38]

For a few years in the 1970s, there were loud calls to abolish plea bargaining. Public outrage reached its peak in 1973, when Vice President Spiro Agnew, in perhaps the most famous plea bargain of all time, avoided going to prison on extortion charges by pleading no contest to a lesser charge. In 1973 the National Advisory Commission on Criminal Justice Standards and Goals recommended that plea bargaining be abolished within five years.[39] Plea bargaining, of course, continues. In 2000, 95 percent of all felony cases in large urban counties were settled by a guilty plea (up from 91 percent in 1996).[40] When we take a closer look at plea bargaining, including some of the attempts to abolish it, we can understand why.

Alaska Bans Plea Bargaining

The most celebrated attempt to abolish plea bargaining occurred in Alaska, when Attorney General Avrum Gross abolished plea bargaining in the entire state.[41] On July 3, 1975, he issued a memorandum that read, in part,:

> I wish to have the following policy implemented with respect to all adult criminal offenses in which charges have been filed on or after August 15, 1975:

> 1) District Attorneys and Assistant District Attorneys will refrain from engaging in plea negotiations with defendants designed to arrive at an agreement for entry of a plea of guilty in return for a particular sentence. . . . (4) . . . While there continues to be nothing wrong with reducing a charge, reductions should not occur simply to obtain a plea of guilty. (5) Like any general rule, there are going to be some exceptions to this policy [which must be approved by the attorney general's office].

The new policy attacked plea bargaining in three ways: forbidding "sentence bargaining" and "charge bargaining," and establishing procedures for supervising plea negotiations. Gross's action was possible in part because of the special structure of Alaska's criminal justice system. Local prosecutors are appointed by and work under the supervision of the state attorney general. In other states, local prosecutors are elected and enjoy almost complete political and administrative independence.

What happened when Alaska banned plea bargaining? Contrary to popular expectations, the criminal courts did not collapse. The traditional defense of plea bargaining is that it is necessary to handle the heavy load of cases and that the courts will grind to a halt if it is abolished. The Alaska courts, however, continued to function pretty much as they had before. Additionally, there was little change in the rate of guilty pleas. Trials increased, from 6.7 to only 9.6 percent of all cases.[42]

Other dire predictions also did not come true in Alaska. Many experts argue that discretion cannot be eliminated and that attempts to abolish it only serve to move it to other parts of the justice system. Restricting a prosecutor's discretion to accept guilty pleas, according to this argument, will shift discretion "upstream" to police officers or "downstream" to judges.[43] Specifically, some experts believe that banning plea bargaining will give judges more discretion and lead to more sentence bargaining.

No radical shift in discretion occurred as a result of the ban in Alaska. One way to measure this effect is to examine the pattern of rejections and dismissals of cases. Some experts believe that if a prosecutor cannot settle cases by accepting pleas to lesser offenses, more cases will be dismissed altogether. The rate of dismissals in Alaska, however, remained consistently high: about 52 percent before and after the ban. Dismissals in drug possession and morals cases increased, but this seemed to be a function of the low priority prosecutors gave these cases rather than anything related to the ban on plea bargaining.[44]

One surprising result of the ban was that cases actually moved through the courts faster than before. This was contrary to the expectation that there would be more delay because of more trials and a greater backlog of cases. In Anchorage, the mean disposition time for felony cases was cut in half, dropping from 192.1 months to 89.5 months. Case processing time also dropped in Fairbanks and Juneau. We can explain this unexpected outcome. Restrictions on plea bargaining eliminate certain alternatives and uncertainties about which one to choose. With less to negotiate, the prosecutor and defense attorney reach agreements more quickly. Or to put it another way, the courtroom work group has a smaller menu to choose from.[45]

For our purposes, the most significant result was that the ban on plea bargaining had no impact on cases involving defendants charged with serious crimes or those with substantial criminal records. An evaluation concluded that "the conviction and sentencing of persons charged with serious crimes of violence such as murder, rape, robbery, and felonious assault appeared completely unaffected by the change in policy." In short, dangerous offenders had not been beating the system beforehand through plea bargaining (any more than they had in San Diego), and the ban did not change that.

The ban did, however, have an unexpected effect on less serious cases, and resulted in more severe sentences. This is another variation of the "bait and switch" problem. Our wedding cake model helps explain this process. Policies directed toward second-layer cases actually have their greatest impact on third-layer cases. As Zimring and Hawkins argue, "bait and switch" occurs when a new policy promises to deal with serious crime but ends up affecting mainly less serious ones.[46] Under normal circumstances, third-layer cases—low-level assaults or burglaries where little of value is stolen—are often settled with pleas to even lesser offenses and sentences of probation. A "get tough" policy, such as a ban on plea bargaining, however, closes off this avenue of mitigation and produces both convictions on more serious charges and harsher sentences than would normally be the case. Third-layer cases are moved into the second layer, where they are treated more harshly. The problem, of course, is that these third-layer cases were not the original target of the policy change, and there is no impact on serious crime.

From the standpoint of our inquiry, the important question is whether the Alaska ban on plea bargaining affected the crime rate. The evaluation did not examine this issue. Nonetheless, the mere fact that the ban had no real effect on the disposition of cases involving serious crimes suggests that it probably had no impact on the crime rate.

Other Experiments

Other attempts to ban plea bargaining have focused on specific crimes. When Michigan enacted a law mandating prison terms for people convicted of gun-related crimes ("one with a gun gets you two"), the Wayne County (Detroit) prosecutor supplemented it with a ban on plea bargaining. They would no longer drop gun-related charges in return for a guilty plea. This seemed to be an important step, because many people believe that weapons charges are frequently dropped in return for a plea to a nongun charge (for example, from armed robbery to simple robbery) as a way of avoiding a prison sentence. Some people believe this is how mandatory sentencing laws are evaded.[47]

An evaluation of the Michigan law found no significant change in the minimum sentences for homicide and armed robbery cases. The going rate for armed robbery was about six years in prison both before and after the law's passage. In other words, Wayne County prosecutors had not been lenient in plea bargaining with defendants charged with robbery beforehand. Once again, there was no loophole to be closed.

The Michigan policy also had a "bait and switch" effect, however. Defendants charged with aggravated assault began to receive higher minimum sentences. Why? Prosecutors had previously treated aggravated assaults as third-layer cases, accepting pleas to lesser charges. The new law closed off this avenue and (as in Alaska) produced convictions on higher charges and longer sentences.

In Search of Plea Bargains

Plea bargaining has proven to be a phantom loophole. Despite the criticisms, it is not a device by which large numbers of serious offenders are beating the system. Attempts to abolish it either have no effect whatsoever or produce changes that are contrary to the intended result.

Our discussions of the criminal justice wedding cake (Chapter 2) and the role of the courtroom work group (Chapter 3) help explain why plea bargaining survives. As Malcolm Feeley suggests, we should think of the criminal courts as *supermarkets,* handling a high volume of business with fixed prices.[48] Once the work group reaches a consensus about the proper "going rate" for different kinds of cases, not much actual bargaining is necessary. A National Center for State Courts report characterizes this consensus as a shared "norm of proportionality" about the seriousness and worth of different cases.[49]

Virtually all of the studies of plea bargaining have found a high degree of regularity and predictability in the disposition of cases. One of the most systematic studies concluded that you can predict the outcome if you know the seriousness of the top charge and the defendant's prior record.[50]

Courtroom work groups have accommodated themselves to sentencing guideline laws. Many observers have feared that by restricting the discretion of judges, these laws would radically shift power to prosecutors and result in more charge bargaining and/or more trials. Studies of the impact of sentencing guideline jurisdictions, however, have found that most courtroom work groups conduct their business pretty much as before, with relatively little change.[51] This is but another example of both the enduring strength of routine plea bargaining practices and the power of the courtroom work group to accommodate major change.

The evidence is overwhelming: Plea bargaining is not a loophole that lets many dangerous offenders beat the system. Therefore, we can safely conclude:

PROPOSITION 26

Abolishing plea bargaining will not reduce serious crime.

RESTRICT APPEALS

Conservatives believe that post-conviction appeals undermine the criminal justice system in several ways. First, some offenders win and thereby escape punishment altogether. Second, appeals delay final resolution of a case and undermine the deterrent effect of the law. Deterrence theorists believe that punishment must be swift and certain for the deterrent effect to work. Third, appeals transform the criminal process into a "sporting contest," a game rather than a search for truth. Liberals, on the other hand, see the absence of finality as a virtue. Protection of individual rights requires recognition of the possibility of error in the criminal justice process.[52]

Years ago, Judge Macklin Fleming argued that granting numerous postconviction appeals represented a quixotic search for "perfect justice."[53] He listed 26 possible challenges available in California on search-and-seizure grounds alone, including moving for dismissal of all charges at the preliminary examination; appealing a denial of that motion to the state supreme court; moving to have the case transferred to federal court on grounds that federal civil rights had been violated; objecting to admission of the evidence at trial; if convicted, appealing for postconviction relief in the state supreme court; and if that failed, appealing the conviction in federal court.

Nor is this all. Fleming points out that "in almost every one of the foregoing steps the losing defendant can petition for a rehearing or reconsideration by the court that ruled against him."[54] Thus, innumerable potential challenges to a criminal charge can be made just on Fourth Amendment search-and-seizure issues. If these fail, many postconviction appeals are possible—for example, on grounds of inadequate assistance of counsel in violation of the Sixth Amendment. For the imaginative and determined offender, the possibilities are seemingly endless. As we shall see, however, the key word here is *seemingly.*

Limiting Appeals

Conservatives believe that limiting appeals will close a loophole that undermines the criminal justice system. The 1981 Attorney General's Task Force on Violent Crime recommended a three-year statute of limitations on habeas corpus petitions and a prohibition on federal courts' holding evidentiary hearings "on facts which were fully expounded and found in the state court proceeding."[55]

Habeas corpus is one of the cornerstones of Anglo-American law. The British Parliament formalized it with the Habeas Corpus Act of 1679, and Americans wrote it into the U.S. Constitution. Article III, Section 9, of the Constitution reads, "The privilege of the writ of habeas corpus shall not be suspended, unless when in case of rebellion or invasion the public safety may require it." The writ of habeas corpus is a device to challenge the detention of a person taken into custody. A person under arrest or in prison may demand an evidentiary hearing before a judge to examine the legality of the detention. The writ of habeas corpus is purely procedural: It guarantees only a right to a hearing and says nothing about the substance of the issues in the case.

The Supreme Court greatly expanded the ability of an offender convicted in a state court to obtain a rehearing in federal court in the 1963 decision *Fay v. Noia.*[56] One of the underlying issues here is the role of the Supreme Court in a federal system. Conservatives have long argued that the Court, particularly under Chief Justice Earl Warren, intruded into matters that should be left to the states and to legislatures. Liberals, on the other hand, saw the Court as the principal guardian of individual rights.

The Reality of Postconviction Appeals

In actual practice, postconviction appeals play a very minor role in the administration of criminal justice. A national study of 10,000 habeas corpus petitions filed in federal district courts by offenders challenging their convictions found that only 1 percent succeeded. Federal judges dismissed 63 percent (usually for failing to exhaust state remedies) and ruled against the offender on the merits of the case in 35 percent. The typical habeas corpus petition was filed by someone convicted of a violent offense (23 percent had been convicted of murder) and sentenced to a long prison term. The most frequent claim raised was ineffective assistance of counsel.[57]

How many convicted offenders "abuse" the right to appeal? The study found a rate of 14 habeas corpus petitions for every 1,000 prisoners—or only 1.4 percent of all imprisoned offenders. This figure confirms what we have already learned: that most convictions are obtained through plea bargains in which the facts of the case are not seriously contested. The study also found that the impact of habeas corpus petitions on the workload of the courts has been greatly exaggerated. These appeals represented only 4 percent of the civil case filings in U.S. District Courts.

In short, Macklin Fleming's nightmare vision of convicted offenders endlessly filing appeals on all of the theoretically possible issues is pure fantasy. Appeal of felony convictions through habeas corpus petitions is very much like the insanity defense: a procedure that raises a lot of fascinating legal issues but is rarely used in practice and rarely successful even when tried. There are two important exceptions to this rule. People on death row do exhaust every possible appeal, and appeals may drag on for 15 years or longer. The fact is that mistakes do occur with the death penalty. In early 2000, the governor of Illinois ordered a halt to all executions in the state because 13 people sentenced to die had their convictions overturned—as many as had actually been executed since the death penalty was restored in that state. The possibility that innocent people might be wrongfully executed dramatizes the importance of keeping open all possible avenues of appeal.

A second exception involves the "writ writers," prisoners who file innumerable appeals in federal court challenging their conviction or prison conditions. These individuals represent a tiny proportion of all inmates. The few who succeed in winning their release make a negligible contribution to the crime rate, even in the worst circumstances.

The available facts about the use of appeals do not support the conservative argument that multiple appeals contribute to crime. Conservatives argue that appeals delay "finality" and thereby undermine the deterrent effect of the criminal process. Several things are wrong with this argument. First, appeals are filed in so few cases that they cannot have any broad impact on criminal justice. Second, as we have also learned, many factors affect the deterrent effect (low probability of arrest, a relatively high probability of the charges being rejected or dismissed, whether the threat of punishment even works for certain categories of offenders, and so forth). Appeals are at best a very minor factor.

Like the insanity defense, postconviction appeals are mainly a *symbolic* issue. On occasion, a convicted offender is released through a successful appeal. But these are the few celebrated cases that do not represent the general pattern in the criminal justice system. Therefore, our proposition is:

PROPOSITION 27

Limiting habeas corpus appeals of criminal
convictions will have no effect on serious crime.

CONCLUSION

We will not reduce serious crime by trying to close alleged loopholes in the criminal justice system. The reason for this is simple: Those loopholes do not exist. The idea that thousands of criminals beat the system through the insanity defense, or plea bargaining, or some other loophole is a perception based in a very small number of unrepresentative celebrated cases. The justice system is actually fairly harsh in dealing with those serious offenders who are arrested.

NOTES

1. U.S. Department of Justice, *An Exemplary Project: Major Violator Unit—San Diego, California* (Washington, DC: Department of Justice, 1980).

2. Some examples are described in William F. McDonald, *Plea Bargaining: Critical Issues and Current Practices* (Washington, DC: Department of Justice, 1985).

3. McDonald, *Plea Bargaining.*

4. Bureau of Justice Statistics, *Felony Defendants in Large Urban Counties, 2000* (Washington, DC: Department of Justice, 2003), Table 30. NCJ 202021.

5. Eleanor Chelimsky and Judith S. Dahmann, *National Evaluation of the Career Criminal Program: Final Report* (McLean, VA: MITRE, 1979).

6. Allan F. Abrahamse, Patricia A. Ebener, Peter W. Greenwood, Nora Fitzgerald, and Thomas E. Kosin, "An Experimental Evaluation of the Phoenix Repeat Offender Program," *Justice Quarterly* 8 (June 1991): 141–168.

7. The Sentencing Project, *Crime Punishment and Public Opinion: A Summary of Recent Studies and Their Implications for Sentencing Policy* (Washington, DC: The Sentencing Project, 2001). Available on the Sentencing Project website.

8. Jack Hinckley, *Breaking Points* (Grand Rapids, MI: Chosen Books, 1985).

9. Randy Borum and Solomon M. Fulero, "Empirical Research on the Insanity Defense and Attempted Reforms: Evidence Toward Informed Policy," *Law and Human Behavior,* 23.1 (1999): 117–135.

10. Reported in Rita J. Simon and David E. Aaronson, *The Insanity Defense: A Critical Assessment of Law and Policy in the Post-Hinckley Era* (New York: Praeger, 1988), p. 166.

11. Simon and Aaronson, *Insanity Defense,* Table 3.2, p. 40.

12. Borum and Fulero, "Empirical Research on the Insanity Defense," p. 120.

13. Ibid., pp. 27–28.

14. American Psychiatric Association, *American Journal of Psychiatry* 140 (1983): 681–688.

15. Valerie Hans, "An Analysis of Public Attitudes toward the Insanity Defense," *Criminology* 24 (May 1986): 393–414.

16. Jeffrey S. Janofsky, Mitchell H. Dunn, and Erik J. Ruskes, "Insanity Defense Pleas in Baltimore County: An Analysis of Outcome," *American Journal of Psychiatry,* 153.11 (1996): 1464–1468.

17. *Newsweek,* 24 May 1982.

18. For a good study of this subject, see Egon Bittner, "Police on Skid Row: A Study in Peacekeeping," *American Sociological Review* 32 (October 1967): 694–715.

19. *Rights of the Mentally Disabled: Statements and Standards,* rev. ed. (Arlington: American Psychiatric Publishing, 2002).

20. *Baxstrom v. Herold,* 383 U.S. 107 (1966).

21. Henry J. Steadman et al., *Before and After Hinckley* (New York: Guilford, 1993), pp. 58–61, 97–99.

22. Henry J. Steadman, *Beating a Rap? Defendants Found Incompetent to Stand Trial* (Chicago: University of Chicago Press, 1979), p. 104.

23. Terence P. Thornberry and Joseph E. Jacoby, *The Criminally Insane: A Community Follow-up of Mentally Ill Offenders* (Chicago: University of Chicago Press, 1979). For another study with similar results, see Henry J. Steadman and James J. Cacozza, *Careers of the Criminally Insane* (Lexington, MA: Lexington Books, 1974).

24. Borum and Fulero, "Empirical Research on the Insanity Defense," p. 121.

25. Norval Morris, *Madness and the Criminal Law* (Chicago: University of Chicago Press, 1982).

26. Ibid.

27. Ibid.

28. Grant H. Morris, *The Insanity Defense: A Blueprint for Legislative Change* (Lexington, MA: Lexington Books, 1974).

29. Bureau of Justice Statistics, *Mental Health Treatment in State Prisons, 2000* (Washington, DC: Department of Justice, 2001). NCJ 188215.

30. Bureau of Justice Statistics, *Sourcebook of Criminal Justice Statistics, 1997* (Washington, DC: Department of Justice, 1998), p. 13.

31. John Klofus and Ralph Weisheit, "Guilty but Mentally Ill: Reform of the Insanity Defense in Illinois," *Justice Quarterly* 4 (March 1987): 39–50.

32. Ibid.

33. Kurt M. Bumby, "Reviewing the Guilty but Mentally Ill Alternative: A Case of the Blind 'Pleading' the Blind," *Journal of Psychiatry and the Law* 21.2 (1993): 191–220.

34. Moran, "Insanity Defense," p. 81.

35. Ibid., pp. 77–78.

36. Borum and Fulero, "Empirical Research on the Insanity Defense," p. 133.

37. The most critical view of plea bargaining is Abraham Blumberg, *Criminal Justice: Issues and Ironies,* 2nd ed. (New York: New Viewpoints, 1979). The best recent study is McDonald, *Plea Bargaining.*

38. On the "copout" ceremony, see Jonathan D. Casper, *American Criminal Justice: The Defendant's Perspective* (Englewood Cliffs, NJ: Prentice Hall, 1972), pp. 81–86.

39. National Advisory Commission on Criminal Justice Standards and Goals, *Courts* (Washington, DC: Government Printing Office, 1973), p. 46.

40. Bureau of Justice Statistics, *Felony Defendants in Large Urban Counties, 2000* (Washington, DC: Department of Justice, 2003). NCJ 202021.

41. Michael L. Rubinstein, Stevens H. Clarke, and Teresa J. White, *Alaska Bans Plea Bargaining* (Washington, DC: Department of Justice, 1980).

42. Rubinstein et al., *Alaska Bans Plea Bargaining.*

43. Norval Morris and Gordon Hawkins, *Letter to the President on Crime Control* (Chicago: University of Chicago Press, 1977), p. 61.

44. Rubinstein et al., *Alaska Bans Plea Bargaining.*

45. This point is argued in Samuel Walker, *Taming the System: The Control of Discretion in Criminal Justice, 1950–1990* (New York: Oxford University Press, 1993), pp. 95–96.

46. Franklin E. Zimring and Gordon Hawkins, *Crime is not the Problem, Lethal Violence in America* (New York: Oxford University Press, 1997), p. 19.

47. Colin Loftin and David McDowall, "One with a Gun Gets You Two: Mandatory Sentences and Firearms Violence in Detroit," *The Annals of the American Academy of Political and Social Science* 455 (May 1981): 150–167.

48. Malcolm W. Feeley, "Perspectives on Plea Bargaining," *Law and Society Review* 13 (Winter 1979): 199.

49. Brian J. Ostrom and Roger A. Hanson, *Efficiency, Timeliness, and Quality: A New Perspective from Nine State Criminal Courts* (Williamsburg, VA: National Center for State Courts, 1999). Available on the National Center for State Courts website.

50. Peter F. Nardulli, James Eisenstein, and Roy B. Flemming, *The Tenor of Justice: Criminal Courts and the Guilty Plea Process* (Urbana: University of Illinois, 1988).

51. Bureau of Justice Assistance, *National Assessment of Structured Sentencing* (Washington, DC: Government Printing Office, 1996), pp. 98–100. NCJ 153853. Jeffrey T. Ulmer, *Social Worlds of Sentencing* (Albany: State University of New York Press, 1997).

52. Herbert Packer, "Two Models of the Criminal Process," in Packer, *The Limits of the Criminal Sanction* (Stanford, CA: Stanford University Press, 1968), pp. 149–173.

53. Macklin Fleming, *The Price of Perfect Justice* (New York: Basic Books, 1974).

54. Ibid.

55. U.S. Department of Justice, *Attorney General's Task Force on Violent Crime* (Washington, DC: Government Printing Office, 1981), p. 58.

56. *Fay v. Noia,* 372 U.S. 391 (1963).

57. Bureau of Justice Statistics, *Federal Habeas Corpus Review: Challenging State Court Criminal Convictions* (Washington, DC: Department of Justice, 1995). NCJ 155504. See also Victor E. Flango, *Habeas Corpus in State and Federal Courts* (Williamsburg, VA: National Center for State Courts, 1994).

PART III

The Middle Ground:
Guns and Victims

On one thing, conservatives and liberals agree: Guns are a major part of the crime problem. They disagree, however, on the exact nature of the problem and the solution to it. Liberals focus on guns and want to limit their availability. Conservatives focus on criminals who use guns and want to get tough with them. The policies each side recommends reflect their fundamentally different assumptions about crime and criminals. There is also a certain amount of agreement with respect to crime victims. Both sides support certain programs designed to assist victims. In this section we will examine policies directed toward the victims of crime, guns, and gun-related violence.

9

Protect Crime Victims

I n 1982, the chair of the President's Task Force on Victims of Crime declared:
"The neglect of crime victims is a national disgrace."[1] More than two
decades later, that charge is no longer valid. The victims' rights movement
has resulted in a broad array of new laws and programs designed to help crime
victims. The Justice Department established the Office for Victims of Crime
(OVC) in 1983 to provide a broad range of services and information. Thirty-
three states have amended their constitutions to include provisions related to
crime victims, and all states have passed victims' rights laws. The OVC estimates
that there are 27,000 victims' rights laws across the country.[2]

THE VICTIMS' RIGHTS MOVEMENT

The crime victim was long the forgotten person in American criminal justice.
In modern Anglo-American law, the crime victim has had no formal role in
the criminal process. The prosecutor represents the public interest, including
that of the victim. This is why, in some states, cases are formally titled "The
People versus. . . ." As an American Civil Liberties Union (ACLU) handbook
on *The Rights of Crime Victims* explains, "The victim is not a formal party to
a criminal proceeding."[3] It was not always this way. Until the mid-nineteenth
century, crime victims represented themselves, bringing their own cases before
magistrates and judges. The office of the modern prosecutor gradually emerged

in the nineteenth century, assuming the role of representing the public in general and crime victims in particular.[4]

Having a professional public official handle criminal cases serves two important purposes. First, it establishes the idea that a crime is an offense against society as a whole and not just an individual. Second, it removes the element of vengeance from the handling of a case. A public official is more likely to be free of anger and personal animosity toward the offender. The desire to keep emotionalism out of the criminal justice process explains why in two cases the U.S. Supreme Court has ruled that victim impact statements at sentencing in death penalty cases are unconstitutional.[5] (The concept of restorative justice, which we will examine in Chapter 14, represents an attempt to de-bureaucratize the criminal justice system and bring back some of the older informal and communal approaches to justice.)

Another reason that crime victims have had no formal role in the criminal justice process is that Anglo-American law places a high priority on protecting individual rights against possible violations by the state. For this reason, the Bill of Rights includes specific protections for criminal suspects and defendants: due process of law, the right to an attorney, protection against self-incrimination, and so on.

In the 1970s, however, the victims' rights movement emerged, pushing for recognition of and services to victims. The movement found fault with all parts of the system: Police and prosecutors did not inform victims about the progress of cases; victims had no say in plea bargain agreements, sentencing, or parole decisions. An early survey found that in Alameda County, California (Oakland), only about 12 percent of victims had ever been notified that an arrest had been made in their case. Also, 45 percent of those who appeared in court had not been informed of the nature of their appearance, and about 42 percent were never notified of the outcome of the case.[6]

Although conservatives have dominated the victims' rights movement, groups with other political perspectives have also been active. Feminists have helped to secure new laws and policies to protect the victims of domestic violence and rape. These include mandatory arrest laws for domestic violence, shelters for victims and counseling programs for offenders. Mothers Against Drunk Driving (MADD) led a national anti–drunk driving crusade to protect the victims of drunk driving (see Chapter 6). The wave of "three strikes" laws was spurred by public outrage over victims such as Polly Klaas, who was murdered by a recent parolee (see Chapter 7). Even the ACLU, which vigorously opposes many victims' rights proposals as unconstitutional, published a handbook on *The Rights of Crime Victims* in 1985.[7] In the same year, the United Nations adopted a Declaration of Basic Principles of Justice for Victims of Crime and Abuse of Power.

New Laws and Programs

The victims' rights movement has been very successful in achieving its legislative goals. By the early 1990s, every state had passed some kind of victims' rights law, and 29 had amended their constitution to include some victims' rights.

Meanwhile, a series of federal laws included the 1970 Crime Insurance Act, the 1982 Victim Witness Protection Act, the 1984 Victims of Crime Act, the 1984 Justice Assistance Act, the 1990 Victims' Rights and Restitution Act, and the 1994 Violent Crime Control Act.[8]

Typical of many new state laws is the 1986 North Carolina Fair Treatment for Victims and Witnesses Act. The law guarantees a victim's right to information about emergency medical assistance, protection from harm, and financial compensation; a secure area in the courthouse; the right to make a victim impact statement at sentencing; information about the final disposition of the case; and notification about the offender's release or escape.[9]

Critics of the Movement

The victims' rights movement has many critics. Civil libertarians in particular have criticized proposals to limit individual rights in the name of helping crime victims. The most sweeping criticism has been made by Robert Elias. In a series of books, Elias has argued that victims have been manipulated to serve a conservative political agenda, that most of the new victims' rights laws and policies have not provided much in the way of tangible help, and that many serious forms of victimization (workplace injuries, environmental pollution, unsafe products, false advertising, among others) have been ignored despite their enormous toll in terms of peoples' health and costs to communities. As Elias sees it, the victims' rights movement has been largely an exercise in "symbolic politics" that leaves crime victims "victims still."[10]

Sorting Out the Issues

The victims' rights movement does not have a single agenda. Programs and services represent a variety of approaches. It is useful to divide them into three general categories.

Victims' Services   One set of programs involves services for crime victims. The most important are financial compensation and counseling. Women's groups have led the fight for rape and domestic violence hotlines, counseling programs, and shelters.

Victims' Voice Laws   A second group includes laws to enhance the role of victims in the criminal justice system, in particular to allow them to make a formal statement in court about bail setting or plea bargain agreements, or at sentencing or parole hearings.

"Get Tough on Crime" Laws   A third group includes "get tough" ideas similar to ones we have considered in other chapters. These include proposals to deny bail to dangerous offenders, close loopholes in the criminal justice system, and give longer prison sentences. They usually do not mention crime victims directly, but the underlying assumption is that getting tough on criminals will reduce the number of crime victims.

VI. Respecting the victim in the criminal justice process

19. Provide for hearing and considering the victims' perspective at sentencing and at any early release proceedings.

20. Provide victim-witness coordinators.

21. Provide for victim restitution and for adequate compensation and assistance for victims and witnesses.

22. Adopt evidentiary rules to protect victim-witnesses from courtroom intimidation and harassment.

23. Permit victims to require HIV testing before trial of persons charged with sex offenses.

24. Notify the victim of the status of criminal justice proceedings and of the release status of the offender.

FIGURE 9.1 Recommendations related to crime victims

SOURCE: U.S. Department of Justice, *Combating Violent Crime* (Washington, DC: Government Printing Office, 1992), p. xii.

The six recommendations of the Attorney General's Task Force on Violent Crime listed in Figure 9.1 include three in the area of victims' services, one related to victims' voices, and two designed to get tough on crime.

Criteria for Evaluation

Four different criteria can be used to evaluate the various crime victims' programs and services.

Implementation The first issue, of course, is whether a law or policy is in fact being implemented or is likely to be implemented. As we have learned with other laws and policies so far in this book, the courtroom work group has tremendous power to block or frustrate new policies if it upsets the established going rate. If a victims' rights law is not implemented, it will not have any impact on crime.

Impact on Crime Victims A second issue is the impact of a crime victims' law on crime victims themselves. Does a particular law help them deal with the trauma of victimization, return to their normal lifestyle, and improve their evaluation of the criminal justice system?

Impact on the Criminal Justice System A third issue is whether laws and policies designed to help crime victims have undesirable effects on the criminal justice system. Many, for example, call for radical changes in constitutional law. Even if they might reduce crime or help victims, the cost to the justice system may be too great. Remember that our goal in this book is to find policies that are effective, practical, and sound.

Crime Reduction The fourth issue is the concern of this book: Do victims' rights laws help to reduce serious crime? Some of the proposals we will examine may be sound, humane ideas that will genuinely help victims deal with their suffering. They should be supported for that reason. But the relevant question for us is whether they will reduce crime.

VICTIM ASSISTANCE PROGRAMS

Perhaps the most popular victims' rights idea has been victim/witness assistance programs. By the late 1980s an estimated 4,000 such programs existed around the country. The 1984 Victims of Crime Act provides about $50 million a year for local programs; by 1987, 1,364 programs were receiving federal funds. By 1997, one-third of all city police departments and sheriffs' departments had a special unit for victim assistance.[11]

Table 9.1 presents the range of services required by law in 2,282 prosecutors' offices in 1994. Note that the survey asked prosecutors only what services they were required to provide. It is not clear that all of these services were, in fact, provided. The survey found, for example, that some information, although required, was provided only upon the request of a victim.[12]

Victim/witness programs vary widely. Many provide emergency services in the form of shelter, security repair, financial assistance, and on-the-scene comfort. One national survey found that most provide follow-up counseling. Nearly all have some form of advocacy and support services, such as intervening with the victim's employer or landlord. Many help with insurance claims or efforts to obtain restitution. Nearly all provide court-related services concerned with the victim's role as witness for the prosecution, such as orienting victims or witnesses to court procedures, notifying them of court dates, providing transportation to court, escorting them at the court, and providing child care.

How well do these programs work? A survey of 62 victim service programs in North Carolina found that the state's 1986 Fair Treatment for Victims and Witnesses Act was meeting the needs of victims "only minimally."[13] Almost all of the programs were providing referral to social, restitution, and compensation services; notification about court cases; and allowances for victim impact statements. Nonetheless, 59 percent of crime victims surveyed in the state expressed dissatisfaction with the criminal justice system. Particularly significant was the fact that about one-third were not even aware of their right to make a victim impact statement. This suggests that a major provision of the law was not being fully implemented. An evaluation concluded that the programs provided primarily *witness* assistance rather than *victim* assistance.

A national evaluation of victims' rights laws found that in many cases the laws were not fully implemented. Even in states with "strong" victims' rights laws, for example, 60 percent of victims were not given advance notice about offenders' pretrial release hearings, as required by law. Over 90 percent received

Table 9.1 Victim services that jurisdictions require prosecutors' offices to provide, 1994

Type of service	Percentage of offices			
		Full-time office (population served)		
	All offices	500,000 or more	Less than 500,000	Part-time office
Notification/alert				
Notify victim	82	87	85	73
Notify witness	55	67	59	42
Orientation/education				
Victim restitution assistance	60	62	62	55
Victim compensation procedures	58	73	65	41
Victim impact statement assistance	55	78	60	40
Orientation to court procedures	41	57	48	24
Public education	15	20	17	9
Escort				
Escort victim	23	39	28	9
Escort witness	17	31	19	9
Counseling/assistance				
Property return	38	46	39	35
Referral	32	46	37	18
Personal advocacy	17	26	22	5
Counseling	10	21	12	5
Crisis intervention	10	19	14	0
Number of offices	2,282	119	1,480	683

SOURCE: Bureau of Justice Statistics, *Prosecutors in State Courts, 1994* (Washington, DC: Government Printing Office, 1996), p. 9.

notification about the arrest and trial date of the offender in these states, but compliance was much lower for all other stages in the criminal process.[14]

What about the impact of victim/witness services on crime? Because most victim assistance programs operate after the crime has occurred, we have little reason to assume that they will reduce crime. We should not ignore one possible exception to this rule. Shelters for the victims of domestic violence may in fact protect women from immediate violence. This aspect of shelters has not been evaluated, however. Even if they prove effective, shelters have no relationship to the crimes of robbery and burglary, which are the focus of this book. This leads us to the following proposition:

PROPOSITION 28

With the possible exception of domestic violence shelters, social service programs for crime victims will not reduce serious crime.

Police/Victim Recontact

A slightly different service for crime victims is to provide more contact between them and the police. The President's Task Force on Victims of Crime recommended that police departments establish procedures for informing victims of violent crime about the status of the investigation of crimes.[15] Known as victim recontact programs, they are designed to overcome the problem of victims feeling alienated from the system because they never hear from the police.

Victim recontact is a sound and humane idea that is probably long overdue. There is absolutely no reason that the police should not keep victims informed and many reasons that they should. Mainly it would help build positive police/community relations. By 1997, about one-third of all city police departments and county sheriffs' departments had some kind of victim assistance program.[16] Meanwhile, almost all state prosecutors (93 percent) reported in 1990 that they informed victims of the outcome of cases. This compares with only 35 percent in 1974.[17]

Victim recontact may not deliver what its advocates expect, however. In one component of the Houston "fear reduction" experiment, police officers contacted crime victims to express sympathy and ask whether they needed any further assistance or information. An evaluation found that the program achieved none of its goals. Victims who were contacted did not express any less fear of crime or greater confidence in the police, compared with victims who were not contacted. Victims with poor English skills were actually more fearful than those who were not recontacted. They did not understand why the police were contacting them and became more fearful as a result.[18]

The Houston data suggest that perhaps victims' rights advocates have misinterpreted the victims' feelings about the criminal justice system. Many people may prefer just to be left alone. We should remember that according to the National Crime Victimization Survey, victims do not report 61 percent of all crimes. Many regard the crime as a private matter or say that it just was not important enough. In other words, even though something bad has happened to them, these people do not want any involvement with the criminal justice system.[19]

Most important, as far as we are concerned, victim recontact is not going to reduce crime. The evidence leads us to the following proposition:

PROPOSITION 29
Victim recontact programs do not reduce crime.

VICTIM COMPENSATION

The most popular victims' rights program involves financial compensation. California passed the first crime victims' compensation law in 1965. By the 1980s, 44 states and the District of Columbia had similar laws. The 1984 Victims of Crime Act provides federal financial support for state and local programs.

The Office for Crime Victims publishes a bulletin on restitution, *Making it Work,* on programs for obtaining restitution from offenders.[20]

Victim compensation can be seen as a government-supported insurance program, providing funds to help people recover from their losses. (The 1970 Crime Insurance Act was passed to provide insurance for businesses and individuals in high-crime areas who could not get coverage through private insurance companies.)[21] These losses include medical bills, lost wages, and other expenses. The Justice Department estimates that medical costs of crime are $18 billion a year.[22] State programs typically provide between $10,000 and $25,000, although at least two have no upper limit. Many programs limit compensation to victims of particular crimes, and virtually all have time limits on when people must file claims as well as procedures for documenting actual losses.

The national evaluation of victims' rights laws found, paradoxically, that victims in states with "strong" laws were less likely to have the judge order restitution than victims in states with "weak" laws. Moreover, when judges did order restitution, only 37 percent of the victims in "strong" law states actually received it.[23]

Evaluations of victim compensation programs have not been overly favorable. Many requests are denied. The New York State Crime Victims Board denied as many as 60 percent of all requests in the late 1980s. The most common reason for denying claims is the failure to provide sufficient documentation.[24] Even more disturbing, according to William Doerner's study of Florida crime victims, those who did receive compensation did not have more favorable attitudes toward the criminal justice system than did victims whose claims were denied.[25] This failure to affect the attitudes of crime victims is one of the reasons that Robert Elias feels that the victims' rights movement is largely an exercise in symbolic politics.[26]

Despite these problems, victim compensation is a worthy idea that is long overdue. The heavy toll that crime takes on people gives the government good reason to maintain some kind of insurance or compensation program. Yet, we have no reason to believe that compensation will reduce crime in any way.

PROPOSITION 30
Victim compensation programs may provide some help
for crime victims, but they do not reduce serious crime.

EXPANDING THE VICTIM'S VOICE

One of the major goals of the victims' rights movement has been to expand the role of victims in the criminal justice process, giving them a greater voice in bail decisions, plea bargains, sentencing, and parole release decisions. The President's Task Force on Victims of Crime recommended amending the Sixth

Amendment to read: "Likewise, the victim in every criminal prosecution shall have the right to be present and to be heard at all critical stages of judicial proceedings."[27]

The idea of expanding victims' voices has two goals. One is to give crime victims a feeling of participating in the justice system and to end their feelings of isolation and alienation. We should see this as a victim service program. The other goal is to ensure that offenders are properly punished and not allowed to get off too easily. The assumption is that the victim will object to a too lenient plea bargain or sentence. We should regard this as a "get tough" program.

Several states have enacted victims' voice laws. Proposition 8, adopted by California voters in 1982, provided that "the victim of any crime, or the next of kin of the victim . . . has the right to attend all sentencing proceedings . . . [and] to reasonably express his or her views concerning the crime, the person responsible, and the need for restitution."[28] The judge is required to take the victim's views into account in imposing sentence. The Office for Victims of Crime publishes a bulletin on *The Crime Victim's Right to be Present,* with current information on laws and procedures. A second bulletin covers victim input into plea agreements.[29]

Opponents of victims' voice laws fear that it brings vengeance (as opposed to justice) into the criminal process. One of the functions of a professional criminal justice bureaucracy is to ensure fair and impartial treatment of all accused persons. A professional is someone who is not emotionally involved in a case and acts impersonally on the basis of the facts and circumstances. A lawyer, for example, has a professional obligation to prosecute or defend a criminal defendant regardless of his or her personal feelings about the person or what he is accused of doing.

The Supreme Court has shared some of these fears about the danger of vengeance and emotionalism distorting the criminal process. In *Booth v. Maryland* (1987) and *South Carolina v. Gathers* (1989), the Court reversed death sentences because of statements read to the jury about the victim. In *Gathers,* for example, the prosecutor read from religious material that had been in the possession of a murder victim and also mentioned that he was a registered voter.[30] The Court ruled that this information was not related to the circumstances of the crime. Two years later, however, in *Payne v. Tennessee* (1991), the Court ruled that victim impact statements were not unconstitutional.[31]

The Impact of Victims' Voice Laws

There is very mixed evidence about the impact of victims' voice laws. On the one hand, many victims do not take advantage of the opportunities to participate in the process. Also, those who do are not always seeking severe punishment. Nonetheless, some evidence exists of harsher punishment for offenders in cases in which victims do in fact participate.

A recent national study found that among those victims who were notified about hearings (and many were not, as we have seen), over 90 percent chose to make an impact statement at sentencing. Participation was much lower for other stages in the criminal process, however. Less than 40 percent of those who were notified made a statement at bail hearings, and less than 20 percent chose to attend parole hearings.[32]

Does victim participation make a difference in the outcome? A study of 500 Ohio felony cases between June 1985 and January 1989 found several notable effects. First, victim impact statements (VISs) were submitted in about half (55 percent) of all cases. Under the program, VIS staff solicited information from victims at the time of grand jury hearings. Only 18 percent of victims appeared at trial or sentencing, and only 6 percent exercised their right to speak. Victim participation was heavily influenced by the seriousness of the crime. VISs were filed in 73 percent of "aggravated or special felony" cases, including 81 percent of sexual offenses, but only 49 percent of property crime cases, and only 13 percent of those that were handled as misdemeanors. Somewhat surprisingly, 61 percent of male victims filed a VIS, compared with only 28 percent of females.[33]

Of those who did submit a VIS, 60 percent requested that the offender be incarcerated. Convicted offenders were somewhat more likely to be incarcerated if a VIS was filed or if the victim appeared in court or requested incarceration (but, surprisingly, not if the victim only spoke in court). Also, filing a VIS statement, appearing in court, and requesting incarceration were associated with longer prison terms. The overall impact of the VIS law was somewhat limited, however. Case outcomes were affected primarily by offense severity and offenders' prior record.[34]

An earlier study of sexual assault cases in Ohio found that 60 percent of the victims made statements at sentencing. This study concluded that the statements had little effect on sentencing. A high level of agreement was noted between the sentence the victim recommended and the sentence the judge considered appropriate.[35]

A study of parole hearings in Pennsylvania, however, found that victim impact statements had a very significant effect on the chances of an offender being paroled. The Pennsylvania Board of Probation and Parole denied parole in 43 percent of 100 cases in which there was some victim input but in only 7 percent of a comparable set of 100 cases in which there was no input.[36] These findings lend support to concerns about the possible undesirable effects of victim impact statements. Whether a victim makes a statement may be a matter of chance, and it means that one offender will serve longer than another who committed the same crime because of an arbitrary factor unrelated to the crimes they committed.

In any event, apart from the satisfaction that VISs may give to the victims themselves, no evidence indicates that they have any effect on serious crime. Some offenders may serve longer prison terms, but, as we have already seen, there is no evidence that they are any less likely to eventually recidivate.

> ## PROPOSITION 31
> **Victim impact statements do not reduce crime.**

SPEEDY TRIALS

Holding speedy trials is another popular victims' rights proposal. The underlying assumption appears to be that justice delayed is justice denied for the victim as well as the defendant. The irony is that the speedy trial has traditionally been seen as a defendants' rights issue, since the Sixth Amendment guarantees a speedy trial for the accused.

As we learned in Chapter 7, there is some evidence that speedy trials—that is, trials that are speedier than usual—could be an effective crime reduction policy. The likelihood that a defendant released on bail will commit another crime increases the longer he or she is out on release. Holding trials earlier would mean that a number of them would be tried, convicted, and imprisoned before they had time to commit another crime. In Chapter 7 we offered this as a reasonable alternative to preventive detention.[37] Even in the best of circumstances, however, we should not expect too much crime reduction here. As we have also learned, crimes committed by persons out on bail are a small proportion of the total.

Congress passed a federal speedy trial law in 1974 and several states have enacted their own laws. As we have already learned, however (Chapter 3), these laws have not worked as intended. Courtroom work groups frequently subvert the laws, often because attorneys on both sides have reasons for wanting to delay the case.[38] In short, it is not true that everyone wants a speedy trial or that holding a speedy trial is in the best interest of crime victims.

GETTING TOUGH ON CRIME

Many victims' rights proposals are essentially designed to "get tough on crime." The President's Task Force on Victims of Crime, for example, recommended legislation "to abolish the exclusionary rule," "to abolish parole," to permit hearsay evidence at preliminary hearings, and to authorize preventive detention.[39] Few of these proposals address crime victims directly. The underlying assumption is that locking up more offenders will reduce crime and therefore result in fewer crime victims.

We have considered many of these proposals in other chapters. Our conclusion has been that they will not reduce serious crime. In Chapter 5, we found that repealing the exclusionary rule or the *Miranda* warning will not reduce crime. In Chapter 7, we found that limiting the right to bail through preventive detention is not likely to reduce violent crime. In Chapter 11, we will examine whether abolishing parole would have any effect on crime.

Modifying the exclusionary rule may in fact backfire on victims. California's Proposition 8 attacked the exclusionary rule with a "truth-in-evidence" section, permitting introduction of "all relevant evidence." This provision was designed to close an alleged loophole and tip the balance in favor of the prosecution. Within weeks of the proposition's enactment, it was clear that the truth-in-evidence clause might benefit suspects more than victims. The term "all relevant evidence" covers a lot of territory. It could include questions about a rape victim's background and character, allowing the defense to raise doubts about the victim's innocence. Although Proposition 8 specifically excludes the admission of evidence concerning a rape victim's past sexual activity, other evidence about her lifestyle is admissible. One defense attorney obtained an acquittal by introducing evidence concerning the victim's "colorful" background. The result has undermined years of progress toward the elimination of questioning about the past sexual conduct of rape victims.[40]

Equally dangerous is the President's Task Force recommendation that hearsay evidence should be admissible at preliminary hearings. The idea is that this will protect the victim from the trauma of testifying in person. Relaxing the established rules of evidence to permit hearsay testimony at any stage in the criminal justice process sets a dangerous precedent. Allowing it only at preliminary hearings, moreover, is silly and misleading. It will be little help in convicting the offender if it is inadmissible at trial. This leads us to the following conclusion:

PROPOSITION 32
Policies intended to get tough on crime will not reduce crime or help crime victims, and may instead damage the criminal justice system.

Mandatory Arrest for Domestic Violence

Mandatory arrest for domestic violence is designed to protect female victims of crime. Feminists argued that police failure to arrest men for domestic assault left women at risk of being attacked again. Women's groups successfully sued police departments over their failure to arrest, charging denial of equal protection of the law. One of the major results of this movement has been the development of mandatory arrest policies. By 2000, 91 percent of all local police departments had a written policy on arrest for violence, and 72 percent had a mandatory arrest policy.[41] Some of these policies are for mandatory arrest, whereas others are for arrest preferred.

The first study of the impact of arrest on domestic violence, the Minneapolis Domestic Violence Experiment, concluded that arrest deterred violence over the next six months more effectively than either mediation or separation. These findings encouraged the rapid spread of mandatory arrest policies.[42] Unfortunately, subsequent studies in Charlotte, Milwaukee, Omaha, and other cities found that arrest was no more effective in deterring violence than the other alternatives. The Milwaukee study, in fact, found that for certain groups of offenders, arrest actually led to higher levels of repeat violence.[43]

Even more generally, as research and policy debates on domestic violence have progressed since the 1980s, many experts on the subject have increased doubts about the wisdom of absolute mandatory arrest laws.

CONCLUSION

The victims' rights movement is one of the more significant developments in recent criminal justice history. Twenty years ago, there was little concern about crime victims and few programs to assist them. Today new crime victim laws and programs are found in every jurisdiction.

Some of these laws and programs are good ideas, providing valuable assistance to people who have been harmed by crime. Some have not been fully implemented, however. Some of the others are positively dangerous, undermining important constitutional principles and likely to damage the justice system. Most important for our purposes, none of the programs we have discussed is likely to have any impact on serious crime.

NOTES

1.   President's Task Force on Victims of Crime, *Final Report* (Washington, DC: Government Printing Office, 1982), p. vii.

2.   Office for Victims of Crime, *Report to the Nation 2003,* p. 3. Available on the Office for Victims of Crime website.

3.   James H. Stark and Howard Goldstein, *The Rights of Crime Victims* (New York: Bantam, 1985), p. 19.

4.   Allen Steinberg, *The Transformation of Criminal Justice: Philadelphia, 1800–1880* (Chapel Hill. University of North Carolina Press, 1989).

5.   *South Carolina v. Gathers,* 490 U.S. 805 (1989); *Payne v. Tennessee,* 501 U.S. 808 (1991).

6.   R. Lynch, "Improving Treatment of Victims: Some Guides for Action," in William McDonald, ed., *Criminal Justice and the Victim* (Beverly Hills, CA: Sage, 1976), pp. 165–176.

7.   Stark and Goldstein, *Rights of Crime Victims.*

8.   Emilio C. Viano, "The Recognition and Implementation of Victims' Rights in the United States: Developments and Achievements," in E. C. Viano, ed., *The Victimology Handbook: Research Findings, Treatment, and Public Policy* (New York: Garland, 1990); Dean G. Kilpatrick, David Beatty, and Susan Smith Howley, *The Rights of Crime Victims—Does Legal Protection Make a*

Difference? (Washington, DC: Department of Justice, 1998). NCJ 173839.

9.   Robert A. Jerin, Laura J. Moriarty, and Melissa A. Gibson, "Victim Service or Self Service: An Analysis of Prosecution Based Victim-Witness Assistance Programs and Providers," *Criminal Justice Policy Review* 7.2 (1995): 142–154.

10. Robert Elias, *Victims Still: The Political Manipulation of Crime Victims* (Newbury Park, CA: Sage, 1993), *The Politics of Victimization: Victims, Victimology and Human Rights* (New York: Oxford University Press, 1990), and *Victims of the System* (New Brunswick, NJ: Transaction, 1984).

11. Bureau of Justice Statistics, *Law Enforcement Management and Administrative Statistics, 1997* (Washington, DC: Government Printing Office, 1999), p. xix.

12. Bureau of Justice Statistics, *Prosecutors in State Courts, 1994* (Washington, DC: Department of Justice, 1996), p. 9. NCJ 145319.

13. Jerin et al., "Victim Service or Self Service," p. 152.

14. Kilpatrick et al., *The Rights of Crime Victims,* p. 5.

15. President's Task Force on Victims of Crime, *Final Report.*

16. Bureau of Justice Statistics, *Law Enforcement Management and Administrative Statistics, 1997,* p. xix.

17. Bureau of Justice Statistics, *Prosecutors in State Courts, 2001* (Washington, DC: Department of Justice, 2002). NCJ 193441.

18. Lee P. Brown and Mary Ann Wycoff, "Policing Houston: Reducing Fear and Improving Service," *Crime and Delinquency* 33 (January 1986): 71–89.

19. Bureau of Justice Statistics, *Criminal Victimization in the United States, 2003* (Washington, DC: Government Printing Office, 2004). NCJ 205455.

20. See the website of the Office for Victims of Crime.

21. Data on victim compensation programs and money awarded to victims are available on the website of the federal Office for Victims of Crime. Office for Victims of Crime, *Victims of Crime Act Crime Victims Fund* (Washington, DC: Office for Victims of Crime, 2002). FS 000281.

22. Miller et al., *Victim Costs and Consequences,* p. 17.

23. Kilpatrick et al., *The Rights of Crime Victims.*

24. Andrew Karmen, *Crime Victims: An Introduction to Victimology,* 2d ed. (Pacific Grove, CA: Brooks/Cole, 1990), p. 321.

25. William Doerner, "The Impact of Crime Compensation on Victim Attitudes toward the Criminal Justice System," *Victimology* 5.2 (1980): 61–77.

26. Elias, *Victims Still,* p. 42.

27. President's Task Force on Victims of Crime, *Final Report,* p. 114.

28. Edwin Villmoare and Virginia V. Neto, *Victim Appearances at Sentencing under California's Victims' Bill of Rights* (Washington, DC: Government Printing Office, 1987); Candace McCoy, *Politics and Plea Bargaining: Victims' Rights in California* (Philadelphia: University of Pennsylvania Press, 1993).

29. These and other bulletins can be found on the Office for Victims of Crime website.

30. *South Carolina v. Gathers,* 490 U.S. 805 (1989); *Booth v. Maryland,* 482 U.S. 496 (1987).

31. *Payne v. Tennessee.*

32. Kilpatrick et al., *The Rights of Crime Victims,* p. 6.

33. Edna Erez and Pamela Tontodonato, "The Effect of Victim Participation in Sentencing on Sentence Outcome," *Criminology* 28.3 (1990): 451–474.

34. Ibid.

35. Anthony Walsh, "Placebo Justice: Victim Recommendations and Offender Sentences in Sexual Assault Cases," *Journal of Criminal Law and Criminology* 77 (Winter 1986): 1126–1141.

36. William H. Parsonage, Frances Bernat, and Jacquelin Helfgott, "Victim Impact Testimony and Pennsylvania's Parole Decision Making Process: A Pilot Study," *Criminal Justice Policy Review* 6.3 (1994): 187–206.

37. Bureau of Justice Statistics, *Pretrial Release of Felony Defendants, 1992* (Washington, DC: Department of Justice, 1994).

38. Malcolm Feeley, *Court Reform on Trial* (New York: Basic Books, 1982).

39. President's Task Force on Victims of Crime, *Final Report,* pp. 17–18.

40. Cassia Spohn and Julie Horney, *Rape Law Reform* (New York: Plenum, 1992).

41. Bureau of Justice Statistics, *Local Police Departments 2000* (Washington, DC: Department of Justice, 2004), Table 58. NCJ 196002.

42. Lawrence W. Sherman and Richard A. Berk, *The Minneapolis Domestic Violence Experiment* (Washington, DC: Police Foundation, 1984).

43. Lawrence W. Sherman, *Policing Domestic Violence* (New York: Free Press, 1992). Christopher D. Maxwell, Joel H. Garner, and Jeffrey A. Fagan, *The Effects of Arrest on Intimate Partner Violence: New Evidence from the Spouse Assault Replication Program* (Washington, DC: Department of Justice, 2001). NCJ 188199.

10

Control Gun Crimes

THE PROBLEM WITH GUNS—AND GUN POLICY

Firearms, especially handguns, are a serious problem in the United States. Even with the recent decline in violent crime, firearms are associated with thousands of deaths and injuries every year. In 2002 there were 18,289 firearm homicides in the United States. Handguns were used in 40 percent of all robberies.[1] The dollar cost to society of firearms-related violence is enormous. Cook and Ludwig's study of "The Real Costs" of gun violence concludes that costs, including medical expenses, lost wages, and security costs, total about $100 billion a year.[2] Gun-related homicides victimize African Americans at an extremely disproportionate rate. In 1999, for example, gun murders were the leading cause of death for 15- to 34-year-old African American men.[3]

The good news is that gun violence declined dramatically in the 1990s as part of the great crime drop. The victimization survey reports that firearms violence fell 63 percent between 1993 and 2001. Most of this reduction involved gun-related homicides among 18- to 24-year-old men.[4]

The Policy Questions

This chapter addresses two policy questions. The first is, What accounts for the high level of gun-related violence in the United States? The second is, What policies are effective, or are likely to be effective in reducing gun-related violence?

Table 10.1 Major sources of data on firearms

Firearms production

Bureau of Alcohol, Tobacco and Firearms, *Annual Firearms Manufacturing and Exportation Report*

Firearms ownership

National Opinion Research Center, *General Social Survey*

Public attitudes about firearms and firearms policy

Gallup Poll, periodic surveys

Bureau of Justice Statistics, *Sourcebook of Criminal Justice Statistics*

Firearms-related deaths

Center for Disease Control and Prevention, National Vital Statistics system

Firearms use in crime

Bureau of Justice Statistics, annual National Criminal Victimization Survey

Bureau of Justice Statistics, *Weapons Use in Crime*

Federal Bureau of Investigation, Uniform Crime Reports, Supplemental Homicide Reports

Federal Bureau of Investigation, *Annual Report on Law Enforcement Officers Killed or Assaulted*

SOURCE: National Academy of Sciences, *Firearms and Violence: A Critical Review* (Washington, DC: National Academy Press, 2005), pp. 22–31.

Liberals claim that the reduction in gun violence over the past decade is the result of a combination of new gun control laws, such as the Brady Law and the assault weapons ban, together with innovative community policing and problem-oriented policing programs. Conservatives say that tough sentencing laws and the incapacitation of career criminals are responsible.[5] Basically, liberals believe that guns are the problem and support *supply* reduction policies designed to reduce their availability.[6] As they put it, "Guns kill people." Conservatives, on the other hand, believe that criminals are the problem and support *demand* reduction policies designed to either deter or incapacitate them. As they put it, "Guns don't kill people—people kill people."[7] We will encounter the distinction between supply reduction and demand reduction when we discuss drug policy in Chapter 13. As Mark Moore suggests, it is helpful to think comparatively about strategies for controlling guns, drugs, and alcohol.[8]

The gun control issue arouses passionate debate among Americans. With the possible exception of drinking and driving, no other issue discussed in this book directly affects so many people as gun ownership. In 2003, 34 percent of all homes had some kind of firearm, with about 20 percent having a handgun. (Interestingly, the percentage of households with firearms has declined significantly, from 47 percent in the mid-1970s to the current 34 percent).[9] And while no one argues that drunk driving is acceptable, many people believe they have a right to own a gun. Gun owners argue that the Second Amendment establishes a constitutional right to own a gun, although the Supreme Court has never accepted that interpretation.[10]

The National Academy of Sciences lists 35 different sources of data on firearms and firearm-related violence. The most important are listed in Table 10.1.

GUN OWNERSHIP AND
GUN-RELATED VIOLENCE

Much misunderstanding persists about the exact nature of the problem related to guns, gun ownership, and gun-related violence. The leaders of both sides of the issue have often distorted the evidence to support their respective positions. Let us try to clear the air by establishing a few basic facts.

Types of Guns

The first problem is that there is a lot of confusion about exactly which weapons we are talking about. A basic distinction is among rifles, shotguns, and handguns.[11] Virtually everyone agrees that handguns are the real problem with respect to crime. Ninety-six percent of the firearms used in robberies are handguns. The so-called "Saturday night special" is one kind of handgun—small, easily concealed, and cheap. Assault weapons, meanwhile, are rifles or pistols that are capable of rapid-fire action. We will look at specific policy proposals directed at both the specials and assault weapons.

Gun Ownership

The Bureau of Alcohol, Tobacco, and Firearms (BATF) estimates there are currently over 258 million firearms in circulation in the United States. About 93 million are handguns, and 1.5 to 2 million new handguns are manufactured or imported every year.[12] It is important to keep these 93 million handguns in mind throughout this chapter, since any effective gun control policy has to take them into account.

Despite the tremendous increase in the total number of firearms, the percentage of households with some kind of firearm has declined significantly in recent years, falling from 47 percent in the mid-1970s to 34 percent in 2002. The percentage with a handgun has dropped to about 20 percent of all.[13] Handgun ownership is higher among men than women (44 percent of men own any kind of gun, compared with 12 percent of women), and among white households than African American. The most important variable is region: People in the southeastern United States are the most likely to own a handgun, in large part because the region is predominantly rural and has a strong tradition of hunting. Handgun ownership is lowest in the urbanized Northeast. Data from the National Opinion Research Center's General Social Survey indicate that gun ownership is highly correlated with people "who are members of social groups where gun ownership is the norm." With respect to attitudes, gun owners are more likely to distrust government and be part of a cultural tradition of private retribution.[14]

Handgun-Related Violence

The facts about handgun violence in the United States are grisly. In 2003, 24 percent of all violent crimes were committed with a firearm, and 80 percent of those crimes involved a handgun[15] (see Table 10.2). This included 13,200 murders, or almost 60 percent of all murders; 11,800 rapes; 339,000 robberies;

Table 10.2 Presence of a weapon in violent crimes, 2003

	All violent crimes	Rape/ sexual assault	Robbery	Simple or aggravated assault
No weapon	69%	84%	41%	72%
Firearm	24	3	25	5
Knife	7	6	10	6

SOURCE: Bureau of Justice Statistics, *Criminal Victimization, 2003* (Washington, DC: Department of Justice, 2004).

and 566,800 assaults. In addition, two-thirds of all police officers feloniously killed in the line of duty are slain by handguns.

Note that we use the term *gun-related fatalities*. To say that guns "are responsible for" or "caused" deaths is to accept a particular point of view on the issue, namely the liberal gun control position. *Gun-related* is a policy-neutral term.

GUN-RELATED LAWS

It is a myth that the United States has no laws designed to control gun-related crime. In fact, we have innumerable federal, state, and local laws regulating ownership and use of guns, along with sentencing statutes that impose harsher punishment for weapons crimes. (The BATF publishes an annual compilation of *State Laws and Published Ordinances* on its website. Another convenient source is the website of the pro–gun control Brady Campaign.) The important question is whether these laws are effective in accomplishing their stated purposes.

State and local laws vary considerably. Some are far more restrictive than others. Some cities have banned the ownership of handguns, and at least 14 have outlawed the sale of Saturday night specials. The result is that someone can easily buy a handgun in a state with weak regulations and carry it to a state or city with very restrictive laws. A congressional report issued in 1997 found that many guns sold in Virginia, Florida, South Carolina, Georgia, and Texas—states with some of the weakest laws—ended up being seized in other states. In one report, the BATF identified 1,234 guns sold in Florida that were later used by criminals in other states, including 181 in New York.[16]

Policy Attitudes toward Gun Control

It is often reported that a majority of Americans favor gun control. This statement is only partly true. When some people say they favor "gun control," they may mean only restrictions on the purchase of guns rather than a ban on ownership, or they may actually mean tough penalties for criminals who use guns. It depends on exactly which gun control policy you are referring to. Thirty-nine percent of Americans favored banning the possession of handguns in 1999 (a figure that has not changed in about 20 years). More (54–58 percent) favor banning "small, easily concealed, and inexpensive handguns," and 67 percent favor outlawing the sale of all high-capacity gun magazines. A large majority of the public supports regulation of gun ownership: 82 percent support requiring a police permit to buy a gun, and 81 percent favor a background check and a five-day waiting period for a gun purchase. Similar majorities support mandatory gun safety training and designing guns so they cannot be fired by children. Finally, large majorities favor tough criminal penalties: 78 percent support doubling prison terms for crimes committed with a gun.[17]

Now let us review the various policy alternatives and see whether any evidence indicates that they work or might work.

BAN HANDGUNS

The most extreme gun control proposal is to ban handguns The idea of "banning" handguns actually consists of several different policies: outlawing possession, outlawing bullets, prohibiting the manufacture and sale of handguns, and banning only Saturday night specials or assault weapons.

Ban Possession

A few cities have actually banned the possession of handguns. Their experience gives us some idea of what this approach can and cannot accomplish. The District of Columbia banned the purchase, sale, transfer, and possession of all handguns in 1975. It exempted handguns and long guns previously registered under a 1968 gun registration law. The nation's capital represents a tough test of banning handguns because it is a major city with a lot of violent crime.

What happened as a result of the law? The U.S. Conference of Mayors, a leading gun control advocate, claimed that the law was responsible for a "significant reduction in both firearm and handgun crime." Other analysts, however, believe that the mayors' report was flawed and inconclusive. Edward Jones found that comparable cities experienced even greater reductions in gun-related crime during the same period, without the benefit of gun control. Jones conceded that the law may have made some contribution to reducing handgun crime, but it was impossible to argue that it was the only or even the most important cause.[18]

Murder trends in Washington over the last 20 years suggest that the 1975 law was not effective. Murders declined significantly in the late 1970s and early 1980s, reaching a low of 147 in 1985. They skyrocketed to 482 by 1991, mainly as a result of the arrival of crack. Clearly, young men in Washington who wanted to obtain a handgun had little trouble getting one. Murders then declined to 239 in 2000, as part of the national reduction in violent crime.

After an exhaustive review of all studies of the DC handgun ban, the National Academy of Sciences found "no conclusive evidence" regarding the impact of the law.[19]

The Limits of Banning Handguns

The Washington, DC, experience illustrates the limits of attempting to outlaw possession of handguns. The main problem is the 93 million handguns that already exist. No one has offered a realistic plan for how they might be removed from circulation. As law professor John Kaplan once pointed out, crusaders who seek to outlaw a product (alcohol, drugs, guns) always focus on the alleged dangers of the item and spend "little time and energy" estimating the costs of enforcement and the likelihood of effectiveness.[20]

A sizable black market in handguns and other weapons already exists. Surveys consistently indicate that criminals obtain their guns through the illegal firearms market. Over half of arrestees in one study (55 percent) reported that guns were easy to obtain: More than a third (37 percent) said they could obtain one in less than a week, and 20 percent said they could get one in a day or less. Thirteen percent said that they had stolen a gun at some point in their life. A complete federal ban on handgun possession would probably foster the growth of the black market, just as the prohibition of alcohol (1920–1933) stimulated the growth of organized crime. We will discuss the consequences of attempting to outlaw certain products—alcohol, guns, drugs—in more detail in Chapter 13.

Any truly effective attempt to ban ownership of guns would require a federal law. No strong support for such a law exists at present, however. Also, it is safe to predict that millions of gun owners would refuse to turn in their weapons. Not only do about 20 percent of all American households currently have handguns, but many of those people fiercely believe that they have a constitutional right to own those weapons. (Go to the National Rifle Association website for its views on this issue.) A federal ban would create a situation resembling Prohibition in the 1920s, when tens of millions of people drank alcoholic beverages despite a constitutional amendment prohibiting them. Any attempt to enforce such a ban would inevitably require highly intrusive measures by the police. Many right-wing groups already express intense hostility toward the BATF, and a federal ban would only inflame the situation further.

Ban Bullets

Some groups, including the U.S. Conference of Mayors and the Consumer Product Safety Commission, have recommended banning the manufacture and sale of bullets on the grounds that they are a health hazard. This is a politically motivated strategy designed to sidestep the strong public opposition to outlawing guns themselves. The obvious problem with this approach is that bullets are easily made at home. Many hunters already pack their own. Outlawing bullets would only stimulate a large cottage industry in homemade bullets and a black market.

A variation of the bullet ban is a 1986 federal law prohibiting the manufacture, importation, and sale of so-called cop-killer bullets. These bullets are made of hard metals capable of piercing the bulletproof vests worn by police officers. Law enforcement organizations actively supported the law. When pressed, however, advocates of the law could not cite any cases of a police officer's actually being killed by one of these bullets. Meanwhile, only 18 cases were reported of criminals caught in possession of such bullets over an 18-year period.[21]

The cop-killer bullet issue is a classic example of a general phenomenon in crime control policy debates: the habit of some activists and politicians to seize on a small but seemingly important part of the problem. It is usually a cop-out: a way of appearing to have a solution to the problem while actually ignoring the hard questions related to the larger problem.

Ban the Manufacture and Importation of Handguns

Another way to reduce the availability of handguns in the United States is to outlaw their manufacture and importation. This approach is designed to dry up the supply of handguns over the long run. In practice, however, it would only stimulate an international black market like the one that already dominates the drug trade. Also, it has been estimated that the current supply of 93 million handguns is enough to last for the next hundred years.[22]

Buy Back Handguns

Another strategy for drying up the supply is for law enforcement officials to buy back handguns, offering either cash or coupons good for discounts at local stores in exchange for handguns. St. Louis conducted two buy-back programs, bringing in 7,500 guns in 1991 and another 1,200 in 1994. Richard Rosenfeld evaluated the program and found "little evidence" of any impact on gun assaults or homicides in the city. An evaluation of a buy-back program in Seattle also failed to find any reduction in crime.

Trying to put a more optimistic interpretation on his findings, Rosenfeld argues that buy-back programs are more likely to be effective in achieving other goals such as strengthening community bonds and building support for community leadership and that they should be evaluated on those terms.[23]

Buy-backs have serious limitations. The available supply of guns is so huge that it is probably impossible to significantly reduce the number in any community. Many guns are turned in by people who are among the least likely to commit a gun crime (e.g., the elderly). Many simply want to dispose of an unwanted weapon. In St. Louis, 62 percent of those turning in a gun retained another weapon in the home. In short, there is no evidence that buy-back programs reduce crime.

The National Academy of Sciences has concluded that the theory underlying buy-back programs is flawed in three ways. First, the guns that are turned in are those least likely to be used in crime. Second, replacement guns can be easily obtained. Third, the likelihood of any one gun being used in a crime is very low (it based this conclusion on the estimates of 70 million guns; 6,500 handgun homicides in 1999).[24]

Ban Saturday Night Specials

A compromise strategy for banning handguns advocated by some liberals is to outlaw only Saturday night specials.[25] The BATF defines the special as a gun of 0.32 caliber or less, with a barrel less than 3 inches in length and priced at $50 or less. In 1996, Los Angeles became the fourteenth city in the United States (along with the state of Maryland) to outlaw the sale of specials, specifically prohibiting 23 different weapons.[26] Advocates of outlawing the specials believe these weapons are favored by criminals because of their price and concealability.

Outlawing only Saturday night specials probably will not accomplish what many people think it would. The role of the specials in crime has been greatly exaggerated. Gary Kleck found that far from being the "preferred" weapon of criminals, they represent only between 10 and 27 percent of all handguns used in crime.[27] Banning only the specials might produce a *substitution effect,* in which criminals simply move up to a larger weapon.

Kleck further argues that specials are the primary self-defense weapon for low-income people. Banning them would deprive poor people, who are victimized by violent crimes more than middle-class people, of one of their principal means of self-protection.[28]

The proposal to ban only the Saturday night specials is essentially a political cop-out. It allows people to appear to be doing something about the gun problem without directly threatening most gun owners. The same can be said about banning cop-killer bullets: It focuses on a small part of the problem, one that has high symbolic power, while avoiding the hard questions associated with the real problem.

Ban Assault Weapons

The rise of gang-related violence in the 1980s aroused public concern about so-called assault weapons. There was much publicity about gangs being heavily armed with Uzis, AK-47s, and similar weapons. The term *assault weapon* generally refers to "semiautomatic firearms with a large magazine of ammunition that [are] designed and configured for rapid fire and combat use."[29] They can be pistols, rifles, or shotguns. The BATF estimated in 1993 that about 1 percent of the 200 million guns in private hands were assault weapons. Many people want to ban them because they are not legitimate hunting weapons and have no purpose other than killing people. In the 1999 national opinion survey, 66.6 percent supported a ban on "all high capacity ammunition magazines."[30] The 1994 Violent Crime Control Act outlawed the manufacture and sale of 19 specific types of assault weapons.

A 1999 evaluation of the assault weapons ban found no persuasive evidence that it reduced violent crime. At best, the report concluded that "the ban *may* [emphasis added] have contributed to a reduction in the gun murder rate and murders of police officers by criminals armed with assault weapons," but the evidence was far from conclusive.[31] As with Saturday night specials, the importance of assault weapons has been greatly exaggerated. Kleck points out that the ordinary handgun remains the gun of choice among robbers. Virtually all of the police officers feloniously killed are killed with handguns. In short, although extremely deadly, assault weapons are not the real problem in gun-related crimes.

Summary

All of the policies designed to eliminate the possession of handguns or certain types of guns run up against the same basic problems: Millions of these weapons already are in circulation (including 70 million handguns), there is no practical plan for eliminating them, a black market already exists, and any kind of ban would only foster the growth of the black market. This leads us to the following conclusion:

> ### PROPOSITION 33
> Attempts to ban handguns, or certain kinds of guns, or bullets, are not likely to reduce serious crime.

REGULATE THE SALE AND POSSESSION OF HANDGUNS

The basic American strategy for controlling handguns is to regulate their sale, purchase, and ownership. Innumerable federal, state, and local laws are designed to keep handguns out of the hands of convicted offenders, people with a history of mental illness, and juveniles. This is essentially a "bad person" strategy. The 1993 Brady Law requires a five-day waiting period so that a background check can be conducted on applicants. The 1994 Youth Handgun Safety Act outlaws possession of handguns by juveniles and the private sale or transfer of a handgun to a juvenile. The 1996 Lautenberg Amendment, meanwhile, outlaws gun ownership by anyone convicted of a domestic violence crime. The law had enormous implications for police officers and members of the military who must use weapons as part of their jobs. (For information on the Lautenberg Amendment, go to the BATF website and click on "Firearms FAQs.")

Regulate Gun Dealers

Another strategy involves regulating gun dealers. Federal law requires all commercial gun dealers, including pawn shops, to obtain a federal license to sell guns. In 1992 there were about 284,000 federally licensed gun dealers (referred to as FFLs, for Federal Firearms Licenses). Many of these were individuals, however, and one BATF survey found that 46 percent had sold no guns in the previous year. A series of reports found that many FFLs failed to comply with various federal regulations. Additionally, data indicated that a very small number of "problem" dealers were responsible for a very high percentage of guns used in crime. The BATF traced half of all seized guns back to less than 1 percent (0.4 percent) of all the licensed dealers.[32]

Beginning in 1993 a new set of laws and policies tightened up the regulation of FFLs (higher license fees; a requirement that they submit photographs and fingerprints of gun buyers; that they report gun thefts within 48 hours, etc.). As a result, the number of FFLs dropped 70 percent, to about 180,000 by 1998. An evaluation by Christopher Koper found that while the new regulations did eliminate a large number of problem FFLs, it is not clear that this had a direct impact on gun-related crime. The changes occurred during the great crime drop (see Chapter 1) and may have contributed in some marginal way to that decline.[33]

Background Checks: The Brady Law

The 1994 Brady Handgun Violence Prevention Act requires background checks and a one-week waiting period for all handgun purchasers. The law forces 32 states to adopt new procedures; the others already had similar laws. The law specifically prohibits certain classes of people from purchasing handguns: convicted felons, people with mental disabilities, and known drug addicts. In 1996 the Lautenberg Amendment prohibited persons with domestic violence convictions, including even misdemeanors, from owning guns. This had serious potential implications for police officers and military personnel for whom carrying a gun is part of the job.

Did the law prevent crime by keeping guns out of the wrong hands? The Clinton administration, which sponsored the law, cited data that 2.2 percent of all gun purchase applicants were rejected under the law; this involved 66,000 would-be gun buyers in 2001. Over half (58 percent) were rejected because of a felony conviction. Cook and Ludwig compared violent crime trends in the 32 Brady states (the experimental "treatment" group) with those in the 18 states unaffected by the law (the "control" group). They found no significant differences in crime trends.[34]

The gun black market is a major issue affecting all current or proposed gun policies. Mark H. Moore estimates that between 500,000 and 750,000 gun transactions take place between private individuals every year.[35] Many of these do not involve active or potential criminals: They are sales or gifts between friends, family members, gun collectors, and hunters. But many do involve illegal sales among active criminals. James D. Wright found that only one-sixth of all gun-using felons acquired their guns through legal, retail transactions. Half had stolen a gun at one time or another.[36] Additionally, an estimated 341,000 firearms, including 180,000 handguns, are stolen every year. By definition, these guns go directly into the hands of people (thieves) who are barred from owning them.[37]

A Bureau of Justice Statistics report on gun use by criminals supports the idea that regulations on the commercial sales of guns can be easily evaded.

It found that 14.2 percent of first-time offenders in prison purchased their weapon from a retail store, compared with only 6 percent of recidivists. Thirty-one percent of the first-time offenders got their weapon from an illegal source, while 42 percent of the recidivists did. Two points are important here. First, the number of offenders who obtained their weapon from a regulated retail outlet is extremely small. Second, people with criminal records readily shift to illegal sources.[38]

The Brady Law also stumbles over some serious problems with official criminal history data. Offenders whose records do not show up in the files will not be rejected. Some other people are incorrectly listed as having a criminal record (through mistaken identity, data that were entered inaccurately, mistakes that were not expunged, and so forth). The mentally disturbed gun buyer represents an even more serious problem. There is no national data file of people with mental health problems—and some serious civil liberties questions exist about whether we would want such a file. What is meant by having a history of mental illness? Being hospitalized? That covers only a small number of people with problems. What about people who were treated by a private physician or counselor? Requiring these professionals to report all of their clients would be a serious invasion of privacy. And what level of seriousness would trigger the ban on gun ownership? Mild depression? That covers a lot of people. And of course millions of people with serious mental health problems never see a doctor or counselor.

Summary

For all of the same reasons that banning ownership of handguns seems futile, regulations designed to deny ownership to certain categories of "bad" people are not likely to succeed. Seventy million handguns are in existence, an active black market thrives in guns, and criminals themselves say that they have or would have no trouble quickly obtaining a weapon. People intent on committing a crime are particularly motivated to obtain a gun. In short, it is not very efficient or sensible to try to control ownership of guns by the public at large when the real problem is the behavior of a very small part of the population—violent criminals.[39]

PROPOSITION 34
Attempts to deny ownership of handguns to certain categories
of "bad" people are not likely to reduce serious crime.

RESTRICT THE USE OF HANDGUNS

Instead of attempting to deny ownership of handguns, another serious group of policies is aimed at limiting how people *use* handguns. Let us take a look at this approach.

Restrict the Carrying of Handguns

Most states have traditionally had laws regulating the carrying of handguns outside the home, usually by prohibiting the carrying of concealed weapons or by requiring some kind of permit. The most famous variation of this approach was the 1975 Massachusetts Bartley-Fox Law, which mandates a one-year prison term for people who are caught carrying a handgun outside their homes without a permit. (Nationally, about 10 percent of adults reported carrying a hand gun outside their home in 1999. Sixty-three percent of them carried it for self-protection.) The Massachusetts law prohibits plea bargaining to a lesser offense and denies the possibility of either probation or parole. The intent was simple: "If you are caught with a gun, you will go to prison for a year and nobody can get you out."[40]

The Bartley-Fox Law is closely related to other crime control policies we discuss in this book. First, it is an exercise in mandatory sentencing (Chapter 7). It is also a strategy of deterrence, seeking to prevent crime through the threat of certain punishment (Chapter 6). Finally, it is an attempt to close the alleged loophole of plea bargaining (Chapter 8). Here we are interested primarily in its impact on crime and on gun-related crime in particular.

As a gun control measure, Bartley-Fox is a strategic compromise. It does not challenge people's right to own guns. Thus, it sidesteps much of the opposition from gun owners. It attempts to reduce gun-related crime by keeping the guns at home. This strategy has strong empirical support. Many violent crimes are unplanned, spontaneous events: The person left home with no intention of committing a crime. As interviews with criminals have found, most carry a gun for self-defense. Nonetheless, some of these people end up committing a gun crime. Having the gun may have emboldened them to commit a crime once a situation arose. As we have already argued, guns are terribly efficient as threats. Without the gun, a robber may not have attempted or completed the crime. Thus, a strategy to deter people from carrying a gun in the first place might reduce crime.

Bartley-Fox has been intensively evaluated. The data on crime trends indicated that in Boston assaults with a gun declined by 13.5 percent between 1974 and 1975 and by 11.7 percent between 1974 and 1976. Four other cities, however, experienced even greater reductions in gun assaults without the benefit of a similar law. They went down 21.3 percent in Philadelphia and 26 percent in Chicago. Meanwhile, in Boston assaults with other kinds of weapons went up by 40.4 percent between 1974 and 1976. Thus, there may have been a substitution effect as people kept their guns at home and shifted to other weapons.[41]

Gun robberies in Boston went down a substantial 35.5 percent in the 1974–1976 period, whereas robberies committed without guns increased slightly. Again, however, other cities that did not have a similar law experienced even greater reductions. Armed robberies went down 43.5 percent in Chicago and 36.7 percent in Philadelphia. Meanwhile, gun murders declined by 55.7 percent in Boston. This decrease was part of a national decline in murders; the comparison cities had reductions of between 30 and 45 percent. An *announcement effect* (see Chapter 6) may have been at work. Gun-related crimes began to decline in the months just before the law went into effect, perhaps as a result of all the publicity (as has been the case in some drunk driving crackdowns), but this point is not entirely clear.

Some evidence indicates that officials undermined the "mandatory" provisions of Bartley-Fox, as police officers reportedly became a little more cautious about frisking people for weapons. Police reports on gun incidents declined by 25 percent in Boston between 1974 and 1976. Seventy of 79 officers interviewed admitted to being more selective because they did not want to catch "otherwise innocent" people violating the law. This is a classic example of how police officers' discretion reflects their judgment about the moral character of possible suspects. Meanwhile, the percentage of cases dismissed went from 18 to 38 percent. Despite its attempt to close plea-bargaining loopholes, the law did not restrict outright dismissal. Acquittals in the remaining cases increased from 16 percent in 1974 to 40 percent in 1975 and then declined to 33 percent in 1976. Finally, the number of appeals of convictions went from 21 to 96 percent.[42]

The net effect was that fewer people were sentenced for carrying a gun. The percentage of defendants actually sentenced dropped from 41 percent in 1974 to only 17 percent in 1976. This appears to be a classic illustration of criminal justice thermodynamics at work: As the nominal punishment went up, actual punishment went down. A follow-up study of the law in six Massachusetts counties found that it was still being implemented, with no evidence of systematic lowering or dropping of charges.

Guns at Airports and Schools

Another set of laws attempts to keep people from carrying guns in certain places, such as airplanes and schools.

Airports A federal law prohibits the carrying of a weapon on an airplane, and all passengers are electronically screened at the gate. The electronic screening at airports makes enforcement fairly effective. In 2002 the new Transportation Security Administration seized about 1,000 firearms. This was about half the average seized in pre-9/11 years, so the publicity about the tighter security procedures did have some effect. (Some people just didn't get it. On Thanksgiving weekend 2002, despite all the publicity about the new post-9/11 security procedures, airport personnel seized 15,982 pocket knives, 98 box cutters, 6 guns, and a brick.)[43] Many of the people detained in these seizures apparently forgot that they had a gun with them. This point is a testimony to the prevalence of guns in American society, the casualness with which they are carried around, and the limited deterrent effect of a well-known law. Nonetheless, the law has been effective in curbing airplane hijacking. The number of hijackings decreased from 40 in 1969 to only one attempted hijacking each in both 1990 and 1991, and none in either of the next two years.[44]

The strategy of preventing airplane hijackings by prohibiting guns on planes is consistent with the place-oriented approach discussed by the University of Maryland *Preventing Crime* report.[45] The antihijacking effort appears to have been successful, but there are serious limits on its application to other areas of society. Airports are special locations: confined spaces, involving a very small number of people, all of whom can be channeled through a metal detector. It is not clear how this strategy could be applied to society at large for the purpose of reducing ordinary robbery and burglary.

Schools   Another problem involves guns in school. Because of a series of sensational crimes—the 1999 massacre in Littleton, Colorado, and several other highly publicized incidents—there has been great national concern about guns and violence in public schools. Several strategies have been adopted to keep guns out of schools. The 1994 Gun Free Schools Act requires schools receiving federal education funds to have a policy mandating the expulsion of students who bring firearms to school. Some schools have instituted metal detectors similar to those used at airports.

The evidence, however, indicates that this is yet another example of the celebrated case phenomenon discussed in Chapter 2. Surveys of students consistently find that less than 10 percent have ever taken a gun to school. Between 1993 and 2003 between 7 and 9 percent of students reported being threatened with a weapon—knife or gun—in the previous twelve months.[46]

Get Guns off the Street: The Kansas City Experiment

The most innovative recent approach to reducing gun crimes is the Kansas City Gun Experiment. The experiment involved intensive enforcement of existing laws on the illegal carrying of handguns. Funded by the federal Weed and Seed program, it represents a combination of two important innovations in policing: *problem-oriented policing,* in which the police focus on a specific problem, and *hot spots,* in which patrols focus on a particular area (see Chapter 5).[47]

The experiment was conducted in a particularly high crime precinct in Kansas City, Missouri, where the 1991 murder rate was 177 per 100,000, or about 20 times higher than the national average. Two two-officer patrol cars, working overtime, patrolled for six hours every night, concentrating exclusively on detecting and seizing illegally possessed guns. The officers would stop cars on legitimate legal grounds (for example, a traffic violation) but focus on weapons seizures. Almost half (45 percent) of all the guns eventually seized were found through a search incident to arrest, another 21 percent were found in plain view, and 34 percent were found in frisks as authorized by the Supreme Court in the 1968 *Terry* decision.

Over the course of 29 weeks, the gun unit officers seized a total of 29 guns. Meanwhile, regular patrol officers in the target beat seized another 47 guns, for a combined total of 76. The number of gun crimes in the target beat declined by 49 percent, but only by 4 percent in a control beat. The experiment controlled for a possible displacement effect and found that gun crimes went up in some of the neighboring beats and down in others. The reduction in gun crimes could have occurred as a direct result of removing guns from the area, or through deterrence, or through the incapacitation of potential offenders who were arrested and imprisoned.

The Kansas City Gun Experiment seems to suggest that a clearly focused program to remove guns from the streets can reduce gun-related crime. A number of questions about the program remain, however. It is extremely expensive when measured in terms of the cost per gun seized or crime prevented. It is not clear that a police department could afford to run such a program as a part of normal operations. Also, when Sherman replicated the program in Indianapolis, some serious questions were raised about the data and some of the claims made for its success.[48]

The Boston Gun Project

The most successful gun violence reduction program has been the Boston Gun Project, which incorporates the principles of problem-oriented policing. Because it is closely related to other community-focused crime policies, we discuss it in detail in Chapter 14.

Summary

The safest conclusion at this point is that the gun seizure approach may prove to be an effective strategy for reducing gun-related violence, but more research is needed.

PROPOSITION 35
Focused, proactive enforcement strategies may be effective
in reducing gun-related crime in targeted areas.

More Guns? Right-to-Carry Laws

Some gun owners believe that the best way to reduce crime and protect law-abiding citizens is to have more guns on the street. Using county-level data on crime, Lott and Mustard estimated that if states without "shall issue" (i.e., right-to-carry) laws adopted them, it would prevent about 1,570 murders, 4,177 rapes, and over 60,000 aggravated assaults every year. The debate over guns and crime took a new direction in 1998 with John R. Lott's book, *More Guns, Less Crime,* arguing that allowing people to carry concealed weapons would deter violent crime.[49] The policy recommendation is that states should enact shall-issue laws allowing people to carry concealed weapons. Lott's research indicated that such laws were associated with lower crime rates.

Lott's proposal generated enormous controversy and sparked further studies attempting to replicate his research. The controversy over both the proposal and the subsequent studies was so great that the National Academy of Sciences undertook its own study and devoted an entire chapter to the issue. After reviewing all the research, they concluded that studies were highly sensitive to the model and control variables employed (with the result that studies produced very different findings) and that, in the end, it was not possible to determine a causal link between right-to-carry laws and the crime rate.[50]

> ## PROPOSITION 36
> Right-to-carry laws will not reduce crime.

Handguns as Self-Protection

The underlying assumption in Lott's argument is that people will successfully use their guns to defend themselves against criminals. What is the evidence on this? The National Academy of Sciences found wildly varying estimates of the number of defensive gun use incidents per year. One survey estimated 116,000 incidents a year, while another put the figure at 2.5 million.[51] Analyzing data from the *National Crime Victimization Survey* from 1979 to 1985, Gary Kleck and Miriam DeLone found that robbery victims used a gun to resist the offender in only 1.2 percent of all robberies (this figure included both completed and attempted robberies). Very few of these incidents involved a shootout between victim and offender. Nonetheless, Kleck and DeLone argued that when victims did use guns, they were frequently successful in preventing a completed robbery. In short, victims use them in the same way that armed criminals do: to intimidate the other person.[52]

Most of those arrestees who carry a weapon say they do so for protection or self-defense. The result is a self-perpetuating gun culture. As more juveniles carry guns, their peers feel the need to carry one also for self-protection. As James D. Wright explains, these individuals "live in a very hostile and violent environment, and many of them have come to believe, no doubt correctly, that their ability to survive in that environment depends critically on being adequately armed."[53] They are "highly motivated gun owners who are not easily persuaded that they should not have one."

GET TOUGH ON WEAPONS OFFENSES

The primary conservative policy on gun-related crimes is to get tough on offenders convicted of using guns. This approach reflects two basic conservative assumptions about crime, and the criminal justice system: first, that criminals and not guns commit crimes; and, second, that the criminal justice system is soft on crime and criminals. The basic policy recommendation calls for mandatory prison terms for gun-related crimes and longer prison terms. Such laws are extremely popular. In 1994, 41 states had mandatory minimum sentencing laws for illegal weapons possession.[54] A 1975 Florida law is typical of those in other states. It imposed a mandatory minimum sentence of three years in prison for use of a weapon in the commission of certain crimes and prohibited the granting of certain types of good-time credit during the mandatory minimum period.

National data indicate that, contrary to widespread belief, the criminal justice system is not soft on gun-related crimes. In 1994, 69 percent of all persons convicted of a weapons offense in state courts were incarcerated—the same figure as for drug offenses. The average prison sentence was four years, and the average jail term was 6 months. Federal courts were considerably tougher, sentencing 77 percent to prison, for average terms of just over six years. (State court sentences have been getting shorter, down from an average of 56 months since 1985, whereas federal prison sentences have been getting longer, up from 42 months in 1985.) But both state and federal prisoners serve about the same amount of time: 22 months for state prisoners and 23 months for federal prisoners.

Getting Tough in Detroit

In 1977, Michigan passed a law mandating two years in prison for any gun-related crime. The law precluded either probation or parole and was advertised as "One with a gun gets you two." At the same time, the Wayne County (Detroit) prosecutor announced a new policy prohibiting plea bargaining of gun charges under the new law.

An evaluation by Colin Loftin and David McDowall focused on two questions: Did the law increase the certainty and severity of punishment? and did it lower the crime rate? The key issue in regard to the severity of sentences concerned the effective minimum prison terms; that is, how much time could a convicted offender reasonably expect to do before becoming eligible for release, when reductions for both good time and parole were taken into account? They found "no statistically significant change in the expected minimum sentence" for gun-related murders and armed robberies, but a significant increase in the expected minimum sentences for gun-related assaults.[55]

Two factors—the going rate and the trickle-up phenomenon—explain what happened in Detroit. The expected minimum sentences for murder and robbery did not increase because the going rate for these crimes was already high. Armed robbers in Detroit had been serving prison terms averaging six years before the new law, and few convicted robbers ever got probation. The system was not soft on crime beforehand, and the supposed get tough law did not change things.

Sentences for assaults increased because the going rate for those offenses had been rather low. Probation and suspended sentences were common, and incarcerated offenders got an average of six months. Much of this seeming leniency stemmed from the ambiguity of the crime of assault. The nature of the act is often difficult to specify with precision; it may also be difficult to determine who initiated the altercation. Moreover, as we argued in Chapter 3, criminal justice officials routinely treat assaults between people who know each other as essentially private disputes and frequently dismiss the charges or settle the case with a plea to a lesser offense. The new law raised the severity of sentences by eliminating this opportunity for mitigating punishment.

Loftin and McDowall also found that "the gun law did not significantly alter the number or type of violent offenses committed in Detroit." Murder, robbery, and assault did decline, but the decrease in the rate had begun five months before the law went into effect—long enough in advance to rule out the possibility of the announcement effect that has appeared with other laws toughening criminal penalties.[56]

The impact of mandatory sentences for gun crimes is extremely complex. When McDowall and Loftin (in collaboration with Brian Wiersma) pooled the results from six different studies, they reached somewhat different conclusions.[57] Mandatory sentencing appeared to reduce homicides in all six cities. In Detroit, there was a 14 percent reduction, with an average of 5.5 lives saved each month. On the other hand, there were no significant reductions in gun assaults or robberies in any of the sites. The authors characterized the results as a "logical puzzle," conceding that they did not know which features of the sentencing policy were "responsible for the preventive effects." More research is clearly needed, and we should be cautious about simplistic assertions on either side of the debate: that mandatory sentencing deters crime or that it does not work at all.

Project Exile in Richmond

A more recent get tough program was Project Exile in Richmond, Virginia. This involved transferring firearms cases to federal court for prosecution, where defendants faced a possible mandatory five years in prison, a far harsher sentence than in state court. (A similar policy was part of the Boston Gun Project, which we will discuss in Chapter 14.)

Richmond officials claimed that Project Exile produced a 40 percent reduction in firearms-related murders. An independent analysis, however, concluded that this reduction would have occurred anyway. In part this was because of the general reduction in firearms homicides nationally. But also, the baseline year prior to implementation of the new policy had an unusually high number of firearms homicides, with the result that a natural regression to the mean occurred.[58]

Evidence from California also suggests that the system is not overly soft on gun-related crimes. Gun-related crimes were 34 percent more likely to be accepted for prosecution at the initial screening than were nongun crimes and 24 percent more likely to be accepted at the preliminary hearing stage. Gun users were less likely to plead guilty, and 67 percent of the gun wielders who were convicted at trial went to prison, compared with only 33 percent of other offenders. Moreover, the use of a gun added nearly two years (600 days) to the average sentence. Pleading guilty did not help defendants accused of gun crimes. Seventy-four percent of those who pleaded guilty went to prison, compared with 45 percent of all others who copped a plea. And for their plea they got 400 additional days of prison time. These figures hardly paint a picture of a system soft on gun crimes.[59]

In short, as we argued in Chapter 2, the justice system has always been tough on gun-related crimes. Trying to get tough(er), especially through mandatory sentences, will not produce any additional reductions in crime.

> ### PROPOSITION 37
> Trying to "get tough" on gun crimes, especially through mandatory prison sentences, will not reduce gun-related crime.

CONCLUSION

Gun-related violence is a serious problem in American society. There is no obvious solution, however. Banning guns is an empty gesture, given the number of handguns already in circulation. Trying to keep guns out of the hands of "bad" people also appears to be futile. Nor does it appear that threats of severe punishment will deter or incapacitate offenders in a way that will significantly reduce crime. Policies directed at how people use guns, such as the Bartley-Fox Law and the approach taken in the Kansas City Gun Experiment, might have some positive impact on reducing the number of guns on the street and, as a consequence, gun-related crimes.

NOTES

1.   Centers for Disease Control and Prevention, *National Vital Statistics Reports,* vol. 52, no. 3, Sept. 18, 2003. Available on the Center for Disease Control website. The best overview of the problem of guns and violence is National Academy of Sciences, *Firearms and Violence: A Critical Review* (Washington: National Academy Press, 2005).

2.   Philip J. Cook and Jens Ludwig, *Gun Violence: The Real Costs* (New York: Oxford University Press, 2000).

3.   National Center for Health Statistics, 2002.

4.   Bureau of Justice Statistics, *Weapon Use and Violent Crime* (Washington, DC: Department of Justice, 2003). NCJ 194820.

5.   Check the website of the National Rifle Association (NRA) for their views and other related publications.

6.   Check the website of Handgun Control, Inc., for their views and other related materials.

7.   Philip J. Cook and Mark H. Moore, "Gun Control," in James Q. Wilson and Joan Petersilia, eds., *Crime* (San Francisco: ICS Press, 1995), p. 271. The most comprehensive treatment of gun violence and gun control policies is Gary Kleck, *Point Blank: Guns and Violence in America* (New York: Aldine de Gruyter, 1991).

8.   Mark H. Moore, "Controlling Criminogenic Commodities: Drugs, Guns, and Alcohol," in James Q. Wilson, ed., *Crime and Public Policy* (San Francisco: ICS Press, 1983).

9.   Bureau of Justice Statistics, *Sourcebook of Criminal Justice Statistics Online,* Table 2.57. Available on the web either through NCJRS or The University at Albany. The figures cited here are from the National Opinion Research Center. For a detailed report, see Tom W. Smith, *1999 National Gun Policy Survey of the National Opinion Research Center: Research Findings* (Chicago: National Opinion Research Center, 2000).

10. For a useful collection of articles on the debate, see Jan E. Dizard, Robert Merrill Muth, and Stephen D. Andrews, Jr., eds., *Guns in America: A Reader* (New York: New York University Press, 1999).

11. A basic classification scheme is in Bureau of Justice Statistics, *Guns Used in Crime* (Washington, DC: Department of Justice, 1995).

12. National Academy of Sciences, *Firearms and Violence: A Critical Review,* "Defensive Gun Use," pp. 103–108.

13. Smith, *1999 National Gun Policy Survey of the National Opinion Research Center: Research Findings.* Bureau of Justice Statistics, *Sourcebook of Criminal Justice Statistics Online,* Table 2.57.

14. Edward L. Glaeser and Spencer Glendon, "Who Owns Guns? Criminals, Victims, and the Culture of Violence," *American Economic Review* 88 (May 1998): 458–462; Gary Kleck, "Crime, Culture Conflict and the Sources of Support for Gun Control, *American Behavioral Scientist* 39 (February 1996): 387–404.

15. Bureau of Justice Statistics, *Weapon Use and Violent Crime* (2003). NCJ 194820.

16. "Report Links Crimes to States with Weak Gun Controls," *New York Times,* 9 April 1997.

17. Smith, *1999 National Gun Policy Survey.*

18. Edward D. Jones, "The District of Columbia's 'Firearms Control Regulations Act of 1975': The Toughest Handgun Control Law in the United States—Or Is It?" *The Annals* 455 (May 1981): 138–149.

19. National Academy of Sciences, *Firearms and Violence: A Critical Review,* pp. 97–98.

20. John Kaplan, "The Wisdom of Gun Prohibition," *The Annals* 455 (May 1981): 11–23.

21. LaPierre, *Guns, Crime, and Freedom,* pp. 82–83.

22. James D. Wright, Peter H. Rossi and Kathleen Daly, *Under the Gun: Weapons, Crime, and Violence in America (New York: Aldine de Gruyter, 1983),* p. 320.

23. The St. Louis and Seattle evaluations, along with other articles, are in Martha Plotkin, ed., *Under Fire: Gun Buy-Backs,*

Exchanges, and Amnesty Programs (Washington, DC: Police Executive Research Forum, 1996).

24. National Academy of Sciences, *Firearms and Violence: A Critical Review,* p. 95.

25. Robert Sherrill, *The Saturday Night Special* (New York: Charterhouse, 1973).

26. "Los Angeles Bans the Sale of Inexpensive, Small Guns," *New York Times,* 8 September 1996.

27. Kleck, *Point Blank,* p. 85; see also "Los Angeles Bans the Sale of Small, Inexpensive Guns."

28. Kleck, *Point Blank,* pp. 85–86.

29. Bureau of Justice Statistics, *Guns Used in Crime,* p. 6.

30. Smith, *1999 National Gun Policy Survey of the National Opinion Research Center: Research Findings.*

31. Jeffrey A. Roth and Christopher S. Koper, "Impacts of the 1994 Assault Weapons Ban: 1994–96," (Washington, DC: Department of Justice, 1999).

32. National Academy of Sciences, *Firearms and Violence: A Critical Review,* "Regulating Gun Dealers," pp. 89–90.

33. Christopher Koper, "Federal Legislation and Gun Markets: How Much Have Recent Reforms of the Federal Firearms Licensing System Reduced Criminal Gun Suppliers?" *Criminology and Public Policy* 1 (2002): 151–178. And see also the comments by Deborah S. Azrael and James B. Jacobs.

34. Cook and Ludwig J. *Gun Violence: The Real Costs.*

35. Mark H. Moore, "Keeping Handguns from Criminal Offenders," *Annals* 455 (May 1981): 92–109.

36. Wright et al., *Under the Gun.*

37. Bureau of Justice Statistics, *Guns Used in Crime,* p. 4.

38. Bureau of Justice Statistics, *Firearm Use by Offenders* (Washington, DC: Department of Justice, 2001). NCJ 189369.

39. Bureau of Justice Statistics, *Guns Used in Crime.*

40. Glenn L. Pierce and William J. Bowers, "The Bartley-Fox Gun Law's Short-Term Impact on Crime," *The Annals* 455 (May

1981): 120–137. The national data are from Smith, *1999 National Gun Policy Survey of the National Opinion Research Center: Research Findings.*

41. Ibid.

42. Ibid.

43. "Airports' Thanksgiving Seizures: 15,982 Knives and a Brick," *USA Today,* 3 December 2002.

44. Bureau of the Census, *Statistical Abstract of the United States, 1995.*

45. University of Maryland, *Preventing Crime: What Works, What Doesn't, What's Promising?* (Washington, DC: Department of Justice, 1997), chap. 7; airports are covered on pp. 7–29 to 7–30. NCJ 165366.

46. Bureau of Justice Statistics, *Indicators of School Crime and Safety, 2004* (Washington, DC: Department of Justice, 2004). NCJ 205290.

47. Lawrence W. Sherman, James W. Shaw, and Dennis P. Rogan, *The Kansas City Gun Experiment* (Washington, DC: Department of Justice, 1995). NCJ 150855.

48. Ibid.

49. John R. Lott, *More Guns, Less Crime: Understanding Crime and Gun-control Laws* (Chicago: University of Chicago Press, 1998).

50. National Academy of Sciences, *Firearms and Violence.*

51. National Academy of Sciences, *Firearms and Violence.*

52. Gary Kleck and Miriam A. DeLone, "Victim Resistance and Offender Weapon Effects in Robbery," *Journal of Quantitative Criminology* 9 (1993): 55–81.

53. James D. Wright, "Ten Essential Observations on Guns in America," *Society* (March/April 1995): 66.

54. Bureau of Justice Statistics, *National Assessment of Structured Sentencing* (Washington, DC: Department of Justice, 1996), pp. 24–25. NCJ 153853.

55. Colin Loftin and David McDowall, "'One with a Gun Gets You Two': Mandatory Sentencing and Firearms Violence in Detroit," *The Annals* 455 (May 1981): 150–167.

56. Ibid.

57. David McDowall, Colin Loftin, and Brian Wiersma, "A Comparative Study of the Preventive Effects of Mandatory Sentencing Laws for Gun Crimes," *Journal of Criminal Law and Criminology* 83.2 (1992): 378–394.

58. National Academy of Sciences, *Firearms and Violence: A Critical Review,* "Sentencing enhancements," pp. 223–230.

59. Alan Lizotte and Marjorie S. Zatz, "The Use and Abuse of Sentence Enhancement for Firearms Offenses in California," *Law and Contemporary Problems* 49 (1986): 199–221.

PART IV

Reform: The
Liberal Prescription

L iberals take a very different approach to crime policy than do conservatives. As we indicated in Chapter 1, liberals are much more optimistic about our capacity to reduce crime by changing either people or society. In the two chapters that follow, we will take a close look at the two most important components of liberal crime policy. Chapter 11 examines both the concept of rehabilitation and specific programs designed to change criminal offenders into law-abiding citizens. Chapter 12 looks at potential reforms by increasing public confidence in the criminal justice system and as a consequence increasing commitment to lawful behavior.

11

Treat 'Em!

REHABILITATING CRIMINALS

The concept of *rehabilitation* is the cornerstone of traditional liberal crime control policy. Although the rhetoric has changed over the years, the basic idea remains the same: reduce crime by treating criminals and "correcting" their behavior. The terminology used by state agencies reflects the continued commitment to rehabilitation. We have departments of "corrections" but no departments of "punishment." Why do we use this terminology? The term *corrections* carries the aura of healing and helping people, placing corrections officials on the same professional status as medical doctors and social workers.[1]

The Philosophy of Rehabilitation

What exactly is rehabilitation? The National Academy of Sciences defines it as "any planned intervention that reduces an offender's further criminal activity."[2] The key words here are *planned* and *intervention*. As Wolfgang's career criminal research indicates (see Chapter 4), most lawbreakers stop sooner or later. It is well established that criminal activity peaks between the ages of 14 and 24 and then declines sharply. Aging is the best crime reduction policy we know about.[3] The goal of rehabilitation is to make offenders stop sooner rather than later through a planned intervention program. As we explained in Chapter 1, rehabilitation is a crime prevention strategy; it simply takes a different approach than punishment-oriented strategies.

Old and New Programs

The principal strategy for rehabilitating offenders is to reintegrate them into the community and help them establish law-abiding lives. The current buzzword for this is *reentry*. The federal government has made offender reentry programs a top priority and is supporting many reentry programs across the country. Because of its special attention to the community context, we will examine reentry in Chapter 14 along with other new community-focused crime policies. In this chapter we will examine traditional rehabilitation programs.

Traditional correctional institutions offer several programs designed to reintegrate offenders into the community. Prisons offer academic and vocational education programs, drug and alcohol counseling, anger management and other forms of individual counseling, and work experience. Community-based correctional programs—probation and parole—place offenders in the community under some kind of supervision, on the assumption that offenders will respond more effectively to this more normal setting than the very abnormal setting of a prison.

Since the 1990s, a new set of *intermediate punishments* have appeared, designed to place offenders in the community but under much closer surveillance than traditional probation and parole.[4] These programs include boot camps, electronic monitoring, home confinement, and intensive supervision on probation or parole. Some observers believe that these measures represent a revival of rehabilitation as criminal justice policy. Others, however, are not so sure. This chapter examines first traditional rehabilitation-oriented programs and then looks at the new intermediate punishments to see if they are more effective. Our goal is to identify correctional treatment programs that are relatively more effective than others and that, if adopted, would help reduce crime.

The Politics of Rehabilitation:
The Willie Horton Furlough

Rehabilitation-oriented programs are often the subject of bitter political controversy. The 1988 presidential election campaign is one of the most famous examples, and in fact may be the only time in our history where a particular criminal justice case was a major issue in a presidential election campaign. Republican candidate George Bush ran a television ad about a convicted murderer, Willie Horton, who had been released from prison into the community on a weekend furlough during which he raped a woman. Bush used the incident to attack his opponent, Michael Dukakis, as a liberal Democrat who was soft on crime. The fact that Horton was African American and the rape victim a white woman injected a divisive racial element into the election campaign.[5]

Furloughs are a classic type of rehabilitation program. They are designed to reintegrate a prisoner into the community through gradual release. They have been used for many years and are very common. In 1996, about 140,000 prisoners were granted furloughs through programs in 41 states (although more than half were in Florida, which furloughed over 87,000 offenders). Generally, furloughed offenders behave themselves. A 1990 survey found that only 31 of the 96,745 Florida offenders "failed." In Illinois, all of the 13,785 participants successfully completed the program. Connecticut had the highest failure rate, but even there only 29 of 3,398 inmates furloughed were arrested for a new crime. In Massachusetts, scene of the Willie Horton incident, none of the 438 furloughed inmates was rearrested while on release.[6] (The hysteria over furloughs has passed and there are no more recent data available, unfortunately.)

The Willie Horton story is a classic example of the celebrated case in the top layer of our criminal justice wedding cake, which we discussed in Chapter 1. As David C. Anderson observes in his thoughtful review of the case, exaggerating its significance and treating it as typical of general patterns is a "gross insult to truth."[7] The case dramatizes the political controversy over rehabilitation. Liberals believe that furloughs are an effective program for reintegrating offenders into the community, while conservatives believe that they are a soft-hearted and misguided method of turning dangerous people loose on the community.

THE "NOTHING WORKS" CONTROVERSY

Over 30 years ago criminologist Robert Martinson defined the terms of the debate over rehabilitation. In a 1974 article (and later a book), he concluded that "with few and isolated exceptions, the rehabilitative efforts that have been reported so far have had no appreciable effect on rehabilitation."[8] The so-called Martinson Report was an early example of the new evidence-based style of crime policy analysis. Conducting a meta-analysis, he reviewed all of the available evaluations of correctional treatment programs.

Martinson's conclusions were a bombshell, although the report as a whole was widely misinterpreted. The title of his original article was "What Works?" Many people, however, interpreted it to mean that "nothing works." He did not actually say that. In fact, he found positive outcomes in 48 percent of the program evaluations he reviewed. And a few years later, he unequivocally stated that "some treatment programs do have an appreciable effect on recidivism," adding, "The critical fact seems to be the conditions under which the program is delivered."[9]

The Martinson report is a classic example of how social science research is often misinterpreted (and misused) in the political arena. Many people wanted to believe that "nothing worked" because they were disillusioned with rehabilitation. They were angry over (by then) ten years of soaring crime rates. Conservatives blamed rehabilitation programs for being soft on crime, whereas liberals attacked the same programs for violating standards of due process. The disillusionment with rehabilitation was part of a more general conservative mood that arose in the mid-1970s and continues today.[10]

The story of Martinson's report is fascinating in itself. His team reviewed all evaluations of correctional programs published in English between 1945 and 1967. In important respects, his report was a precursor to the current evidence-based policy movement, which we discussed in Chapter 1. They were able to find only 231 that were acceptable by rigorous scientific standards. Most evaluations they rejected because these tests used unreliable measures, failed to specify the "treatment," did not use proper control groups, or drew questionable conclusions from the data.[11] Martinson exposed a scandalous case of professional irresponsibility: the correctional community's failure to develop a systematic process of evaluation. Programs routinely claimed "success" without any legitimate basis for doing so. The academic community shared much of the responsibility, as formal evaluations were done either by researchers under contract or by in-house professionals with academic training. Because his findings were so threatening, the state of New York did not release the report and even denied Martinson permission to publish it. He sued and eventually forced the report's release.

Was Martinson Right?

Was Martinson's assessment of correctional programs accurate? The National Academy of Sciences' Panel on Research on Rehabilitative Techniques reviewed his work and concluded that he was "essentially correct."[12] It supported Martinson's view that there was little evidence "to allay the current pessimism about the effectiveness of institutional rehabilitation programs as they now exist."

The debate sparked by Martinson continues to rage. Some criminologists, including Logan and Gaes, agree with Martinson that there is no convincing evidence about the effectiveness of correctional treatment.[13] Daniel Glaser and others, however, believe that there is enough evidence of success of particular programs to justify continued support for rehabilitation as a crime control strategy.[14] Glaser states that "certain sentencing and correctional policies, which differ according to the criminalization of the offender, are more likely than their alternatives to reduce recidivism rates."[15]

How can we sort our way through this debate? As a first step, it is important to recognize, as Logan and Gaes point out, that the debate is as much ideological as it is empirical. Some advocates of rehabilitation regard it as a morally superior social policy regardless of the evidence about its success. Logan and Gaes, on the other hand, regard punishment as a morally legitimate social policy. "Legal punishment," they argue, "is a legitimate and . . . even a noble aspect of our culture."[16] No empirical evidence is going to resolve this aspect of the debate. It is a question of what values should underlie social policies.

The Prediction Problem Revisited

Glaser's defense of rehabilitation illustrates the problem that lies at the core of all treatment-oriented programs. It assumes a good match between offender and treatment program. It is certainly true that *some* programs are effective for *some* offenders. Achieving the proper match, however, brings us back to our old friend the prediction problem (Chapter 4). Sentencing a convicted offender to a community-based drug treatment program represents a prediction that he or she (1) is not a serious danger to the community, and therefore does not need to go to prison, and (2) will respond positively to the drug treatment. Drawing on the work of John Hagan, Glaser argues that some individuals are more deeply "embedded in crime" than others.[17] Those who are less deeply embedded are more "amenable" to community-based treatment. So far, so good.

The crucial question is whether judges and correctional officials can correctly identify the more "amenable" offenders and sentence them to the right treatment program. We have already criticized conservative programs because of their inability to accurately predict which offenders are the really high risk ones who should be sentenced to long prison terms (Chapters 4, 7). Choosing which offenders to place on probation is simply the other side of the same sentencing coin. The criticisms we made of conservative punishment-oriented programs apply with equal force to liberal rehabilitation-oriented programs.

TRADITIONAL REHABILITATION PROGRAMS

Let us now examine the traditional rehabilitation-oriented programs—diversion, probation, and parole—to see what evidence there is regarding their effectiveness.

Diversion

Diversion was one of the great reforms of the 1960s. The President's Crime Commission gave it a strong endorsement in 1967, and in the 1970s an estimated 1,200 diversion programs were established.[18] A diversion program is a planned intervention with a treatment component and the goal of getting offenders out of the criminal justice system as early as possible.

Actually, diversion was nothing new in the 1960s. Historically, many offenders have been diverted from the criminal justice system at an early stage. Police officers routinely decide not to arrest someone even though they have probable cause to, and prosecutors routinely dismiss cases when prosecution would not serve the "interests of justice." We call these practices the *old* diversion. The *new* diversion programs are characterized by several formal program elements: officially stated goals, a professional staff, and treatment services.[19] Drug courts are simply the latest form of diversion.

Diversion programs are designed to rehabilitate offenders (and thereby reduce crime) in two ways. First, they keep people accused of relatively minor offenses out of jails and prisons. This reflects labeling theory in criminology, which holds that formal processing in the criminal justice system (and imprisonment in particular) only accentuates a person's tendency toward criminal behavior. The President's Crime Commission argued: "Institutions tend to isolate offenders from society, both physically and psychologically, cutting them off from schools, jobs, families, and other supportive influences and increasing the probability that the label criminal will be indelibly impressed upon them."[20] The Wolfgang cohort data we examined in Chapter 4, moreover, suggest that most juveniles "mature out" in relation to criminal behavior. Diversion programs assume that the best approach is to intervene in people's lives as little as possible.

Second, diversion programs are designed to provide the treatment services that address the offender's real problems: drug or alcohol treatment, employment counseling, anger management, and so forth. Advocates of diversion believe that arrest, prosecution, and punishment aggravate rather than treat those problems (while at the same time overloading the criminal justice system).

Finally, diversion programs are intended to reduce the costs of the criminal justice system, by avoiding the expenses of full criminal prosecution and imprisonment.

In short, diversion promised the best of all possible worlds—an approach that was more effective, more humane, and cheaper. An old adage says that if something seems too good to be true, it probably is. Let us take a look at diversion in practice.

The Manhattan Court Employment Project The earliest and most influential diversion program was the Manhattan Court Employment Project. Sponsored by the Vera Institute, the project provided employment services to arrested persons. The basic assumption was that because unemployment is a major cause of crime, facilitating employment will reduce subsequent criminal activity. Although it is an old program, it is worth taking a close look at it because it illustrates a number of important issues.

Each day staff members of the Court Employment Project reviewed the arrest docket and identified defendants who met the program's criteria: resident of New York City, between the ages of 16 and 45, unemployed or earning less than $125 a week, and charged with a felony other than homicide, rape, kidnapping, or arson. In addition, the defendant must have not had prior jail or prison experience of one year or longer. With the prosecutor's consent, the case was suspended for 90 days while the defendant received counseling, assistance in obtaining any short-term public assistance for which he or she might have been eligible, and referral to a job opening with one of the 400 cooperating employers. Charges were dropped completely if the defendant "succeeded" by keeping a job. If the person "failed" to secure employment, the case was prosecuted.

An early evaluation declared the Manhattan Court Employment Project a huge success. In its first three years, the project accepted 1,300 clients, about half of whom (48.2 percent) succeeded. About 70 percent of these 626 people had been unemployed at the time of arrest. Fourteen months later, about 80 percent of those who could be located were still employed. Only 15.8 percent of these successful clients committed another crime in the twelve months following their release from the program. This recidivism rate was half of that for both offenders who failed in the program and a control group. The program cost only $731 per client, or $1,518 per success.[21]

A subsequent evaluation, however, reached very different conclusions. It found that the project did not reduce recidivism and had no discernible effect on the employment record or the behavior of its clients. Moreover, it did not reduce pretrial detention time or lower the number of convictions. A major problem was that about half of the clients served by the program would not have been prosecuted at all if there had been no court employment project.[22] This is a classic example of "net widening." Because this phenomenon affects so many well-intentioned reforms, we need to discuss it in detail.

The Net-Widening Problem *Net widening* is the process by which more people are brought under some form of social control through the criminal justice system. The unwritten law of net widening is that less punitive alternatives tend to be applied to people who would otherwise not be under any social control at all—that is, they would be truly diverted and not arrested, prosecuted, or incarcerated.

Evaluations of early diversion programs found that they led to substantial net widening. More than half of the juveniles referred to 15 diversion projects in California would not have been committed to any kind of program under traditional practice. Thomas G. Blomberg found that juvenile diversion programs produced a 32 percent increase in the total number of juveniles under some form of control. Other evaluations have found varying degrees of net widening.[23] And as we shall see, net widening has plagued many of the new intermediate punishments such as boot camps.

A study of reforms in the San Francisco juvenile justice system in the mid 1990s that included new prevention and intervention systems and cost $20 million found a significant increase in the detention of juvenile arrestees, even though juvenile arrests declined by about half. And in fact, the average length of detentions increased despite the original goal of diverting juveniles from the system.[24]

The dynamics of net widening are easy to understand. Officials continue to use severe sanctions (e.g., prison) for offenders they regard as dangerous and use new and less punitive programs for less serious offenders. Thus, instead of diverting less serious offenders completely out of the system, they "divert" them into a treatment program. As a result, more people are under control of the criminal justice system. The problem, of course, is that most of those low-risk offenders would have succeeded without the benefit of the program. The treatment, therefore, provides no added crime reduction effectiveness.

The net-widening phenomenon suggests that the old diversion did a better job of achieving the basic goal of keeping people out of the system. When a police officer does not make an arrest, that person is truly diverted; when a prosecutor dismisses all charges, that defendant is genuinely diverted. New diversion programs, however, keep people under some form of control, thereby maintaining or even increasing the total costs to the system.[25]

Does Diversion Rehabilitate? The most important question for us is whether diversion programs effectively rehabilitate offenders. More precisely, the question is: Do diversion programs provide a treatment or intervention that reduces future criminal behavior more effectively than normal prosecution? A number of evaluations have found that they do not. The Law Enforcement Assistance Administration touted the Des Moines (Iowa) Adult Diversion Project as an "exemplary project" that other communities should adopt. An evaluation, however, found that it had "little impact in reducing recidivism among diverted, compared to nondiverted offenders." In another program, diverted offenders had lower recidivism rates than did juveniles sent to juvenile court but, alas, had higher recidivism rates than did kids released outright without the benefit of any "treatment."[26] More recent reviews have found similarly disappointing results.

The failure of diversion programs is the result of a number of problems. First, many do not actually deliver the treatment services they claim to deliver. Some intensive probation supervision programs, for example, promised a high rate of contacts between probationers and probation officers but did not achieve that goal.[27] Second, even when treatments are delivered, there are questions about the content of those treatment services. Do the drug and alcohol treatment components of a diversion program effectively reduce substance abuse? How many of the offenders who succeed would have done so on their own, without the benefit of the treatment?

Additionally, if net widening occurs, the promised cost savings will not result because there are now more rather than fewer people under the control of the criminal justice system. (In Chapter 14, we will find that the innovative community courts in New York City did not save money as intended.)

Finally, diversion programs introduce serious due process considerations. A person who agrees to enter a treatment program in the expectation of having criminal charges dropped is, in effect, admitting guilt. Rather than contest the charge, the person is saying, "Yes, I have done something wrong, and you have a right to force me to undergo treatment." By offering a seemingly more attractive alternative to prosecution and possible incarceration, the program coerces this tacit admission of guilt in a subtle but powerful way. In addition, the selection of the program's clients may be unfair.[28]

In the end, diversion offers a false promise. It fails to achieve its own goals, may in fact contradict them, and does not offer a realistic solution to the problem of serious crime. Diversion is not really used for persons charged with robbery or burglary. Nor is there persuasive evidence that it rehabilitates lesser offenders in a way that keeps them from becoming serious offenders.

An evidence-based crime policy approach leads us to the following proposition:

PROPOSITION 38
Diversion programs do not reduce serious crime.

Drug Courts as Diversion Programs   Diversion enjoyed a revival, although in somewhat disguised form, in the 1990s as drug courts. Drug courts emphasize the treatment of offenders for their substance abuse problems rather than full criminal prosecution. We could discuss drug courts in Chapter 13, which covers drugs, but we include them here because for all practical purposes they represent a form of correctional treatment and diversion in particular.

The drug court idea was born in 1989 in Miami. It spread rapidly and enjoyed significant financial support from the U.S. Department of Justice. By 2005 there were over 1,500 drug courts operating or being planned across the country. (Details and current data can be found on the website of the National Association of Drug Court Professionals.)

A drug court is a specialized court that handles substance abuse cases through a comprehensive program of treatment, supervision, and alternative sanctions. Basically, if an offender successfully completes a treatment program, the drug court has the option of dismissing the original criminal charges, reducing or setting aside a sentence, or providing a lesser penalty, or some combination of these alternatives.[29] These options represent the basic idea of diversion programs: getting offenders out of the system early in return for participating in treatment. There are variations among drug courts in terms of how they implement their goals. One important innovative aspect of drug courts is greater involvement of judges in overseeing the progress of cases. They engage in close cooperation with prosecutors, defense attorneys, and correctional treatment personnel in all aspects of cases. This is a non-traditional role for judges. Additionally, drug courts utilize frequent drug testing to ensure that offenders remains drug free.

It is interesting that the official literature on drug courts rarely if ever mention the word "diversion," even though that is what they are really doing. This silence is probably due to the bad reputation that diversion acquired by the 1980s when research did not find that programs achieved their goals.

As with other correctional treatment programs, drug courts have multiple goals. They are designed to reduce crime by providing the treatment that offenders need, save money by reducing jail prison populations, and provide closer supervision and control of offenders who are released to the community (mainly through drug testing and other forms of intensive supervision). These multiple and often conflicting goals are also found in the new intermediate punishments that we will examine later.

Are drug courts effective? The evidence is mixed. Offenders who complete drug court programs do have lower recidivism rates than those who do not participate at all. In one early study, drug court graduates had a recidivism rate of 29 percent, compared with 49 percent for the control group. A later and more comprehensive evaluation by the Urban Institute found that although there was considerable variation among drug courts, recidivism rates in general were lower than would otherwise have been the case. Many offenders who are offered the option of a drug court program decline to participate.[30] (As with some intermediate punishments we will look at shortly, such a program often involves more intrusive control than does conventional jail or prison time.) Many of those who enter drug court programs drop out.

The lesson seems to be the same as for all treatment programs: Some programs work for some offenders. The problem, however, is in matching individual offenders to the right program. And matching offenders to programs is yet another variation of the prediction problem.

Probation

Probation is the most widely used rehabilitation program in the criminal justice system. In 2003, 4 million adults were on probation in the United States, 1 million more than in 1995.[31] Thirty-two percent of all convicted felons are sentenced to "straight probation," and another 28 percent receive split sentences, i.e., a jail term followed by probation.[32]

Probation embodies the philosophy of rehabilitation by keeping convicted offenders in the community rather than sending them to prison. Probation "treatment" generally consists of supervision by a probation officer and some formal restrictions on a probationer's behavior: being required to report regularly to a probation officer, not leave the area without permission, take drug or alcohol counseling, furnish employment verification or evidence of seeking a job, and so on. Traditionally, probation was designed to help rehabilitate offenders by having probation officers assist them in finding a job and dealing with other personal problems.

Probation serves a number of different purposes. It is often an appropriate sentence for someone convicted of a less serious offense or for a first-time offender. In this respect it serves the goal of proportionality in sentencing. It is also far cheaper than imprisonment—less than $1,000 a year per probationer, compared with $26,000 per prisoner. Finally, we use probation as a matter of necessity. We simply could not afford to imprison all convicted felons even if we wanted to.

The Effectiveness of Probation Does probation work? Is it effective in rehabilitating offenders and reducing crime? Actually, there are two separate questions related to effectiveness: Is probation more effective than incarceration? and are some kinds of probation programs more effective than others? There is much debate over the effectiveness of probation. Evaluations have found failure rates that range from 65 to 12 percent.[33] Where does the truth lie?

The Rand study of felons on probation in California found very depressing results. After 40 months on probation, 65 percent of the probationers had been rearrested, and 51 percent had been reconvicted of a new offense. Moreover, one-third of those reconvicted (18 percent of the original sample) were reconvicted of a serious violent crime. Nor do they wait very long to fail. Probationers reconvicted of a violent crime took an average of only eight months to recidivate, while those reconvicted of property offenses took an average of only five months (see Figure 11.1).

In short, most felons placed on probation fail; they do not become law-abiding citizens. Why? Many experts argue that traditional probation programs do not provide any kind of meaningful supervision or treatment. The level of supervision has always been very minimal, involving a meeting with a probation officer (PO) perhaps once a month. The PO fills out the required reports, and that is that. Joan Petersilia found that offenders on regular probation in Los Angeles County met with their POs only once a month. Another report

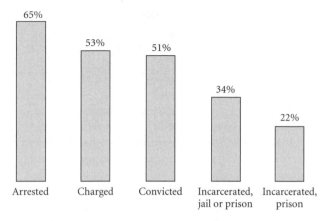

FIGURE 11.1 Probation outcomes after three years, California

SOURCE: Joan Petersilia, *Granting Felons Probation* (Santa Monica: Rand Corporation, 1985).

indicated that because some PO caseloads exceeded a thousand probationers, POs in Los Angeles spent an average of 1 hour and 47 minutes *per year* with each offender.[34] The level of supervision has gotten even worse in recent years because of the increase in caseloads. The total number of people on probation quadrupled between 1979 and 2003, from 1 to 4 million. The "war on crime" has resulted not just in a soaring prison population but also in a huge increase in the probation population.[35]

A third issue involved the quality content of treatment services. Even assuming that a probationer is officially enrolled in a drug treatment or anger management program, it is not clear that this particular program is well run or that any kind of service—in and of itself—can overcome the problems that led the probationer to commit crime in the first place. As we will see in Chapter 13, the evidence on the effectiveness of drug treatment programs is very weak.

In the long run, most probationers eventually rehabilitate themselves, through maturation, finding a job, getting married, and so on. John Hagan argues that whether a person becomes law abiding or continues in a life of criminal activity depends on the extent to which he or she is "socially embedded" in either legitimate or criminal opportunities. Some individuals have more contacts— with family members or people in the neighborhood—that lead to jobs. These contacts, moreover, tend to multiply: A job results in additional contacts that lead to other and often better job opportunities. Individuals who are embedded in these kinds of networks are far more likely to establish law-abiding lives than those who are not—regardless of the kind of probation or parole services they receive. Generally, white youths are more embedded in positive networks than African American or Hispanic youths. Whites are simply more likely to have a family member, friend, or acquaintance who can refer them to a job opening that is the case with young men of color, who are more likely to live in economically devastated neighborhoods.[36]

Research related to offender reentry programs (which we will examine in Chapter 14) provides a valuable glimpse into the lives of criminal offenders. Although the research is specifically related to parole, it has direct relevance to probation. Interviews with 400 recently released offenders who returned to Chicago found that they suffered from major problems that made readjustment to a normal life very difficult: 30 percent had "significant" health problems, but 81 percent had no health care; about half (48 percent) had no close friends, and among those with friends, 40 percent had a friend who had also been in prison. And as we will see in Chapter 14, all convicted felons face restrictions on employment, housing, welfare, and voting. In short, they are embedded in social experiences that impose many hurdles but offer few supports.[37]

The evidence leads us to the following conclusion:

PROPOSITION 39
Probation is an appropriate sentence for many offenders, but there is no evidence that one kind of probation treatment is more effective in reducing crime than other kinds.

Parole

Parole is the second most prevalent rehabilitation program. Most offenders sent to prison are released early under some form of supervision. Parole is seen as a rehabilitation program because, like probation, it seeks to reintegrate the offender into the community. In 2003, 775,000 adults were on parole in the United States, almost 100,000 more than in 1995.[38] The use of discretionary release parole has been declining as a result of the growth of sentencing guidelines. Sixteen states have abolished discretionary parole. One study found that more offenders left prison each year through supervised mandatory release (51 percent) than discretionary parole release (39 percent).[39]

When it was first developed, experts believed that parole would facilitate rehabilitation by placing a prisoner's future in his own hands. The possibility of gaining an earlier release would, they believed, encourage good behavior. Despite these promises, parole has always been the unloved child of the criminal justice system. Ever since it was fully established in the 1920s, it has been criticized from all directions. Conservatives argue that it allows dangerous offenders to get out of prison early, while liberals argue that parole release decisions are made without any scientific foundation, and are thus arbitrary and often discriminatory.[40] Despite persistent criticisms, however, parole survives, because it serves a number of purposes unrelated to rehabilitation: It offers prisoners an incentive to behave in prison, gives prison officials some power to control them, and serves as a safety valve for prison overcrowding.

Table 11.1 Parole-outcome recidivism rates of prisoners released in 1994 from prisons in 15 states

	CUMULATIVE PERCENT OF RELEASED PRISONERS WHO WERE—		
	Returned to prison[a,b]	Rearrested	Reconvicted[a,c]
Time after release			
6 months	29.9%	10.6%	5.0%
1 year	44.1	21.5	10.4
2 years	59.2	36.4	18.8
3 years	67.5	46.9	25.4

[a]With new sentence, including to state or federal prisons but not to local jails.

[b]Because of missing data, prisoners released in Ohio and Virginia were excluded from the calculation of those returned to prison with a new prison sentence.

[c]Because of missing data, prisoners released in Ohio were excluded from the calculation of percent reconvicted.

SOURCE: Bureau of Justice Statistics, *Recidivism of Prisoners Released in 1994* (Washington, DC: Department of Justice, 2002).

Does Parole Work? Do prisoners who are released on parole have lower recidivism rates than those who serve longer prison terms? Does parole supervision facilitate rehabilitation? Do some forms of parole supervision work more effectively than others? It is important to recognize that parole consists of two elements: *discretionary release* and *postrelease supervision,* which is supposed to deliver treatment services and ensure that the parolee does not engage in wrongdoing.

The effectiveness of parole has traditionally been measured in terms of the recidivism rate.[41] As with probation, an offender can fail either by being arrested for a new crime or through a technical violation of parole conditions. In terms of a new crime, it depends on whether we measure failure in terms of being rearrested, reconvicted, or reincarcerated (see Table 11.1).

The data on parole outcomes are as discouraging as those for probation. The most recent and most thorough study of parole outcomes found that within three years 62.3 percent were rearrested for either a felony or a serious misdemeanor. This was little different from the 64.8 rearrest rate for offenders released unconditionally. About 47 percent were convicted of a new offense, and 41 percent were imprisoned for a conviction or a technical violation of their conditions of release.[42] These figures lend a great deal of support to the widespread belief that neither prison nor parole are successful in rehabilitating offenders. The policy question is whether parole can be made to work more effectively.

The problems with parole are similar to the problems with probation. First, parole supervision is generally pretty minimal. Petersilia reports that in California, 85 percent of parolees are on regular supervision, with each parole officer carrying an average caseload of 66 parolees and an average of 1.7 contacts per month. The remaining parolees are on intensive supervision with an average of 5.6 contacts per month and parole officer caseloads of 25 per officer.[43]

Second, there are serious questions about the availability and content of treatment services. A California study estimated that 10,000 parolees were homeless but only 200 shelter beds were available to them. Similarly, only four mental health clinics were available for an estimated 18,000 parolees with psychiatric problems. And there were only 750 beds in treatment programs for 85,000 parolees with alcohol or drug problems.[44] Even if there were more of these services available, there is no strong evidence that we successfully match offenders to the specific treatment they need. This leads us again to our old friend the prediction problem.

Research on offender reentry confirms the inadequacy of treatment services. The Urban Institute interviewed 400 released offenders who returned to Chicago. Although 87 percent had participated in prerelease programs related to such practical matters as finding a job, obtaining a photo ID, and finding a place to live, once they were home only 25 percent received an actual referral to a job; only 15 percent received a referral to a substance abuse treatment program; and only 22 percent contacted a community program based on a referral from the prerelease program.[45]

The Prediction Problem Again Parole is where criminal justice officials first encountered the prediction problem, beginning in the 1920s (see Chapter 4 for our first discussion of this problem). For about 90 years, parole officials and criminologists have tried to develop formulas for predicting success on parole and to ensure that parole is granted only to those offenders who are rehabilitated and ready for release into the community. The sad fact, however, is that criminologists have been searching for better parole release criteria since the 1920s. They are no closer to a successful formula today than they were then.[46]

Repeatedly, research has confirmed the basic finding reported by Martinson: that some programs work for some offenders. The problem, of course, is in matching offenders to the right programs. Petersilia reports that California uses risk prediction instruments, but there is no evidence that they are any more effective in predicting success than the tools used in earlier decades.[47]

Abolish Discretionary Parole? Disillusionment with parole reached such a point in the 1970s that several jurisdictions simply abolished discretionary parole release (although some kept postrelease supervision). The 1976 California Determinate Sentencing Law abolished discretionary parole release. Release dates are mandatory once a prisoner has served the sentence imposed by the judge and good time has been deducted. A one-year period of parole supervision remains, however. The federal sentencing guidelines that took effect in

1987 also abolished discretionary parole release and replaced it with a system of presumptive sentences. Sixteen states have now abolished discretionary parole release.

Abolishing parole may not be an effective crime reduction policy. Bureau of Justice Statistics data indicate that in 1999 54 percent of the prisoners released through discretionary parole were successful (that is, not rearrested), compared with 33 percent who left prison through mandatory release. The Bureau of Justice Statistics uncovered the astonishing fact that when the state of California is excluded the national success rate for mandatory release *doubles,* from 33 to 66 percent. This is due to both the enormous size of the California parole population, and its consequent impact on national data, but also to the extremely high parole revocation rate in California.[48] Joan Petersilia calls for a return to discretionary parole release, but the evidence on whether it is indeed more effective than mandatory release is still very inconclusive.[49]

For the moment, however, the evidence leads us to conclude that:

> ### PROPOSITION 40
> Abolishing parole will not reduce crime; and in fact
> it appears to lead to higher recidivism rates.

THE NEW INTERMEDIATE PUNISHMENTS

In their 1990 book *Between Prison and Probation,* Norval Morris and Michael Tonry leveled a major criticism at criminal sentencing in America. They argued that at sentencing, judges faced a stark choice between two extremes: probation or prison. In many cases, however, prison is too harsh a punishment, while probation is too lenient. Their argument exposed the problem that probation involves neither meaningful treatment nor effective control of offenders in the community. Consequently, they called for the development of a range of intermediate punishments that would be less extreme than prison but with more content that traditional probation.[50]

Correctional officials and politicians across the country responded to Morris and Tonry by developing a set of new programs called *intermediate punishments.* They include boot camps, shock incarceration, intensive probation/parole supervision, home confinement, and electronic monitoring. These programs often overlap, and sentences typically include two or more different programs. Boot camps are often defined as a form of shock incarceration and frequently include a period of intensive parole supervision following release. Intensive probation/parole supervision might include home confinement, which may be enforced through electronic monitoring.[51] All of these programs may include frequent random drug tests. In examining a particular intermediate punishment, therefore, it is important to look beyond the label and determine exactly what program elements it contains.

Ted Palmer and some others regard the new intermediate punishments as a revival of rehabilitation. Is this true? Palmer's own choice of words raises some doubts. He refers to *correctional intervention* instead of *rehabilitation*. The difference is more than a matter of semantics. As we shall see, the new intermediate punishments emphasize surveillance and control of offenders, often with little emphasis on traditional treatment components. Joan Petersilia argues, as have other critics, that parole has become largely devoted to the surveillance and control of parolees and that services designed to help them adjust to society have decreased and in many instances vanished altogether.[52] This trend reflects the extent to which recent developments in corrections have been completely dominated by the conservative crime control agenda.

We now have 15 years of experience with the new intermediate punishments. Let's see what the evidence is on their effectiveness.

Boot Camps

Beginning in the mid-1980s, the most highly publicized new intermediate sanction was the boot camp. By 2000, there were a total of 95 boot camps in the country, enrolling 12,751 prisoners.[53] What exactly is a boot camp? Generally it involves (1) a short period of incarceration (typically three to six months), (2) in a facility separate from a regular prison, (3) for young first-time offenders (many exclude offenders convicted of violent crimes), (4) with a program of rigorous physical, educational, and substance-abuse-prevention programs, followed by (5) a period of intensive supervision in the community.

Many of the initial boot camps emphasized the purely military aspects:"military drill and ceremony, hard labor, physical training, and strict rules and discipline."[54] As time passed, correctional officials gave more emphasis to the treatment elements, such as drug counseling. As is the case with other intermediate punishments, boot camps have multiple and conflicting goals. They are simultaneously intended to rehabilitate, punish, control, and reduce prison overcrowding.

The basic idea underlying boot camps is nothing new. Judges have routinely given split sentences: short periods of incarceration followed by probation. Boot camps are different primarily by virtue of the military rhetoric that surrounds them and the intensive probation supervision that usually follows release.

Boot camp programs vary considerably in terms of how participants are selected, the content of the boot camp program, and the nature of the postrelease supervision. In some states, judges sentence offenders directly to boot camp (these are sometimes referred to as *front-end* intermediate punishments). In others, correctional officials select participants (referred to as *back-end* programs). In some states, boot camp participation is voluntary, meaning that an offender must choose it. In others, it is mandatory for those sentenced to it. Offenders in some states can voluntarily drop out of the boot camp and return to prison.[55]

In terms of content, Doris Mackenzie and her colleagues found that one of the greatest differences among the boot camps in the eight states they evaluated was "the amount of time in the daily schedule that is devoted to work, drill, and physical training versus such treatment-type activities as counseling, drug treatment, or academic education."[56] Some boot camps are almost entirely military-style programs, whereas others put much more emphasis on traditional rehabilitation efforts.

Do boot camps work? Are they more effective than other forms of correctional treatment in reducing recidivism? The good news is that boot camps have been subject to rigorous evaluations. The bad news is that they do not reduce recidivism rates. In an assessment of ten years of experience with boot camps, a Department of Justice report found that they generally produced "positive short-term changes in attitudes and behaviors" among their participants but that "with few exceptions, these positive changes did not lead to reduced recidivism." The graduates of some boot camps did have lower recidivism rates, but they participated in camps with more treatment services, more intensive sessions, and more intensive postrelease supervision. In short, there is today no consistent evidence that boot camps are more effective in reducing recidivism than are other types of correctional programs.[57]

A number of problems affect boot camp programs. The Department of Justice report concluded that "the length of stay in boot camps—usually from 90 to 120 days—was too brief to realistically affect recidivism." In short, as with many other correctional programs there was not much "treatment." The report also found that there was "little or no postrelease programming to prepare [boot camp] graduates to lead productive lives."[58] Increasing recognition of this problem has heightened interest in reentry programs which we will examine in Chapter 14. One-third to half of offenders fail to complete the program. There also appears to be significant net widening, as judges or correctional officials place low-risk offenders in boot camp programs. As a result, overall system costs often increase rather than decrease. One problem that has affected all new intermediate punishment programs is that the intensified surveillance (e.g., more contacts with parole officers, frequent drug tests) identifies more technical violations of the conditions of release. This increases the failure rate and results in sending more offenders back to prison, a development that eliminates the potential cost savings.

Some critics argue that the emphasis on military drill may be fundamentally misguided. Yelling at inmates, treating them with disrespect, and forcing them to undergo painful physical exercises may be counterproductive, teaching inmates that disrespect and verbal abuse are the keys to success in life. Such programs also value the most aggressive definition of masculinity. Finally, the legendary rigors of Marine boot camp at least offer a reward at the end: entry into the proud fellowship of the Corps. If prison boot camps offer nothing of comparable positive value at the end but only a return to the same neighborhood with the same bleak prospects (what Hagan refers to as a life socially embedded in crime), they are not likely to have a long-term positive impact on the people who pass through them.[59]

The evidence leads us to the following conclusion:

PROPOSITION 41
Boot camps do not reduce crime.

Intensive Parole Supervision

Intensive probation supervision or intensive parole supervision (IPS) is one of the new intermediate punishments designed to improve both probation and parole. It is frequently combined with other intermediate sanctions (boot camps, home confinement, and electronic monitoring) and applied to high-risk offenders.[60]

The basic idea of intensive supervision is nothing new. California developed a pioneering Special Intensive Parole Unit (SIPU) program in the mid-1950s and maintained it for ten years. Martinson reviewed the SIPU evaluations and found that three of the four phases produced no meaningful improvement in parolees' behavior. The phase involving smaller caseloads yielded some positive results. Parolees in this phase were returned to prison more often for technical violations. Martinson concluded that this was a deterrent rather than a rehabilitative effect. Parolees behaved themselves a little better when they knew that they faced a real prospect of being sent back to prison.[61]

The federal probation system, meanwhile, developed the San Francisco Project in the 1960s. Two IPS groups had caseloads of only 20 probationers, while two other groups had caseloads of 40, and another group had caseloads of several hundred clients. All other offenders were assigned to groups with normal levels of supervision, meaning that probation officers had between 70 and 130 clients.[62] An evaluation found no significant difference in the recidivism rates of offenders in the various groups. IPS did not consistently reduce the failure rate. And in fact, anticipating a problem that would affect the intermediate sanction programs of the 1980s and 1990s, intensive supervision resulted in a higher rate of technical violations of the conditions of probation.

The original IPS programs rested on a flawed assumption that increasing the intensity of supervision simply by lowering case loads and increasing the frequency of contact would enhance effectiveness.[63] Mere contact with a probation or parole officer, however, has little impact on an offender's behavior, and increasing the number of contacts makes no difference. The new IPS programs attempt to overcome some of this problem by incorporating other intermediate sanctions such as home confinement, mandatory drug and alcohol tests, and electronic monitoring.[64] One important aspect of this approach is that intensive supervision has become primarily enforcement oriented rather than treatment oriented. The basic goal is to control the offender.

Are the new IPS programs effective? That is, are they more effective than traditional probation? Joan Petersilia found the results in three California programs "particularly discouraging." After one year, about 35 percent of the IPS probationers had been rearrested, another 40 percent committed technical violations of probation conditions, and only 25 percent had no violations of any sort. Admittedly, the offenders assigned to these IPS programs were labeled high risk, but a 75 percent failure rate after only one year is a very poor showing. Perhaps even more significant, their rearrest rates were no different from those of other probationers. This outcome suggests that the intense supervision did not stop them from committing crime. Once again, more intensive supervision resulted in much higher rates of technical violations. This result is hardly surprising, because that is what frequent contacts and drug tests are designed to detect.[65]

Why are IPS programs no more successful than regular probation in reducing recidivism? The answer may be that no form of probation supervision—intensive or minimal—has any real impact on the lives of people who are embedded in environments with few positive opportunities, weak or nonexistent family supports, and many dysfunctional peer influences such as friends involved in drugs and crime. The "treatment" of intense supervision may not be able to overcome the real problems that offenders have. We will examine these issues in more detail when we look at the new reentry programs in Chapter 15.

This leads us to the following conclusion:

PROPOSITION 42
Intensive supervision, with either probation or parole, will not reduce crime.

Home Confinement and Electronic Monitoring

Home confinement (HC) and electronic monitoring (EM) are designed to keep the offender under fairly strict surveillance and control. HC is essentially a curfew. In some cases, is enforced through EM; in others, it is not. Both HC and EM have the same mixture of goals as does IPS. They are designed to simultaneously reduce prison overcrowding and both control and rehabilitate the offender.

Electronic monitoring emerged in 1983 when Judge Jack Love of Albuquerque adopted the Gosslink system for a convicted offender. The idea quickly caught on. By 1996, there were 13,868 probationers and 8,491 parolees in EM programs.[66] An early report found EM to be far cheaper than imprisonment: as low as $1,350 per year, versus $20,000 for prison. Basically two different EM technologies are available. *Passive monitoring radio frequency systems* place a transmitter on the offender (a tamper-proof bracelet or anklet) and a dialer on the telephone. If the probationer leaves the premises, the signal is interrupted, and the dialer automatically calls the probation office. *Active monitoring programmed contact systems* involve periodic, usually random telephone calls to the probationer's home. The calling may be done automatically by machine or by the PO's personal phone call.

Initially, the largest group of offenders in EM programs were traffic violation offenders. By 1989, property offenders and drug offenders had become the two largest categories. Sentences generally ran from 60 to 120 days. A Justice Department survey found that most failures occurred within the first two months. About 4 percent of the total sample committed a new offense, and half of those occurred in the first 60 days. About 22 percent of the sample committed a technical violation of the terms of their confinement.[67]

Many people initially opposed EM because it conjured up images of George Orwell's famous novel *1984,* with Big Brother continuously monitoring everyone's private behavior. In actual practice, EM may not deliver on its promises.

Although advertised as a technological "fix" for the crime problem, EM systems often have serious technical and administrative problems. The signal can be disrupted by certain kinds of housing construction; random calls in the middle of the night disrupt the probationer's sleep (not such a good idea if we want that person to hold a steady job) and require that a staff person be on duty to respond to a violation. The cost savings are also relatively small. The 12,000 offenders in EM programs in 1992 (probation and parole combined) represented a minuscule fraction of the 4.8 million under correctional supervision that year.[68]

The intensive surveillance that EM (and IPS) provides creates a special problem for the criminal justice system. It does succeed in detecting violations of probation or parole conditions, and many of the offenders are returned to prison. As the report *Performance Measures for the Criminal Justice System* points out, there is serious disagreement over whether a high rate of technical violations indicates success or failure. If the purpose of EM is to control offenders and detect misbehavior, then EM is a success. But if the purpose is to control costs and reintegrate the offender into the community, then it is a failure.[69]

Most important for our purposes, evaluations indicate that offenders under IPS, HC, and EM are no more effective in reducing crime than conventional prison or probation programs. Offenders in these programs have the same rearrest rate as those on conventional probation or parole.

This leads us to conclude:

PROPOSITION 43
Home confinement and electronic monitoring do not reduce crime.

Lessons of the Intermediate Punishment Movement

Reviewing the first 10 to 15 years of the intermediate punishment movement, Joan Petersilia reached some sobering conclusions. Most of the programs were "more symbolic . . . than substantive."[70]

Most seriously, there was no evidence that intermediate sanctions were more effective than traditional programs in reducing recidivism. In many cases, this was the result of implementation problems: lack of adequate funding and program resources; selection of inappropriate offenders, and so on. The one "tantalizing" positive finding, Petersilia concluded, was the evidence that offenders who participated in a range of programs—substance abuse treatment, community service, employment programs—had lower recidivism rates than comparable offenders who did not.[71] This finding is a central element of the new prisoner reentry programs that are discussed in Chapter 14.

Confused Goals

IPS suffers from both confused goals and exaggerated promises. Its advocates claim it will rehabilitate offenders, keep them under control, reduce prison overcrowding, and save money—all at the same time. As some critics point out, if all this were true, IPS would be "the wonderchild of the criminal justice system."[72] Yet, as many observers have pointed out, current IPS programs emphasize surveillance and control rather than rehabilitation. A Justice Department report on *Performance Measures for the Criminal Justice System* argues that if the goal is surveillance and control, then a high failure rate is a positive indicator of the program's performance: Offenders who violate the terms of probation or commit another crime are taken off the streets and sent to prison.[73]

Many IPS programs do not necessarily serve the clients for whom they were designed. Although generally intended for those designated high-risk offenders, only 20 percent of the clients in the Georgia and New Jersey programs fit that definition. Georgia officials privately conceded that 25 percent of the IPS clients were not "true" diversions from prison. There were also rumors that New Jersey judges sentenced some offenders to prison only to make them eligible for "diversion" through IPS.[74]

The very intensity of the supervision in IPS programs has introduced an entirely new problem. Joan Petersilia reports that one-third of those offenders eligible for intensive probation in Marion County, Oregon, chose to go to prison. In New Jersey, 15 percent of those who applied for IPS withdrew their applications when they found out what IPS would be like.[75]

It is easy to see why offenders choose prison. The Oregon IPS program included home visits two or three times a week, with telephone checks on other days, unannounced searches for drugs, and periodic urine tests for drug use. Offenders were required to perform community service work and were forbidden to associate with certain people. This regime would last for two *years*. The alternative was a two- to four-year prison sentence that usually resulted in three to six *months* of actual time served, followed by two years of routine parole supervision, which meant only one visit per month and none of the other IPS requirements. The IPS program was far more intrusive and punitive than prison and parole.[76]

Innovative Roles for Probation and Parole

In Chapter 15 we will examine the role of probation and parole officers in the innovative and successful Boston Gun Project. While they played an enforcement role, they were part of a broader and carefully planned strategy for addressing gun crimes, one that included partnerships with other agencies and community groups and innovative tactics.

SPECIAL TREATMENT PROGRAMS

Treatment for Domestic Violence Batterers

A variety of treatment programs have been used for offenders with a record of violence. Sentencing offenders to anger management programs is an increasingly popular alternative. For about 30 years, batterer treatment programs have been used for men guilty of domestic violence. The most famous of these is the so-called Duluth Model, originally developed in Duluth, Minnesota. It is based on the assumption that men who commit domestic assault basically want to control their partners. The program's curriculum uses a "power and control wheel" to outline the various tactics used by assailants and to help them understand and ultimately control their behavior. (You can find the wheel and other information about the program through a Web search for the "Duluth Model.")[77]

A National Institute of Justice evaluation of two batterer programs based on the Duluth Model, however, found that they were not effective. The Broward County, Florida, program had "little or no effect" on its clients. The program was evaluated in terms of several measures, including clients' attitudes toward the role of women and subsequent violations of probation or rearrest. Twenty-four percent of the members of the treatment group and a control group were rearrested in the following 12 months while on probation. The evaluation did find lower levels of violence among those who were employed, married, and owned their own homes. But these understandable factors were unrelated to participation in the treatment program.

The second program, in Brooklyn, New York, resulted in "only minor improvements in some subjects." An interesting natural experiment occurred after the local prosecutor objected to the length and cost of the original 26-week treatment program. The program was shortened to eight weeks, resulting in two treatment groups. The clients participating in the 26-week program were less likely to be arrested than either the 8-week participants or the control group. This finding did provide some glimmer of hope, suggesting that perhaps a longer period of treatment might be effective.

A meta-analysis of 22 batterer programs concluded: "Overall, effects due to treatment were in the small range, meaning that the current interventions have a minimal impact on reducing recidivism beyond the effect of being arrested."[78]

A CONSERVATIVE VARIATION:
FAITH-BASED TREATMENT

While treatment for offenders has always been the preferred policy for liberals, the idea now has support among conservatives. They believe that faith-based treatment services will be effective in reducing criminal behavior among adults and juveniles. President George W. Bush created the Office of Faith-Based and Community Initiatives in January 2001 and has spent several billion dollars on programs such as "abstinence only" education ($31 million in grants in 2004, for example). (For more details, check out the official website of the Office.) Across the country there are now many treatment programs—drug abuse treatment, alcohol treatment, employment counseling, etc.—that have some kind of religious component.

What exactly is faith-based treatment? Like most of the programs considered in this book, it is surrounded by a lot of myths and misunderstandings. Let's begin by sorting out the issues so we can focus our attention on the effectiveness of faith-based correctional treatment.

Sorting Out the Issues

Faith-based treatment involves several different kinds of programs incorporating religious belief. The most general kind of faith-based program is derived from *organic religion*. This means that religion is an integral part of a person's life, independent of any deviant or criminal behavior. Byron Johnson reviewed 669 studies of the impact of organic religion and found a consistent positive impact on a wide range of conditions. People who indicated religious faith and/or activity were less likely to experience hypertension, depression, suicidal thoughts, or alcohol or drug use or be involved in delinquent or criminal behavior. This finding is consistent with criminological theories associating criminal activity with anomie, a lack of positive attachment to family, differential association with offenders, and so on.[79]

The second general category of faith-based program is *intentional religion*. This is defined as "exposure to religion . . . at a particular time in life for a particular purpose."[80] An example would be a religiously centered drug treatment program in a prison setting. The religious component is introduced to the participants in the program with the specific intent of helping them overcome their drug abuse problem.

Actually, there are two kinds of intentional religion programs. One would be a social service program provided by a faith-based organization that has no religious content. A good example would be a homeless shelter or soup kitchen run by a church where people can get a bed for the night and a meal without having to participate in any religious activity. Many advocates of faith-based programs argue that religious organizations can deliver these services more efficiently and effectively than government-based programs.

A different form of intentional religion program is one in which the program includes religious content. A good example would be the drug treatment program that includes religious services, in which the underlying assumption is that developing religious commitment will help the clients overcome their drug dependency. (In the case of old-fashioned homeless shelters, this is referred to as "soup, soap, and salvation." To get the food and the bed you have to participate in religious services.)

Are Faith-Based Programs Effective?

Our focus here is on the latter category: intentional religion programs with religious content. Is there any evidence that they are effective in treating criminal offenders? And are they more effective than secular programs? Byron R. Johnson conducted a thorough review of the literature for the Center for Research on Religion and Urban Civil Society. His 2002 report is consistent with the standards of evidence-based crime policy, and we should take a close look at his findings.[81]

Johnson's most notable finding was that the impact of intentional religion has not been extensively studied by social scientists. While there were 669 studies of organic religion, he could find only 97 studies of intentional religion, and only 25 of those examined program effectiveness. These 25 studies also suffered from a number of weaknesses. Some did not describe their methodologies. Only a few were published in refereed journals. Many used qualitative methods and cases studies, as opposed to quantitative studies with random assignment to treatment and control groups. Also, the studies were not rigorous in defining and measuring the "faith" component of faith-based programs. It is not always clear exactly what the religious part of a particular program was. Nor is it always clear how significant the religious component was compared with other aspects of the program.

Of the eleven studies that did involve a multivariate analysis, ten found the faith-based program to be effective in terms of lower recidivism rates. For example, the participants in a Bible study group run by the group Prison Fellowship were less likely to be rearrested during the one-year follow-up period. A study of Teen Challenge, a faith-based alcohol abuse treatment program, found that its clients were more likely to remain sober and maintain employment than a comparison group who participated in a secular treatment program.

PROPOSITION 44
There is no evidence that faith-based treatment programs are any more or any less effective in reducing crime than are secular treatment programs.

OFFENDER REENTRY

The current innovation in correctional treatment is reentry programming. Each year almost 600,000 offenders leave prison and return to society. Reentry programs seek to better prepare them for establishing law-abiding lives. The U.S. Justice Department created the Reentry Partnership Initiative in 1999 and has funded a number of policy papers and research studies. (Go to The U.S. Justice Department's website and look for the reentry page.) Of course, correctional treatment always sought to "reintegrate" (to use the old phrase) offenders into the community. The innovative aspects of reentry programming involve an emphasis on the *community* aspects of offender rehabilitation, with special attention to the role of other criminal justice and social service agencies, and the importance of neighborhood and family influences. Because of this community orientation, reentry programs are discussed at length in Chapter 15.

CONCLUSION: ANY FUTURE FOR REHABILITATION?

In the end, the evidence on rehabilitation does not look very promising. It is true that most offenders eventually stop their lawbreaking. Most simply mature out of crime. Unfortunately, we do not have any "planned interventions" (recall that this is our definition of correctional treatment) that consistently cause them to cease their criminal activity earlier than they otherwise might. None of the highly publicized innovations such as boot camps or intensive supervision seem to be more successful than traditional programs. It is indeed true that some programs do work. As Glaser and others argue, some programs work for some offenders. The problem, however, is that we do not have diagnostic tools to match individual offenders with the right programs. This is our old friend the prediction problem. In the end, liberals who advocate rehabilitation are no more effective in predicting future behavior than are the conservative advocates of incapacitation.

NOTES

1. Charles H. Logan and Gerald G. Gaes, "Meta-Analysis and the Rehabilitation of Punishment," *Justice Quarterly* 10 (June 1993): 245–263.

2. Lee B. Sechrest, Susan O. White, and Elizabeth Brown, *The Rehabilitation of Criminal Offenders: Problems and Prospects* (Washington, DC: National Academy of Sciences, 1979), pp. 18–19.

3. Michael Gottfredson and Travis Hirschi, "The True Value of Lambda Would Appear to be Zero: An Essay on Career Criminals, Criminal Careers, Selective Incapacitation, Cohort Studies, and Related Topics," *Criminology* 24 (1986): 213–234.

4. Michael Tonry and Mary Lynch, "Intermediate Sanctions," in Michael Tonry, ed., *Crime and Justice: A Review of Research,* vol. 20 (Chicago: University of Chicago Press, 1996), pp. 99–144.

5. David C. Anderson, *Crime and the Politics of Hysteria* (New York: Times Books, 1995); The Sentencing Project, *The Lessons of Willie Horton: Thinking about Crime and Punishment for the 1990s* (Washington, DC: The Sentencing Project, 1989).

6. The 1996 data are in Bureau of Justice Statistics, *Sourcebook of Criminal Justice Statistics—1997* (Washington, DC: Government Printing Office, 1998), pp. 513–514. The 1990 data are in Bureau of Justice Statistics, *Sourcebook of Criminal Justice Statistics—1991* (Washington, DC: Government Printing Office, 1992), p. 130.

7. Anderson, *Crime and the Politics of Hysteria,* pp. 270–271.

8. Robert Martinson, "What Works? Questions and Answers about Prison Reform," *Public Interest* 35 (Spring 1974): 22–54.

9. Robert Martinson, "Symposium on Sentencing: Part II," *Hofstra Law Review* 7.2 (1979): 243–258. The full report is published as Douglas Lipton, Robert Martinson, and Judith Wilks, *The Effectiveness of Correctional Treatment* (New York: Praeger, 1975).

10. Samuel Walker, *Popular Justice: A History of American Criminal Justice,* 2nd rev. ed. (New York: Oxford University Press, 1998).

11. Lipton et al., *The Effectiveness of Correctional Treatment.*

12. Sechrest et al., *The Rehabilitation of Criminal Offenders,* pp. 14, 31, 102.

13. Logan and Gaes, "Meta-Analysis and the Rehabilitation of Punishment."

14. Daniel Glaser, "What Works, and Why It Is Important: A Response to Logan and Gaes," *Justice Quarterly* 11 (December 1994): 711–723.

15. Glaser, "What Works?" p. 721.

16. Logan and Gaes, "Meta-Analysis and the Rehabilitation of Punishment," p. 255.

17. Glaser, "What Works?"; see also John Hagan, "The Social Embeddedness of Crime and Unemployment," *Criminology* 31 (November 1993): 465–491.

18. Raymond T. Nimmer, *Diversion: The Search for Alternative Forms of Prosecution* (Chicago: American Bar Foundation, 1974).

19. Nimmer, *Diversion,* pp. 11–18, 41–51.

20. President's Crime Commission, *The Challenge of Crime in a Free Society* (Washington, DC: Government Printing Office, 1967), p. 165.

21. Vera Institute of Justice, *The Manhattan Court Employment Project: Final Report* (New York: Vera Institute of Justice, 1972).

22. U.S. Department of Justice, *Diversion of Felony Arrests: An Experiment in Pretrial Intervention* (Washington, DC: Department of Justice, 1981).

23. Thomas G. Blomberg, "Widening the Net: An Anomaly in the Evaluation of Diversion Programs," in Malcolm W. Klein and K. S. Teilman, eds., *Handbook of Criminal Justice Evaluation* (Beverly Hills, CA: Sage, 1980), pp. 572–592.

24. Jacqueline Sullivan, *Widening the Net in Juvenile Justice and the Dangers of Prevention and Early Intervention* (San Francisco: Center of Juvenile and Criminal Justice, 2002). Available on the website of the Center of Juvenile and Criminal Justice.

25. Eugene Doleschal, "The Dangers of Criminal Justice Reform," *Criminal Justice Abstracts* 14 (March 1982): 133–152. A different perspective on criminal justice reform is in Samuel Walker, *Taming the System: The Control of Discretion in American Criminal Justice, 1950–1990* (New York: Oxford University Press, 1993).

26. Blomberg, "Widening the Net," p. 592.

27. Joan Petersilia and Susan Turner, *Intensive Supervision Probation for High Risk Offenders: Findings from Three California Experiments* (Santa Monica, CA: Rand, 1990).

28. Jamie Gorelick, "Pretrial Diversion: The Threat of Expanding Social Control," *Harvard Civil Rights—Civil Liberties Law Review* 10 (1975): 180–214.

29. Bureau of Justice Statistics, *Defining Drug Courts: The Key Components* (Washington, DC: Department of Justice, 1997), p. 7. NCJ 165478.

30. John Roman, Wendy Townsend, and Avinash Singh Bahti, *Recidivism Rates for Drug Court Graduates: National Estimates* (Washington, DC: The Urban Institute, 2001). Available on the NCJRS and the Urban Institute websites.

31. Bureau of Justice Statistics, *Probation and Parole in the United States, 2003* (Washington, DC: Department of Justice, 2004). NCJ 205336.

32. Bureau of Justice Statistics, *Felony Sentences in State Courts, 2000* (Washington, DC: Department of Justice, 2003). NCJ 198821.

33. Todd R. Clear and Anthony A. Braga, "Community Corrections," in James Q. Wilson and Joan Petersilia, eds., *Crime* (San Francisco: ICS Press, 1995), p. 431.

34. Petersilia and Turner, *Intensive Supervision Probation for High Risk Offenders,* p. 47.

35. Bureau of Justice Statistics, *Probation and Parole in the United States, 2003* (Washington, DC: Department of Justice, 2004). NCJ 205336.

36. Hagan, "The Social Embeddedness of Crime and Unemployment."

37. Nancy G. La Vigne, Christy Visher, and Jennifer Castro, *Chicago Prisoners' Experiences Returning Home* (Washington, DC: The Urban Institute, 2004). Available on the Urban Institute website.

38. Bureau of Justice Statistics, *Probation and Parole in the United States, 2003.*

39. Ibid.

40. David J. Rothman, *Conscience and Convenience: The Asylum and Its Alternatives in Progressive America* (Boston: Little, Brown, 1980); Jonathan Simon, *Poor Discipline: Parole and the Social Control of the Underclass, 1890–1990* (Chicago: University of Chicago Press, 1993).

41. Joan Petersilia, "Measuring the Performance of Community Corrections."

42. Ibid., p. 512.

43. Joan Petersilia, *When Prisoners Come Home* (New York: Oxford, 2003), p. 85.

44. Ibid., p. 81.

45. La Vigne et al., *Chicago Prisoners' Experiences Returning Home.*

46. Walker, *Popular Justice.*

47. Petersilia, *When Prisoners Come Home,* p. 71.

48. Bureau of Justice Statistics, *Trends in State Parole, 1990–2000* (Washington, DC: Department of Justice, 2001). NCJ 184735.

49. Petersilia, *When Prisoners Come Home.*

50. Norval Morris and Michael Tonry, *Between Prison and Probation* (New York: Oxford University Press, 1990).

51. Richard A. Ball, C. Ronald Huff, and J. Robert Lilly, *House Arrest and Correctional Policy* (Beverly Hills, CA: Sage, 1988).

52. Petersilia, *When Prisoners Come Home,* p. 80.

53. Bureau of Justice Statistics, *Census of State and Federal Correctional Facilities, 2000* (Washington, DC: Department of Justice, 2003), Table 18. NCJ 198272.

54. Doris Layton MacKenzie, Robert Brame, David McDowall, and Claire Souryal, "Boot Camp Prisons and Recidivism in Eight States," *Criminology* 33 (August 1995): 351.

55. For a discussion of the distinction between front end and back end, see Tonry and Lynch, "Intermediate Sanctions," pp. 110–111.

56. MacKenzie et al., "Boot Camp Prisons and Recidivism in Eight States."

57. Dale G. Parent, *Correctional Boot Camps: Lessons from a Decade of Research* (Washington, DC: Department of Justice, 2003). NCJ 197018. Doris Layton MacKenzie, David B. Wilson, and Suzanne B. Kider, "Effects of Correctional Boot Camps on Offending," *The Annals* 578 (November 2001): 126–143.

58. Parent, *Correctional Boot Camps: Lessons from a Decade of Research.*

59. Merry Morash and Lila Rucker, "A Critical Look at the Idea of Boot Camp as a Correctional Reform," *Crime and Delinquency* 36 (April 1990): 204–222.

60. Bureau of Justice Statistics, *Correctional Populations in the United States, 1996* (Washington, DC: Department of Justice, 1999), p. 124.

61. Robert Martinson and Judith Wilks, "Save Parole Supervision," *Federal Probation* 41 (September 1977): 23–27.

62. J. Banks, A. A. Porter, R. L. Rardin, T. R. Silver, and V. E. Unger, *Evaluation of Intensive Special Probation Projects* (Washington, DC: Department of Justice, 1977).

63. Todd Clear and Patricia Hardyman, "The New Intensive Supervision Movement," *Crime and Delinquency* 36 (January 1990): 42–60.

64. Petersilia and Turner, *Intensive Supervision Probation for High Risk Offenders.*

65. Ibid.

66. Bureau of Justice Statistics, *Correctional Populations in the United States, 1996,* p. 124.

67. Marc Renzema and David T. Skelton, *Use of Electronic Monitoring in the United States: 1989 Update* (Washington, DC: Department of Justice, 1990).

68. Bureau of Justice Statistics, *Correctional Populations in the United States, 1992.*

69. Bureau of Justice Statistics, *Performance Measures for the Criminal Justice System* (Washington, DC: Department of Justice, 1993), pp. 67–68.

70. Joan Petersilia, "A Decade of Experimenting with Intermediate Sanctions: What Have We Learned?" in National Institute of Justice, *Perspectives on Crime and Justice: 1997–1998* (Washington, DC: Department of Justice, 1998). p. 3. NCJ 172851.

71. Ibid., p. 6.

72. Todd Clear, S. Flynn, and C. Shapiro, "Intensive Supervision in Probation," in Belinda McCarthy, ed., *Intermediate Punishments* (Monsey, NY: Willow Tree Press, 1987), pp. 10–11.

73. Petersilia, "Measuring the Performance of Community Corrections," p. 67.

74. Clear and Hardyman, "The New Intensive Supervision Movement."

75. Joan Petersilia, "When Probation Becomes More Dreaded than Prison," *Federal Probation* 54 (March 1990): 23–27.

76. Ibid.

77. National Institute of Justice, *Do Batterer Intervention Programs Work? Two Studies* (Washington, DC: Department of Justice, 2003). NCJ 195079.

78. J. C. Babcock, C. E. Green, and C. Robie, "Does Batterers' Treatment Work? A Meta-analytic Review of Domestic Violence Treatment," *Clinical Psychology Review* 23 (January 2004): 1023–1053.

79. Byron R. Johnson, *Objective Hope: Assessing the Effectiveness of Faith-Based Organizations: A Review of the Literature* (Philadelphia: Center for Research on Religion and Urban Civil Society, 2002).

80. Ibid., p. 8.

81. Ibid.

12

Gain Compliance
with the Law

THE BASIS OF AN ORDERLY SOCIETY

Compliance with the Law

The ultimate goal of the criminal justice system—and of all social institutions, including schools, fire departments, health systems, and all government agencies—is to create and maintain an orderly society in which people are free to go about their lives. In this book we are examining a variety of different crime policies designed to achieve that goal. The book is organized around a dichotomy of conservative and liberal strategies, which we described in Chapter 1. Basically, conservative strategies want to hold individuals accountable for their actions, through programs designed to enhance punishment, deterrence, and incapacitation. Liberals, on the other hand, focus on social and environmental factors. They support programs designed to help offenders adjust to their social environment and other programs designed to change the environment itself and eliminate barriers to individual fulfillment such as poverty, unemployment, lack of educational achievement, and so on.

The common theme that unites both the conservative and liberal programs we have covered so far is that they rely on external authority to cause people not to commit crime: the police, the courts, correctional programs, and so on. Some programs operate through coercion; some operate by treatment. Recent research on procedural justice, however, broadens the focus to consider preventing crime by instilling self-control in individuals and cultivating voluntary compliance with the laws.

How can this be achieved? How can we make people law abiding? The research by Wolfgang that we considered in Chapter 4 clearly suggests that most people do obey the law—well, at least most of the laws most of the time. Further, many of those who do break the law (or have a contact with the police, in Wolfgang's study) eventually stop and become law abiding. This chapter examines the recent research suggesting that the conduct of criminal justice agencies themselves can help instill law-abiding behavior.

Legitimacy and Compliance

The most important research on achieving voluntary compliance with the law is in the field of social psychology, by Tom Tyler in particular. Tyler argues that a critical factor in people's complying with the law is the *perceived legitimacy* of the law and the justice system.[1] That is, if they believe the system is just, they are more likely to obey the law. If they feel the police, the courts, and other criminal justice institutions are fair and effective, they will respect them, cooperate with them, regard them as legitimate, and be more inclined to obey the law.

The National Academy of Sciences report on policing makes an important distinction between *lawfulness* on the part of criminal justice agencies and *legitimacy*. Lawfulness refers to the behavior of criminal justice agencies in an objective sense. That is, do police departments treat people equally and not use excessive force? Do prosecutors handle cases fairly and give everyone the same breaks in plea bargains? Do the courts hand down sentences that are equal? Legitimacy, on the other hand, refers to public perception of the lawfulness of these agencies. Even if a department never engages in profiling or other forms of race discrimination, if people believe it does, it does not gain legitimacy.[2]

The issue of legitimacy can be traced back to the founding of the field of sociology and the work of Max Weber. Weber argued that the social dynamics of authority in society involve not just the coercive power of social institutions to force people to do things, but the voluntary obligation that people feel to do those things—that is, to comply with the law.[3]

Does Legitimacy Matter? The Evidence

The concept of procedural justice holds that people's satisfaction with the justice system depends heavily on how they feel they were treated by the system. The important factor is the process. Of particular importance is whether people feel they had a chance to tell their side of the story and that someone listened to them. Procedural justice is distinct from *distributive justice,* which involves actual case outcomes (see Figure 12.1).

Think of it in terms of your grade in a course. The grade you receive represents distributive justice. But let's say you appeal the grade. How you are treated in that appeal represents procedural justice. The concept of procedural justice holds that *having an opportunity* to tell your side of story (e.g., a meeting or hearing) is more important to you than the actual outcome of the appeal.

FIGURE 12.1 Procedural justice model of crime prevention

You may still be unhappy about your grade, but you feel that at least the process was fair. As a result, your confidence and trust in the teacher, the course, and the university will be positive, or at least not as negative as it would have been if no one listened to your side of the story. But let's say the instructor just turns you away, without any explanation. Your attitude will be very negative. And, in fact, you are likely to be even more upset than you were based only on the grade.

An important application of this concept involves traffic stops by the police. A number of experts argue that many drivers are upset mainly over the manner in which the officer treated them and not because of the stop itself. In fact, many drivers admit they were doing something wrong (speeding, rolling through a stop sign, etc.). They are often upset because the officer was rude or refused to answer their questions. Many of these experts further argue that officer behavior during the process of stops of African Americans leads to allegations of racial profiling. To correct this problem, the report on racial profiling by the Police Executive Research Forum offers a model policy for traffic stops that emphasizes respectful behavior on the part of officers. It recommends that officers introduce themselves, explain the basis for the stop, and offer an apology if the person has been mistakenly stopped.[4]

Does a sense of fairness and justice make a difference in terms of law-abiding behavior? Tyler investigates this question in his book *Why People Obey the Law*.[5] Tyler's study was based on interviews with 1,575 Chicago residents, 804 of whom were reinterviewed a year later. Respondents were asked about their own lawbreaking (e.g., speeding, littering, shoplifting) and their perceptions of and experience with the police and the courts. The latter questions were designed to determine respondents' sense of the legitimacy of the justice system. Tyler concluded: "Citizens who view legal authority as legitimate are generally more likely to comply with the law."[6]

One of the important implications of Tyler's study—and of the entire field of procedural justice—is that we have placed too much emphasis on deterrence, a coercive approach, in our effort to make people law abiding. We have invested too much in trying to scare people by attempting to raise the risk of arrest or increasing the severity of punishment. We have not invested the same amount of resources in making people feel positively about the law and the criminal justice system. The procedural justice perspective says that people are not motivated primarily by fear of punishment, but are more likely to be influenced by positive attachments and feelings of loyalty.

In another study, Casper, Tyler, and Fisher found that among several hundred male felony defendants in three cities, procedural justice issues were associated with their evaluation of their experience in criminal court. Particularly important was how they felt they were treated by the police (e.g., did the officer "treat you in a businesslike manner" or "use disrespectful language?") and the amount of time their lawyer spent with them. Interestingly, defendants' evaluations were not affected by whether they had a private attorney or a public defender, or whether they pled guilty or went to trial. In short, how they felt they were treated shaped their level of satisfaction with the system.[7]

Finally, a reanalysis of the Milwaukee Domestic Violence Experiment found that aspects of procedural justice were associated with lower recidivism rates. Arrestees who felt they were treated in a procedurally fair manner had recidivism rates that were as low as the rates for those given a more favorable outcome (e.g., warned but not arrested).[8]

In the end, does justice matter? There is persuasive evidence to support Tyler's argument that a *sense of justice* does contribute to law-abiding behavior. The major limitation in his Chicago study was that he asked people about relatively minor offenses. The most serious crime was shoplifting an inexpensive item. It did not investigate the relationship between perceptions of the fairness of the justice system and serious crimes such as robbery and burglary. Nonetheless, it is reasonable to speculate that perceptions of discrimination do make a difference and that people who feel that the criminal justice system is unfair—and that American society in general offers them no place—are more likely to break the law. This leads us to the following conclusion:

PROPOSITION 45

Creating a greater sense of the legitimacy of the criminal justice system may encourage law-abiding behavior and reduce crime.

BUILDING LEGITIMACY

If greater legitimacy is likely to result in less lawbreaking, how can criminal justice agencies build and maintain legitimacy? There are several different approaches. Some involve programs that we will consider in more detail in Chapter 14 on the community context of crime policy. In this chapter we will discuss them briefly in order to put them in context.

Building Outreach to Citizens and Communities

The victims' rights movement we examined in Chapter 9 involves a major effort to build legitimacy. All of the programs we discussed represent an effort to overcome the traditional view that the victim is the "forgotten person" in the criminal justice system. Particularly important are the victims' voice laws and programs that give crime victims an opportunity to express their views in plea bargains, at sentencing, and at parole hearings. Procedural justice experts argue that one of the key variables in peoples' satisfaction with a system or organization is their sense that they have an opportunity to participate and express their point of view.

Building good relations with the community is one of the principal goals of community policing. The community policing movement arose out of recognition that, first, the police were isolated from the public and, second, the police depended heavily on citizen cooperation to enforce the law and maintain order. Consequently, community policing and problem-oriented policing projects emphasize developing partnerships with community groups. In Chapter 14 we will examine how partnerships with neighborhood religious groups was an important element of Operation Cease Fire in Boston.

Attempting to develop better relations with the community has not been confined to the police. Innovative community prosecution programs have the same goal and seek to develop partnerships with neighborhood residents and businesses. We will examine community prosecution programs in Chapter 14.

Finally, in the area of corrections, some of the new offender reentry programs involve partnerships with community groups. In the next chapter, we will also examine problem-solving parole programs that include meetings between community groups, corrections officials, and parolees in a manner that is very similar to problem-oriented policing.

Eliminating Bias and the Perception of Bias

One of the most important ways to build trust in the criminal justice system is to eliminate injustice—and the perception of injustice—in the everyday operations of the system itself. The most important injustices involve discrimination based on race and ethnicity, gender, or social class. As Chapter 1 explained, many critics believe that the war on drugs involves serious patterns of racial and ethnic discrimination in the criminal justice system. Injustices, both real and perceived, exist in all components of the justice system.

Policing The most serious injustices are believed to occur in policing. This is partly because the police are the most visible part of the justice system—with patrol cars and uniformed officers dispersed through the community. The most inflammatory controversies involve police use of deadly force and excessive physical force. There has been considerable progress in reducing racial disparities in fatal shootings. For example, a recent Bureau of Justice Statistics report found that the racial disparity in persons shot and killed by the police is half what it was 25 years ago.[9] Nonetheless, fatal shootings of African Americans continue to provoke anger and accusations of racism in the African American community.

The newest controversy involves the issue of racial profiling, defined as police making traffic stops based on race or ethnicity rather than genuine lawbreaking. Public opinion surveys consistently indicate a widespread belief that racial profiling exists, even though the official data on stops have found it difficult to prove that belief conclusively.[10] As we mentioned earlier, some of the hostility toward the police is based on the manner in which stops are conducted and not necessarily the reasons for stops.

Finally, there is evidence of significant disparity in drug enforcement. African Americans represent 33 percent of all drug arrests (in 2002) despite the fact that the National Household Survey of Drug Abuse (see Chapter 13) finds only slight differences in illegal drug use between African Americans and whites.[11] This disparity may be due to the fact that the police concentrate their drug enforcement efforts in minority communities while ignoring drug offenses in other communities. Jerome Miller characterizes the justice system's approach to young African American men as one of "search and destroy."[12]

The Courts There is widespread belief among African Americans that the courts engage in racial discrimination in plea bargaining and sentencing. The most persuasive evidence of race discrimination involves sentencing for drug offenses. The most glaring example involves sentences for cocaine-related offenses in the federal sentencing guidelines, with much longer sentences for crack cocaine, which is more heavily used by African Americans, than for powder cocaine, which is more heavily used by whites. The evidence of systematic discrimination in sentencing for routine felonies is modest at best.[13]

Cumulative Disadvantage The data on discrimination in the criminal justice system needs to be understood in terms of cumulative disadvantage. Marjorie Zatz persuasively argues that relatively small amounts of discrimination at different points in the system have an enormous cumulative effect.[14] That is, some racial disparity takes place in arrests, but when this is combined with equally modest disparities in the decision to prosecute, to convict, and to sentence to prison and in the length of prison sentences, the end result is a significant disparity overall.

This leads us to the following proposition:

PROPOSITION 46

Elimination of discrimination and the perception of injustice is likely to reduce alienation from the criminal justice system and as a consequence help to increase law-abiding behavior.

DECRIMINALIZATION

New Perspective on an Old Issue

The question of legitimacy puts the old policy issue of decriminalization in a new perspective. In previous editions of this book, we discussed decriminalization in terms of its direct impact on serious crime (and also in terms of increasing the efficiency of the justice system). We should now look at it in terms of its indirect effect on serious crime. From the procedural justice perspective, decriminalizing certain offenses may reduce the alienation of groups of people from the criminal justice system and as a result enhance their inclination to obey the law.

For decades, decriminalizing certain offenses was a major liberal policy recommendation. In their 1970 book *The Honest Politician's Guide to Crime Control,* Norval Morris and Gordon Hawkins called decriminalization a "first principle." Specifically, they proposed removing criminal penalties on (1) public drunkenness; (2) purchase, possession, and use of all drugs; (3) all forms of gambling; (4) disorderly conduct and vagrancy; (5) abortion; (6) private sexual activity between consenting adults; and (7) juvenile "status" offenses.[15]

We should clarify exactly what kinds of behavior are involved in the list offered by Morris and Hawkins. Public drunkenness is included but not drunk driving. The person drunk on the street may be a nuisance but poses no real threat of harm to anyone else. The drunk driver does pose such a threat. Sexual activity between consenting adults is covered but not sex between an adult and a child. Adults have the capacity to make choices; children are vulnerable and need the protection of the law. In short, the standard decriminalization proposal covers a limited range of activity and not a general repeal of all criminal laws governing drinking or sex.

While decriminalization has generally been a liberal policy recommendation, libertarian conservatives also support decriminalizing some offenses. A number of prominent conservatives now support the legalization of drugs, for example. In short, just as many liberals have adopted traditional conservative crime control ideas, so have some conservatives embraced some traditional liberal ideas. Decriminalization or legalization of drugs is a major policy alternative today. We will consider that issue in detail in Chapter 13, which deals with drugs and drug policy. This chapter places the issue of decriminalization in a broader perspective, examining the likely impact on crime of decriminalizing other offenses.

The Rationale for Decriminalization

The basic assumption underlying decriminalization is the long-standing belief among liberals that the criminal law in the United States covers too much behavior. This is referred to as the *overreach* of the criminal law. In his classic work *The Limits of the Criminal Sanction,* Herbert L. Packer argues, "The criminal sanction is indispensable, [but] we resort to it in far too indiscriminate a way."[16] His point is that we should use it more sparingly and focus it on offenses that do genuine harm and about which there is a broad social consensus.

The overreach of the criminal law has several undesirable consequences.[17] First, it overburdens the justice system with relatively minor offenses, such as public drunkenness, leaving it with less resources for the really serious crimes of murder, rape, robbery, and burglary. Public drunkenness is a good example. A 1971 book published by the American Bar Foundation defined the problem as

Two Million Unnecessary Arrests.[18] Actually, the number of arrests for drunkenness has been declining steadily, from 1.2 million in 1975 to 713,000 in 1994 to 572,735 in 2002.[19] Nonetheless, 700,000 arrests consume a large amount of police and court resources. We can legitimately ask whether this effort is worth the cost.

A second problem is that no strong public consensus prevails about whether some behavior should be criminalized. Packer argues that "the criminal sanction should ordinarily be limited to conduct that is viewed, *without significant social dissent,* as immoral" (emphasis added).[20] The problem, however, is that there is much dissent on many issues. Americans have very mixed attitudes about gambling, for example; they feel that something is immoral about it, but they love to bet on sports nonetheless.

This relates directly to the legitimacy issue as defined by Tyler. If people feel that the law is intruding on behavior they believe is harmless and they want to engage in, their respect for the law will suffer. One good example of this is the medical use of marijuana. Many people feel that use of marijuana is a legitimate and effective treatment for relieving the pain of certain illnesses. They object to the fact that it is illegal.

One result of conflicting public attitudes is selective and often arbitrary law enforcement. This practice violates the principle of equal protection of the law and leads to cynicism about law enforcement among the public and police officers. Packer argues that "respect for law generally is likely to suffer."[21]

This issue is also at the heart of legitimacy as defined by Tyler. Racial and ethnic discrimination is the central controversy in the administration of justice. Public opinion polls consistently indicate that African Americans and Latinos have lower levels of confidence in the police and other parts of the justice system than do white Americans.[22]

A third problem is that making certain activities illegal leads to the development of criminal syndicates that provide the goods and services people want. Thirty years ago, the President's Crime Commission argued, "The core of organized crime activity is the supplying of illegal goods and services . . . to countless numbers of citizen customers."[23] Gambling was historically the principal source of revenue for organized crime, and the United States demand for illegal drugs sustains vast international networks and neighborhood drug gangs. In this sense, the law becomes criminogenic, creating forms of criminal behavior.

Fourth, the criminal syndicates that are created by making gambling and other activities illegal corrupt the justice system. The Knapp Commission investigation into police corruption in New York City in the early 1970s found that police officers were receiving a weekly "pad" of between $300 and $1,500 a month for protecting illegal gambling.[24] Twenty years later, the Mollen Commission found that the worst forms of police corruption and brutality in New York City were associated with drug trafficking.[25] Finally, the huge corruption and brutality scandal that was discovered in the Los Angeles Police Department in 1999 was clearly associated with the war on drugs, which created a climate in which LAPD officers felt they could get away with anything.[26]

Fifth, many people believe that certain kinds of recreation—sex and the use of some substances—is a matter of private choice that should be protected by the law. The overwhelming majority of Americans believe that sex between two adults of the opposite sex should not be a crime. About half of all Americans today now believe that sex between two adults of the same sex should not be a crime. Over 80 percent of Americans believe that women have a right to terminate a pregnancy by abortion.[27] This can have a profound effect on the perceived legitimacy of the criminal justice system. If a lot of people feel that the law is intruding on their privacy, they will lose respect for the law and the system.

Sixth, many criminal justice and public health experts believe that the problems associated with drinking, gambling, and sex are really social, psychological, and medical problems that should not be addressed through the criminal law. The President's Crime Commission concluded that the criminal justice system "is not in a position to meet [the chronic alcoholic's] underlying medical and social problems."[28] Many drug policy reform experts have been arguing for decades that drug abuse is a medical problem that should be treated as such and not be made a crime. Arrest and prosecution do nothing to help the chronic alcoholic deal with his or her drinking problem, and in many cases they make matters worse. Medical and social services would be a far more effective response.[29]

The Terms of the Debate

Not everyone agrees with the traditional arguments in favor of decriminalization. The debate between advocates and opponents of decriminalization raises fundamental questions about the role of the criminal law, involving issues of moral standards and the practical effects of criminalization.

Everyone does agree with the principle that the criminal law expresses (or should express) the basic values of society and defines the boundaries of acceptable conduct. Robbery is a crime because we believe that taking something that belongs to another person is wrong. Murder is a crime because taking another person's life is wrong. As Patrick Devlin puts it, "The criminal law as we know it is based upon moral principle."[30]

The question is not *whether* the law should express the values of society but *which values* it should express. As Packer says, "Whose morality are we talking about?"[31] Is gambling morally wrong or a legitimate form of entertainment? Is homosexual behavior morally wrong or a matter of private choice? Is abortion morally wrong (murder, in the eyes of anti-abortion activists) or a constitutionally protected private choice? Conservatives generally believe that these behaviors are morally wrong and therefore should be prohibited by the criminal law. Liberals generally believe that there is nothing immoral about these same behaviors and therefore they should not be made illegal. According to criminologist Gilbert Geis, certain forms of behavior are "not the law's business."[32]

Whether certain forms of behavior are wrong depends on how you define "harm." Advocates of decriminalization believe that gambling, for example, is a "victimless crime." Advocates of criminal prohibition believe that it produces real harms: that people can become addicted to gambling, that it can ruin their personal finances and harm their families, that it can lead to other crime as people try to pay off their gambling debts. Advocates of drug decriminalization believe that marijuana, for example, does not do the harm that it is alleged to do. Supporters of the current drug laws, on the other hand, believe that marijuana does real physical, psychological, and social harm. Devlin sums up the prohibitionist position by arguing that "society is entitled by means of its laws to protect itself from dangers, whether from within or without."[33]

Decriminalization is also debated in terms of the practical consequences of making certain behavior illegal. As we mentioned earlier, advocates of decriminalization believe that criminal prohibition overburdens the justice system, leads to arbitrary enforcement, encourages corruption, and does not help people who have a medical or psychological problem. The advocates of criminalization would reply that the moral issues at stake outweigh the bad consequences. Even if the law does not completely deter drug abuse, society should still condemn this behavior through the criminal law.

The Potential Impact of Decriminalization

Now let us take a look at some of the specific items on the traditional decriminalization agenda and discuss them in terms of both the potential direct impact on serious crime and the procedural justice perspective.

Public Disorder Crimes Public drunkenness, disorderly conduct, and vagrancy are essentially public nuisances rather than predatory crimes. They may offend our sensibilities, but they do not inflict tangible harm on someone the way robbery and burglary do.[34]

The crime control strategy underlying decriminalization of these offenses assumes that it would give the police more time to concentrate on serious crimes. As we indicated, 572,735 arrests were made for drunkenness in 2002, representing slightly less than 5 percent of all arrests and almost as many arrests as for all violent Index crimes.[35]

The basic assumption is flawed. As we learned in Chapter 5, adding more patrol officers will not prevent more crime, and adding more detectives will not raise clearance rates. Insofar as decriminalization of public drunkenness saves police time and resources, it might be desirable as a cost-saving measure. We have no reason to assume, however, that it will help reduce serious crime.

Not everyone agrees with our analysis. Public-order offenses such as drunkenness and urinating in public are a central part of the zero-tolerance policy adopted by then New York City police commissioner William Bratton. He and others claim that aggressively enforcing the law on these minor crimes has contributed directly to the reduction of murder and other serious crimes.[36] Critics, however, point out that crime has also fallen in cities that do not have the zero-tolerance policy and that the decline began before Bratton became police commissioner.[37]

Arrest trends indicate that we have been de-emphasizing public order arrests for many years. As we have already noted, between 1975 and 1997, the number of arrests for drunkenness fell from 1.2 million to 509,764. Several factors accounted for this decline. First, some court decisions held that arresting someone because of a medical condition—as opposed to some behavior—was unconstitutional. In 1966, the U.S. Court of Appeals for the District of Columbia ruled in *Easter v. District of Columbia* that DeWitt Easter could not be convicted for public intoxication.[38] Second, states have decriminalized public intoxication (in part due to court rulings). Third, police departments informally de-emphasized public order offenses and concentrated on serious crimes.

In the end, there may be good reasons for decriminalizing or de-emphasizing public disorder crimes, but doing so is unlikely to have any notable effect on serious crime.

Abortion Abortion was decriminalized by the famous 1973 Supreme Court decision *Roe v. Wade,* which declared existing criminal abortion laws unconstitutional.[39] We will not debate the morality of abortion here. It is important, however, to note that this issue dramatizes better than any other the moral basis of the criminal law and the conflict between different moral perspectives in our society. If you believe that the fetus is a human being, then it logically follows that abortion is murder. But if you believe that the fetus is not a human being, then it follows that the abortion decision is a private choice.[40]

In one of the most controversial pieces of criminological research in recent years, economists John J. Donohue, III, and Steven D. Levitt argued that the legalization of abortion did reduce crime. They conclude that the 1973 *Roe v. Wade* decision, which has resulted in about a million and a half abortions a year has reduced the number of unwanted children, and as a result reduced the size of the crime-prone age cohort (14–24 years old). They argue that legalized abortion accounts for as much as 50 percent of the crime drop of the 1990s. Despite the controversy over their argument (it was criticized by both pro-abortion and anti-abortion activists), it has not been replicated by other studies.[41]

Sex Between Consenting Adults States traditionally outlawed different kinds of sexual behavior, including activity between consenting adults such as adultery, cohabitation, homosexuality, and sodomy (which in some states includes "unnatural" sexual acts as well as acts between people of the same sex). By the mid-1980s, 13 states still had laws making it illegal for unmarried people to live together, and 13 had laws against "fornication" (sexual intercourse between people who are not married).[42] The 1910 Mann Act makes it a federal crime to take someone of the opposite sex across state lines for "immoral purposes." These laws are another good example of how the criminal law is used to define the moral boundaries of society.

In actual practice, the laws on sexual activity were rarely enforced, and as public attitudes about sex began to change in the 1960s, enforcement dropped even further. Between the 1960s and 2003, 35 states abolished their sodomy laws. Then in 2003, the U.S. Supreme Court declared sodomy laws unconstitutional on the grounds that they violated the right to privacy (*Lawrence v. Texas*).[43]

Whatever your views on adultery, cohabitation, or homosexuality, it is impossible to establish any connection between these activities and serious predatory crime. Legalizing or criminalizing cohabitation will have no effect on burglary or robbery.

One possible exception to this rule might be prostitution. In some instances, prostitution facilitates ancillary crimes: Customers are robbed; prostitutes are beaten by their pimps. It is possible that a system of legalized and regulated prostitution would remove streetwalkers from the streets and reduce some of these crimes.

Gambling   The legal status of gambling in the United States has undergone a massive change in recent years. The old moralistic objections to gambling have collapsed as many states have created lotteries and authorized casino gambling.[44] Many Native American tribes have established betting casinos on tribal lands that are exempt from federal and state gambling laws. Despite the spread of legal gambling, however, many of the popular forms of illegal gambling—sports betting pools, the numbers game—continue to flourish.

Advocates of decriminalizing gambling see a number of possible benefits: saving scarce resources, ending arbitrary law enforcement, and undercutting the economic basis of organized crime, for instance. There is no expectation, however, that it would reduce predatory crime, which is the issue that concerns us.[45]

Some opponents of legalized gambling believe that it might actually lead to an increase in crime. They argue that gambling casinos attract a criminal subculture that involves more thefts, robberies, and other crimes. Several studies have examined this issue. The Illinois Criminal Justice Information Authority found that the advent of riverboat gambling had no impact on crime in Joliet, Illinois.[46] David Giacopassi and B. Grant Stitt found that casino gambling had a mixed impact on crime in Biloxi, Mississippi. Auto theft and larceny did rise, but no significant changes were noted for other crimes.[47] Finally, crime did increase in Atlantic City, New Jersey, after gambling was legalized there in 1976, but it was primarily "in-house" crime inside the casinos themselves. No increase occurred in the community generally.[48] In short, no consistent evidence indicates that legalized gambling leads to higher crime rates.

Summary

Many arguments exist for and against criminalizing the different kinds of behavior we have discussed. We can debate this issue on moral grounds, on grounds of the practical consequences of criminal penalties, or on both grounds. It seems very clear, however, that we have no reason to expect any direct reduction in serious crime. This leads us to the following conclusion:

PROPOSITION 47
With the possible exception of drugs, decriminalization will not reduce serious crime.

There is some possibility that decriminalizing certain offenses will decrease the alienation of some people from the legal system and, according to the theories of procedural justice, increase their perception of the legitimacy and their tendency to obey the law. The evidence on this is speculative at best, however.

CONCLUSION

The emerging procedural justice perspective suggests that reforming the criminal justice system may in fact make a difference. Eliminating the sense of injustice, including the perceptions of discrimination, may enhance the legitimacy of the law and the justice system and promote law-abiding behavior. Though still very limited, there is some evidence that justice does make a difference—and potentially makes a difference in terms of serious crime. The decriminalization of offenses other than those related to drugs, however, is unlikely to make any difference with respect to serious crime.

NOTES

1. Tom R. Tyler, *Why People Obey the Law* (New Haven: Yale University Press, 1990).

2. National Academy of Sciences, *Fairness and Effectiveness in Policing: The Evidence* (Washington, DC: National Academy Press, 2004).

3. Ibid., p. 297.

4. Lorie Fridell et. al., *Racially Biased Policing: A Principled Response* (Washington, DC: Police Executive Research Forum, 2001), chapter 4.

5. Tyler, *Why People Obey the Law.*

6. Ibid., p. 62.

7. Jonathan D. Casper, Tom Tyler, and Bonnie Fisher, "Procedural Justice in Felony Cases," *Law and Society Review* 22.3 (1988): 484–507.

8. Raymond Paternoster, Robert Brame, Ronet Bachman, and Lawrence W. Sherman, "Do Fair Procedures Matter? The Effect of Procedural Justice on Spouse Assault," *Law and Society Review* 31 (1997): 163–204.

9. Bureau of Justice Statistics, *Policing and Homicide, 1976–1998: Justifiable Homicide by Police, Police Officers Murdered by Felons* (Washington, DC: Department of Justice, 2001). NCJ 180987.

10. Lorie Fridell, *By the Numbers* (Washington, DC: Police Executive Research Forum, 2005).

11. Department of Health and Human Services, 2003 *National Household Survey of Drug Abuse and Health* (Washington, DC: Author, 2004).

12. Jerome G. Miller, *Search and Destroy: African-American Males in the Criminal Justice System* (New York: Cambridge University Press, 1996).

13. Cassia Spohn, *How Do Judges Decide?* (Thousand Oaks, CA: Pine Forge Press, 2002).

14. Marjorie Zatz, "The Changing Forms of Racial/Ethnic Biases in Sentencing," *Journal of Research in Crime and Delinquency* 24 (February 1987): 69–92.

15. Norval Morris and Gordon Hawkins, *The Honest Politician's Guide to Crime Control* (Chicago: University of Chicago Press, 1970), p. 3.

16. Herbert L. Packer, *The Limits of the Criminal Sanction* (Stanford, CA: Stanford University Press, 1968), p. 364.

17. The best overview of this issue is still Packer, *The Limits of the Criminal Sanction*.

18. Raymond T. Nimmer, *Two Million Unnecessary Arrests* (Chicago: American Bar Foundation, 1971).

19. Federal Bureau of Investigation, *Crime in the United States, 1975* (Washington, DC: Government Printing Office, 1976), p. 179; Bureau of Justice Statistics, *Sourcebook of Criminal Justice Statistics 2002* (Washington, DC: Government Printing Office, 2002). Available online on the FBI website.

20. Packer, *Limits of the Criminal Sanction,* p. 264.

21. Ibid., p. 287.

22. Timothy J. Flanagan and Dennis R. Longmire, eds., *Americans View Crime and Justice: A National Public Opinion Survey* (Thousand Oaks, CA: Sage, 1996). Until recently, most surveys did not investigate the attitudes of Latino/Hispanic Americans.

23. President's Commission on Law Enforcement and Administration of Justice, *The Challenge of Crime in a Free Society* (New York: Avon, 1968), p. 437.

24. Knapp Commission, *Report on Police Corruption* (New York: Braziller, 1973).

25. Commission to Investigate Allegations of Police Corruption and the Anti-Corruption Procedures of the Police Department, *Report* (New York: City of New York, 1994).

26. Los Angeles Police Department, Board of Inquiry, *Rampart Area Corruption Incident* (Los Angeles: Author, 2000).

27. Bureau of Justice Statistics, *Sourcebook of Criminal Justice Statistics—1995* (Washington, DC: Government Printing Office, 1996), p. 228.

28. President's Commission on Law Enforcement and Administration of Justice, *Task Force Report: Drunkenness* (Washington, DC: Government Printing Office, 1967), p. 3.

29. Nimmer, *Two Million Unnecessary Arrests.*

30. Patrick Devlin, *The Enforcement of Morals* (London: Oxford University Press, 1965), p. 7.

31. Packer, *Limits of the Criminal Sanction,* p. 263.

32. Gilbert Geis, *Not the Law's Business* (New York: Schocken, 1979).

33. Devlin, *Enforcement of Morals,* p. 13.

34. President's Commission, *Task Force Report: Drunkenness.*

35. Federal Bureau of Investigation, *Crime in the United States, 2002* (Washington, DC: Department of Justice, 2002). Current data are available on the FBI website.

36. George L. Kelling and Catherine Coles, *Fixing Broken Windows* (New York: Kessler, 1996).

37. John E. Eck and Edward Maguire, "Have Changes in Policing Reduced Crime?," in Alfred Blumstein and Joel Wallman, *The Crime Drop in America* (New York: Cambridge University Press, 2000), pp. 207–265.

38. *Easter v. District of Columbia,* 361 F.2d 50 (D.C. Cir. 1966).

39. *Roe v. Wade,* 410 U.S. 113 (1973).

40. Lawrence H. Tribe, Abortion: *The Clash of Absolutes* (New York: Norton, 1990).

41. John J. Donohue, III, and Steven D. Levitt, "The Impact of Legalized Abortion on Crime," *Quarterly Journal of Economics,* 66 (no. 2, 2001): 379–420.

42. Mitchell Bernard, Ellen Levine, Stefan Presser, and Marianne Stecich, *The Rights of Single People* (New York: Bantam, 1985), pp. 12–13.

43. *Lawrence v. Texas,* 539 U.S. 558 (2003). Vincent J. Samar, *The Right to Privacy: Gays, Lesbians, and the Constitution* (Philadelphia: Temple University Press, 1991). A Web search for the term "sodomy laws" will yield websites that provide current information.

44. John D. Rosecrance, *Gambling without Guilt: The Legitimation of an American Past-time* (Pacific Grove, CA: Brooks/Cole, 1988).

45. Earl L. Grinois, *Gambling in America: Costs and Benefits* (New York: Cambridge University Press, 2004).

46. Illinois Criminal Justice Information Authority, *Riverboat Gambling and Crime in Illinois* (Springfield: Author, 1994).

47. David Giacopassi and B. Grant Stitt, "Assessing the Impact of Casino Gambling on Crime in Mississippi," *American Journal of Criminal Justice* 18 (1994): 117–131.

48. Daniel Curran and Frank Scarpitti, "Crime in Atlantic City: Do Casinos Make a Difference?" *Deviant Behavior* 12 (1991): 431–450.

PART V

The Drug Problem

One of the ground rules for this book is a focus on robbery and burglary. We are now going to violate that rule by examining drug policy. The drug crack was closely associated with the surge in gun violence in the 1980s. The Sentencing Project bluntly declares: "No issue has had more impact on the criminal justice system in the past two decades than national drug policy. The 'war on drugs' that was declared in the early 1980s has been a primary contributor to the enormous growth of the prison system in the United States since that time and has affected all aspects of the criminal justice system."[1]

Drug arrests tripled between 1975 and 2003, with the result that drug offenders went from 6 to 21 percent of all state prisoners; in the federal prisons they rose from 25 to 57 percent of prisoners. Prison terms also lengthened, from an average of 22 months for federal drug offenders in 1999 to 62 months today. Additionally, most of these prisoners are low-level dealers; only 11 percent of federal drug defendants are major dealers.[2] Let us take a look at the problem of drugs, the drug–crime connection, and the larger question of drug policy.

13

Sense and Nonsense about Drugs

THE DRUG PROBLEM

To talk seriously about crime policy, we have to address the issue of drugs and drug policy. Drugs have been the focal point of the crime problem in the United States for many years. Directly or indirectly, they were responsible for the dramatic rise in the murder rate in the 1980s, gang violence, the soaring prison population, the worsening crisis in race relations, and the steady erosion of individual rights in Supreme Court rulings.[3]

Discussing drug policy allows us to apply much of what we have learned so far. Conservative drug policies emphasize getting tough with drug offenders through more arrests and tougher punishments, while liberal policies prefer prevention, education, and treatment. Have we learned anything so far about policies that would effectively address the drug problem?

Hysteria over Drugs

Public hysteria over drugs and drug-related crime prevents sensible discussion of policy. This has long been the case. In the 1930s, a wave of national hysteria arose over "reefer madness," with wild stories about the alleged dangers of marijuana. Rent the hilarious *Reefer Madness* (1938) video and see for yourself. A similar scare erupted in the 1980s over "crack babies." Sensational news media stories appeared in 1988 about 375,000 crack babies born to addicted mothers. Reports claimed that these infants had severe physical and psychological

Table 13.1 Sources of data on drug use

National Survey of Drug Use and Health
Monitoring the Future (MTF)
Drug Abuse Warning Network (DAWN)
Arrestee Drug Abuse Monitoring (ADAM) [Terminated in 2003.]

damage, would never develop normally, and would be a permanent burden to society. One medical expert said, "It's as if the part of the brain that makes us human beings capable of discussion or reflection is wiped out."[4]

The truth turned out to be very different. The number of babies possibly affected by crack was grossly exaggerated. The original reports counted all babies who had been exposed to drugs during pregnancy, not just those who were genuinely addicted or even harmed. Some hospitals included mothers who had used marijuana. Later research found that the long-term damage even to addicted babies had been exaggerated. One study found no performance differences in crack and noncrack children by age four. (Check the website of Drug War Facts for more information on this issue.) Other studies found that the problems attributed to crack exposure were due primarily to inadequate prenatal care, a problem associated with low-income parents. Some studies suggest that alcohol does more harm to a fetus than cocaine. Among adults, the Sentencing Project points out that there are far more alcohol-related deaths every year (94,000) than drug-related deaths (21,000), but the criminal justice system is far harsher on drug offenses.[5]

Myths and Realities about Drugs and Crime

To help sort our way through the debate over drug policy, we need to establish some basic facts about drugs and crime. As with most criminal justice issues, many myths about drugs and crime inhibit the development of sound and effective policies on this problem. Let us begin by exploring some of the facts about the extent of illegal drug use, drug use trends, and the relationship between drugs and crime.

The Extent of Illegal Drug Use

The first question is: How extensive is illegal drug use? We currently have four different surveys (Table 13.1). Two are general social surveys, while two are surveys of specific subgroups of the population. There is much disagreement over what these four surveys say. There are problems with the methodology of each survey. In terms of the findings, it is important to distinguish between first-time use, continued use, and abuse (as indicated by some harm to the individual or society).[6]

The broadest general survey is the National Survey on Drug Use and Health (formerly known as the National Household Survey), which collects self-report data on a sample of the general population. (Check the most recent survey on the SAMSHA website.) The flaw in its methodology is similar to that of the National Crime Victimization Survey: First, respondents may not truthfully report their illegal drug use, and second, it surveys households and misses many of the most serious drug abusers, who are transients, homeless, or in prison.

The National Survey data indicate that illegal substance use is fairly widespread. In 2003 about 20 million Americans, or 8.2 percent of the population, used an illicit drug in the past month. This was down from 11.2 percent in 1997. Marijuana was the most commonly used drug, with 14 million users in 2003, while 2.3 million used cocaine and about 600,000 used crack cocaine. Illicit drug use peaks at among 18–20 year olds and then declines steadily as people get older.[7] About 46 percent of the adult population have used an illegal drug at least once in their lifetime, with 40 percent having used marijuana and 14.7 percent having used cocaine.

The Monitoring the Future (MTF) survey provides self-report data from about 48,500 students enrolled in grades 8, 10, and 12 in 392 public and private schools.[8] (Check the Monitoring the Future website for the most recent reports.) Students represent an important segment of the at-risk population. The major weakness is that it misses kids who have dropped out of school—precisely those who are most likely to be the heaviest drug abusers. The MTF data indicate that illegal drug use declined among young people between the late 1970s and about 1992, as it did for the general population, but then began increasing again. The prevalence of illicit drug use peaked in 1981 at 66 percent of all young people, declined to 41 percent in 1992, and rose to 51 percent by 2003.[9]

A third survey, the Drug Abuse Warning Network (DAWN), uses a different methodology and tells a very different story. In 2001, DAWN collected data on alcohol and drug-related admissions to emergency rooms and substance-related deaths from over 470 emergency departments (EDs) at 470 hospitals in 21 metropolitan areas and from 87 medical examiners (or coroners) in 27 metropolitan areas. While DAWN obviously does not estimate general patterns of illegal drug use, it does indicate trends in the most serious consequences of drug abuse. (One major limitation is that it reports *mentions* of drugs in a medical report, which does not necessarily mean that a drug *caused* the medical emergency.) DAWN presents a very grim picture. Cocaine- and heroin-related ED admissions quadrupled between the early 1980s and 1989, declined in 1990, and then continued to rise significantly to the present. Deaths have also risen significantly since 1980.[10]

The trends indicated by the DAWN survey are clearly at odds with those from the National Survey on Drug Use. This divergence suggests that while illegal drug use declined for the general population between the late 1970s and the 1990s, it became far more acute for one segment of the population. This supports our argument in Chapter 1, following on Elliott Currie's analysis, that we really have two separate drug problems, one related to the general population where the immediate harms are limited and another that affects the poorest minority communities with very serious immediate consequences.[11]

Finally, until its termination in 2003, the Arrestee Drug Abuse Monitoring (ADAM) program (formerly known as DUF, or Drug Use Forecasting) collected urine specimens and self-report data on drug use from arrestees. In 2003, ADAM collected data on adults in 39 cities. Although not a representative sample of the population, it provided useful data on drug use among criminal offenders. In New Orleans, for example, 78 percent of all male arrestees tested positive for one of five drugs, and 30 percent tested positive for multiple drugs. In Miami, 47 percent of male arrestees tested positive for crack cocaine, compared with only 10 percent in San Diego.[12]

One of the most important contributions of the ADAM data has been to document the significant reduction in crack usage in many major cities in the 1990s.[13] Many criminologists believe that this reduction is closely associated with—and may be the major cause of—the drop in the crime rate.[14] We will look at this issue in more detail later in this chapter.

The various measures of illegal drug use lead us to three general conclusions. First, illegal drug use has declined among the general population since the late 1970s (although usage of some drugs has increased among teenagers since 1992). Second, drug abuse increased sharply among a particular segment of the population between 1985 and the early 1990s. Third, crack use has declined significantly in many cities in recent years, and this reduction appears to be associated with the reduction in serious crime. As we pointed out in Chapter 1, the decline in crack usage and serious crime appears to be genuine and long-term. The important—and still unanswered—question is: What caused the decline in crack use?

The Drug–Crime Connection

A second important question involves the relationship between drugs and crime. Many people believe that drugs *cause* crime and that if we reduced illegal drug abuse, we would have much less crime. The myth persists of the "drug-crazed criminal" who robs and murders while high on drugs. This is similar to the old reefer madness view that women become sexually promiscuous because of marijuana. The federal Office of National Drug Control Policy published a frightening graphic purporting to show the direct and harmful "Consequences of Drug Use" on "family, crime, violence, health, economic [circumstances, and] community."[15] In short, drugs are commonly seen as the cause of almost all of our problems.

Drugs and crime are related, but the relationship is very complex.[16] Crime associated with drugs falls into three categories. First, there are *drug-defined* crimes: the possession and sale of illegal substances. Second, there are *drug-related* crimes, including violent behavior caused by the pharmacological effects of a drug or robberies committed to get money to buy drugs. Third, there are crimes *associated with drug usage,* meaning that an offender was using drugs around the time he or she committed an offense, but the crime was not caused by drug use.[17]

The ADAM data confirm the fact that a large percentage of arrestees are involved with both drug and alcohol use. Merely testing positive for drugs, however, does not mean that the crime was *caused* by drugs. This is similar to the problem we discussed in Chapter 6: Just because a driver tests positive for alcohol does not mean that his or her driving was impaired by drinking. Only 17 percent of prison inmates say they committed their offense to get money to buy drugs.[18] A survey of offenders on probation found that half admitted to being under the influence of drugs or alcohol at the time they committed the offense for which they were convicted. Two-thirds reported they had used drugs in the past and about one-third admitted they had used drugs in the month before they committed the offense for which they were convicted.[19] This involvement with drugs does not, however, mean that the crimes these individuals committed were caused by drugs.

The federal government's national drug control strategy regards many substances—alcohol, tobacco, marijuana—as "gateways" to more serious drug abuse and criminal behavior. (A Web search for "gateway drugs" will find a number of organizations that advance this idea.) The evidence does not support this view. Studies of high-rate offenders have found that many began their criminal activity before they began using drugs. But for others drug use preceded their criminal activity. Still others became involved in crime and drugs at about the same time. As a Justice Department report concludes, "For some individuals drugs use is independent of their involvement in crime. These people may continue to commit crimes even if drugs were unavailable."[20] David Farrington argues that "violent youth have many other 'co-occurring problems.'" These problems include truancy, early sexual initiation and sexual promiscuity, unstable employment records, bad relations with parents, and many other factors.[21] It is impossible to say that any one (e.g., drug use) *caused* subsequent violent criminal behavior.

The National Survey data provide further evidence that illegal drug use does not lead to criminal activity. Few of the estimated 110 million people who reported ever having used an illicit drug in their life in 2003 became either addicts or career criminals. Most drug use is casual and recreational and does not have serious antisocial consequences.

The lack of a direct causal link between drugs and crime has important implications for crime policy. It means that even if we succeeded in substantially reducing illegal drug use, we would not necessarily reduce crime to the same degree. Crimes related to drug trafficking would certainly be reduced, but the impact on crimes associated with deviant lifestyles, which include the vast majority of robberies and burglaries, would be very limited. And by the same token, reducing crime would not necessarily reduce drug use. A causal relationship between the two behaviors simply does not exist.

The Drug Policy Choices

What should we do about drugs and crime? Peter Reuter classifies policy advocates into three groups: hawks, doves, and owls (these categories are borrowed from the debate over the Vietnam War in the 1960s and 1970s).[22] Hawks emphasize law enforcement to eradicate drug abuse, believing that we simply need to get tougher than we have been. Enforcement strategies include both supply reduction, designed to reduce the availability of drugs, and demand reduction, designed to decrease peoples' desire to use drugs.[23] American drug policy is dominated by the hawk approach, with most of the emphasis on supply reduction.

Owls prefer prevention and treatment of drug abuse, which are essentially demand-reduction strategies. Current drug policy includes prevention and treatment, but they have always received less emphasis than supply reduction–oriented law enforcement approaches.

Doves, meanwhile, believe that we should completely rethink our national drug policy. In general, they would prefer to define drug abuse as a public health problem. The National Council on Crime and Delinquency asserts that it "should be defined primarily as a health-related problem that should reside in the public health domain."[24]

The radical dove approach is to legalize drugs. We discuss legalization later in this chapter. A more moderate approach is generally referred to as *harm reduction,* which means keeping the criminal penalties for drugs on the books, but not enforcing them as intensively. The title of Mark A. R. Kleiman's book, *Against Excess,* expresses this point of view. Both the war on drugs and legalization are radical policies, and he argues in favor of a middle range.[25] Harm reduction essentially represents the drug policies of many European countries, particularly the Netherlands.[26]

To a certain extent, the drug policy debate is a discussion about what causes the greatest harm: drugs or drug policy. Hawks believe that drugs are the problem. Doves believe that drug policy is the problem, causing more harm than good.

The hawk/owl/dove categories do not conform to the conservative/liberal dichotomy we have used in this book. The Reagan and Bush administrations (1981–1993) put tremendous emphasis on tough law enforcement, but First Lady Nancy Reagan simultaneously led a highly publicized "Just say no" antidrug education campaign. The policies of the liberal Clinton administration included tough sentencing measures for drug offenders and postconviction restrictions on offenders' rights (see Chapter 15), but also more money for drug prevention programs.

THE WAR ON DRUGS:
POLICY AND CONSEQUENCES

Since passage of the 1914 Harrison Act, the hawks have dominated American drug policy. That is, we have defined certain substances as illegal and attempted to suppress their use though criminal law enforcement. Over the past 30 years, our policy has become increasingly hawkish, as a succession of presidents have declared "war" on drugs, and arrests and imprisonment for drug possession and sale have soared.[27]

Table 13.2 Illicit drug use,* by race and ethnicity, 2002

	Ever	Past Year	Past Month
White (non-Hispanic)	48.5%	14.9%	8.5%
Hispanic or Latino	38.9	15	7.2
African American	43.8	16.8	9.7

*Any illicit drug.

SOURCE: Substance Abuse and Mental Health Services Administration, *National Survey on Drug Use and Health, 2002* (Washington, DC: SAMHSA, 2004).

The 2004 program of the Office of National Drug Control Policy includes a mix of education, treatment, and law enforcement. The three parts are: "Stopping Use Before it Starts" (including education and student drug testing, an antidrug media campaign, and $10 million for antidrug community projects), "Healing America's Drug Users" (drug treatment and drug courts), and "Disrupting the Market" (law enforcement programs).[28]

The Impact of the War on Drugs

As we argued in Chapter 1, the war on drugs has had an enormous impact on U.S. society, on the criminal justice system, and on racial minorities in particular. The number of persons arrested for drug offenses almost tripled, from 601,000 in 1975 to 1.7 million in 2003. Persons convicted of drug offenses are the primary factor in the spectacular increase in the prison population. About 60 percent of all federal prisoners today are there for drug offenses, compared with only 25 percent in 1980.[29]

Many critics argue that racial minorities are the primary victims of the war on drugs. The National Criminal Justice Commission argues that "we are on the verge of a social catastrophe because of the sheer number of African-Americans behind bars."[30] Some would argue that the catastrophe is already here. Data compiled by The Sentencing Project (see Chapter 1, Figure 1.4) indicate that African Americans are treated more harshly at every stage of the criminal justice system. Yet the National Survey on Drug Use and Health indicates that this group is only somewhat more likely to use illegal drugs. Hispanics are even less likely than whites to use drugs. In 2002, 8.5 percent of whites used drugs in the past month, compared with 7.2 percent of Hispanics and 9.7 percent of African Americans (see Table 13.2).[31]

Illegal Drug Use by Race and Ethnicity Racial bias is particularly blatant at two points in the criminal justice system. With respect to policing, the National Criminal Justice Commission argues that street-level drug enforcement "focus[es] almost exclusively on low-level dealers in minority neighborhoods."[32] With respect to sentencing, the federal sentencing guidelines include differential penalties for powdered and crack cocaine. Possession of 5 grams of crack nets a mandatory minimum sentence of five years, whereas possession of the same amount of powdered cocaine carries a maximum sentence of only one year. This has a grossly disparate racial impact, as crack is favored by African Americans and powdered cocaine is preferred by whites.[33] Yet, Congress and the courts have refused to revise the guidelines.

Arrest and imprisonment have become extremely common experiences in underclass neighborhoods. As we pointed out in Chapter 6, some deterrence theorists argue that arrest loses its deterrent effect when it becomes a common experience for a group.[34] And as we argued in Chapter 12, the racial disparities associated with the war on drugs undermines the legitimacy of the criminal justice system in the eyes of many African Americans.

In short, the war on drugs has undoubtedly had a tremendous impact on U.S. society and on racial minorities in particular. Whether it has succeeded in reducing illegal drug use or serious crime associated with drug use is another question. Now let us take a look at some of the major components of the drug war.

Police Crackdowns

The principal police strategy for reducing drug abuse is aggressive law enforcement. One variation is the *crackdown,* an intensive, short-term, geographically focused effort.[35] (See our earlier discussion of crackdowns in Chapter 5.) One well-known crackdown was Operation Pressure Point (OPP) on New York City's Lower East Side. Directed at an open-air drug market, OPP flooded the area with police officers, produced a high volume of arrests, and sought to scare away drug buyers.

Evaluations of OPP claimed some short-term benefits: an end to open drug dealing and a reduction in crime. Many important questions remain unanswered, however. The enforcement effort may have displaced drug dealing to other areas. Even within the targeted area, drug dealers adapted their procedures to insulate themselves from the police. The evaluations made no serious attempt to assess the outcomes of the arrests. Improper police tactics may have been used, particularly the harassment of potential buyers who drove in from suburban areas. There was also no serious discussion of the long-term cost-effectiveness of a mass arrest policy.[36]

The most telling criticism of OPP is that the drug problem in New York City worsened dramatically over the next few years with the arrival of crack. Open-air drug markets spread to many neighborhoods. Even the New York City police department tacitly admitted that the crackdown strategy was futile, and in the early 1990s it reduced both the number of officers assigned to the tactical narcotics teams (TNTs) and the number of drug arrests.[37] Many street-level police officers candidly admitted that they could make all the arrests they wanted, but new dealers and buyers would just take the place of those arrested. Other crackdowns, such as Operation Hammer in Los Angeles, had little impact on drugs or gang activity and were done mainly for the short-term publicity effect.[38] The University of Maryland report concludes, "The evidence on drug crackdowns shows no consistent reductions in violent crime during or after the crackdown."[39] We agree.

In fact, no local law enforcement efforts have much impact on the availability of drugs on the street. A 2002 survey asked undercover police officers in 25 cities how difficult it was to obtain various drugs. On a scale of 0 to 10, with 0 meaning not difficult at all, officers in Dallas, New York City, and Phoenix gave ratings of 0 for heroin, crack, and marijuana; no city gave a rating higher than 1.75 for marijuana; the overall rating for crack was 0.7 in the 25 cities.[40] In short, police officers themselves do not believe that their intensive antidrug efforts reduce the availability of drugs. This is a damning indictment of police crackdowns.

PROPOSITION 48
Police crackdowns will not reduce illegal drug use
or serious crime associated with drugs.

This does not mean that no police antidrug efforts work. As we found in Chapter 5 and will discuss again in Chapter 14, some problem-oriented policing programs have shown some signs of success. The SMART (Specialized Multi-Agency Response Team) program in Oakland, California, reduced drug-related activity without displacing it to neighboring areas. The difference is that SMART (and other problem-oriented policing programs) involves more than just the police and more than law enforcement strategies. Taking a multiagency approach, it mobilizes other government agencies to attack a range of neighborhood problems, particularly housing. Instead of relying solely on arrest and prosecution, like traditional crackdowns, it uses a combination of criminal and civil law strategies such as enforcing housing codes and cleaning up the physical appearance of neighborhoods, to address underlying community problems.[41]

Interdiction and Eradication

Two major supply-reduction efforts by the federal government include *interdiction,* stopping the flow of drugs entering the country, and *eradication,* reducing the production of drug plants in the field. The conservative policy advocates William J. Bennett, John J. DiIulio, and John P. Walters argue that interdiction of drugs should be a "top national security priority" for the United States.[42] In fact, the federal government has made a huge and steadily increasing effort at interdiction.

In 2002 the DEA (U.S. Drug Enforcement Administration) seized 61,594 kilograms of cocaine, up from 28,630 in 1998 (but not as much as the 75,051 seized in 1994). Heroin seizures (705 kilograms in 2002) have fluctuated in a similar fashion.[43] The U.S. State Department's Plan Colombia gives $129 million to that country to halt the production and export of cocaine; it gives an additional $30 million for voluntary eradication by Colombian farmers. (See the entire Plan on the State Department website.) And as the survey of undercover police officers we mentioned above indicates, these efforts have no impact on the availability of drugs on the street. Many experts believe that the combined efforts of federal, state, and local law enforcement succeed in seizing only about 10 to 15 percent of the total supply.

The failure of interdiction is easy to understand. The 20,000-mile border of the United States is too great, the possible methods of smuggling drugs too many, and the people engaged in the trade too numerous. Increased enforcement, moreover, produces a variety of adaptations: new points of entry, new methods of smuggling, shifts in drug use as prices change, and so on. Insofar as tougher enforcement raises the risks of drug trafficking, it drives the trade into the hands of those who are better organized, more heavily armed, and willing to take the risks—in short, the cartels that dominate the international cocaine market. Despite increased federal interdiction efforts, total worldwide production of drugs increased significantly between 1987 and 1991 alone. Production of marijuana rose from 13,000 to 23,000 metric tons, while coca leaf production increased from 291,000 to 337,000 metric tons.[44] A Rand report concludes, "Increased drug interdiction efforts are not likely to greatly affect the availability of cocaine in the United States."[45]

PROPOSITION 49
Drug interdiction and eradication efforts are doomed to fail.

Tougher Sentencing

Tough sentencing policies for persons convicted of drug offenses have been another major strategy of the war on drugs. This represents the incapacitation and deterrence we studied in Chapters 6 and 7. Our conclusion in those chapters was that neither strategy is effective in reducing crime. In the case of drugs, incapacitation is often undermined by the *replacement effect*. Persons who are imprisoned for drug offenses are replaced by someone else who is willing to take the risks. The lack of legitimate opportunities (e.g., jobs, prospects for upward mobility) creates a substantial pool of potential new offenders.

It is important to note that drug use and crime associated with drugs has remained highest among the underclass, the very group that has been the primary target of the war on drugs. Arrest and imprisonment have obviously not had deterrent or incapacitative effects on that group. And while it is true that the crack epidemic has passed, this was primarily the result of a cultural shift away from crack and toward other drugs, rather than as a result of tough enforcement.[46]

PROPOSITION 50
Tougher sentencing is not likely to reduce illegal
drug use or serious crime associated with drugs.

LIMITS OF THE CRIMINAL LAW:
THE LESSONS OF HISTORY

Many critics of current drug policy argue that a war-on-drugs approach is doomed to fail. History provides a valuable perspective on this issue by offering a number of examples of attempts to control products or services through the criminal law. Let us take a look at some of the more notable ones.

Prohibition Between 1920 and 1933, the manufacture and sale of alcoholic beverages were illegal under the Eighteenth Amendment to the U.S. Constitution. Stories from Prohibition have entered the national folklore: speakeasies, Al Capone, gangland shootouts, and so on. Prohibition did reduce drinking and probably contributed to the decline in deaths from cirrhosis of the liver (from 13.3 per 100,000 in 1910 to 7.2 per 100,000 in 1930).

Citing these figures, some historians argue that Prohibition was a success.[47] Other historians, however, argue that Prohibition clearly did not end all drinking and inflicted enormous collateral damage on the country.[48] By turning millions of casual drinkers into criminals, it undermined respect for the law. (It would be interesting to write a history of Prohibition from the procedural justice perspective we discussed in Chapter 12.) It created a vast illegal market that was filled by criminal syndicates, which corrupted police and politicians. Prohibition enforcement was accompanied by widespread abuses, particularly illegal searches and seizures.

Social Gambling Gambling is big business in the United States. This was not always so. Gambling policy has undergone a revolution in recent years, with the spread of state lotteries and casinos. Until recently, it was a heavily restricted activity, confined to a small number of racetracks, Las Vegas, and church-based bingo games. Nonetheless, millions of Americans routinely engaged in illegal betting—on athletic events, the "numbers," and so on. The laws restricting gambling had many of the same collateral effects as Prohibition. Gambling has long been the primary source of revenue for organized crime and was the main cause of police corruption.[49]

Gun Control As we learned in Chapter 10, we have many laws barring certain people from owning guns, especially criminals. Yet active criminals have no trouble obtaining weapons through friends, the black market, or theft.

The Old Criminal Abortion Laws Before the 1973 *Roe v. Wade* decision, abortion was a criminal offense in every state (several states did liberalize their laws between 1967 and 1973). But these laws did not eliminate abortions; in fact, as many as a million illegal abortions may have been performed a year. The harmful consequences included death and permanent injury to women from unsanitary back-alley abortions.

Sodomy, Fornication, Adultery, and Prostitution Laws Various forms of sexual activity have traditionally been illegal in the United States: sex between members of the same sex (sodomy), sex between unmarried people of different sex (fornication), sex between a married person and someone other than his or her spouse (adultery), and sex for pay (prostitution). The law has been changing rapidly on some of these issues, however. The Supreme Court declared sodomy laws unconstitutional in 2003. To put it mildly, none of these laws ever stopped people from engaging in these forms of sexual behavior. All of these behaviors have occurred since the beginning of recorded history.

The Lessons of History

These examples suggest the following four conclusions about the limits of the criminal law in controlling products or services that a large number of people want:

1. If a large number of people want a product or service, someone will try to supply it.
2. Efforts to suppress that supply will result in massive evasion and the creation of criminal syndicates.
3. The enforcement effort itself will generate secondary crime (e.g., turf wars between gangs, corruption of law enforcement), abuse of individual rights (e.g., illegal searches and seizures), and loss of respect for the law.
4. Intensifying the enforcement effort encourages adaptations, either substitution of products (as in the case of some drugs) or transfer of the service to people more willing to take the increased risks.

In short, criminal law enforcement is inherently weak in the face of a strong public demand for a product or service. This point helps explain the failure of the war on drugs. Shortly, we will look at some policies designed to reduce the demand for drugs.

When Social Control Does Work

It is not true that *all* efforts to prevent undesirable behavior fail. In principle, some prohibitions are good. The criminal law defines the basic standards of society. As children, we learn that stealing things and hitting people are wrong. To the extent that the criminal law shapes the values and habits of most people, it does work. The problem, of course, is that this process of socialization fails for a number of people.

The case of smoking offers an interesting example of an apparently successful attempt at curbing harmful behavior. Smoking among adults has declined significantly in recent years. Between 1965 and 2001, the percentage of American men who smoked fell from 52 to 24 percent. Among women it declined from 34 to 20 percent.[50] This sharp decline is the result of both formal restrictions on smoking in many buildings and public areas and a massive public education effort (including warning labels on cigarette packages).

We have not completely eliminated smoking, and we have not tried to. The new restrictions attempt only to regulate and restrict it. In many respects, they have reinforced changing public attitudes about health. It is reasonable to speculate that a complete prohibition on smoking (similar to the one on alcohol in the

1920s) would produce a backlash that might only reinforce pro-smoking attitudes. We might speculate on what would happen if tobacco were outlawed. Would prohibition succeed? Would the results be like those during Prohibition in the 1920s and like the current prohibition of drugs? Or would they be different?

It is also worth noting that smoking has recently increased among white teenagers, particularly females.[51] In other words, the national antismoking effort has not affected one major at-risk group, indicating that there are some limits as to what restrictions and education can accomplish. We will have more to say about this subject when we turn to the question of drug education programs.

The decline in automobile fatalities we discussed in Chapter 6 offers another useful example. This remarkable achievement in saving lives was the result not of traffic enforcement crackdowns, but of a number of social policies working in combination: improved roads, better-designed cars, seat belts, and so on. When we focus on alcohol-related fatalities, the use of the criminal law is now the most effective approach.

DEMAND REDUCTION: DRUG EDUCATION

The owl drug policy favored by most liberals includes demand reduction through education and treatment. Let us take a look at drug education programs.

"Just Say No"

The most widely used demand reduction programs involve public education efforts designed to persuade people not to use drugs. The most famous was Nancy Reagan's "Just say no" campaign in the 1980s. The first priority of a drug control policy proposed by conservatives William J. Bennett, John J. DiIulio, and John P. Walters is: "Teach the young that drug use is wrong."[52] The relevant question, however, is whether drug education efforts actually work. Educational programs employ one or more of four different strategies.[53]

The most common strategy is *information dissemination*. This approach seeks to change behavior simply by providing information. Sex education programs, for example, discuss the basic facts about reproduction, while health education programs explain cholesterol.

A second strategy is *fear arousal*, which attempts to change behavior by frightening people. Safe-sex education programs emphasize the danger of getting AIDS from unprotected sex. In the Scared Straight program we discussed in Chapter 6, adult prisoners told juvenile offenders about the horrors of imprisonment.[54]

A third strategy is *moral appeal*, emphasizing the idea that certain behavior is wrong—that sex outside of marriage is a sin or that gambling is immoral, for example.

A fourth strategy is known as *affective education*. This approach attempts to develop personal and social skills that will help people resist certain behavior. Sex education programs, for instance, try to teach teenagers how to say no to someone who is pressuring them to have sex.

Nancy Reagan's "Just say no" campaign combined fear arousal and moral appeal. The famous "This is your brain—this is your brain on drugs" ad campaign developed by the Partnership for a Drug-Free America also used fear arousal.

We have good reasons for questioning the effectiveness of antidrug educational programs. The problems are similar to the ones we discussed in Chapter 6 regarding deterrence theory: The message has to reach the intended audience, members of that audience have to perceive a real personal risk, and they have to make rational decisions to change their behavior.

First, many antidrug messages probably do not even reach their target audience. For example, the National Campaign for a Drug-Free America runs expensive full-page ads in the *Wall Street Journal*. But how many teenagers or low-income people—those most at risk for illegal drug use—read the *Wall Street Journal*? Second, many members of the target audience do not think that a real risk exists. Teenagers especially tend to believe that they are invulnerable— that they will not be caught by the police, that they are not too drunk to drive, that drugs will not hurt them, and so on. Also, as with deterrence theory, the risk has to be perceived in a cost-benefit context, as being worse than the alternative (see our discussion in Chapter 6). But many people trapped in very poor neighborhoods do not perceive any realistic long-term hopes for economic advancement. Consequently, the short-term benefits of immediate gratification weigh much more heavily for them.

Some of the education program messengers, meanwhile, are not credible. Was Nancy Reagan, for example, an influential role model for low-income teenagers in the 1980s? Another problem is that some fear arousal programs backfire by glamorizing the forbidden behavior. They may heighten the allure of drinking, smoking, sex, and drugs by portraying them as adult-only activities. In fact, the famous "This is your brain on drugs" concept became the subject of many parodies that undermined the purpose of the original campaign.[55]

Third, we cannot assume that the members of the target audience will make rational decisions even if they hear the message. Teenagers, as we mentioned, are notoriously focused on short-term gratification rather than long-term consequences. Anti-smoking campaigns have been least successful with this group. An education program is only one small factor influencing behavior and is likely to be very weak in the face of peer group influence.

Evaluation of a Major Media Campaign   The National Youth Anti-Drug Media Campaign sponsored paid advertisements targeted at young people between ages of 9 to 18, with a special focus on 14- to 16-year-olds, along with parents of youth in these age groups. A major component of the campaign was a special Marijuana Initiative. An evaluation surveyed a representative sample of several thousand young people and adults.[56]

How effective was the campaign? Most parents (70 percent) and youth (80 percent) surveyed recalled having seen the ads at least once. Parents consistently had a favorable reaction to them. The impact on young people, however, was not positive. And among the primary target audience of 14- to 16-year-olds, marijuana use actually increased. With respect to attitudes, young people who were more exposed to the campaign were no more likely to express opposition to marijuana than were those who were less exposed.

DARE: Success or Failure?

The most popular antidrug education program in recent years has been DARE (Drug Abuse Resistance Education). Created by the Los Angeles police department and school system in 1983, the program consists of seventeen 45- to 60-minute classes, taught by sworn police officers, for fifth- and sixth-grade students. It relies primarily on affective education, attempting to provide the "skills for recognizing and resisting social pressures to experiment with tobacco, alcohol, and drugs" and "developing skills in risk assessment and decision making."[57]

DARE is extremely popular with parents, politicians, and the police. DARE bumper stickers can be seen everywhere. The program is currently operating in 80 percent of all school districts, at a total cost of an estimated $750 million a year. The official DARE website estimates that 36 million students will participate in the program in the 2004–2005 school year. Eighty percent of all local law enforcement agencies reported having a special unit for in-school drug education.[58]

Evaluations of DARE have not found it effective, however. Evaluations have measured students' knowledge about drugs, attitudes toward drug use, social skills in resisting pressure to use drugs, and actual drug usage. A meta-analysis of 18 evaluations by the Research Triangle Institute of North Carolina concludes that the program's effect on drug use is "slight, and except for tobacco use, not statistically significant."[59] Studies that have followed DARE and non-DARE students for up to five years after the program have consistently found that "DARE does not have long-term effects on drug use." A ten-year follow-up study of 1,002 people who had experienced the DARE program or an equivalent drug education program found that "in no case did the DARE group have a more successful outcome than the comparison group."[60] It is worth pointing out, too, that the recent increase in teenage drug use has occurred in spite of the massive DARE effort directed at precisely that audience.

There are several possible reasons why DARE does not affect drug use. The teaching method used, primarily classroom lectures, is inherently less effective than participative methods used in other kinds of programs. Some critics suggest that police officers may not be well trained for this activity and may not be effective role models. A more fundamental question is whether 17 hours of classroom lectures can overcome the other influences in a teenager's life—family (perhaps a dysfunctional family), peer group, neighborhood, and so on. It is likely that the program works only where it supplements existing positive influences such as a strong family and peer group environment. The evidence on DARE leads us to the following conclusion:

PROPOSITION 51

There is no evidence that DARE or other drug
education programs reduce illegal drug use.

But *Some* Education Programs Do Work

Not all education programs are worthless. Some are effective, but it is important to examine why certain kinds of programs work for certain audiences.

AIDS education programs are a good example. Good evidence exists indicating that safe-sex education programs have changed behavior. In New York, the average number of unsafe sexual encounters per person dropped from eleven to only one per year between 1980 and 1991. As a result, the incidence of new AIDS cases among adult gay men also dropped. Nationally, the number of AIDS cases has dropped significantly since 1993.[61] Unfortunately, unsafe activity has continued among people in the underclass, including both unprotected sex and the use of unclean needles. As a result, AIDS has spread from male drug addicts to their female sexual partners and on to other men. Surveys of members of the underclass have found an incredible indifference to the known risks of using unclean needles and engaging in unprotected sex.[62]

Deaths related to AIDS rose sharply in the 1980s, peaked in 1994, and then began an equally dramatic decline. The number of deaths in 1998 equaled the number in 1988. (It is worth noting that these trends parallel almost exactly the trends in gun-related deaths among young African American men during the same years.) Education efforts have to be maintained and retooled for new generations, however. In early 2005 a new strain of drug-resistant HIV appeared, leading health officials to realize that members of a younger generation were engaging in risky sexual activities.

In 1990 50 percent of all AIDS diagnoses involved whites and 28 percent involved African Americans. By 1999 the distribution was reversed: 48 percent African American and 28 percent white.[63] Why the difference between the two groups? The adult gay community is a relatively successful group in U.S. society, with relatively high levels of education and professional careers. That segment of the gay community is also very cohesive, with a strong self-identity, networks of community institutions, and strong peer group support. Needle-drug users are at the other end of the social scale: They are unemployed, with little if any education, substantial criminal records, and no community identity or institutions. It is reasonable to conclude that successful, educated people are more likely to respond to information dissemination programs: to receive the information, process it, and make a rational decision to change their behavior. This process reflects a sense of empowerment and capacity to control one's own life. That sense of power and control is precisely what people at the bottom of society do not have.

Despite the early success of safe-sex education programs, disturbing recent evidence indicates that they are not having the same degree of success with a younger generation of gay men. The reasons are not yet clear, but the situation does highlight the fact that people's behavior is influenced by a complex mix of personal and social factors. We cannot assume that education programs, by themselves, will have a dominant influence on behavior.[64]

Another example is the antismoking crusade, which we have already discussed. As we mentioned earlier, smoking has increased among teenagers recently, despite a significant decline among adults. Why the difference? We can argue that adults, especially successful, middle-class, and professional adults, are more likely to make rational choices about their behavior. Teenagers are far more likely to make reckless decisions, to consider themselves invulnerable, and to fail to think about either the immediate or the long-term consequences of their actions.

The response of different groups to education programs is closely related to the problems associated with deterrence theory, which we have already considered. Just as some people are more likely to be deterred by the threat of criminal sanction than others, so educational programs will be more effective with some groups than others. People with a stake in society are likely to respond very differently than people at the very bottom who feel they have nothing to lose.

DRUG TREATMENT

Along with education, drug treatment represents the prevention and demand-reduction approach favored by most liberals. Treatment raises all of the issues related to rehabilitation that we discussed in Chapter 11. It is a planned intervention designed to change behavior. Treatment makes a lot of economic sense, even though many treatment participants fail. One study estimated the cost of treatment for an offender at $2,941 and that the benefit to society in terms of reduced crime, arrest, prosecution, and imprisonment amounted to $9,177.[65]

One of the major issues related to drug treatment is the availability of treatment programs. Critics of current drug policy argue that programs are not adequately funded and that many people who want treatment cannot receive it. Their proposal calls for funding to provide "treatment on demand." Slightly more than 900,000 people have been enrolled in alcohol and drug treatment programs per year since the early 1990s. About 30 percent of them are receiving drug treatment only.[66] It has also been estimated, however, that about three or four times as many people need drug treatment as are currently receiving it.[67] One of the main arguments by the advocates of rehabilitation is that we have never adequately funded treatment programs to meet current needs. The fact of the matter is that few prisoners get drug treatment. It is estimated that between 70 and 85 percent of state prisoners need drug treatment, but only 11 percent actually participate in treatment programs.[68]

Varieties of Treatment

As with drug education, several different kinds of drug treatment programs are available.[69]

Methadone Maintenance   This treatment provides methadone as a substitute for heroin. A supervised medical treatment maintains the addiction at a steady level to prevent deeper dependency, eliminates the addict's need to turn to crime, and presumably reduces his or her association with drug addicts and criminals (and their peer influence). A supervised program of withdrawal can also be included. Because it involves providing an addictive drug, methadone maintenance is the most controversial of the three major forms of treatment.

Therapeutic Communities These are residential programs using intensive individual or group counseling techniques. Their primary goal is to temporarily remove the external influences that contribute to drug dependency and through counseling restructure the client's personality. Some of the more famous therapeutic communities include Synanon and Phoenix House. The therapeutic community is the most expensive of the three major types of programs.

Outpatient Drug-free Programs These programs provide counseling and other services to clients who remain in the community. Services include individual and group counseling on drug abuse and counseling or training for employment and family and other problems. Because they are the least expensive and least controversial type of program, outpatient programs are the most common.

Drug users can get into treatment in a variety of different ways. They can enter a program voluntarily. Many celebrities, for example, go to the Betty Ford Clinic, which is a therapeutic community. Others are compelled to enter treatment through the criminal justice system. Drug abuse counseling is often a condition of a diversion program, probation, or parole. Most of the new intensive probation supervision and boot camp programs (see Chapter 11) include drug and alcohol counseling. Opponents of drug legalization argue that the coercive aspect of the criminal law is necessary to get most people into treatment.

Drug Courts We examined drug courts in Chapter 11 because they represent a form of correctional treatment. Recall that drug courts provide a combination of treatment and services for substance abuse offenders and offer dismissal of criminal charges or reduced sentences to participants who successfully complete the treatment program. As we found, the evidence on the success of drug courts is mixed. Among those who successfully complete drug court programs, the recidivism rate is generally lower than those who do not participate. But there is often a high dropout rate among offenders who enter drug court programs, a fact that undermines the overall effectiveness of programs.

Faith-based Treatment A number of religious organizations operate faith-based drug treatment programs. As we learned in Chapter 11, however, there have been very few evaluations of any faith-based programs, and at this point there is no persuasive evidence that they are any more effective than secular programs.

Does Treatment Work?

The evidence on the effectiveness of treatment programs is very mixed. One review concludes that "all" the major types of programs "have been shown to be successful."[70] Another survey concludes optimistically that "research provides convincing evidence for the effectiveness of treatment for drug abuse."[71]

Evaluations of drug treatment programs generally show that clients who successfully complete the programs are less likely to use illegal drugs and to commit crimes than before treatment. An evaluation of one Philadelphia methadone maintenance program found that clients averaged nine "crime days" per month before treatment but only three after treatment; their average number of days per month employed went from three to eleven. Of 202 men who completed the Phoenix House therapeutic community program, 72 percent were arrested in the three years before entering the program, whereas 41 percent were arrested in the three years afterward. Outpatient treatment in the Drug Abuse Reporting Program reduced the arrest rate of clients from 87 percent beforehand to 22 percent after three years.[72]

Upon closer inspection, however, these claims are less impressive than they first appear to be. First, few if any programs claim to reduce completely illegal drug use or criminal activity. Especially disturbing are the high dropout rates in virtually all programs. Program evaluations that include only those who complete the program are artificially inflating their success rate.

Even more seriously, treatment programs report high rates of relapse into drug use. The report that says treatment is effective also states that "relapse to drug use is the rule."[73] National data indicate that almost half of all heroin users in treatment have previously been in treatment three times or more. And almost 40 percent of cocaine users in treatment have previously been in treatment two or more times.[74] It is not exactly a ringing endorsement to say that failure is "the rule." Treatment programs seem to work for those clients who have made a personal commitment to get off drugs. Interviews with ex-addicts repeatedly reveal that they decided that the drug life was too much hassle, that they could not put up with it anymore. In other words, treatment works for those who have decided to make it work. But treatment programs do not seem to be able to produce that change in personal commitment.[75]

The relapse problem arises with programs designed to treat alcoholism, smoking, weight problems, and criminal behavior. Millions of people try to give up smoking or lose weight every year. Most of them fail. In fact, most fail many times. We all know people who have made several efforts to quit smoking or lose weight. In some cases, however, they succeed. They finally quit smoking or lost the 20 pounds they always wanted to lose.

The challenge for effective treatment is to match the right program with the right client.[76] To a great extent, the "right" client is the person who has already made a commitment to change his or her life. But as one treatment expert put it, "Little progress has been made in classifying drug users to identify what kinds of users will benefit most from particular kinds of programs."[77] If this sounds familiar, it is because it is another version of the prediction problem we have encountered several times before. As we have seen, bail decisions, selective incapacitation, probation, and parole all depend on identifying just the right people and only those people. Overpredicting produces false positives; underpredicting leads to false negatives. And as we have seen, the data and diagnostic tools are not available to us to make the precise predictions we want. This leads us to the following proposition:

PROPOSITION 52

Drug treatment can help committed individuals end their drug use.
But there is no evidence that any treatment program consistently
reduces drug use for all persons enrolled in the program.

But Something Positive *Has* Happened

Our review of drug policies so far has not turned up any policies that have demonstrated consistent effectiveness. But wait a minute: Something positive *has* happened. Use of crack has declined substantially in many cities in the mid-1990s, and many criminologists believe that this is one of the factors—perhaps *the* factor—in the drop in the crime rate. In short, something has worked.

The ADAM program gives us very good data on illegal drug use among persons arrested. Several points need to be emphasized. First, Manhattan is typical of many other cities in that the decline began first and was steepest among youthful (under age 18) offenders. This effect suggests that overall crack use in the city is likely to continue to drop as each cohort ages into adulthood.

Second, crack use declined in Washington, DC, despite the fact that its police department during these years was widely criticized for being disorganized and ineffective in dealing with crime. This effect suggests that the decline in crack usage is unrelated to police enforcement patterns. Third, crack use remained stable in Phoenix. In some other cities it rose during this period (Indianapolis, for example). This effect suggests that patterns in crack usage are highly sensitive to local factors, with very different trends in different cities.

What the ADAM data do *not* tell us is *why* crack usage has declined so significantly in so many cities. As we suggested in Chapter 1, several explanations are possible. New York City officials claim that it is because of their zero-tolerance crime policy. But as we have already suggested, this does not account for similar trends in other cities with very different enforcement patterns. Many advocates of community policing claim that the 80,000 new police officers hired under the COPS program are responsible. But the General Accounting Office and other critics point out that most of those officers have been hired in cities and towns that never had a serious drug or crime problem in the first place, and as we learned in Chapter 5 there is very mixed evidence about the impact of community policing programs across the country. Still others claim that our sentencing policies have reduced both drug use and crime through a combination of deterrence and incapacitation. But as we found in Chapters 6 and 7, there is no strong evidence to support that argument.

Another possible explanation is that crack has simply gone out of style—that it is no longer regarded as cool among those most likely to use it. An ethnographic study of young adults in New York City found that crack users had become negatively stereotyped as "crack heads" in their peer group and that they took pride in not using the drug. In particular, they defined "crack heads" as people who had lost control over their lives: They could not control their drug habit and often lost their apartments and custody of their children. In short, control of crack use was the result of peer pressure and a strong concern for self-image among one's peers, and not a result of law enforcement. A *New York Times* article suggested: "The crack epidemic behaved much like a fever: It came on strong, appearing to rise without hesitation, and then broke, just as the most dire warnings were being sounded."[78] Law enforcement undoubtedly played some role in changing attitudes toward crack as people saw the effect of arrest and incarceration on friends and other people they knew, but at best this was only one factor in their decision not to use crack.

LEGALIZE DRUGS?

By the 1980s, many thoughtful observers had concluded that the war on drugs was a disaster, particularly in terms of the impact on racial minority communities and the economic cost of the soaring prison population.[79]

These criticisms gave new life to the call to legalize drugs. Legalization is no longer something advocated by hippies left over from the 1960s. The advocates include prominent conservatives, such as the Nobel Prize–winning economist Milton Friedman and writer William F. Buckley. They are joined by civil libertarians, who agree with these conservatives on almost no other criminal justice issue.[80] The American Civil Liberties Union adopted a policy in 1994 calling for the "full and complete decriminalization of the use, possession, manufacture and distribution of drugs."[81]

The debate over legalization was sparked by Ethan Nadelmann's 1989 article in *Science* magazine, "Drug Prohibition in the United States."[82] His case for legalization includes the following points: Criminal prohibition has not eliminated or even reduced drug use; we spend billions of dollars a year in this seemingly futile effort; the war on drugs produces numerous harmful side effects, including corruption and damage to poor and minority neighborhoods, prohibition of potentially beneficial medical uses of marijuana, and so on. The "logic of legalization," he argues, consists of two main points: that "most illegal drugs are not as dangerous as is commonly believed" and that abuse of the most dangerous drugs will not rise significantly under legalization.[83]

Public opinion on legalization is very mixed. Public opinion surveys have generally found that only about a quarter of the public support full legalization of marijuana, the softest of all drugs.[84] Yet nearly half approve of legalizing the medical use of marijuana.

Varieties of Legalization

The debate over legalization has been confused because the term means different things to different people. It is often used interchangeably with *decriminalization*. Both terms embrace a variety of specific proposals. The basic point of both is the removal of criminal penalties for the possession and sale of at least some currently illegal drugs. Beyond that, however, much disagreement prevails over four issues: (1) Are all drugs to be legalized, or only some? (2) Are possession *and* sale to be legalized, or only possession? (3) Will legalization apply to adults *and* juveniles, or just adults? (4) Will some kind of regulation replace criminal penalties, and if so, what kind?[85] As Nadelmann points out, "There is no one legalization option."[86]

Legalization *maximalists* take the extreme position, advocating legalization of both sale and possession of all drugs for juveniles as well as adults. Legalization *moderates* want to remove criminal penalties for the possession of many drugs and the sale of some drugs, but for adults only. Legalization *minimalists,* meanwhile, would eliminate penalties only for adult possession of marijuana and perhaps other less dangerous drugs. Finally, *agnostics* have not taken a final position on legalization but are convinced that current policy has failed and that we need a national debate on a new approach to drugs.[87]

Within this general framework are a number of different policy options. One approach is to give states the right to set their own drug policy, allowing them to experiment as they see fit. Doing this would abandon a national policy. Under a proposal drafted by Daniel K. Benjamin and Roger Leroy Miller, any conflict between federal and state laws would be resolved in favor of state law.[88] Another alternative would be to legalize particular drugs for medical use only. California and Arizona took a step in this direction in 1996. A more comprehensive option would have the government-issue "user's licenses" to individuals who pass a required test.[89]

Except for radical libertarians, most legalization proposals would maintain some government regulation over drugs. The issue of regulation, however, is widely misunderstood. A wide range of legal products today are regulated (for example, tobacco and alcohol). Similarly, you cannot just buy a cow and sell milk from your front porch. These regulations are ultimately backed up by criminal penalties. It is illegal to sell cigarettes or beer to minors. Thus, legalization does not necessarily mean the complete elimination of all forms of government control or the threat of criminal punishment. But it does represent a shift in the basic direction of drug policy.

Medical Marijuana   The one legalization proposal that has gained some ground is to legalize marijuana for medical purposes. In 1996 the voters in California passed Proposition 215, the Compassionate Use Act, by a margin of 56 to 44 percent. That same year, Arizona passed Proposition 2000 by a margin of 65 to 35 percent. Several other states have since passed similar laws. Because these state laws permitting use of marijuana conflict with federal law, there has been considerable conflict with federal authorities over their legality. A case involving the California law reached the Supreme Court in late 2004. (For additional information on these and other legalization efforts, go to the NORML website.)

The Impact of Legalization   What would happen if we legalized drugs? Obviously, the answer depends on which form of legalization we are talking about. The effect of radical legalization would be very different from the moderate or conservative alternatives.

Whichever policy were adopted, these questions arise: (1) Would drug use increase or decrease? (2) Would predatory crime such as robbery and burglary increase or decrease? (3) How much money would in fact be saved? (4) What would happen to the drug-related criminal syndicates? (4) What would be the overall impact on the criminal justice system? (6) Would there be fewer violations of individual rights? (7) Finally, what would be the overall effect on the quality of life in the United States?

A Specific Proposal To focus our discussion of these questions, let us examine a specific legalization proposal drafted by Richard B. Karel that appears in a collection of essays on the legalization debate.[90]

Karel proposes legalizing drugs only for adults and making distinctions among various drugs based on their toxicity and potential harm. He would completely legalize coca leaves, which could be sold in supermarkets "as tea is now sold." Granular cocaine would be illegal, but people could obtain cocaine gum similar to the nicotine gum currently available. Access would be rationed through an Automated Teller Machine (ATM)–type system. You would have a card and you could "withdraw" so much per day or week. Crack cocaine would be completely illegal. Smokable and edible forms of opium would also be available through an ATM system. Heroin would be available to addicts, through either medical prescription or the ATM system, but PCP would remain illegal. Psychedelic drugs would be legally available to people who could demonstrate "knowledge as to their effects" through a written test and interview. The government would regulate the market by controlling distribution and ensuring product purity, much as the government now regulates alcohol and tobacco.

Karel's proposal falls somewhere in the moderate-to-conservative range of legalization alternatives. The most dangerous drugs—crack and PCP—would still be illegal. All drug use by and sale to juveniles would be illegal.

What would be the result? First, there would be an immediate and significant reduction in the number of arrests and persons sent to prison. This outcome would reduce the workload of the justice system and save a certain amount of money, particularly in terms of imprisonment costs. The dollar savings would be a lot less than many legalization advocates believe, however. With cocaine still illegal for adults and all drugs illegal for juveniles, we would still maintain most of the present law enforcement apparatus. And we should not forget that police do a lot of other things besides investigate drug crimes. Criminal syndicates would probably not disappear, because they would still try to serve the demand for cocaine and other drugs that were still illegal. In short, many of the gains promised by legalization advocates—the dollar savings, the disappearance of the drug profits and the criminal syndicates—would not materialize.

Karel's proposal also makes some assumptions about drug users that are debatable. His scenario assumes that they are basically rational people, deciding to go to the clinic to get their ration of gum cocaine or methadone, much the way middle-class yuppies decide whether to buy domestic or imported beer. This scenario does not come to grips with the irrational and self-destructive nature of drug abuse. Among teenagers, drug and alcohol abuse are acts of rebellion. Among the underclass, heroin and cocaine abuse is a way of retreating from a brutal world with no apparent opportunities.

Would Karel's proposal reduce crime? In one limited sense, yes. By definition, it eliminates certain drug-defined crimes involving possession and sale. It is not likely to reduce drug-associated crimes such as robbery and burglary, however. As we already noted, most of this criminal behavior is part of a deviant lifestyle that is the product of many different factors. Relatively little predatory crime is directly caused by drugs, and legalization will not end that criminal behavior. Because crack would still be illegal, drug gangs would still engage in the same violent struggle for control of the market.

Let us move beyond Karel's proposal and discuss the legalization of all drugs. Would drug use increase? Much controversy exists over this question. Even Ethan Nadelmann, one of the leading legalization advocates, concedes, "It is thus impossible to predict whether or not legalization would lead to much greater levels of drug abuse."[91]

Opponents of legalization argue that a tremendous increase in drug use would result. They believe that existing criminal penalties curb drug use, both by the threat of arrest and punishment and because the criminal law represents a statement about society's values.[92] Some evidence, however, suggests that drug use would not increase. The National Household Survey clearly indicates that millions of Americans use illegal drugs every year without becoming heavy users, addicts, or criminals. They do not because the process of socialization operates somewhat effectively. They may engage in some minor deviance—casual drug use, vandalism, even some petty theft—but they do not cross over the line into addiction or criminality. Moreover, drug abuse is not rampant in those European countries that have relatively tolerant drug policies. These countries do not have the same level of crime the United States has, and their example may not be relevant in this context.

The danger, however, is that the mechanisms of socialization might be overwhelmed by legalization. In a suburban high school, for example, drug use could become so prevalent that peer pressure encourages pervasive cocaine use. As drug use increases, academic performance could decline, leading to a complete change in the culture of the school.

To a great extent, this is exactly what has already happened in many schools and neighborhoods. Drug use is so pervasive that it is extremely difficult for young people to resist the pressures to join. Drug-related crime contributes to the dreadful quality of neighborhood life. This is one of the main reasons that African American leaders are some of the most vocal opponents of legalization. People such as Representative Charles Rangel, whose district includes Harlem, see a covert form of racism in the legalization idea.[93] They argue that it would abandon their communities to drugs.

The legalization issue is not completely polarized along racial lines. Kurt Schmoke, former mayor of Baltimore and an African American, is one of the leading advocates of an alternative to our current drug policy. In fact, his firsthand experience as a prosecutor convinced him of the futility of the war on drugs.[94] He and others argue that the war on drugs has already failed to protect poor neighborhoods. The calamity Rangel describes—of open drug trafficking and abuse, of rampant crime and violence—is already here in many neighborhoods.

One of the strongest arguments against the war on drugs is that it converts many otherwise law-abiding people into criminals. The Rand Corporation interviewed people arrested for drug offenses in Washington, DC, and found that two-thirds held regular jobs. Drug dealing was essentially a part-time job. Their regular jobs paid an average of $11,000 to $14,000 a year, while they said they made an average of $24,000, tax free, from their drug dealing. The illegal drug markets represented a very tempting way to supplement their annual income. Looking at it another way, their $7-per-hour jobs were not adequate to support a decent lifestyle.[95] Legalizing drugs would eliminate this temptation to engage in criminal activity and save thousands of people from arrest and imprisonment and the subsequent problems associated with having a criminal record.

The full impact of legalization remains entirely a matter of speculation. It depends on which drugs would be legalized and whether they would be fully legalized or regulated. This leads us to the following conclusion:

PROPOSITION 53
The impact of legalizing drugs on serious crime is not known at this time.

CONCLUSION

In the end, what can we recommend in the way of a sensible drug policy? The first step should be to face squarely the fact that we do not have any convincing evidence of a program or policy that has been proven effective in reducing drug abuse and crime associated with drugs. Politicians continually restate the same old policies ("longer prison terms," "more treatment") without any evidence regarding their effectiveness.

The starting point should be to recognize that we really do not have the answers at the moment. The major contribution of the advocates of legalization has been to force a wide-ranging discussion of our current drug policy.

The purpose of this book is to find policies that will reduce serious crime. As we have found, the drug–crime relationship is extremely complex. It does appear that most of the serious crime associated with drug use is not directly caused by drugs. Thus, even if we found a solution to the drug problem, we would probably still be faced with the crime problem.

NOTES

1.   Sentencing Project, *Drug Policy and the Criminal Justice System* (Washington, DC: The Sentencing Project, 2001). Available on the Sentencing Project website.

2.   United States Sentencing Commission, *Cocaine and Federal Sentencing Policy* (Washington, DC: Author, 1995), p. 172.

3.   Elliott Currie, *Reckoning: Drugs, the Cities, and the American Future* (New York: Hill & Wang, 1992); Steven R. Donziger, ed., *The Real War on Crime: The Report of the National Criminal Justice Commission* (New York: HarperPerennial, 1996).

4.   Dale Gieringer, "How Many Crack Babies?" in Arnold Trebach and Kevin B. Zeese, eds., *Drug Prohibition and the Conscience of Nations* (Washington, DC: Drug Policy Foundation, 1990), pp. 71–75.

5.   The Sentencing Project, *Does the Punishment Fit the Crime? Drug Users and Drunk Drivers, Questions of Race and Class* (Washington, DC: The Sentencing Project, 1993). Available on the Sentencing Project website.

6.   Peter Reuter, "Drug Use Measures: What Are They Really Telling Us?" *National Institute of Justice Journal* (April 1999): 13. An extended discussion of methodologies and findings is in Thomas Mieczkowski, "The Prevalence of Drug Use in the United States," in Michael Tonry, ed., *Crime and Justice: A Review of Research,* vol. 20 (Chicago: University of Chicago Press, 1996), pp. 349–414.

7.   U.S. Department of Health and Human Services, *Results from the 2003 National Survey on Drug Use and Health: National Findings* (Washington, DC: Author, 2004).

8.   Monitoring the Future, *National Survey Results on Drug Use, 1975–2003* (Ann Arbor, MI: Author, 2004). Available on the Monitoring the Future website.

9.   Ibid.

10. Reuter, "Drug Use Measures: What Are They Really Telling Us?"

11. Currie, *Reckoning.*

12. National Institute of Justice, *Drug and Alcohol Use and Related Matters Among Arrestees, 2003* (Washington, DC: Author, 2004).

13. Andrew Lang Golub and Bruce D. Johnson, *Crack's Decline: Some Surprises Across U.S. Cities* (Washington, DC: Government Printing Office, 1997). NCJ 165707.

14. Jeremy Travis and Michelle Waul, *Reflections on the Crime Decline* (Washington, DC: Urban Institute, 2002). Available on the Urban Institute website.

15. A series of Fact Sheets on drug-related issues is available on the website of the Office of National Drug Control Policy.

16. David N. Nurco, Timothy W. Kinlock, and Thomas E. Hanlon, "The Drugs–Crime Connection," in James A Inciardi, ed., *Handbook of Drug Control in the United States* (New York: Greenwood, 1990), pp. 71–90.

17. This typology is taken from the Office of National Drug Control Policy, *Fact Sheet: Drug-Related Crime* (Washington, DC: Author, 2000). NCJ 181056.

18. The data in this paragraph are summarized in ibid.

19. Bureau of Justice Statistics, *Substance Abuse and Treatment of Adults on Probation, 1995* (Washington, DC: Government Printing Office, 1998).

20. Bureau of Justice Statistics, *Drugs, Crime, and the Justice System* (Washington, DC: Government Printing Office, 1992), p. 2.

21. David P. Farrington, "Predictors, Causes, and Correlates of Male Youth Violence," in Michael Tonry and Mark H. Moore, eds., *Youth Violence* (Chicago: University of Chicago Press, 1998), p. 431.

22. A good discussion of the different positions on drug policy is Peter Reuter, "Hawks Ascendant: The Punitive Trend of American Drug Policy," *Daedalus* 121 (Summer 1992): 15–52.

23. Mark H. Moore, "Controlling Criminogenic Commodities: Drugs, Guns, and Alcohol," in James Q. Wilson, ed., *Crime and Public Policy* (San Francisco: ICS Press, 1983), chapter 8.

24. Marsha Rosenbaum, *Just Say What? An Alternative View on Solving America's Drug Problem* (San Francisco: National Council on Crime and Delinquency, 1989), p. 17.

25. Mark A. R. Kleiman, *Against Excess: Drug Policy for Results* (New York: Basic Books, 1992).

26. Ed Leuw, "Drugs and Drug Policy in the Netherlands," in Michael Tonry, ed., *Crime and Justice: A Review of Research,* vol. 14 (Chicago: University of Chicago Press, 1991), pp. 229–276.

27. Jerome G. Miller, *Search and Destroy: African American Males in the Criminal Justice System* (New York: Cambridge University Press, 1996); Donziger, ed., *The Real War on Crime.*

28. Office of National Drug Control Policy, *Program.* Available on the website of the Office.

29. Office of National Drug Control Policy, *Drug Treatment in the Criminal Justice System* (Washington, DC: Department of Justice, 2001). NCJ 181857.

30. Stephen R. Donziger, ed., *The Real War on Crime,* p. 99.

31. Department of Health and Human Services, *2003 National Survey of Drug Abuse and Health* (Washington, DC: Department of Health and Human Services, 2004). Available on the HHS website.

32. Donziger, *The Real War on Crime,* p. 115.

33. Michael Tonry, *Malign Neglect: Race, Crime, and Punishment in America* (New York: Oxford University Press, 1995), pp. 188–189; Bureau of Justice Statistics, *Sentencing in the Federal Courts: Does Race Matter?* (Washington, DC: Government Printing Office, 1993).

34. Daniel S. Nagin, "Criminal Deterrence Research at the Outset of the Twentieth Century," in Michael Tonry, ed., *Crime and Justice: A Review of Research,* vol. 23 (Chicago: University of Chicago Press, 1998), pp. 1–37.

35. Lawrence W. Sherman, "Police Crackdowns: Initial and Residual Deterrence," in Michael Tonry and Norval Morris, eds., *Crime and Justice: A Review of Research,* vol. 12 (Chicago: University of Chicago press, 1990), pp. 1–48.

36. Lynn Zimmer, "Proactive Policing Against Street-Level Drug Trafficking," *American Journal of Police* 9 (1990): 43–74.

37. "How Much Bang from TNT?" *Law Enforcement News,* 31 December 1992.

38. Paul Hoffman, "The Feds, Lies, and Videotape," *Southern California Law Review* 66 (May 1993): 1453–1532.

39. University of Maryland, *Preventing Crime: What Works, What Doesn't, What's Promising* (Washington, DC: Government Printing Office, 1997), pp. 8–24.

40. Office of National Drug Control Policy, *Pulse Check: Drug Markets and Chronic Users in 25 of America's Largest Cities* (Washington, DC: Author, 2004). NCJ 201398.

41. Lorraine Greene, *Policing Places with Drug Problems* (Thousand Oaks, CA: Sage, 1996).

42. William J. Bennett, John J. DiIulio, and John P. Walters, *Body Count: Moral Poverty . . . And How to Win America's War Against Crime* (New York: Simon & Schuster, 1996), p. 189.

43. Office of National Drug Control Policy, *Drug Snapshot: Drug Abuse in America, 1998.* For the latest DEA data, go to its website.

44. Bureau of Justice Statistics, *Drugs, Crime, and the Justice System,* p. 36. For efforts by the U.S. Customs Bureau, go to its website.

45. Peter Reuter, Gordon Crawford, and Jonathan Cave, *Sealing the Borders: The Effects of Increased Military Participation in Drug Interdiction* (Santa Monica, CA: Rand, 1988), p. xi.

46. Travis and Waul, *Reflections on the Crime Drop.*

47. Mark H. Moore, "Actually Prohibition Was a Success," in Rod L. Evans and Irwin M. Berent, eds., *Drug Legalization* (LaSalle, IL: Open Court, 1992), pp. 95–97.

48. Samuel Walker, *Popular Justice: A History of American Criminal Justice,* 2nd ed. (New York: Oxford University Press, 1998), pp. 158–159.

49. The Knapp Commission, *The Knapp Commission Report on Police Corruption* (New York: Braziller, 1973).

50. Bureau of the Census, *Statistical Abstract of the United States* (annual). The latest data are available on the Bureau's website.

51. See the latest data on the Monitoring the Future website.

52. Bennett et al., *Body Count,* p. 187.

53. Gilbert J. Botvin, "Substance Abuse Prevention: Theory, Practice, and Effectiveness," in Michael Tonry and James Q. Wilson, eds., *Crime and Justice: An Annual Review of Research,* vol. 13 (Chicago: University of Chicago Press, 1990), pp. 474–477.

54. James O. Finckenauer, *Scared Straight and the Panacea Phenomenon* (Englewood Cliffs, NJ: Prentice Hall, 1982).

55. Jesse Greene, "Flirting with Suicide," *New York Times,* 15 September 1996: 41.

56. National Institute on Drug Abuse, *Evaluation of the National Youth Anti-Drug Media Campaign: 2003 Report of Findings Executive Summary* (Rockville, MD: Westate, 2003).

57. Bureau of Justice Assistance, *An Introduction to DARE,* 2nd ed. (Washington, DC: Government Printing Office, 1991). Information about the program is available on the official website of DARE, Inc.

58. Bureau of Justice Statistics, *Law Enforcement Management and Administrative Statistics, 1997* (Washington, DC: Government Printing Office, 1999), p. xix. Current data are on the official DARE website.

59. Susan T. Emmett, Nancy Tobler, Christopher Ringwalt, and Robert L. Flewelling, "How Effective Is Drug Abuse Resistance Education? A Meta-Analysis of Project DARE Outcome Evaluations," *American Journal of Public Health* 84 (September 1994): 1394–1401.

60. Five-year follow-up: Richard R. Clayton, Carl G. Leukefeld, Nancy Grant Harrington, and Anne Cattarello, "DARE (Drug Abuse Resistance Education): Very Popular but Not Very Effective," in Clyde B. McCoy, Lisa R. Metsch, and James A. Inciardi, eds., *Intervening with Drug-Involved Youth* (Thousand Oaks, CA: Sage, 1996), p. 104. Ten-year follow-up: Donald R. Lyman, "Project DARE: No Effects at 10-years Follow-up," *Journal of Consulting and Clinical Psychology,* 67 (August 1999): 590–593.

61. Greene, "Flirting with Suicide"; Bureau of the Census, *Statistical Abstract of the United States, 1998,* pp. 146–147.

62. Currie, *Reckoning,* pp. 247–251.

63. The most recent data are available on the website of the Centers for Disease Control and Prevention.

64. Greene, "Flirting with Suicide."

65. Office of National Drug Control Policy, *Drug Treatment in the CJ System* (Washington, DC: Author, 2001). NCJ, 181857.

66. Office of National Drug Control Policy, *Data Snapshot: Drug Abuse in America, 1998,* plates 84, 86.

67. Bureau of Justice Statistics, *Drugs, Crime, and the Justice System,* p. 109.

68. Office of National Drug Control Policy, *Drug Treatment in the CJ System.*

69. George De Leon, "Treatment Strategies," in James A. Inciardi, ed., *Handbook of Drug Control in the United States,* pp. 115–138; Bureau of Justice Statistics, *Drugs, Crime, and the Justice System,* pp. 107–111.

70. M. Douglas Anglin and Yih-Ing Hser, "Treatment of Drug Abuse," in Tonry and Wilson, eds., *Drugs and Crime* (Chicago: University of Chicago Press, 1990), p. 393.

71. De Leon, "Treatment Strategies," p. 120.

72. Ibid.

73. Ibid., p. 127.

74. Office of National Drug Control Policy, *Data Snapshot: Drug Abuse in America, 1998,* panels 89, 90.

75. Currie, *Reckoning,* pp. 154–155.

76. Ibid., pp. 132–133.

77. Anglin and Hser, "Treatment of Drug Abuse," p. 395.

78. R. Terry Furst, Bruce D. Johnson, Eloise Dunlap and Richard Curtis, "The Stigmatized Image of the 'crack head:' A Sociocultural Exploration of a Barrier to Cocaine Smoking among a Cohort of Youth in New York City," *Deviant Behavior,* 20 (1999): 153–181. Timothy Egan, "A Drug Ran Its Course, Then Hid with Its Users," *The New York Times,* 19 September 1999: I.

79. Miller, *Search and Destroy.*

80. A history of the debate over decriminalization/legalization of drugs is

in Ronald Bayer, "Introduction: The Great Drug Policy Debate—What Means This Thing Called Decriminalization?" in Ronald Bayer and Gerald M. Oppenheimer, eds., *Confronting Drug Policy: Illicit Drugs in a Free Society* (New York: Cambridge University Press, 1993), pp. 1–23.

81. American Civil Liberties Union, Board of Directors, "Minutes, April 9, 1994," *ACLU Briefing Paper 19, Against Drug Prohibition* (New York: Author, n.d.).

82. Ethan A. Nadelmann, "Drug Prohibition in the United States: Costs, Consequences, and Alternatives," *Science* 245 (September 1, 1989): 939–947.

83. Ibid., p. 943.

84. Bureau of Justice Statistics, *Sourcebook of Criminal Justice Statistics, 1998* (Washington, DC: Department of Justice, 1999), p. 146. Current edition is available on the website of The University at Albany (formerly SUNY Albany).

85. See the questions posed by James A. Inciardi, "The Case against Legalization," in Inciardi, ed., *The Drug Legalization Debate* (Newbury Park, CA: Sage, 1991), pp. 45–79.

86. Nadelmann, "Drug Prohibition in the United States," p. 939.

87. Drug Policy Foundation, *National Drug Reform Strategy* (Washington, DC: Drug Policy Foundation, 1992).

88. Cited in Arnold Trebach, "Thinking Through Models of Drug Legalization," in *The Drug Policy Newsletter* 23 (July/August 1994): 12.

89. These options are discussed by Trebach, "Thinking Through Models of Drug Legalization."

90. Richard B. Karel, "A Model Legalization Proposal," in Inciardi, ed., *The Drug Legalization Debate,* pp. 80–102.

91. Nadelmann, "Drug Prohibition in the United States," p. 944.

92. James Q. Wilson, "Against the Legalization of Drugs," *Commentary* 89 (February 1990): 21–28.

93. See the thoughtful discussion in William Kornblum, "Drug Legalization and the Minority Poor," in Bayer and Oppenheimer, eds., *Confronting Drug Policy,* pp. 115–135.

94. Kurt L. Schmoke, "Drugs: A Problem of Health and Economics," in David Boaz, ed., *The Crisis in Drug Prohibition* (Washington, DC: Cato Institute, 1990), pp. 9–12.

95. Peter Reuter, Robert MacCoun, and Patrick Murphy, *Money from Crime: A Study of the Economics of Drug Dealing in Washington, DC* (Santa Monica, CA: Rand, 1990).

PART VI

Conclusions

14

Crime and Community: Putting It All Together

THE NEW COMMUNITY FOCUS
ON CRIME CONTROL

A strong consensus has emerged among criminologists that effective crime control requires a focus on communities. This new paradigm is the product of several developments: a new theoretical perspective in criminology, research on criminal behavior, the community policing movement, and applications of community policing principles to courts and corrections. Summarizing this new thinking, Joan Petersilia points out: "Research has long documented how the social organization of neighborhoods—particularly poverty, ethnic composition, and residential stability—influences crime."[1]

The new consensus includes several basic operating principles for crime policies. First, *no single crime policy* holds the key to crime reduction. Effective crime prevention and control requires the simultaneous application of several policies.[2] This is an important departure in crime policy. As we have seen again and again in this book, the advocates of particular policies have focused very narrowly on their particular idea, giving almost no attention to the role of other policies.

A second operating principle is, of course, the *community or geographic focus.* All of the programs discussed in this chapter focus on particular neighborhoods and communities. In policing, many new programs focus on "hot spots," areas where crime and disorder are concentrated.

A third principle is the *need for partnerships* among different agencies, including both criminal justice and non–criminal justice agencies. This idea originated with the community policing movement, which began with the recognition that the police cannot control crime by themselves but need the cooperation of citizens and neighborhood groups. Problem-oriented policing, meanwhile, contributed the idea of police cooperation with non–criminal justice agencies.

Housing code enforcement agencies, for example, can help deal with apartments that are centers of drug trafficking; sanitation departments can clean up neighborhoods and eliminate the signs of disorder and neglect (the "broken windows" that invite lawbreaking). Faye Taxman, one of the leading experts on offender reentry programs, explains: "The underlying premise of the reentry partnership is that each component of the criminal justice system . . . plays a role" in dealing with released offenders and also that "criminal justice agencies cannot do this alone, and must engage family, community-based service providers, the faith community and other sources of formal and informal support in reintegrating offenders."[3]

Fourth, many of the new policies utilize *non–criminal law remedies.* This is particularly true with problem-oriented policing where programs include better street lighting and sanitation services as part of a larger effort to improve the quality of life in a neighborhood. Improving these services necessarily includes partnerships with other government agencies.

Fifth, the new community focus embraces the *evidence-based policy movement* (see our discussion in Chapter 1) and insists that policies be supported by empirical research demonstrating effectiveness. It is no longer acceptable to base policies on myths, hopes, and good intentions.

The Goals of This Chapter

This chapter will attempt to pull together all the different strands of community-focused crime policy development. This includes clarifying the theoretical and practical links between developments in the different components of the criminal justice system: community policing, community prosecution, and reentry programs in corrections.

This chapter is also a critical review of the new community focus in crime policy. In this regard, we are going to hold it to the standards of evidence-based crime policy. The theoretical basis for this new orientation is clear. And there is evidence that some programs have been effective. But does it all hold together? Will the successful programs continue to be effective in the future? Most important, can all the different elements be coordinated to form a comprehensive crime control effort?

There are many reasons for skepticism about the new community focus, and the jury is still out on the long-term impact on crime. First, the supporting evidence is preliminary at best. Some programs appear to work, but more research is still needed. Second, there are serious questions about the implementation and continuity of many programs. There is a long history in criminal justice of exciting innovative programs fading away as funding or the program's founders move on.

The Theoretical Background

The community focus of crime control is grounded in the most important recent developments in theoretical criminology. Sociologist Robert J. Sampson, arguably the most influential scholar on this subject, argues: "'Community' now reigns as the modern elixir for much of what allegedly ails American society." Sampson proposes the concept of "ecometrics" to measure the social ecology of the individuals being studied. This approach emphasizes direct observation of people in their social environment. The new community orientation represents a turning away from the University of Chicago–style research that emerged in the 1960s. Relying primarily on survey research, it focused on individuals, both as "units of data collection and targets of theoretical inference."[4]

In terms of crime control, Sampson and others propose the concept of *collective efficacy*, which includes *trust among residents* in a neighborhood and their *shared expectations about their social control,* meaning their capacity to exercise some control over their neighborhood.[5] The importance of collective efficacy represents a radical reorientation of thinking about crime control. As the earlier chapters of this book make clear, the traditional approach places primary responsibility on criminal justice agencies: on police patrol to deter crime, on the courts to convict and punish offenders, on sentencing policy to incapacitate career criminals. The new approach emphasizes the role of citizens as "co-producers" of crime control efforts.

An important aspect of the theory is that collective efficacy mediates the impact of environmental factors. Criminologists have long held that poverty, high rates of unemployment, and other social problems are associated with high crime rates. Recent research, however, indicates that neighborhoods with collective efficacy have lower crime rates than similarly poor neighborhoods with no sense of collective efficacy.

An important policy implication of collective efficacy is that people need to have trust in local criminal justice agencies. Sampson argues that if people do not trust the police, it will be impossible to develop effective neighborhood crime prevention policies. The same point holds true for the justice system as a whole. As we saw in Chapter 12, Tom Tyler's research on procedural justice indicates that distrust of the justice system increases peoples' tendency to break the law.[6] The concept of collective efficacy suggests that if they trust the police and other agencies, they will be more likely to cooperate with the police and their neighbors in programs to control crime.

With respect to attitudes toward the police, Sampson challenges the prevalent stereotype that the entire African American community distrusts the police. Forty years of public opinion poll data consistent show that while African Americans are more likely to distrust the police, a majority nonetheless have a positive attitude.[7] This evidence suggests that there is a vast resource that police departments can tap into to develop effective crime prevention programs.

The Empirical Basis

The concept of collective efficacy is supported by empirical research. Sampson's work is based on the Chicago Project on Human Development in Chicago Neighborhoods. It studied seven cohorts of children and their families, involving about 6,500 children.[8] The project also involved systematic observation of conditions in neighborhoods, including the videotaping and rating of over 23,000 different "street segments" in Chicago. Measures of social and physical disorder were developed and applied to 196 neighborhoods.

Finally, more than 3,500 area residents were surveyed. Collective efficacy was defined in terms of the cohesion among residents and their shared expectations about their ability to control public space. In practical terms, this involved the extent to which residents worked together on neighborhood problems (for instance, to get street lights or broken park equipment repaired) and whether they felt they could exercise some control over areas such as street corners or parks (by calling the police to get rid of drug dealers, for instance).[9]

The data indicate that collective efficacy explains lower rates of crime and observed neighborhood disorder, even after controlling for the economic conditions of neighborhoods.[10] The implications for crime policy are clear and powerful. Poverty alone does not determine crime rates. Within limits, residents have some impact on the level of crime. Collective efficacy emphasizes what citizens believe and do. Traditional crime policies focus entirely on what criminal justice agencies do.

Another study found that domestic violence was lower in neighborhoods where there were higher levels of collective efficacy. It concluded: "Collective efficacy also increases the likelihood that women will disclose conflict in their relationships to various potential sources of support."[11] A study in Detroit, meanwhile, found collective efficacy associated with lower burglary rates in Detroit. "Neighborhoods with active community organizations and a politically active citizenry were better able to control crime than others."[12]

The Basic Paradigm: Operation Cease Fire in Boston

The Boston Gun Project's Operation Cease Fire is in many respects a paradigm for community-focused crime control policy.[13] When Boston experienced a surge in gun homicides of young men in the late 1980s, community leaders brought together a broad coalition of criminal justice officials, neighborhood leaders, and academic experts to seek an innovative and effective response. In the end, it worked; youth homicides dropped dramatically.

Operation Cease Fire incorporated all the elements of the new community focus to crime control. First, it was a highly focused effort, concentrating on a particular problem—youth gun violence—on particular neighborhoods, and ultimately on particular offenders. Since research indicated that much of the gun violence was associated with particular gangs, those gangs and their leaders were targeted for special attention. This kind of focused effort was quite different from the traditional police "crackdowns" we discussed in Chapter 5, which have generally been unfocused and often involve indiscriminate mass arrests.

Second, it was a multiagency effort, involving partnerships among police and correctional agencies and local and federal criminal justice agencies. In 1995 Police Commissioner Paul Evans convened a working group of representatives from all the relevant agencies to plan a coordinated and innovative effort. This included coordinating the efforts of federal, state, and local law enforcement agencies on gun trafficking and gun crimes. Under the federal sentencing guidelines, prison terms are much longer than under state law. Coordinated efforts referred major gun dealers for federal prosecution.

Third, it involved the active participation of community groups. In this case, religious leaders in the African American community, organized as the Ten Point Coalition, played a major role in working with criminal justice officials and communicating with neighborhood residents.

Fourth, it adopted innovative strategies and tactics, rejecting the traditional approach of unfocused arrest, prosecution, and imprisonment. Some of the most important innovations were characterized as "pulling levers": using a variety of legally available sanctions against gang leaders. Gang members with outstanding warrants were arrested; those whose driver's licenses had been suspended had their cars impounded; in Operation Night Light, probation and parole officers made home visits to gang members and enforced violations of the conditions of release; gang members under the supervision of the Department of Youth Services were arrested and taken off the street. (These efforts obviously involved partnerships among criminal justice agencies.) And in another innovative approach, gang members were summoned to meetings and directly told about the enforcement effort and that there would be no deals if they were arrested.

A Justice Department report on an Operation Cease Fire program in Los Angeles, modeled after Boston's, defined pulling levers as "[a] crime deterrence strategy that attempts to prevent violent behavior by using a targeted individual or group's vulnerability to law enforcement as a means of gaining their compliance."[14]

Finally, it included the active participation of academic experts, who not only brought expert knowledge to the program but undertook a rigorous evaluation of its impact. Scholars from Harvard University's Kennedy School of Government were actively involved in planning the project—bringing their expertise in research on problem-oriented policing, gangs, and gun violence—and in evaluating the impact of the project.

The evaluation found a 63 percent decrease in youth homicides per month; a 32 percent decrease in the number of calls to the police regarding shots fired; a 25 percent decrease in gun assaults per month; and a 44 percent decline in youth gun assaults in the district with the highest levels of violence. The researchers controlled for other factors that might explain these results, including changes in the employment rate, the relative percentage of youths in the population, violent crimes in the entire city, homicides among older people, and the level of drug activity. And because the nation as a whole was experiencing a decline in violent crime, they compared Boston's trends with those in other cities. The reduction in violent crime was greater than in the United States generally and in other New England cities. In this respect, Operation Cease Fire met the standard of evidence-based policymaking (see Figure 14.1).

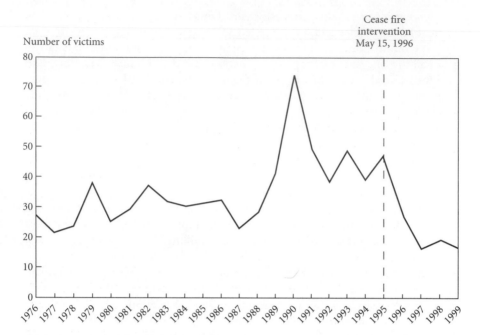

FIGURE 14.1 Youth homicide victims ages 24 and under in Boston, 1976–1999

SOURCE: Bureau of Justice Statistics, *Reducing Gun Violence: The Boston Gun Project's Operation Cease Fire* (Washington, DC: Department of Justice, 2001).

The tremendous success of the Gun Project was referred to as the "Boston Miracle." It became the basis for a national program sponsored by the U.S. Justice Department, Project Safe Neighborhoods (although its funds were abruptly cut in 2004).

INNOVATIONS IN POLICING

The Boston Gun Project is one of the most notable innovations in policing labeled *community policing* or *problem-oriented policing* (POP). In many important respects, police innovations are the parent of the other new community-focused crime policies. They have provided the key term and orientation—community—and have defined and tested the basic operating principles, particularly the idea of developing close partnerships with community groups and other criminal justice and non–criminal justice agencies. (Check the Center for Problem Oriented Policing website for the latest information about POP.)

Community policing originated in the early 1980s, rising from the ashes of traditional police practices. Research in the 1970s demolished the traditional assumptions underlying preventive patrol (see the Kansas City Patrol Experiment in Chapter 5), the goal of reducing response time, and the myths surrounding the effectiveness of detective work. The key insight was that the police cannot fight crime by themselves but need to work closely with other groups and agencies that ultimately influence crime and disorder.[15] The negative findings from the best research coincided with powerful political pressures to do something about high crime rates and at the same time to improve police/community relations. Police research also contributed the concept of "hot spots," the geographic concentrations of very high rates of crime and disorder. Finally, the concept of "broken windows" emphasized the importance of disorder and its impact on the quality of neighborhood life, as opposed to serious crime, as something criminal justice officials should be concerned with.

The Boston Gun Project is perhaps the most well known application of problem-oriented policing. In Chapter 5 we looked at the SMART program in Oakland, California. The next section looks at a successful POP experiment in Jersey City, New Jersey.

Case Study: Problem-Oriented Policing in Jersey City

The POP program in Jersey City first identified 12 pairs of areas in the city where there were high rates of violent crime (hot spots). In each pair, one area received focused crime prevention police work, while the other served as a control. In the analysis phase, officers with the Jersey City Police Department identified the specific problems in each of the 24 areas. In treatment and control areas 1, for example, the problem was robbery of commuters; another pair of treatment and control areas, on the other hand, were afflicted by street fights and drug market violence. The analysis phase was consistent with the basic principle of problem-oriented policing: identifying and addressing particular problems in particular places, as opposed to the traditional approach of fighting "crime" in a general sense.

The police employed 28 different strategies in the experimental areas (see Table 14.1). Some of these strategies involved traditional policing: aggressive order maintenance, drug enforcement, and so on. But eight of the twelve most commonly used strategies involved nontraditional activities: requiring store owners to clean their store fronts, getting the Public Works Department to remove trash from the street, getting more lighting for certain areas. The latter two, of course, involved partnerships with other city agencies.

An evaluation found that the POP program reduced both violent and property crime in the treatment areas compared with their paired control areas. Through direct observation, the evaluation found that observed disorderly behavior declined in 10 of the 12 treatment areas. Signs of physical disorder (uncollected trash, graffiti) also declined in 10 treatment areas, without displacement to neighboring areas.[16]

The evidence on the various problem-oriented policing projects is sufficient to support the following proposition.

PROPOSITION 54
Focused, problem-oriented policing programs that involve partnerships and utilize a range of strategies can reduce serious crime.

Table 14.1 Police strategies used in Jersey City

Strategy	Number of places used
Aggressive order maintenance	12
Drug enforcement	9
Required store owners to clean store fronts	5
Public Works Dept. removed trash from streets	5
Robbery investigations	4
Increased lighting of areas	4
Housing code enforcement	3
Erected fences around vacant lots	3
Vacant lots cleaned	3
Abandoned buildings boarded and fenced	3
Hung signs explaining rules of behavior (e.g., no drinking)	3
Videotape surveillance of places	3

SOURCE: Anthony M. Braga et al., "Problem-Oriented Policing in Violent Crime Places: A Randomized Controlled Experiment," *Criminology* 37:3 (1999): 544, Table 2. Reprinted with permission.

Unanswered Questions about the Future

Despite the successes reported to date, there are a number of unanswered questions about the future of community policing and POP. These questions are extremely important given the fact that so many of the other community-focused crime policies are modeled after community policing and POP principles and practices.

The first question involves the implementation and continuity of both community policing and POP programs. Skogan's research on Chicago indicates that the city has made a decade-long commitment to community policing.[17] Many other programs reported in the scholarly literature, however, involved short-term, grant-funded experiments that were not continued once the grant ended. And in some programs it is not at all clear whether anything new and distinctive was ever implemented in the first place. Is Jersey City continuing to maintain problem-oriented policing, for example? Murders in Boston increased in 2003 and 2004. Is Operating Cease Fire continuing? These questions need to be answered.

The problem of maintaining continuity in innovative programs is pervasive in American policing.[18] Over the years, innumerable promising reforms have simply faded away after a few years. The attempt to transfer the Boston Cease Fire program to Los Angeles ran into a number of problems that limited full implementation of the plan, and the impact on crime and gang-related violence was mixed.[19]

The second question involves continued federal funding. Because of the combined impact of the "war on terrorism" and federal budget deficits, federal funding for the community policing programs has been severely reduced. Such funding was extremely important in providing an incentive for police departments to experiment and attempt innovation. In fact, this may have been a much more important long-term effect than the additional officers hired.

Third, there are a number of powerful countervailing influences at work. The budget constraints that many cities face and temporary loss of officers to National Guard and military reserve duties have disrupted police departments. The war on terrorism has caused police departments to refocus their efforts. Whereas police chiefs talked about community policing in the 1990s, today they are more likely to talk about preparing for possible terrorist attacks.[20]

COMMUNITY PROSECUTION

Community prosecution applies the basic principles of problem-oriented policing to the prosecution stage of the criminal process, doing traditional things (prosecuting offenders) in a new way. Our task here is to take a cold, critical look at it and ask two questions. First, is it really something new and different? Second, is there any evidence that it is effective in controlling crime?

The Concept of Community Prosecution

The American Prosecutors Research Institute (APRI) defines community prosecution as "a long-term, proactive partnership among the prosecutor's office, law enforcement, the community and public and private organizations, whereby the authority of the prosecutor's office is used to solve problems, improve public safety and enhance the quality of life of community members."[21] This definition includes all of the current buzzwords: "community," "partnerships," "quality of life," and so on. In fact, the rhetoric is exactly the same as that of community policing and problem-oriented policing. The APRI explains that the goal of community prosecution is crime prevention, and not merely convicting and punishing offenders.

The idea of community prosecution is extremely popular and has been spreading rapidly. In 1995 there were six programs across the country; by 2001 one survey found that 68 percent of all prosecutors' offices had some kind of community-oriented program.[22]

Problem-Solving Courts Community prosecution programs are sometimes referred to as "problem-solving courts." According to the National Center for State Courts, the basic elements include a focus on less serious "disorder" offenses, which often get lost in a traditional criminal court, the use of community service and other alternatives to incarceration, strict monitoring of sentence conditions, rapid imposition of sentences (to communicate the message that crime has consequences), close relations with community groups, and a goal of improving the quality of life in the immediate neighborhood.[23]

There are considerable variations in community prosecution and problem-solving court programs. Some community prosecution strategies address serious crimes of violence and drugs, while others deal with disorder offenses.[24]

The New York Midtown Community Court

Community prosecution originated in 1993 with the Midtown Community Court (MCC) in New York City. (For the latest information, go to the website of the Center for Court Innovation.) The MCC targeted "quality-of-life offenses, such as prostitution, illegal vending, graffiti, shoplifting, fare-beating [not paying subway fares] and vandalism." It grew out of frustration with the failure of the traditional criminal courts to deal effectively with low-level crime. The problem was not that offenders were not punished or punished severely, but that there were often no consequences of any sort for committing quality-of-life offenses. At most, offenders might get a few days of jail time, but often they received probation with no meaningful restrictions.

Court officials and community residents shared the same frustration. A major part of the problem—which affects courts all across the country—is that courts are swamped with major cases and do not have the time or resources to deal with minor crimes.[25] In important respects, this analysis is similar to the one voiced by Morris and Hawkins about the limited sentencing options facing criminal courts (prison or probation), which led to the development of intermediate sanctions (see Chapter 11).

The MCC gives as its guiding principles: (1) restore the community, (2) bridge the gap between communities and courts, (3) knit together a fractured criminal justice system, (4) help offenders deal with problems that lead to crime, (5) provide better information, and (6) design a physical space to match the court's goals. These are lofty goals. Let's see what actually happens in practice.[26]

To implement these principles, sentences in the MCC typically involve a requirement that offenders repay the neighborhood through community service and also undergo treatment. While performing community service (for example, painting over graffiti), sentenced offenders wear bright blue vests. This is designed to "make justice visible" and communicate the message that crime has consequences. To "make justice swift," offenders begin performing their community service within 24 hours of being sentenced.

"Engaging New Partners" involves partnerships with local businesses and agencies in job training, services for the homeless, and so on. The program element of "Offering Social Services" includes providing drug treatment, job training, and other services for offenders. Finally, "Providing Better Information" involves a computerized management information system that provides judges with better information about offenders to help them develop individualized sentences, and also feedback to police officers about the outcomes of their arrests.

Evaluation of the MCC

An evaluation of the MCC by the National Center for State Courts found mixed results. In some important respects, the MCC did achieve its goals. Sentences involving community service were twice as frequent at the MCC compared with the traditional downtown court. Jail sentences were also less common (9 percent compared with 18 percent in the downtown court). This resulted in a reduction of 27,000 jail-days over three-year period, with the consequent dollar savings. Interestingly, there was some "feedback effect," as downtown court sentences became closer to MCC's, suggesting that the innovations impressed officials in the other court. Court processing also speeded up, with an average arrest-to-arraignment time of 18.9 hours compared with 29.2 hours in the downtown court. There was also a modest increase in dispositions at the arraignment stage, resulting in both time saved and cost savings.[27]

Offenders who received alternative sanctions (that is, alternatives to jail) were more likely to comply with the requirements (75 percent) than offenders sentenced in the downtown court (50 percent). Additionally, offenders in the MCC who did comply with the terms of their sentences were more likely to receive a secondary sentence than offenders in the downtown court. In this respect, offenders were held to a higher standard of accountability.

With respect to conditions in the immediate neighborhood, observations and interviews with residents of local hot spots in the MCC area indicated "substantial reductions" in the concentration of prostitution and unlicensed vending. There was also a reduction in graffiti on Ninth Avenue, a decline in arrests for prostitution, and a noticeable disruption in the neighborhood drug markets (e.g., fewer individuals, offending less frequently)

The anticipated cost savings were not achieved, and in fact the MCC proved to be more expensive. There were tangible savings of about $1.1 to $1.2 million a year because of speedier court procedures and fewer jail sentences, but the innovative aspects of the program added expenses (for personnel, etc.) of $1.8 to $2.2 million.

The impact on recidivism among sentenced offenders was mixed, however. In the first year a large majority of those sentenced to the mandatory case management/drug treatment program as an alternative to jail did not complete the program. There was a lower rearrest rate for those who did, and in particular lower rearrest rates for those who spent over 90 days in treatment. After three years there was an increase in completion rates in the treatment programs and a reduction in the frequency of rearrest.

A Critical Look at Community Prosecution

Like so many innovations, community prosecution promises a lot: reduced crime, improved neighborhood conditions, and cost savings. Let's take a critical look at this program to see if it meets our standard of dealing with serious crime.

First, it is obvious that community prosecution is directed at less serious, quality-of-life offenses: graffiti, prostitution, and so on. It does not claim to deal with robbery, burglary, or other serious felonies.

The second question is whether the focus on quality-of-life issues helps to reduce serious crime. This question lies at the heart of the broken windows and zero-tolerance policing. The advocates of these programs argue that focusing on small crimes and signs of disorder can produce a reduction in serious crime.[28] We need to be fair but also tough-minded here. It is entirely possible that community prosecution does improve neighborhood quality of life. If so, that is a good reason to endorse it. But we also have to ask the tough question of whether it also reduces serious crime. New York City did experience a tremendous reduction in crime that coincided with the operation of the Midtown Community Court. But the direct connection between cracking down on small crimes and a reduction in major crimes remains unproven at this point.

A third question is whether community prosecution effectively treats convicted offenders. For all practical purposes, community prosecution is a form of traditional correctional treatment: probation and parole. The evaluation of the MCC, however, found very mixed results. This leaves us with the same problem we encountered in Chapter 11: Since treatment programs work for those who are ready for treatment, identifying those people and matching them to the right program is the major hurdle. The evidence leads us to the following proposition:

> ## PROPOSITION 55
> Community prosecution is a promising alternative to traditional prosecution for minor offenses, but its impact on serious crime remains unproven.

OFFENDER REENTRY PROGRAMS

The Importance of Offender Reentry

Our soaring use of imprisonment has created a new problem for society and the criminal justice system. Every year about 600,000 adults leave prison and return home (this represents about 1,600 a day). Joan Petersilia regards the reintegration of released prisoners as "[o]ne of the most profound challenges facing American society" today.[29] The steady flood of returning prisoners has particular relevance for community-focused crime policy. As Petersilia points out, it results in "the concentration of ex-prisoners in already fragile communities." The effects are numerous. The concentration of ex-offenders alters the peer culture of the neighborhood, adding one more risk factor to already at-risk young men.

The response to this problem is a new set of programs called Offender Reentry. Petersilia defines reentry as "all activities and programming conducted to prepare ex-convicts to return safely to the community and to live as law-abiding citizens."[30] The U.S. Department of Justice launched the Reentry Partnership Initiative in 1999. (Check the DOJ website for the latest information on its reentry efforts.)[31]

Reentry programming embraces the operating principles that guide problem-oriented policing and community prosecution. First, it builds on criminological research indicating that informal social controls, notably family, peer group, and other community factors, have a more direct influence on offender behavior than formal social controls such as probation and parole supervision.[32] Second, it seeks to develop partnerships with both community groups and other criminal justice agencies. Finally, it is committed to evidence-based practice and seeks to base programming on empirical research about what works and what doesn't.

A Closer Look at Returning Prisoners

The reentry initiative has sponsored detailed research on the circumstances of returning prisoners in several cities. The Urban Institute studied 400 prisoners returning to Chicago.[33] Eighty-three percent were African American. Returning prisoners were concentrated in a few neighborhoods with severe social and economic disadvantages. Interestingly, however, only 45 percent returned to their old neighborhood. Some wanted to avoid trouble, while for others their family had moved. Prior to their release, most expressed a strong desire to improve their lives and change their behavior.

Before their release, 87 percent participated in prerelease programs related to such practical matters as finding a job, obtaining a photo ID, and finding a place to live. But in practice, only 25 percent received an actual referral to a job, only 15 percent received a referral to a substance abuse treatment program, and only 22 percent contacted a community program based on a referral from the prerelease program.

Interviewed four to eight months after their return, the parolees reported that family ties and support were the "most important factor" in their adjustment to society. Data on their behavior confirmed this, finding that those with family support were less likely to be reconvicted than those with weak or no support. Almost all suffered from major problems that made readjustment difficult: 81 percent had no health care, and 30 had significant health problems upon release. About half (48 percent) had no close friends; and among those with friends, 40 percent had a friend who had been in prison. They had very limited success in finding jobs, and 70 percent were not employed after four to eight months. The monthly meeting with their parole officers typically lasted between 5 and 30 minutes. After 13 months, one-third (31 percent) were reincarcerated.

The Chicago returnees are typical of parolees nationally. Petersilia reports that half of parolees have less than a high school education, an estimated 19 percent are completely illiterate, and 40 percent are functionally illiterate. Over half (56 percent in 2002) have a prior criminal record, and 53 percent were on probation or parole at the time of the arrest that sent them to prison. Twenty-one percent have some physical or mental condition (such as a learning disability) that limits their ability to work. Most (60 percent) had used drugs in the month before their arrest, and 25 percent were alcohol dependent at that time.[34]

Participation in prerelease programs continues to be low across the country. Prior to release, only about 29 percent participate in a drug treatment program, 35 percent in education classes, and 27 percent in vocational training programs. In prison, a little more than half (56 percent) had any work assignment.[35]

The Urban Institute conducted similar studies of parolees in Baltimore, New Jersey, Ohio, and Texas. The research confirms what we have long known about parolees. They suffer from a number of personal problems, including both a lack of education and histories of substance abuse, and receive weak support in terms of parole services.[36]

WHAT'S REALLY NEW? A CLOSE LOOK AT JOAN PETERSILIA'S RECOMMENDATIONS

On the issue of prisoner reentry, Joan Petersilia is without question the most authoritative voice. Her ideas on this subject are based on over two decades of research on community-based corrections. Her book *When Prisoners Come Home* is the best overview of the important topic of prisoner reentry, solidly rooted in a comprehensive review of official data and the best research.[37] For precisely this reason we should take a very good look at recommendations for reentry programming. She offers four basic policy recommendations. Let's take a close look at them.

Investing in Prison-Based Rehabilitation Programs

Petersilia makes a persuasive case for investing in prison programs that will provide inmates with meaningful work experience and education, and treatment programs that address substance abuse, anger management, and other problems. Today's prisoners suffer from serious deficiencies in all of these areas: About half have less than a high school education; most have very limited employment experience; most have histories of alcohol or drug abuse; many have records of violent behavior, if not involving the crime that sent them to prison, then episodes of violence in their family or among friends.

It hardly needs to be said that all of these factors make it extremely difficult for a person leaving prison to successfully reenter conventional society and establish productive, law-abiding lives. Few employers are attracted to people without a high school diploma and the lack of basic reading comprehension skills that a diploma implies. Even fewer employers are willing to tolerate tardiness or absenteeism. People with histories of drug or alcohol abuse relapse at a very high rate. And people leaving prison generally return to communities where substance abuse is high and consequently will be subject to all of the wrong influences.

The truth of the matter, however, is that all of these things *have been said* before, for many decades in fact. Petersilia's evidence and recommendations evoke a powerful sense of deja vu, recalling the President's Crime Commission report, *The Challenge of Crime in a Free Society,* from 1967.[38] Many professional associations in the field of corrections have made similar recommendations.

The relevant question is, Why did American society ignore the recommendations of the Crime Commission and other professional associations regarding prison programming and spend the last 30 years just locking up more and more people? This question involves politics rather than criminology. It involves the attitudes of Americans about crime and criminals and how those attitudes are translated into politics. It is fair to ask, What program does Petersilia offer to change the minds of Americans on correctional policy?

A third question is, what evidence does she have that these programs are in fact effective? We might consider the issue of prison industries. There is a long history of the failure to provide meaningful work for inmates. And there are several well-known reasons for this. Restrictive laws limit the kind of industries that prisons can operate. These restrictions reflect the fear among businesses out in the free world that prison industries represent unfair competition. Additionally, many industries provide opportunities for inmate misconduct. Industrial jobs give inmates access to tools that can easily be fashioned into weapons. Contemporary communications jobs, such as telephone calling centers, open the door to telephone abuse. Finally, prison industries that would provide skills relevant to today's job market require all of the basic skills that inmates lack: basic education, work experience, and work habits.

The first edition of this book, published 20 years ago, contained a discussion of prison industries, and in particular a new program called Free Venture that was supposed to overcome the problems that had plagued earlier attempts at developing prison industries. That discussion was dropped, as Free Venture and related 1980s programs proved to be unsuccessful and faded away. But now here we are 20 years later and the subject of prison industries has begun to reappear.

But not that loudly. It is interesting that Petersilia passes over the subject very quickly, with almost no detailed discussion of how we could design effective prison industries that would teach meaningful job skills and instill good work habits in people who do not have them. One suspects that she does not because she is too good a scholar and knows full well that the history of prison industries is a story of repeated failures.

Restoring Discretionary Parole Release

Petersilia calls for a return to discretionary parole release. The elimination of discretionary release was one of the most significant policy changes of the past 25 years. Sixteen states have completely abolished discretionary parole release, and because of mandatory sentencing laws only 39 percent of prisoners in 2003 obtained their release through discretionary parole decision.[39] Petersilia's recommendation is based on data indicating that prisoners obtaining discretionary release are less likely to recidivate than those who "max out" their terms. Michael Tonry, a leading expert on sentencing, called for a return to discretionary parole release several years earlier.[40]

In fact, there is some evidence that prisoners released through discretionary parole are more successful—that is less likely to be rearrested—than prisoners released through mandatory release (54 vs. 33 percent, respectively).[41] This is an important finding, and more research on this subject is needed.

At the same time, however, Petersilia's call for a return to discretionary parole release ignores the serious problems that contributed to its demise in the first place. The two major problems are closely linked. The first is a lack of rational, scientifically based standards for deciding when to release a prisoner. We are back to our old friend the prediction problem (Chapter 4 and elsewhere). Parole officials began the search for guidelines to predict success on parole in the 1920s, but we are nowhere nearer that goal today than they were then.[42] The second is that in the absence of rational and scientifically based standards, parole decision making became arbitrary and often discriminatory. These criticisms were raised in the early 1970s and have not been effectively rebutted in the interim.

Front-Loading Postrelease Services

"Front-loading" postrelease services in the first six months after a prisoner's release is Petersilia's third policy recommendation. Common sense supports this idea. The initial weeks upon return to the community pose the most difficult readjustment problems for ex-offenders. They need adequate preparation in the form of job referrals, photo identification, a place to live, and referral to services such as substance abuse treatment. All of these factors are important to their success on parole.[43]

There are several problems with Petersilia's proposal on this point, however. The first is a problem of implementation. Correctional officials have known this for a long time—from their personal experience, if not on the basis of systematic data. The question is, Why have parole agencies failed to do the obvious? This brings us back to the larger problem of organizing and delivering parole services. One answer is that agencies are so overwhelmed by huge caseloads that they really don't have the staff and resources to shift more effort to the first six months. Remember, an estimated 11,000 offenders leave prison every week across the country.

Reallocating resources calls for good management: an ongoing assessment of current operations, an analysis of the evident problems, and a capacity to plan and implement changes. Many parole agencies simply lack good management. Others may have the potential capacity but are simply overwhelmed by the steady flow of new clients.

And then there is a more fundamental question that has plagued both parole and probation since they were invented: Are the services effective? Let's imagine for a moment a parole agency that is well managed and has reasonably sufficient resources. Let's assume that it follows Petersilia and the other recommendations by reentry experts and front-loads its services in the first six months. Do we have any solid evidence that these services are effective? Petersilia's own evidence is pretty grim on this point. As we learned in Chapter 11, the recidivism rates for offenders on probation are depressingly high. And there is precious little evidence that the actual services are effective treatments for the clients. It is appropriate to ask whether front-loading services is really any different than the old idea of intensive supervision. What services, exactly, are being "loaded"?

This also brings us back to the more specific problem that has bedeviled community correctional services since the very beginning. It is undoubtedly true that *some* offenders succeed; probation and parole are not 100 percent failures. And it is also probably true that some of these offenders succeed because of the help or monitoring they receive from their probation or parole officer. And it is also probably true that more offenders could be helped if we could match offenders with the combination of services and/or monitoring each one needs. (Some may respond better to a more friendly form of supervision, while others may need the guidance of a sterner form of monitoring.)

Eliminate Restrictions on Convicted Offenders

The most devastating section of Petersilia's *When Prisoners Come Home* is chapter 6, on the barriers society places on ex-offenders ("How We Hinder: Legal and Practical Barriers to Reintegration").[44] An Urban Institute report refers to them as "brick walls," creating enormous obstacles for the recently released offender.[45]

Publicly Available Criminal Records Criminal records are increasingly available to the public; 25 states, in fact, make them available on the Internet. While this policy is designed to inform the public and allow crime victims and other people to find out what has happened to an offender, there are potential dangers as well. A report on sex offender notification in Wisconsin found that some offenders had been harassed by neighborhood residents who could find out where they lived.[46]

Employment The barriers to employment are sweeping and have been growing in the last decade. For example, California bars convicted felons from holding jobs in law, real estate, medicine, nursing, physical therapy, and education. Even worse, all states prohibit convicted felons from working as barbers, beauticians, or nurses. The cruel absurdity of this practice is dramatized by the fact that hair care vocational programs are the most popular in the New York City Reformatory![47] Six states permanently deny public employment to felons. This means that a parolee cannot hold the most menial city or county job.

The war on drugs has had a special impact. A 1992 federal law requires states to revoke the driver's licenses of convicted drug offenders or lose 10 percent of their federal highway funds.[48] Given the fact that so many jobs have left the inner city and are now located in suburban areas, lack of a driver's license effectively means that a person cannot even look for a job, much less hold on to one. In addition to the legal restrictions, there are serious informal barriers to finding employment. One survey found that 40 percent of employers would never hire anyone with a felony drug conviction.

Housing Laws also limit the ability of ex-felons to find housing. Public housing agencies are required to refuse housing to certain categories of offenders (mainly drug or sex offenders).

Welfare The 1994 welfare reform law (officially the Personal Responsibility and Work Opportunity Reconciliation Act) requires states to permanently bar drug offenders from receiving federal welfare or public assistance funds (p. 124) (although 9 states have chosen to opt out of this requirement, and 10 made it available if the offender participates in a treatment program). What this means is that a murderer is eligible for public assistance but not someone convicted of possessing a small amount of marijuana.[49]

The Denial of Federal Benefits Program, established by the 1988 Anti-Drug Abuse Act, provides that anyone convicted of a first-offense drug possession in either federal or state court can, at the discretion of the judge, receive one or more of the following sentences: (1) be ineligible for any or all federal benefits for up to one year, (2) be required to successfully complete an approved drug treatment program that includes periodic testing, or (3) be required to perform community service. For a second offense, the person would be ineligible for all federal benefits for up to five years. The law explicitly grants the judge discretion in applying these provisions, and there is good reason to think that they are not using the law. At the end of 2001, there was a total of 6,938 cases in the Denial of Federal Benefits database, and only 765 had been added in the past year.[50]

Offender Registration and Sex-Offender Notification Laws Laws requiring sex offenders to register with local officials and/or that provide public notification of their residence exist in some form in every state (see our discussion in Chapter 6). While designed to protect the public by alerting families and allowing them to take self-protective measures, these requirements also expose offenders to harassment and vigilante action.

Voting Finally, one of the most serious disabilities is the denial of voting rights to convicted offenders. Every state has some form of voting denial. The Sentencing Project estimates that 4.7 million Americans cannot vote because of a criminal record. This includes an estimated 7 percent of all African Americans, and 1.4 million African American males. Denying people the right to vote is perhaps the most dramatic way of telling people that they are outcasts in American society, and an excellent way of keeping them from fully reintegrating into their local communities.[51]

Summary

When we put all this together, the picture looks almost impossible for the parolee. We take people with very limited education, significant histories of drug and alcohol abuse, criminal records, and mental and physical disabilities and proceed to bar them from many jobs, keep them from getting a driver's license so they could find and keep a job, deny them any possibility of public assistance until they find a job, and bar them from public housing. By denying them the right to vote, we tell them that they are not full members of American society.

And remember, they are returning to neighborhoods with high concentrations of similar problems. Is it any wonder that so many fail on parole?

There is a good reason why these restrictions exist: Society has demonized criminals for the last 30 years. What Petersilia, the Urban Institute, and others fail to confront are the political realities that have created these "brick walls." The solution is a technical matter not of correctional programming, but of political action: changing the hearts and minds of the American people and of the officials they elect.

PROACTIVE PAROLE SUPERVISION

The offender reentry movement has introduced the idea of "proactive supervision" in parole. Rejecting the "passive monitoring" of traditional parole, it is modeled after the proactive approach of problem-oriented policing, and in particular the SARA model (scanning, analysis, response, assessment). This includes a risk assessment of a parolee's problems, an analysis of appropriate responses, implementation of those responses, and an assessment of how well they are working. Faye Taxman explains: "The important part of the risk factor assessment is to use the information to develop a crime prevention plan for the offender."[52]

An Indianapolis reentry program applied the problem-solving approach to a group of recently released offenders. The program consisted of a series of neighborhood community meetings for the offenders that also included criminal justice agency officials, community representatives, and social service providers. The goal of the program was to combine deterrence (in the form of parole supervision) with social support from the community and service providers. An evaluation compared a treatment group of 93 ex-offenders who attended between one and five meetings with a control group of 107 ex-offenders released at the same time. The results were not very promising. Forty percent of both groups were rearrested within 10 to 24 months after their release. The treatment group did a little better, lasting an average of 172 days before rearrest, compared with 120 days for the control group.[53]

When we stop to think about the program, there is little reason to expect that it would have much impact. What difference would attending one meeting make to the typical ex-offender? What real difference would five meetings make? Indeed, on closer inspection even the problem-solving aspect of the program seems pretty shallow. The "problem analysis" phase, designed to help tailor the right treatment for each offender, produced the most obvious set of factors: prior criminal histories, employment problems, histories of substance abuse, and so on. The evidence leads us to the following proposition:

PROPOSITION 56
Without major changes in public thinking about crime
and criminals, and accompanying changes in spending
and programming, prisoner reentry programs will not reduce crime.

RESTORATIVE JUSTICE

A radically new approach to criminal justice policy involves the concept of restorative justice. As an alternative to the basic ethos of our legal system, it emphasizes both repairing the harm done to the community and building a sense of responsibility to the community in the offender. As the term *restorative justice* implies, it seeks not so much to punish offenders but to *restore* the bonds between the person who has done wrong, the victim, and the community at large.[54]

Instead of the traditional Anglo-American adversarial process, restorative justice emphasizes dialogue, negotiation, and the reestablishment of a positive relationship between victim and offender. In practice, restorative justice programs have often used financial restitution, community service, and mediation, usually in the form of face-to-face acknowledgment of guilt. The restorative justice movement draws heavily on communal peacemaking traditions among Native Americans and other indigenous peoples.

The chief proponent of restorative justice is John Braithwaite, whose book *Crime, Shame, and Reintegration* sparked the movement. Emphasizing shaming as the key to controlling crime, he argues that informal sanctions "imposed by relatives, friends or a personally relevant collectivity have more effect on criminal behavior than sanctions imposed by a remote legal authority."[55] Although Braithwaite is critical of traditional rehabilitation-oriented programs, his concept of restorative justice can be seen as a form of rehabilitation, particularly with its emphasis on reintegrating offenders into the community. Some programs, in fact, operate as diversion programs, referring cases to mediation conferences as an alternative to prosecution.

Restorative Justice in Operation

In a recent elaboration of restorative justice principles, Braithwaite argues that this approach is more effective in controlling crime than policies based on punishment, deterrence, incapacitation, and even rehabilitation. The U.S. Justice Department has recommended incorporating restorative justice into community policing programs.[56]

How well does restorative justice work in practice? Like many of the so-called new intermediate punishments we discussed earlier, the restorative justice programs of financial restitution and community service are nothing new. They have been used for many years but have been seen primarily as alternative sentences within the basic sentencing framework, appropriate for less serious offenses, and not a radical alternative to the basic principles of the justice system.

Evaluations of experimental restitution, community service, and mediation programs have tended to find slightly lower recidivism rates for offenders compared with traditional sentences of prison or probation. The differences are not always consistent, however, and many questions remain regarding the implementation and outcomes of such programs.[57] Some of the most promising findings are closely related to the concept of procedural justice discussed in

Chapter 12. In the most ambitious experiment, in Australia, preliminary findings indicate that restorative justice conferences result in lower levels of anger, fear, and alienation from the legal system among both victims and offenders than does traditional court processing.

We have many reasons for being skeptical about restorative justice as a response to serious crime. First, although it may well be appropriate for less serious crimes, especially minor property offenses, many people will question whether, from the standpoint of proportionality and just deserts, it is appropriate for serious crimes. Second, although it may be appropriate for first-time offenders, there are questions about whether it is appropriate for fourth- or fifth-time offenders. And finally, there are questions about whether it effectively reduces serious crime. A careful reading of Braithwaite's long 1999 essay in defense of restorative justice reveals that it is long on theory—and discussions of what it might accomplish—and fairly short on proven results.[58]

The most serious problem with Braithwaite's concept is that the necessary conditions he identifies do not exist in modern urban society. Common sense suggests that the informal sanctions of family, friends, or community are likely to be more effective in controlling behavior than the threats and actions of remote official agencies. But a major part of the crime problem in the United States today is the collapse of families, peer groups, and communities for many people. As Hagan's theory of social embeddedness suggests, some individuals are deeply embedded in lives that encourage lawbreaking rather than law abidance.[59] In our poorest, most economically ravaged and drug-ridden neighborhoods, "community," in the positive sense of the term, has disappeared. The structure of families has collapsed for too many people. The peer group influence too often leads to drugs and crime. The concept of restorative justice may well be appropriate and effective for the juvenile delinquent in a middle-class neighborhood but irrelevant for those aspects of our society that are the center of most serious crime.

Not only does restorative justice draw heavily on Native American traditions of communal justice, but it also reflects a nostalgic view of community in the United States. The informal mechanisms of social control that Braithwaite prizes—disapproval by family, friends, and neighbors—were in fact the primary means of crime control in seventeenth-century colonial New England. They worked because those communities were small and extremely homogenous (almost entirely white, English, and Protestant). As the United States grew into a large and diverse nation, characterized not only by different racial, ethnic, religious, and cultural groups but also by largely anonymous social relations, the old mechanisms no longer worked. That is one of the main reasons that Americans created the modern criminal justice system in the early nineteenth century. There is no returning to this vanished society.[60] This leads us to the following conclusion:

PROPOSITION 57

The promise of restorative justice remains unproven in reducing serious crime.

CONCLUSION

In the end, what does the new community focus of crime policy offer? Is it a realistic strategy for reducing crime? Or is just the latest fad, offering false promises? Remember, this movement is still fairly new, and all the evidence is not in. But a careful review of the existing evidence suggests the following tentative conclusions.

First, the most substantial evidence involves innovative police practices following the principles of problem-oriented policing. The Boston Gun Project, the SMART project in Oakland, and the POP experiment in Jersey City have all been subject to rigorous evaluations by some of the best criminologists, with the results published in the best peer-reviewed scholarly journals. This meets one of the basic standards of evidence-based policymaking. The evaluations found all three programs to be effective. The lessons are that the police can be effective in reducing serious crime if they undertake careful planning, involve outside experts, focus on particular problems and/or geographic areas, develop partnerships with other criminal justice and non–criminal justice agencies, establish working relationships with community groups, and allow a rigorous independent evaluation.

Second, the evidence about community prosecution is somewhat weak. The Midtown Community Court in New York City addressed only quality-of-life crimes and not serious crimes, which are our primary focus. There was some evidence of successful outcomes, but the anticipated cost savings were not achieved. A fair conclusion would be that community prosecution is a good idea that can address some problems of crime and disorder, but there is no evidence yet that it can address serious crime.

Third, there is at present no persuasive evidence that offender reentry programs are effective in dealing with serious crime by reducing recidivism rates. The concept of reentry is still in a very early stage; much is promised but the evidence is still not there. Especially troubling is that reentry advocates offer a lot of old wine in fancy new bottles. The goal of reintegrating offenders back into the community is as old as community-based corrections itself. The idea of preparing prisoners for release through educational programs, counseling, and so on is equally old. It is simply not clear what is really new here. Even more serious, the advocates of the movement have not faced up to the political realities that have undermined community-based corrections for the past 30 years.

NOTES

1.   Joan Petersilia, *When Prisoners Come Home* (New York: Oxford University Press, 2004).

2.   Jeremy Travis and Michelle Waul, *Reflections on the Crime Decline: Lessons for the Future?* (Washington, DC: Urban Institute,

2002). Available at on the Urban Institute website.

3.   Faye S. Taxman, Douglas Young, James Byrne, Alexander Holsinger, and Donald Anspach, *From Prison Safety to Public Safety: Innovations in Offender Reentry* (Washington,

DC: Department of Justice, 2002), p. 5. For this and other reports, go to the reentry page on the U.S. Department of Justice website, or the website of the Bureau of Government Research at the University of Maryland.

4.   Robert J. Sampson, " Transcending Tradition: New Directions in Community Research, Chicago Style," *Criminology* 40 (May 2002): 213–230.

5.   Robert J. Sampson and Steven W. Raudenbush, "Systematic Social Observation of Public Spaces: A New Look at Disorder in Urban Neighborhoods," *American Journal of Sociology* 105 (November 1999): 603 651.

6.   Tom R. Tyler, *Why People Obey the Law* (New Haven: Yale University Press, 1990).

7.   Summarized in Samuel Walker and Charles M. Katz, *The Police in America: An Introduction,* 5th ed. (New York: McGraw-Hill, 2005).

8.   Sampson, "Transcending Tradition."

9.   Jeffrey D. Morenoff, Robert J. Sampson, and Stephen W. Raudenbush, "Neighborhood Inequality, Collective Efficacy, and the Spatial Dynamics of Urban Violence," *Criminology* 39 (2001): 517–560.

10   Sampson and Raudenbush, "Systematic Social Observation of Public Spaces."

11.   Christopher R. Browning, "The Span of Collective Efficacy. Extending Social Disorganization Theory to Partner Violence," *Journal of Marriage and Family* 64 (2002): 833–850.

12.   David Martin, "Spatial Patterns in Residential Burglary: Assessing the Effect of Neighborhood Social Capital," *Journal of Contemporary Criminal Justice* 18 (2002): 132–146.

13.   David M. Kennedy, Anthony A. Braga, and Anne M. Piehl, *Reducing Gun Violence: The Boston Gun Project's Operation Ceasefire* (Washington, DC: Department of Justice, 2001). NCJ 188741.

14.   National Institute of Justice, *Operation Cease Fire in Los Angeles* (Washington, DC: Department of Justice, 2005). NCJ 192378.

15.   These developments are best summarized in David Bayley, *Police for the Future*

(New York: Oxford University Press, 1994).

16.   Anthony A. Braga, David L. Weisburd, Elin J. Waring, Lorraine Green Mazerolle, William Spelman, and Francis Gajewski, "Problem-Oriented Policing in Violent Crime Places: A Randomized Controlled Experiment," *Criminology* 37 (1999): 541–580.

17.   Wesley G. Skogan and Susan Hartmann, *Community Policing, Chicago Style* (New York: Oxford University Press, 1997).

18.   This issue is discussed in detail with regard to accountability-related innovations in Samuel Walker, *The New World of Police Accountability* (Thousand Oaks: Sage, 2005). An excellent case study of a lack of continuity is the St. Louis consent-to-search program: Scott Decker, *Reducing Gun Violence: The St. Louis Consent-to-Search Program* (Washington, DC: Department of Justice, 2004). NCJ 191332.

19.   National Institute of Justice, *Operation Cease Fire in Los Angeles.*

20.   See the discussion of "Ashcroft Policing" in David Harris, *Good Cops: The Case for Preventive Policing* (New York: The New Press, 2005).

21.   American Prosecutors Research Institute, "What is Community Prosecution?" on the website of the National District Attorneys Association (NDAA) website.

22.   American Prosecutors Research Institute, "Community Prosecution Programs Across the U.S.," on the NDAA website. The website map has links to programs in each state.

23.   Pamela M. Casey and David A. Rottman, *Problem-Solving Courts* (Williamsburg, VA: National Center for State Courts, 2004). Available on the National Center for State Courts website.

24.   For a description of programs and philosophy, take a look at John S. Goldkamp, Cheryl Irons-Guynn, and Doris Weiland, *Community Prosecution Strategies* (Washington, DC: Department of Justice, 2003). NCJ 195062.

25.   John Feinblatt, Greg Berman, and Michele Sviridoff, *Neighborhood Justice: Lessons Learned from the Midtown Commu-*

nity Court (New York: Center for Court Innovation, 1998).

26. Ibid.

27. Michele Sviridoff, David Rottman, and Rob Weidner, *Dispensing Justice Locally: The Impacts, Costs, and Benefits of the Midtown Community Court* (Williamsburg, VA: National Center for State Courts, 2000).

28. George L. Kelling and Catherine M. Coles, *Fixing Broken Windows* (New York: The Free Press, 1996); William J. Bratton and Peter Knoblach, *Turnaround* (New York: Random House, 1998); James Q. Wilson and George L. Kelling, "Broken Windows: The Police and Neighborhood Safety," *Atlantic Monthly,* 249 (March 1982): 29–38.

29. Joan Petersilia, *When Prisoners Come Home* (New York: Oxford University Press, 2004), p. 3.

30. Ibid.

31. Taxman et al., *From Prison Safety to Public Safety.*

32. Michael R. Gottfredson and Travis Hirschi, *A General Theory of Crime* (Stanford, CA: Stanford University Press, 1990).

33. Nancy G. La Vigne, Christy Visher, and Jennifer Castro, *Chicago Prisoners' Experiences Returning Home* (Washington, DC: The Urban Institute, 2004). Available on the Urban Institute website.

34. Petersilia, *When Prisoners Come Home,* p. 32.

35. Ibid., p. 95.

36. The reports and other information about prisoner reentry can be found on the Urban Institute website.

37. Petersilia, *When Prisoners Come Home,* pp. 140–142.

38. President's Commission on Law Enforcement and Administration of Justice, *The Challenge of Crime in a Free Society* (New York: Avon Books, 1967).

39. Bureau of Justice Statistics, *Probation and Parole in the United States, 2003* (Washington, DC: Department of Justice, 2004). NCJ 205336.

40. Michael Tonry, *Sentencing Matters* (New York: Oxford, 1996).

41. Petersilia, *When Prisoners Come Home,* p. 70; Bureau of Justice Statistics, *Trends in State Parole, 1990–2000* (Washington, DC: Department of Justice, 2001). NCJ 184735.

42. David J. Rothman, *Conscience and Convenience: The Asylum and Its Alternatives in Progressive America* (Boston: Little, Brown, 1980); Samuel Walker, *Popular Justice: A History of American Criminal Justice,* 2nd ed. (New York: Oxford University Press, 1998).

43. The Urban Institute report on parolees in Chicago provides valuable data on these issues. See also La Vigne et al., *Chicago Prisoners' Experiences Returning Home.*

44. Petersilia, *When Prisoners Come Home,* pp. 105–137; Office of the Pardon Attorney, U. S. Department of Justice, *Civil Disabilities of Convicted Felons* (Washington, DC: Department of Justice, 1996).

45. Urban Institute, *Prisoner Reentry and Community Policing* (Washington, DC: Urban Institute, 2004). Available on the Urban Institute website.

46. Richard G. Zevitz and Mary Ann Farkas, *Sex Offender Community Notification: Assessing the Impact in Wisconsin* (Washington, DC: Department of Justice, 2001). NCJ 179992.

47. Petersilia, *When Prisoners Come Home,* p. 114.

48. Ibid., p. 115.

49. Ibid., p. 124.

50. Bureau of Justice Assistance, *Denial of Federal Benefits Program and Clearing House* (Washington, DC: Department of Justice, 2002). NCJ 193770.

51. The Sentencing Project, *Losing the Vote: The Impact of Felony Disenfranchisement Laws in the United States* (Washington, DC: Author, 1998). Available on the Sentencing Project website.

52. Faye Taxman, *Proactive Supervision: Supervision as Crime Prevention* (College Park, MD: University of Maryland, n.d.). Available on the website of the Bureau of Government Research at the University of Maryland.

53. National Institute of Justice, *Applying Problem Solving Approaches to Issues of Inmate*

Re-Entry: The Indianapolis Pilot Project, Final Report (Washington, DC: Department of Justice, 2004). NCJ 203923.

54. John Braithwaite, *Crime, Shame, and Reintegration* (New York: Cambridge University Press, 1989).

55. Ibid., p. 69.

56. Caroline G. Nicholl, *Community Policing, Community Justice, and Restorative Justice* (Washington, DC: Department of Justice, 1999).

57. Burt Galway and Joe Hudson, eds., *Criminal Justice, Restitution, and Reconciliation* (Monsey, NY: Willow Tree Press, 1990).

58. Braithwaite, *Crime, Shame, and Reintegration*.

59. John Hagan, "The Social Embeddedness of Crime and Unemployment," *Criminology* 31 (November 1993): 465–491.

60. Walker, *Popular Justice*.

Index